Questions of Form

Questions of Form
Logic and the Analytic Proposition from Kant to Carnap

Joëlle Proust

Translation by
Anastasios Albert Brenner

University of Minnesota Press　Minneapolis

Published by the University of Minnesota Press
2037 University Avenue Southeast, Minneapolis MN 55414.
Printed in the United States of America.

Library of Congress Catalog Card Number 89-40446

ISBN 0-8166-1760-0   ISBN 0-8166-1761-9 (pbk.)

Contents

Translator's Note

I have employed the plural singular in number "a topics" (with reference to Aristotle and on the analogy of "mathematics") for the comparative inquiry undertaken by the author in order to avoid confusion with the ordinary meaning of the term in English. Whenever available I have followed for the passages quoted in this book the authorized English translations (given in the bibliography), in which a few concepts have been revised according to the author's interpretation.

An unpublished partial translation of Chapter 2 of Section 4 prepared by Francis Harrisson proved helpful.

Abbreviations

A   Rudolf Carnap, *Der logische Aufbau der Welt*. Berlin: Weltkreis, 1928. Translated by R. George as *The Logical Structure of the World*.

Ab   Rudolf Carnap, *Abriss der Logistik*. Vienna, 1929.

Akad Immanuel Kant, *Kants gesammelte Schriften*, volumes I–XXIX. Edition of the Deutsche Akademie der Wissenschaften zu Berlin. Berlin: Walter de Gruyter, 1966.

B   Gottlob Frege, *Begriffsschrift, eine der arithmetischen nachgebildete Formelsprache des reinen Denkens*. Halle, 1879. Translated by T. W. Bynuum as *Conceptual Notation and Related Articles*.

D   *Kant's Inaugural Dissertation and Early Writings on Space*. Translated by J. Handyside. Chicago: Open Court, 1929.

Draft A John Locke, *An Early Draft of Locke's Essay*. Oxford, 1936.

E   John Locke, *An Essay Concerning Human Understanding*. London: Dover, 1959.

EG Bernard Bolzano, *Einleitung in der Grossenlehre*. Stuttgart: Frommann Verlag, 1977.

EHU David Hume, *Enquiries Concerning Human Understanding and Concerning the Principles of Morals*. Oxford: Clarendon Press, 1975.

G   Gottlob Frege, *Grundgesetze der Arithmetic*. Jena: Hermann Pohle, 1892 and 1903. Translated by M. Furth as *The Basic Laws of Arithmetic*.

GA   Gottlob Frege, *Der Grundlagen der Arithmetik*. Breslau: W. Köbner, 1884. Translated by J. L. Austin as *The Foundations of Arithmetic*.

KRV   Immanuel Kant, *Kritik der reinen Vernunft*, 1781, 1786. Translated by N. K. Smith as *Critique of Pure Reason*.

KS   Gottlob Frege, *Kleine Schriften*. Hildesheim: Olms, 1967.

L   Immanuel Kant, *Kants Logik*. Edited by J. B. Jäsche. 1800.

LS   Rudolf Carnap, *Logische Syntax der Sprache*. Vienna: Julius Springer Verlag, 1934. Translated by A. Smeaton.

N   Gottlob Frege, *Nachgelassene Schriften und Wissenschaftlicher Briefwechsel*. Hamburg: Meiner, 1969. Translated by P. Long and R. White as *Posthumous Writings*.

P   Immanuel Kant, *Prolegomena zu einer jeden künftigen Metaphysik*, 1783. Translated by L. W. Beck as *Prolegomena to Any Future Metaphysics*.

PLS   Rudolf Carnap, *Philosophy and Logical Syntax*. London: Paul, Trench, Trubner, 1935.

PM   See *WF*.

PU   Bernard Bolzano, *Paradoxien des Unendlichen*. Leipzig, 1831.

T   David Hume, *Treatise of Human Nature*. Oxford: Clarendon Press, 1978.

W   Bernard Bolzano, *Wissenschaftslehre*. Sulzbach, 1837; Leipzig, 1914. Partially translated by R. George as *Theory of Science*.

WF   Immanuel Kant, *Welches sind die wirklichen Fortschritte . . . ?* 1791. Translated by T. Humphrey as *What Real Progress Has Metaphysics Made . . . ?* (*PM*).

Introduction

"The distinction between synthetic and analytic judgments is not new; it has been known for a long time."[1] Thus Eberhard, in his controversy with Kant, tries to downplay the originality of the *Critique of Pure Reason* by keeping the distinction between the analytic and the synthetic in the well-known setting of dogmatic metaphysics. Here Eberhard is aiming not only to undermine Kant's claim to innovation. He means to suggest that the distinction in question is of little importance. Although it was made by others before Kant—by Wolff, Baumgarten, and Crusius—these authors did not think it important to highlight it. This distinction remained for them simply a paragraph within a chapter on the origin of knowledge. The *Critique*, after all, merely takes up again, without adding anything new, an old theme of metaphysics: the criticism of knowledge with respect to its origin.

How can one answer Eberhard? To say that he missed the historical importance of Kant's "Copernican revolution" in philosophy would be to overlook a more fundamental objection: he misunderstood what might be called the "degree of freedom," the *Spielraum* of a concept or a distinction—what Kant calls "the way it is used." That the contrast between two modes of acquiring concepts, or two modes of predicating, had already been noticed before Kant in no way determines the theoretical role it played. For what is an observation that is not exploited? Is it even legitimate to grant in such a case that the distinction was really made?

We should begin by asking what it means to make a discovery in philosophy. How do we recognize that a concept or distinction was not only mentioned but really used? Even before establishing, against Eberhard, the true novelty of the distinction with which the *Critique* opens, Kant addresses this question of principle: What determines whether an observation is effective in philosophy?

If from an observation presented as new important consequences strike one immediately in the eye, consequences which it would have been impossible to have overlooked had it been made previously, then a suspicion must arise

xi

in regard to the correctness or importance of that division itself, a suspicion which could stand in the way of its use. If, however, this division is put beyond doubt, and at the same time the necessity with which it brings forth from itself these consequences becomes apparent, then one can assume with the highest degree of probability that it had yet not been made. (*The Kant-Eberhard Controversy*, 154)

The criterion for determining the originality of a discovery cannot be reduced to mere chronological antecedence. To have drawn a distinction is not enough; one has to show what its consequences are — that is, *reveal the problems it allows us to bring up*. Going through the table of contents of philosophical works will not tell us who invented the analytic-synthetic distinction. We have to look at what is done with it, the questions it makes possible, and finally how it maps out the very sphere within which these questions should be raised.

In this book I will follow Kant's suggestion and judge by the evidence. Ever since Locke the question of how a priori knowledge is possible has been a subject for philosophical reflection. Had philosophers truly been aware of the distinction between analytic and synthetic judgments, they could not have failed to grasp the particular question this distinction makes it possible to formulate: How are *synthetic* a priori judgments possible? That they did not ask the question shows that they also had not arrived at the analytic-synthetic distinction: "This manner of distinguishing judgments has never been properly conceived."

Does Kant's criterion not deserve to be generalized? We should subject every philosophy to a reading that would seek out behind the explicit theses, the link the concepts bear with a *topics*, understood here neither in the rhetorical nor in the transcendental but in a metasystematic sense: as the locus of a question that determines the urgency of certain problems, mobilizes certain postulates, and fixes certain theses while freeing others — in brief, as the field for a discursive *strategy*.[2] Understood thus, the way Kant marshals his own defense prompts me to attempt a topical reading of the distinction between analytic and synthetic judgments. Yet, as the broad sense of the term "topics" indicates, it is not enough to refer a particular concept or distinction to the transcendental locus that determines, in Kant's view, its problematic relevance. Generalizing the question implies varying the points of view, developing a "comparative topics"; for only a confrontation between distinct arrangements — frameworks of theses, networks of concepts — can fully reveal what it means in philosophy to "conceive a distinction." It is beyond doubt for Kant that the feasibility of applying the distinction between analytic and synthetic judgments to the general question of the possibility of a priori knowledge is evidence of the correct use of this distinction, that is, of its operational comprehensibility. But the fact that the division was used in favor of this powerful antidogmatic war machine does not rule out that it may later, and in different contexts, acquire another crucial function, by determining differently the possibility of inquiry, by mapping out again the field of thought, and by founding on another base the philosophical project itself.

The comparative topics I am proposing must, however, show its worth. Two kinds of objections must be overcome. The first concerns the necessity that it seems to claim unduly. Why have I chosen to examine the topical mutations of the concept of analytic proposition, instead of that of necessity or synthetic proposition, for example? Why have I traced the road leading from Hume's "relations of ideas" to the analytic statements of the Vienna Circle? The second kind of objection aims at exposing the (meta)philosophy on which the project of a comparative topics must secretly rest: Is not this project, in its attempt to discourage the philosopher from "searching for truth," an exercise in skepticism? What else should we expect at the end of this itinerary but a foregone conclusion: as many philosophers as there are views of the world, no progress having been made, no evaluation having become feasible, no discussion having even been started?

Let me begin by making clear the reasons that determined the choice of the concept of "analytic" for this essay on comparative topics. Of the analytic-synthetic pair, "analytic" seems to have played the lesser role in Kant; his true innovation could be summed up as the *synthetic* a priori. His thesis on the apriority of *analytic* judgments contains nothing that could provoke a revolution in philosophy. Simply juxtaposed to the synthetic domain, the analytic mode, as it appears in Kant's philosophy, allows us to define the realm of truths of reason; an analytic truth is, in its main features, a proposition whose treatment belongs to logic in the traditional meaning of the term, that is, Aristotelian "formal" logic. The analytic-synthetic dichotomy thus seems designed to emphasize the synthetic pole of knowledge. The analytic and clarifying dimension of thought is examined only to bring out better the properly synthetic character of the production of knowledge. The locus of truth that Wolff called *veritas logica* is crossed only for the purpose of revealing the larger realm on which it depends, that of *veritas transcendentalis*.[3] In consequence, the *Critique of Pure Reason* distinguishes two kinds of logic: the one "abstracts from all content"; it is general, "formal," logic. The other does not abstract from all content, but is concerned with the origin (*Ursprung*) of knowledge, insofar as the origin "cannot be attributed to the objects" (*Kritik der reinen Vernunft* [hereafter, *KRV*] B 80, Akad, III, 77, 79). The contrast between *analytic* and *synthetic* thus belongs to concepts that only a transcendental logic can produce. General logic being itself included in this contrast, the possibility of its existence is conceived by transcendental logic. The fate of general logic in critical inquiry is therefore determined in the same fashion as the general question of truth that forms one of its chapters: it is "accepted and assumed" (ibid.), the specifically critical task consisting only in knowing what its criterion of scientificity is, which means once again its "origin."

To retain this dualistic presentation, one would have to recognize that the only appropriate perspective on the contrast between judgments is one that shows the specific efficiency of the synthetic part of knowledge and grasps the subsidiary role that belongs to analytic thought and, more globally, to general logic, which controls the formal use of understanding.

If I center this study on the seemingly poorer term of the Kantian distinction, or at least on the one that is not problematic, it is for two reasons, both of which have to do with the relationship that philosophy *after Kant* has with logic. Let me spell them out. After Kant there is a redistribution of tasks, which allows formal logic to replace the transcendental subject, in the foundational role as well as in the architectonic function. Logic becomes in consequence rightfully *philosophical*. In a similar manner, the "analytic-synthetic" pair can be conceived in what Kant called "general logic"—which, as we will see, opens up a novel field of action for the analytic property.

If the post-Kantians neglect general logic and even, to use Hegel's expression, show a "brutal contempt" for it—which the secular petrifaction of the discipline, still largely dominated by Aristotelian syllogistics, seemed to justify— they appear nevertheless to have paved the road to it in their posing the problem of a unitary theory of science.[4] What in Kant's eyes constituted—paradoxically, because of the slight importance that Fichte attached to logic—the chimerical character of the Fichtean project of a theory of science (namely, to promote general logic to the rank of the science of the unity of knowledge, which is in fact to expect of thought that it produce a content, to expect of the analytic that which only the synthetic can give) becomes an enterprise that Hegel and Bolzano both pursue with very different means. Hegel recasts the concept of logic so that the traditional metaphysical oppositions—between form and content, subject and object—are overcome. Bolzano shows that so-called formal logic still has some content, for the most part synthetic, made up of the objective set of propositions in themselves.

The reappearance of logic in the active and architectonic element of philosophical thought is accompanied in this second current by what might be called a "logical revisionism": the important concepts of transcendental logic are taken up and relocated in general logic. If indeed science is represented as a set of propositions, the logician seems to be in the best position to describe the general properties of these propositions, to understand their hierarchy, and to define the boundaries of each science. As soon as they had this premonition—based on the renewal and extension of the conceptual and descriptive means of logic—logicians became philosophers, by challenging the legitimacy of the Kantian or Hegelian philosopher's foundational or systematic concepts. Bolzano illustrates in a characteristic way this anti-Hegelian movement, but he is not alone. Without having attempted to present like Bolzano a "theory of science," Frege places himself at the architectonic level by making analyticity the mortar of the system of arithmetic and the universal element of the a priori legitimation of discourse.

Consequently, logical thought can no longer be content with indicating the rules of conceiving, judging, and reasoning. It must also conceive its own nature, in terms of its own relationship to philosophy. This leads logical thought to define *logically* what should be understood precisely by "analytic proposition" (how are we to define the concept *logically*, eventually so as to be self-descriptive?), and to specify its function (what constitutes the value of analytic propositions; what purpose do they serve? And if logic itself is made up of these propositions, what is the status of logic; what comprises its particular contribution to knowledge as a whole?). It is therefore in the strategy of logicians who come after Kant, and who see in Hegel their main opponent, but also under the impulse of new forces that logic takes from recent discoveries, for the concept of analyticity to play a positive role: no longer just to bring out the synthetic a priori, as in the *Critique*, but as an instrument that makes it possible to describe and to found a science, and in particular to discredit any descriptive or foundational claim on the part of a synthetic a priori.

This is but the second episode of what might be termed the revenge of formal logic: an episode in which logic revises the concept of analytic proposition so as to give it a precise function in the systemization of scientific propositions, and which the different yet kindred projects of Bolzano and Frege let us map out.

The third episode of what might be called the "fate" of the notion of analytic proposition starts in the 1920s. It is characterized by a noteworthy topical shift, which continues to characterize contemporary philosophy. Associated by the Vienna Circle and its followers with an *empiricist* inquiry into knowledge, analytic propositions receive henceforth a new function: that of defining the field of the philosophical, which becomes coextensive with that of the logic of science. "Comparative topics" allows us to bring out the functional mutation that the notion of analytic proposition then undergoes: with "logical empiricism," analyticity is ascribed a task that in Kantian thought should have remained outside its scope, namely, the systematic organization of knowledge, the constitution of experience — the general ability to account for the application of forms to content.

The hypothesis guiding this study consists in challenging in particular the empiricist character involved in this use of the concept of analytic proposition, and more generally in defending the fundamentally rationalist character of the distinction between analytic and synthetic propositions.[5] It could be objected here that it is not Leibniz whom Kant recognizes as having perceived the importance of the contrast between the two types of propositions for understanding the nature of knowledge, but empiricists like Locke and Hume. A close examination of texts shows, however, that neither Locke nor Hume could be said to have "anticipated" the Kantian distinction. Chapter 1 of Section 1 shows that the determining contrast in Locke's thought is that between nominal essence and real essence. If it is true that Locke opposes these two types of essences, it must be observed that he does not seek to derive a distinction between kinds of *propositions*; knowledge of a real essence, if it were possible, would be of the same predicative form as nominal knowledge and would develop what is contained in the essence. As far as the Humean distinction between "relations of ideas" and "matters of fact" is concerned, one may see the Kantian distinction only at the cost of a series of confusions with respect, in particular, to Hume's doctrine of relationships and his theory of mathematical objects.

This does not imply, however, that the Kantian distinction is simply a recovery of the Leibnizian distinction between truths of reason and truths of fact. For as Kant emphasizes, Leibniz's dichotomy of truths is not radical enough because it fails to be followed up by a distinction between discrete sources of knowledge. Leibniz did not accomplish the "Copernican revolution"; he remains on the side of rationalism, moreover of dogmatic rationalism. The Kantian theory of character attempts precisely to discredit the universalist claims of universal characteristics. Kant's subordinating of formal logic to transcendental logic obliges us to divide characters into two types that cannot be combined: analytic and synthetic characters. Composition ceases to be the inverse of decomposition. Similarly the Kantian theory of definition (Chapter 4) demonstrates against Leibniz that it is impossible to transform a nominal definition into a real definition — to build up objects by simple calculation.

"Comparative topics" then faces the task of examining the evolution of the notion, or more exactly the various ways the concept of "analytic proposition" is put to use *after Kant*. The successive examination of the different ways of approaching the "same concept" introduces us into networks of "obligations" and theoretical constraints in which the notion of analyticity receives each time a singular function. Bolzano is concerned with giving a purely logical definition of the concept of analytic proposition. This must be understood as a definition that refers only to the behavior of propositions in respect to truth, without reference to logically impure distinctions (as, for example, that between logical and extralogical types of constituents). The inquiry into the meaning of this definition will perhaps illustrate in the most convincing manner the value of comparative topics. By articulating the various constraints that Bolzano sets on the nature of logical reasoning, I am led to rule out current interpretations of Bolzano's work (which identify his analytic with Quine's "logical truth") and to bring out the fundamental derivational schema from which the very cursory definition of the concept of analytic proposition arises, as a proposition that remains true or false when at least one of its constituents is modified freely (Section 2, Chapter 3).

Whereas analyticity has a merely secondary role in Bolzano's logic as a "pedagogical" instance of submodelization for universal truths, Frege gives it an essential function in his system, as the mortar of the system of logical truths. A proposition is analytic if it is part of the system of logical laws. The analyticity of logical propositions is not itself in question, but it forms the assumption of the enterprise, which concerns the possibility of carrying out the logicist reduction and deduction of mathematical truths. The property of conserving analyticity — "mortar" of the system — together with the constructive nature of the system constitutes the originality of the Fregean construction. Conservation is ensured by *formulary language* designed to guarantee a perfect demonstrative continuity. The notion of identity in conjunction with the Fregean theory of reference plays a fundamental role here by guaranteeing the real (and not purely nominal) scope of constructions. This notion goes along with a new theory of definition, which allows us to associate the two values, regarded as antithetical by traditional thought, of a construction both nominal and real, by imposing restrictions on the current use of definitions. The concept of logical axiom must still be analyzed, in order to understand how it can be considered the "incipient germ" of the system of analytic propositions.

If the parallel between Frege and Carnap makes it possible for comparative topics to outline the logicist project as well as the specificity of each of the two "ventures," the parallel between Bolzano and Frege is no less instructive. In spite of a different conception of foundational instances, the way the question of *Grund* is raised involves more than a formal affinity. It is known that Kant names "transcendental" a principle "through which we represent a priori the universal condition under which alone things can become objects of our cognition generally" (*Critique of Judgment*, v). Bolzano and Frege agree to dismiss the subject from the transcendental function as defined here, and to place in the same role of "constitution" of the object of cognition a set of "propositions" or "thoughts" true eternally and independent of our cognitive grasp. In order to qualify this joint foundational strategy, I will speak of "ontotranscendental," designating thereby not the oxymoronic negation of the critical project but the persistence of the quest for a general a priori condition transposed to a universe that admits objective forms "in themselves."[6] This means, in short, that Bolzano and Frege fix the transcendental *question* so as to give an answer *different* from that of Kant, and not through an inquiry into the a priori powers of knowledge, but by bringing to light the objective logical properties that a set of propositions must have in order to constitute a science.

It remains, then, to explain why I have limited to Carnap the examination of post-Fregean philosophies of analyticity and made the *Logical Syntax* of 1934 the upper bound of my inquiry. Should I not have extended my study of Carnap to his works of the semantic period? Should I not have added Russell, Wittgenstein, and Tarski, in an investigation that seeks to elucidate the origins of analytic philosophy by describing the formation of the concept of "analytic proposition"?

This objection would bear only if my purpose was to retrace exhaustively the history of analyticity. But what I am undertaking is, by nature, *selective*. I have retained the lineage of Frege and Carnap because it seemed to me to have been the determining factor in the logicist breakthrough; I delineate the extension of the logicist project, already represented by the *Aufbau* of 1928; I also attempt to show how the *Logical Syntax* constitutes Carnap's reply to the challenge contained in the last sentence of the *Tractatus* ("What we cannot speak about we must pass over in silence").

Just as I could not claim to be exhaustive with respect to authors who could rightly be considered relevant in this attempt in comparative topics, so too I have chosen not to tackle the "semantic" conception of analyticity that Carnap develops, after the *Syntax*, under Tarski's influence. But the reason for this choice is not wholly negative. It proceeds from the decision I took to describe, by means of an inquiry into the concept of analyticity, the emergence of the logicist thesis. The *Logical Syntax* is certainly, in this respect, a work that portrays the final stage of logicism. Subsequent works can be read as the completion of the project of which the *Logical Syntax* is the first sketch. Semantics takes the place of universal syntax, the problem of induction becoming the focus of a foundational inquiry more than ever dependent on the analytic-synthetic dichotomy.

These objections to the relevance of my enterprise are only "internal," to speak in Carnapian terms. I must now consider briefly the "external" objections mentioned above. What justifies *this* manner of philosophizing? What is to be gained from a "comparative topics"? Is it only a matter of exposing a clockwork, of reducing the quest for truth to a certain arrangement of themes and theses? But why try to comprehend thus each discourse in its own setting? Does it not amount to emptying philosophical inquiry of its *purpose*? Is it not to give up the task of *assessing* a philosophy?

Several problems are implicitly confused in these questions. One assumption concerns the necessary barrenness of a faithful historical description, with which is contrasted the forceful but fruitful intrusion of rational reconstruction. Another assumption touches on what must be chosen as the basic unit of philosophical analysis: if argumentation is favored—taken, that is, as a chain of statements offering a precise solution for a limited question—one will tend to discredit an approach that focuses not on a problem but on a network of problems, or "discursive formation."[7] This tendency is quite often accompanied by the realist illusion according to which the only "useful" philosophical exercise consists in resolving problems, considered, as it were, in themselves and without reference to theoretical and methodological preliminaries.

This question of scale confronts not only the historian of ideas or of philosophy but also the philosopher engaged in systematic elaboration. Historians must delimit a corpus: but should they confine their investigations to one book, to the works of one author, or to the joint productions of several authors? And according to what criterion: temporal, geographical, sociological, or epistemic? Should they go beyond the written work toward biographical, sociological, or institutional data? Likewise, philosophers must determine the scope of their inquiry: Should they merely clarify the meaning of a concept and point to new applications of it? Should they present new arguments for (or against) a problematic thesis? Or should they seek more ambitiously to promote new problems, new theses, and even inaugurate a new manner of philosophizing?

The parallel between the historical and the constructive inquiry shows that, although remaining generally implicit, the unit of analysis chosen depends on a preliminary evaluation of the conceptual importance of a question, that is, on the set of former presuppositions that the proposed solution challenges or on the set of new notions or modes of reasoning that it brings in. Let me remark that philosophers are all the more reserved as to the nature of their investigations the narrower the unit of analysis chosen. Why? They share with their readers more assumptions and, consequently, do not need to develop them. Hence the illusion mentioned above, which transforms the problem examined into an object independent from a context of argumentation and a definite set of problems.

In other words, one could say that by choosing to treat a problem in terms of arguments, philosophers decide implicitly that the question examined calls for a local, not a global, treatment. Yet, scientific research shows that the transition from the local to the global almost always has a heuristic value, not only owing to the new comprehension brought about by the change of scale, but also because it leads in some cases to a modification of the very concept of local analysis. Hence the project of changing or combining scales, of developing a history of philosophy that would be at the same time a reconstruction of arguments and a reconstruction of the particular conditions of their acceptability.

The comparative topics proposed in this book recommends precisely that very close attention be paid to the details of the construction of a concept and to the totality in which it is inscribed. The originality of comparative topics consists in considering what forms the implicit conditions of philosophical debate by choosing as a guideline a particular question, common to several authors: What implications and ''canon'' or set of rules of exposition and reasoning make up the backdrop of the problem considered? What relevance and systematic weight are ascribed to this problem in the general framework of theses? It is undeniable that nuanced attention to the validity that a certain question or distinction is accorded in different philosophies allows us to bring out what an isolated reading cannot reveal: the persistence of certain schemata of problems and certain types of solutions, and—simultaneously—the change in meaning of concepts borrowed from ordinary usage, but actively assimilated, redefined, and arranged in view of a new systematic finality.

What, then, is the specific contribution of this method with respect to the constructive discussion of problems? The effort to clear up presuppositions leads, in the case of philosophical analysis, to the advantage that, from Frege's point of view, justifies in mathematics the task of axiomatization: what goes into an agreement or disagreement becomes clearer when we follow out the relationships of interdependence between the various theses that give body to a particular problem. There is interest in historical reconstruction because it forces one to bring out all the assumptions and claims necessary for the validity of the argumentation under study. In many cases, historical reconstruction reveals the relevant elements that "rational reconstruction" ignores, precisely because it is located at a different level.

. Moreover, comparative study brings out what in general remains if not hidden at least indistinct—namely, forces exerting influence both on the meaning of concepts and on the relevance of questions, as the discussion of a problem evolves and becomes complicated. By directing our reading to a question regarded as crucial, comparative topics adopts a specific point of view on the literature; the worth of a point of view is appreciated by the panorama it opens up. Other points of view, other questions, would have opened different areas of inquiry. But not all concepts are equally "topical," not all questions are equally relevant. By choosing a key question and by delimiting determinately the extension of its domain of application, comparative topics is radically opposed to doxography, which typically refuses to select and delimit.[8]

Exposition difficulties in the history of philosophy result from the necessity of combining analyses carried out in different scales. In the history of philosophy, as in other historical disciplines, there are indeed several types of "temporal duration," several ways to scan phenomena, in some cases a systematic text, in others an economic cycle. In addition to the short duration of the construction of a work—for example, that in which Carnap redefines progressively the scientific content of the logicist venture—there is the "easy-slope" history,[9] which requires relativizing the importance of ruptures brought about in the short lapse of a work. Although he departs from Fregean ontology, Carnap remains, at a deeper level, in agreement with Frege and, through him, in continuity with Kant.

The methodological interest in comparative topics thus lies in the freedom allowed by it of "changing scale," that is, of combining several comparative levels, of discovering in a work superimposed stratifications. This superimposition is not an illusion begot by comparison: textual evidence is here to show it. I leave it to readers to judge for themselves.

This superimposition of what, lacking a better expression, I call the "levels" of conceptual arrangement ultimately throws light on what a specifically discontinuist "structuralist" or "archaeological" history usually leaves in the dark: the conditions of a minimal continuity between works. Without this minimal communication, it is not possible to give meaning to the notion of *philosophical problem*, understanding thereby a complex formation that without being eternal, can in certain cases go beyond the system that gave rise to it and survive doctrinal reworkings and terminological changes for a rather long period. It is true that the notion of "philosophical problem" long ago lost any credibility in the eyes of historians, on account of the continuist naïveté of doxographers. Topical inquiry seems nevertheless capable of giving meaning to the intuitive idea of the inter-systematic permanence of certain questions. I do not mean that philosophical articulation amounts to giving a particular solution to a universal problem whose expression would be literally identical, according to the implicit postulate of doxography, but merely that, in spite of changes affecting the order of precedence of related questions, as well as the definition of essential concepts and the origin of evidence, certain systems appear truly as ways of raising one and the same problem. In this book, I examine the role that the notion of logical form, and more precisely of analytic proposition, plays in the examination of the conditions of objective knowledge. It appeared to me that this problem originated in a post-Kantian reading of Kant, concerned with giving formal logic the attributions of what Kant named "transcendental logic." With stylistic, terminological, and doctrinal differences, the same problem is taken up again by Bolzano, Frege, the early Wittgenstein, Russell, and Carnap.

To return to the objection mentioned above: Am I not giving up the task of assessing? This conclusion would follow if I invited the reader to substitute, in Rorty's terms, "conversation" for "epistemology"[10] — to renounce inquiring into the condition of scientificness (whatever concept we are able to construct of it) in favor of a comprehensive reading of discourses cut off from any objective referent.

Skeptical relativism could appear to be the sole possible route only if a teleological inquiry failed to grasp the meaning of a succession of epistemic configurations. It is the disappointment of not finding in history the triumphant revelation of truth (definitive truth obtained once and for all in the perfect equilibrium of a system of universal knowledge) that seems to dictate that a skeptical conclusion be drawn from the facts. Perhaps nostalgia for the Hegelian *Offenbarung*, which so easily comes to the fore when one ventures to do history, prompts historians who are unable to defend themselves against it to leave to epistemologists the interest for truth (discredited by the multiplicity of its definitions), and to seek to join forces with the latest embodiment of the *Weltgeist*.

Whether historians project comparative constructs on the oriented vector of a dialectic (or more generally of an "edifying" history) they proclaim, in a relativist vein, the forthcoming extinction of foundational soundings, they cannot appeal to de facto proof without contradicting their basic methodological assumptions. For one cannot accept the supposed obviousness of the relativity of truth without conferring on the variation of themes and discursive formations the role of "evidence," of preliminary data for every concept, a procedure moreover whose validity historians refuse when they reconstruct systems. To deny comparatists a teleological and edifying perspective does not therefore amount to forbidding them to raise the question of truth. Comparative construction permits, quite the contrary, its development with all its conditions. The idea that there is a dilemma between comparison and evaluation proceeds thus from a restrictive conception of systematic activity. For it seems difficult to reach a philosophical evaluation without practicing, at least implicitly, the type of conceptual archaeology that I am proposing here under the name of "comparative topics." What does it mean to refute a thesis if not to prove its incompatibility with a given series of theses regarded as foundational? How to assess, for example, the usefulness of the distinction between analytic and synthetic propositions without measuring its intrasystematic significance, without perceiving the relationship it bears with the idea of an a priori foundation of knowledge?

Comparative topics is a discipline at the same time constructive and corrective, but it is not edifying. It offers a reconstruction of systems that reveals their architecture by specifying the nature of the dependence between theses and concepts. It sometimes happens that the result of this kind of inquiry conflicts with the perception that authors have of their own philosophy. For example, the topical approach allows us to question the "empiricist" character of Carnap's *universal syntax*, and to bring out its structural affinity with the (onto)transcendental philosophies that came before it. This shift is one of the contributions of a method that prescribes relating a set of concepts and theses (stated *in* the system) to their own systematic function (stated *with the help of* the system in comparative language and evaluated not according to the aims and allegiances particular to a given strategy, but according to the fundamental lines of force of the philosophy under consideration.

This is not to say that comparison is the last word of philosophy, or that comparison furnishes the historian with a privileged standpoint from which to anticipate the outcome of systems. A more urgent task awaiting the historian consists, rather, in trying to remove the obstacles to the global comprehension of the current philosophical situation. As was said above, the determination of an object of analysis always presupposes a preliminary diagnostic: in one case an incorrectly stated problem, in another an unresolved difficulty. For me the essential problem of contemporary philosophy, rarely stated, is the respective inabilities of "Anglo-Saxon" and "Continental" philosophers to establish between themselves a critical exchange. How can communication be established between two philosophical traditions that are perfectly impervious to one another? By striving, in this study, to make more perceptible the philosophical role allotted since Kant to "formal" logic, and thus to shed light on the genesis of analytic philosophy, the role played by logical elucidation, and the correlative rejection of subjective apriorism, I wish to point out a *common bedrock of philosophical strategies*. If one grasps the continuity of Carnap's project with that of Kant—namely, the attempt to submit to the canons of modern science the concepts and questions of traditional metaphysics, by questioning the general a priori conditions of the possibility of scientific discourse, one should also assess the necessity of widening the debate with the systematic philosophies of our time.[11]

Section 1
Kant and His "Precursors"

1

Locke's "Indication"

Kant's cleavage between analytic and synthetic truths was foreshadowed in Hume's distinction between relations of ideas and matters of fact, and in Leibniz's distinction between truths of reason and truths of fact.
— W. V. Quine, *From a Logical Point of View*

The Kant-Eberhard controversy about the inventor of the analytic-synthetic distinction suggested to us that Kant is interested in analyticity, in the explanatory dimension of judgment, only insofar as it brings out the "real" question. It is not important to insist on the purely resolutive, decompositional character of analytic predication, for the legitimacy of resolution is unproblematic. What is important is understanding that synthetic judgment cannot be founded *on this legitimacy*. For Kant this is precisely the contribution of Locke and Hume: they both suspected that there is a difference of nature between a judgment of observation or causality, on the one hand, and a judgment restricted to developing what is already conceived in the concept of the subject, on the other hand:

> In Locke's *Essay*, however, I find an indication of my division. For in the fourth book (Chapter III, §9ff), having discussed the various connections of representations in judgments, and their sources, one of which he makes "identity or contradiction" (analytical judgments) and another the coexistence of ideas in a subject (synthetical judgments), he confesses (§10) that our (a priori) knowledge of the latter is very narrow and almost nothing. (*Prolegomena*, §3)

Having recognized Locke as the precursor of a distinction that will become "classic," Kant quickly adds—*in cauda venenum*—a remark that amounts to canceling his recognition:

3

But in his remarks on this species of knowledge, there is so little of what is definite and reduced to rules that we cannot wonder if no one, not even Hume, was led to make investigations concerning this sort of proposition.

This page of the *Prolegomena* deserves to be meditated on for its exemplary value. Here Kant is trying to clarify what constitutes the novelty of his distinction. Clearly he hopes to persuade readers of the *Critique* that the contrast between analytic and synthetic propositions goes well beyond a simple terminological innovation. Kant invites his readers to recognize here a *real* distinction, the only one that would allow us to characterize adequately not only *given* types but also *possible* types of knowledge. This passage, thus, has quite precisely a metaphilosophical function, that is, a *topical* one in my sense of the term.

Later I will have the opportunity to encounter in other authors passages similar to this one, texts devoted to a topical comparison between the author's use of the analytic-synthetic distinction, or of the definition of "analytic," and a predecessor's use that had become influential (usually Kant is the reference point that will be retained for some time). Of course, after Kant, and because of the strategic role it plays not only in the *Critique of Pure Reason* but also in post-Kantian debate, the distinction will be most often reconstructed in the terminology inaugurated by the *Critique*. However, all authors, when confronted with problems unknown to their predecessors, will still have to establish, for their readers and for themselves, the exact extent to which their own use of the concept of analytic—or of the analytic-synthetic distinction—agrees with tradition.

In trying to show the scope of their own innovation, authors are subjected to two contradictory tendencies which the text of the *Prolegomena* illustrates. The first tendency is to assimilate: one identifies—in a related system (which must be neither proximate nor antagonistic)—a distinction that "from a particular angle" is analogous to the distinction one wants to introduce. The second tendency is to indicate the inadequacy of the traditional distinction (or definition), either by criticizing it as vague and without foundation, like Kant with respect to Locke, or by condemning it as inexhaustive or insufficiently incorporated into a general theory of the propositions of science.

It may be objected that this vacillation is not in the least surprising. It seems to express the double requirement authors face in locating the originality of their conception: on the one hand, to establish in what respect their thought is a "continuation" of earlier works and, on the other hand, to point out in what respect it goes beyond them. If the succession of acknowledgments and reproofs is worth studying more closely, it is because most often the setting of the standards leading to the final verdict actually starts *with* the phase of assimilation. This prompts us to pay special attention to the historical references an author decides to give: they are suggestive so long as we consider them the expression of a new point of view on the concept or pair of concepts studied; they may well, however, subject the target text to a systematic distortion, which is the retroactive effect that the new topics has on a foreign conceptual scheme.

These remarks acquire their full meaning only when confronted with the facts. Let us reexamine how Kant summarizes Locke in the *Prolegomena*. Surely no one will challenge Kant when he says that Locke speaks very little about "this species of knowledge"—synthetic a priori. One could even say, going beyond Kant's remark, that Locke *does not speak at all* about it. Kant's procedure is to rediscover in empiricism the type of problem that critical rationalism poses. This charitable assimilating phase of Kant's commentary should be compared with the reality of Locke's' philosophy: Is this philosophy adequately represented by what Kant says? Is there truly in Locke a first "indication" of the division of propositions into analytic and synthetic?

In spite of appearances, this question is of more than local interest. It makes it possible to conceive the relationships between two systems of thought as fundamentally distinct in their purposes and their methods of argumentation as classic empiricism and Kantian criticism. Let me state the suspicion that justifies a careful reexamination of the empiricist texts: Has the analytic-synthetic dualism not been purely and simply *smuggled* into philosophies that not only ignore it, but even disclaim in advance its topical use? Is Kant not responsible for having misunderstood *the specific type of empiricist problem*? Did he not for a long time give a "rationalist turn" to the empiricist approach to the question of the limits of knowledge?

Let us enter Locke's *Essays* in Kant's footsteps, so to speak. In what way can it be said that there is in Locke an "indication" of this distinction? In the chapter Kant refers to, Locke examines the different types of knowledge. For Locke, to know is to perceive the agreement or disagreement between two ideas. This expression will be generalized by Leibniz, following in fact an observation of Locke's in §7: to know is to establish between two ideas or two propositions a relationship, which can be "either of comparison or concurrence" (*New Essays*, IV, I, §7). If we decide that *relationship*—the second kind of agreement between ideas—must be understood rather as a generic mark of all knowledge than as a particular cognitive species, three types of knowledge remain: one that presupposes the perception of an *identity* or a "*diversity*" between ideas, one that discovers the *coexistence* of several qualities in a substance, and one that results from judgments of *existence*.

By establishing this taxonomy, Locke means to distinguish the limits within which sure knowledge can be attained, and this is accomplished in his next two chapters. Let me summarize his evaluation. First, propositions of existence do not generally lead to certainty concerning their subject matter, except the Cartesian proposition of the *cogito*, which without being a necessary proposition is indubitable for every thinking being.[1] Identical propositions are certain but "trifling," as Locke will call them in Chapter VIII of Book IV: they carry no "instruction"; they do not at all increase our knowledge. What remains are propositions affirming the connection between ideas. In this area, "our knowledge is very short":

The simple ideas whereof our complex ideas of substances are made up are, for the most part, such as carry with them, in their own nature, no *visible necessary* connexion or inconsistency with any other simple ideas, whose co-existence with them we would inform ourselves about. (*An Essay Concerning Human Understanding* [hereafter, *E*], IV, III, §10; ed. Fraser, 200).

Here Locke wants to insist on the role that secondary qualities play, in our ignorance where we find ourselves of the "necessary" connections between the properties of a substance. Which does not mean that these connections do not exist. But the secondary qualities are only the effect, on us, of primary qualities, which alone are the attributes of things themselves. We do not know what the causal connections between secondary qualities and underlying primary qualities are. We are unable a fortiori to know the structure of primary qualities: what "size, figure, and texture of parts they are, on which depend, and from which result" the secondary qualities that are often our only way of characterizing a substance (IV, III, §11). Thus our inability to derive secondary qualities follows from our ignorance of primary qualities and their "secondary" effects:

Our minds not being able to discover any connexion betwixt these primary qualities of bodies and the sensations that are produced in us by them, we can never be able to establish certain and undoubted rules of the *consequence* or *co-existence* of any secondary qualities, though we could discover the size, figure, or motion of those invisible parts which immediately produce them. We are so far from knowing *what* figure, size, or motion of parts produce a yellow colour, a sweet taste, or a sharp sound, that we can by no means conceive how *any* size, figure, or motion of any particles, can possibly produce in us the idea of any colour, taste, or sound whatsoever: there is no conceivable connexion between the one and the other. (*E*, IV, III, §13; ed. Fraser, 202).

The limitation of our demonstrative knowledge (that is, deductive or mediated knowledge) arises not from the absence of an *objective* connection—whose existence Locke maintains—but from the absence of a connection accessible to *our mind*. The limitation of our knowledge of coexistence is thus in itself a contingent fact: other beings could reach it. As for us, "we are left only to the assistance of our senses" to learn the properties of gold (§14); we must be content with adding one property to another, instead of deriving them from the essence. We may well inquire "what other qualities" a substance has, but not systematically derive the complete set of secondary properties that a substance owes to its primary qualities (§9). But because of this, we never reach a *sure* knowledge of the properties of things: we only have a nominal definition, which means that, in the case of substances, we are not able to frame definitions that would allow us to derive in a necessary and exhaustive manner the whole set of predicates.

The preceding discussion allows us to understand better in what way Locke can be pictured by Kant as having anticipated the analytic-synthetic distinction. As we saw, one of the main aims of the *Essay* is to warn readers to avoid the Scholastic confusion between the arbitrary juxtaposing of simple ideas (of modes) in the complex idea (of substance)—which is the usual way in which we give meaning to words—and the acquiring of objective knowledge. If we follow up this Lockean line of thought, we see that what determines Locke's discourse is not the distinction Kant finds, but rather a distinction that *in a way*—in the use Locke makes of it—is incompatible with Kant's distinction, that is, one between *nominal essence* and *real essence*. Let us try to grasp the originality of this second distinction, and its specific role in Locke's philosophy, before examining the reasons that may explain why Kant banished it, in favor of his own.

The Nominal and the Real

I could say provocatively, that the only way Locke can assign a property to a substance is in the "analytic" manner; but such an interpretation, I must quickly add, might lead us to compare Locke's thought with criteria of intelligibility that are not his own. What makes this assimilation tempting is that Locke seems to consider every universal predication in the mode of *praedicatum inest subjecto*. In the margins of Locke's distinction between nominal and real we learn that a predication can be necessarily true only if it develops the ideas contained in the subject.[2]

When I know the properties of an individual thing by observation, I put in the idea of this thing the corresponding ideas of properties. Assuredly these ideas are not part of the definition, for I form in this case knowledge pertaining not to nominal essence but to something "really existing outside of me" (*An Early Draft of Locke's Essay* [hereafter, *Draft A*], §13). It seems, however, that these properties "are contained" in the individual idea just as the nominal constituents "are contained" in the definition. This condition of inherence applies as well to nominal essences as to real essences, whether it is a matter of explaining the meaning we give to a word, or of discovering the objective properties of a concrete thing. Locke excludes the possibility of reaching knowledge of the real essences of substances precisely because the necessity of a proposition has the same requisites in both cases; we will soon see that this is not the case for real essence of modes. To know a nominal essence is to examine what is contained in the complex idea expressed by a certain word. Such knowledge is thus only verbal; it is the kind of information that a dictionary gives. Here, for example, the nominal essence of gold is specified as the complex idea that the word "gold" represents: a yellow substance, of a certain weight, malleable, fusible, soluble in aqua regia, and so forth. Obviously it is possible to acquire in this kind of "knowledge" complete certainty, because nominal essence follows from an arbitrary decision. Here certainty is directly related to the very triviality of nominal definition.

I may add that such certainty does not mean that different speakers cannot give a different meaning to the same words. On the contrary, such divergences are commonplace, because each speaker has formed each idea in a manner that is singular and contingent. Such divergences are not in fact an obstacle to communication, as long as communication is restricted to ordinary situations of everyday life and makes no scientific claims. In this last case, it is the effort that persons make to *fix* the meaning of words that leads them astray, by attracting their energies to solely verbal and classificatory questions, instead of making them attentive to things themselves.

What does it mean to know a *real* essence? By "real essence" Locke understands "the real constitution of substances, upon which depends this nominal essence, and all the properties of that sort." For example, the real essence of gold is what makes possible nominal definition (in terms of the secondary qualities previously mentioned: yellow, malleable, etc.): "the constitution of the insensible parts of that body, on which those qualities and all the other properties of gold depend" (III, VI, §2). However, as the primary qualities of substances are not accessible to our senses, it is not in our power to form an idea of this real essence. We could express this differently by saying that nominal essence is *abstract, classificatory*, and *variable*, whereas real essence is *concrete, an internal principle of development*, and *unique*. The real essence of substances cannot be reached through our finite means of knowledge; it is held by Locke, however, for the only objective one, the ideal aim of knowledge, which is impossible only "for us" and not "in itself." If we cannot grasp the human essence, for example, it is not the same for the Creator, who has an idea of human nature as different from ours as the clockmaker has of the clock of Strasbourg compared with that of an astonished farmer who only sees "outward appearances" and knows nothing about the mechanism of the clock.

If knowledge of real essence were possible, its form would not be *different* from that of nominal knowledge; such knowledge would, for example, show that the *thing* called "gold" takes its properties from its "genetic definition," meaning a representation isomorphic with the physical constitution of the substance under study. Whether the predication is real or nominal, it continues to appear as the development of what is contained in the essence.

The limit of Kant's interpretation manifests itself clearly in the interpretation that should be given to the "and" of empirical judgment. If I say, "Gold is yellow and malleable and fusible" (being unable to derive these properties from the real essence, which I do not know), I am not *synthesizing* an empirical concept, that is, a "real" concept. In Locke's view, I confine myself to developing what is *contained* in the complex idea that I associate with the word "gold," but to developing it in a typically nominal way. For to develop the real contents would be to allow substituting for the simple coordinative "and" the derivative "therefore," and thus passing from the contingent enumeration of properties to the necessary knowledge of the properties of the substance (*Draft A*, V, §15).

There is therefore no trace, in Locke, of a synthetic *predication* in Kant's sense. Quite on the contrary, we must say that such a predication would, in Locke's eyes, be a purely verbal manner of going beyond the limits imposed on us by nature, a way of replacing the necessary deduction of characteristics, which marks for Locke true knowledge, by a freer mode of connection—not requiring (impossible) recourse to direct observation of primary qualities. In other words, Locke would see in the transcendental a reappearance of the postulate of substance, which would providentially bind the predicates grouped together randomly through experience. In its "topical" function though, we find a feature that links Locke's distinction to Kant's. This function is explicated by Locke in his *Conduct of the Understanding*, where he tries to bring out what constitutes the importance of thought. Interest in the nominal characterizes in Locke's eyes a defect encouraged by Scholastic philosophy, as well as by *formal logic*: Locke's nominal covers what will be for Kant the domain of the thought of understanding.

In Locke's eyes, exclusive interest in logic and analysis of nominal essences is mistaken in two senses. It is not only the result of a confusion between questions having to do with words, and questions having to do with things, but "so obvious a mismanagement of the understanding . . . that it could not be passed by" (§43). "This is no better than if a man, who was to be a painter, should spend all his time in examining the threads of several cloths he is to paint upon, and counting the hairs of each pencil and brush he intends to use in the laying of his colours." No better, and even much worse, for the apprentice painter would eventually discover that what he is doing has nothing to do with painting, whereas "men designed for scholars have often their heads so filled and warmed with disputes on logical questions, that they take those airy useless notions for real and substantial knowledge, and think their understanding so well furnished with science, that they need not look farther into the nature of things, or descend to the mechanical drudgery of experiment and inquiry."

The purpose of the distinction given such importance by Locke, as well as the classification he proposes between various modes of knowledge, is therefore not to distract humankind from experimental research, as a superficial reading of the beginning of Book IV could lead someone to believe, but rather, after having set the limits of this kind of research—in particular, to the extent that certainty should be replaced by probability—to show that it is in these "low" human tasks that the true victories of understanding must be won. We can increase our knowledge only by venturing where purely verbal certainties cease to be relevant. Chapter VIII of Book IV, "Of Trifling Propositions," appears thus clearly to be directed against the Scholastic tradition: nominal predication that only develops in the predicate the ordinary meaning of the subject, whether it is in the form of an identity or a predication using part of the definition of the subject, does not represent true knowledge. This fact is not, remarks Locke, universally accepted. On the contrary, either "in books or out of them," we often encounter propositions that, in the garb of "instructive" propositions, only deal with words and therefore give us merely the illusion of knowledge, thus creating from a certain point of view, a major obstacle for carrying out efficient research. "Trifling" propositions must be recognized for what they are, in order to restore knowledge to its true seriousness.

Mathematical Demonstration

To recognize if we are concerned with an instructive proposition, we cannot rely solely on a contrast of the type that Kant ascribes to Locke in the *Prolegomena*; there are indeed "relational" propositions that are purely verbal, although they seem to refer to some *thing* and although they presuppose "the coexistence of ideas in a subject" (this is the case of all propositions that describe a substance by referring to secondary qualities). On the other hand, there are propositions of identity[3] that are not at all trivial, but constitute true knowledge; this is the case, in particular, of propositions about modes. The complete clarification of the scope of the distinction of nominal essences and real essences in Locke thus supposes that we understand why modes, unlike substances, can be *known with certainty*. A unique feature establishes the possibility of a sure knowledge of modes (whether simple or complex): it is their *abstraction*—in other words, the pureness of the empirical genesis of these ideas, whose classificatory and comparative meaning is in agreement with reality as perceived.

Let us first examine, in the case of simple modes, what follows from their genesis. We acquire, for example, the idea of whiteness by *abstraction* from a concrete substance, say, a white wall. The abstraction from which the mode proceeds guarantees that we have not put *anything* in the idea of whiteness *other than* what the corresponding impression reveals. In this case, there is no middle course between understanding and not understanding the word "white." We understand the word if we remember that it is the color of snow and milk. If, on the other hand, we no longer know what to apply the abstraction to, we will not be mistaken, for that matter, concerning the meaning of the word "white": we will simply admit that we do not understand the word (III, IV, §15).

Mixed modes, which Kant would call "formed concepts," are not "passively" established—that is, from the impressions that a substance, a real being, has caused in the subject; they are "made by the mind," "made very arbitrarily, made without patterns, or reference to any real existence" (III, V, §9). Because these mixed modes are formed concepts—formed not in pure intuition, but simply by free conjunction of simple modes—there is no danger of taking the name for the thing itself: denomination follows abstraction and appropriate composition of ideas; it cannot go beyond them, for there is no substratum to qualify, no *concretum* to describe (IV, IV, §5). This property of mixed modes entitles them, paradoxically, to be known in an "infallibly certain" manner. This certainty, however, does not have the restrictions of solely nominal certainty. Precisely because the ideas of complex modes do not depend for their elaboration on the observation of a concrete complex thing to which they should correspond—which is the case of ideas of substance—what we know about them "reaches things themselves.'' We even have here a necessary property of complex modes: "So that in these we cannot miss of a certain and undoubted reality.''

How are we to understand in what way the modes, simple or complex, make it possible in such a clearly exclusive way to form a sure knowledge that is *not only nominal*? The question appears crucial—that is, if we want to understand what set Locke in a different perspective from Kant concerning the necessity of mathematical propositions, and what allows his definition to be nevertheless reinterpreted by Kant—the nominal being assimilated with the analytic, the real with the synthetic. Mathematical propositions for Locke are propositions based on ideas of modes—in other words, propositions *at the same time* nominal and real. These, with the ideas of moral modes, are the only ones in which demonstration is concerned. Interpreted as a Kantian, Locke seems to be saying that mathematical propositions suppose a synthesis, moreover an a priori synthesis: they are "real," they are "constructed," and they are necessarily true. Is this reading truly correct?

Let me point out right away a possible misinterpretation: to say that mathematical knowledge is real does not mean that mathematical objects exist. They are, rather, *abstract* ideas, which as such were not made "according to nature," that is, with the same type of precision that the characterization of a substance supposes. It is very possible that the rectangle or the circle may not exist in nature or may not be "precisely true," as Locke says, meaning that they are not realized in an exact way in any physical object. They are, nonetheless, perfectly determined, with all their properties and relationships, in the mind of the mathematician (IV, IV, §6). Then how can they be called "real"? First, because they remain bound up with intuition, in a sense that I will have to make clearer. The most obvious simple ideas are for Locke those of numbers, which are even clearer than the idea of extension. What explains this property of number is the perfect agreement between the *notation* and the *idea represented*, which makes the latter intuitively testable (*Draft A*, §68). Thus from the repeated observation of equalities or inequalities follows the perception of the "eternal" truths of arithmetic; in geometry, the relationships of equality or inequality are "less easy to observe or to measure." Locke considers, as will later Hume, the discontinuous conception of numbers as more obvious[4] or at least more definite and more precise than the apprehension of spatial objects, which our inability to discriminate between small differences in a continuum undermines (*Draft A*, §12).

For Locke, as for Descartes, proof consists in a *mediate perception* of a relationship of agreement or disagreement between ideas; it therefore calls for intermediate intuitive stages that allow us to go step by step—from one intuition to the next—from truths immediately known to truths we hope to establish. Although demonstration always depends on the recollection of a chain of intuitions, it seems difficult to infer without further consideration that it follows a "synthetic" line. If we interpret the texts literally, we would have to understand Locke's demonstration in the traditional sense of analysis taken up by Descartes. Locke characterizes it as "the art of finding out those intermediate ideas which may show us the agreement or repugnancy of other ideas which cannot be immediately compared.'' One of Locke's favorite examples is algebra, which ''finds out the ideas of quantities to measure others by'' (IV, XII, §§14–15). Just as an idea of number is no different from a combination of ''undifferentiated unities'' (II, XIV, §5), it seems that Locke conceives the relationships between numerical ideas (or geometrical ones, because he believes that the certainty of geometrical proof depends on arithmetic) along the mode that he conceives the other relationships between ideas: either identity, ''diversity,'' or ''necessary connexion.'' One needs only to examine the number of unities that are represented by a number to be able to prove by how many unities it differs from another number.

If we try to apply to this concept of proof the Kantian question of its ''foundation'' and of the nature of its propositions and theorems, we encounter inextricable difficulties, which suggest that the question is simply not ''translatable'' into Locke's doctrine.[5] If the analytic-synthetic distinction does not seem to be relevant to Locke's conception of mathematical proof, can one nevertheless conceive of the latter in the a priori-a posteriori division? Here again, Locke's texts seem to ''resist.'' First of all, it is clear that for Locke the demonstrative certainty of mathematics does not owe anything to the fact that mathematicians might have over physicists the advantage of being able to grasp their objects in a purely a priori manner. The fact that mathematical objects—numbers and geometrical forms—are modes, and consequently abstract, is not enough to make them pure idealities. *Observation* remains the only source of mathematical obviousness, for it makes it possible to constitute ideas of modes during demonstration and to identify the relationships that these ideas have among themselves (equality, inequality, etc.). It remains now to understand whence mathematical certainty originates, for this certainty is a remarkable exception in the realm of human knowledge.

Locke is strongly opposed to the idea that we may understand mathematical certainty in *purely* nominal terms, that is, in the form of axioms and deduction schemata. In the chapter ''Of Maxims,'' he insists that axioms have no more obviousness than the particular propositions that are supposed to be justified with their help (IV, VII, §6). We can ''find'' the truths generalized in axioms under their ''particular'' form in such a way as to ''force agreement'' and acquire a higher degree of clarity than do axioms. If the demonstrative power of mathematics does not owe anything to the nominal nature of the modes they use, but are indebted to their real essence (which in their case coincides with the nominal essence), it remains to understand what accounts for universality and *real* necessity of proofs. In other words, what keeps observation from falling prey to the usual difficulties of induction? This question will become urgent, starting with Kant, and will motivate recourse to the distinction between the a priori and a posteriori synthetic.

The answer lies in the property of abstraction, which gives rise to the modes: in the property that makes them at once universals *in re* and *in idea*. For the universality of mathematical truths comes from the universality of modes—from their archetypal value. We can judge what distinguishes this empiricism from that of the Viennese of the 1920s; it is not because mathematical truths are nominal (because they only state the meaning arbitrarily associated with a particular word or a particular sign) that they are necessarily true, but because facts of observation, being abstract, are invariable whatever the circumstances. It is not because mathematics has no object (and thus mathematical propositions are without content) that it is certain, but because all possible worlds have the same modes. The necessity of mathematics is not for Locke a grammatical property; it is an ontological property.[6]

Mathematics pertains to nominal essences that are *also* real; the latter are acquired by observation, but are certain, guaranteed by the intuitive continuity characteristic of proofs. A doctrine like this obviously makes the application of a clear analytic-synthetic distinction very artificial, but also that of the opposition between a priori and a posteriori propositions. For Locke there is no *difference of nature* between "proof" in mathematics and "proof" concerning qualitatively "secondary" modes. We can prove with similar certainty that $1 + 1 = 2$ and that blue is distinct from red. On the other hand, although all numerical equalities and inequalities are provable, there are qualitative identities that are not: we lack conclusive means by which to establish with certainty, for example, that two "reds" are of the same hue.[7]

Was Locke on the road to the Kantian division between analytic and synthetic propositions? It might seem more proper to say that it is Leibniz who, in his commentary on the *Essay*, brings in this essential detail, which cannot seriously be accredited to Locke:

> And I add that the immediate apperception of our existence and of our thoughts furnishes us the first truths *a posteriori*, or of fact, i.e. the *first* experiences, as the identical propositions contain the first truths *a priori*, of a reason, i.e. *the first lights*. (*New Essays Concerning Human Understanding*, IV, IX, §2).

I will have to make clear why Kant rejects or, more precisely, denies any relationship between Leibniz's division into truths of reason and truths of fact and his own distinction, in order to put forward a "precursor" like Locke, who develops all the consequences of our inability to know the real essence of substances, without recognizing, even "obscurely," the existence of a difference of nature between a priori and a posteriori knowledge. We already have some inkling as to the answer. I have noted that the main opponents of the *Critique* are Leibnizians who try to minimize Kant's originality by drawing him back to dogmatic philosophy, with which he claims to have broken off. We also know that empiricist philosophy, particularly in the "moderate" skeptical version that Hume offers, represents in Kant's view the possibility of critical awakening. As Kant recalls in the introduction to the *Prolegomena*, "The suggestion of David Hume was the very thing that . . . interrupted my dogmatic slumber, and gave my investigations in the field of speculative philosophy quite a new direction." The retrospective reading that Kant gives of Locke appears thus to pass through the distorting medium of a critical reinterpretation of Hume. Hume's skepticism more than Locke's empiricism pushes Kant to look for the precursors of his distinction in empiricism. Is this not what Kant suggests, when, accusing ultimately Locke of having played his role as a pioneer of this distinction badly, he sees the evident symptom of his failure in the fact that he was unable to lead Hume to "make investigations concerning this sort of proposition"?

It is as if Kant, though admitting that he does not find the least trace of the distinction in Hume, and that he detects only a confused and marginal indication in Locke, insists nevertheless on discovering in empiricism a dualist movement of thought foreshadowing, from his point of view, the objective necessity of the analytic-synthetic contrast—allowing us to justify the thesis of a topical equivalence between the skeptical question and the transcendental question.

2

Hume's "Error"

" . . . errors that at the start were certainly on the track of
truth." (KRV, III, 499)

What I called earlier the "assimilating tendency" (of Kant's reappropriation of
the Lockean movement of thought) appears again in Kant's reading of Hume.
Hume's "philosophical vocation" is from the outset associated with forming a
political constitution for the sciences. The association is legitimate because, for
Kant, "a philosophical history of philosophy is itself possible, neither historically nor empirically, but rationally, that is, a priori" (*Welches sind die wirklichen Fortschritte* . . . [hereafter, *WF*], XX, 341). Hume's skepticism should
therefore be put into perspective with the idea that presides over the development
of philosophy, by an inquiry concerning the power of knowing. Questioning the
right of reason to know, Hume would have unjustly hastened its demission by too
quickly placing mathematics under the heading of analyticity; he would have *isolated* mathematics from the other sciences by making them depend only on a pure
and a priori principle, the principle of contradiction. The natural sciences, on the
contrary, are established on the basis of a subjective principle of experience, causality (a relationship exterior to the objects brought together, between which "no
connection can be discovered") (*Treatise of Human Nature* [hereafter, *T*], 180).

Why is this opposition a "serious error" for Kant? Because by placing mathematics on the side of analytic certainty, Hume failed to see the hypothesis of the
demonstrative capacity suited to the synthetic a priori. Had he recognized the
synthetic a priori nature of mathematics, Hume would not have rejected as unfounded the claims of metaphysics. First, he would have discovered the *importance* of the synthetic a priori for knowledge: not only *causality*, but also number
and space would have appeared to him, in this hypothesis, as equally a priori.
Furthermore, faced with the obligation to point out the origin of the a priori thus

extended, he could not have confined himself to calling upon *experience*, that is, a principle of association exterior to ideas but produced by habit. He could not have done it—precisely because of the privileged status of mathematics: as he sees in arithmetic the best example of a purely demonstrative science, allowing its object to be known with certainty, he would not have thought of connecting it with experience. Being in such "good company," metaphysics, like mathematics, could also have been connected with a pure a priori principle.

Again, Kant's reasoning proceeds in two stages. First, an assimilating stage: although Hume did not use these words, we can translate his theses by saying that mathematics is composed of anlaytic propositions, and metaphysics of synthetic a priori propositions (as is physics, it may be added). The former are certain, being analytic; the latter lack for Hume any objective foundation, being synthetic a priori. The second stage is critical. Kant shows that Hume was not able to apply correctly a distinction, which in itself is essential. As he wrote in the introduction to the *Prolegomena*, "He [Hume] did not recognize the problem in its full significance." In Kant's opinion, Hume limited the extension of the synthetic a priori to the relationship of cause and effect, and in this way was kept from arriving at a transcendental deduction of concepts. On the one hand, Hume missed the real scope of pure understanding; on the other hand, he passed by the very idea of a pure a priori intuition of space and time.

The same critical vacillation is found in another appraisal by Kant of Hume's contribution, no longer in connection with the analytic-synthetic distinction, but in regard to the synthetic a priori judgment. Tribute is first paid to Hume's insight:

> Hume was perhaps aware, although he never followed the matter out, that
> in judgments of a certain kind we pass beyond our concept of the object.
> (*KRV*, III, 499; trans. Smith, 609)

In saying that Hume "never followed the matter out," Kant means that he never described the structure of these types of propositions in their full generality. This does not mean that Hume did not implicitly call on a theory of proposition. If such a theory is not developed for itself, Kant notes its presence as a backdrop for the theory of causal judgment. When Hume emphasizes, for example, that the relationship of causation is not taken from the idea we have of the objects it brings together, he is referring to a model of judgment Kant would call "analytic," in that it develops what is "contained" in ideas, as opposed to the type of judgment Hume seeks to characterize, introducing a new relationship, which is *added* to the objects related. For example, the object identified as the cause does not "contain" its effect; in its concept, one does not find the idea of a "power" that would be part of its essence. The causal judgment must therefore involve an external, nonlogical principle, the adjunction being interpreted as the action of custom on imagination (*T*, 180). Then follows the criticism: Hume did not distinguish between two types of synthetic judgments, those that apply to possible experience, and those that apply to objects that can never appear in experience:

Our sceptical philosopher did not distinguish these two kinds of judgments, as he yet ought to have done, but straightaway proceeded to treat this self-increment of concepts, and, as we may say, this spontaneous generation on the part of our understanding and of our reason, without impregnation by experience, as being impossible. He therefore regarded all the supposed a priori principles of these faculties as fictitious. (*KRV*, III, 499; trans. Smith, 609)

Hume's empiricism leads him to accept no connection between concepts other than the one between ideas "connected in the understanding," as Kant writes elsewhere (*KRV*, III, 105). This restriction goes along with the empiricist radicalization of the understanding-experience dualism: "It never occurred to him that the understanding might itself, perhaps through these concepts, be the author of the experience in which its objects are found" (ibid.).

I may now give a rough sketch of Kant's "Hume," a sketch governed by the rule of pure reason in its polemical use (*KRV*, III, 484ff.). Hume is the philosopher who was able to direct his censorship against dogmatic pretensions. This explains both his clear insights, which cast doubt on the transcendent use of principles, and his shortcomings (failing to subordinate the *facts* of reason to a criticism of its powers, and to substitute for censorship the tracing of the limits of knowledge in general). Hume puts reason in contradiction with itself. This is, however, only a stage that grants a rest from dogmatism, not a "place to take up residence" (III, 497). Kant's attitude toward Hume is determined by the mediatory position he ascribes to him between dogmatism and criticism.[8] Although suspecting the existence of two cognitive functions, one that would be purely explicative, the other extensive (whereby he announces critical philosophy), Hume could conceive propositional "legality" only in its analytic form (which classes him among dogmatic philosophers). The adjunction that the causal synthesis brings in is perceived by Hume as involving a *subservience* of reason to imagination. Hume confused, as equally "imaginary," causal propositions directed toward possible experience and metaphysical arguments having for their object what goes beyond such experience. He put causality on a par with the existence of God, human freedom, or the identity of the self in time. This indiscriminate character of censorship leads ultimately to the ignorance of reason concerning its own power and concerning the limits of possible knowledge.

The division of propositions into analytic and synthetic is in Kant's eyes an "indispensable" division for the critique of understanding, and deserves to be considered as "classic" (*Prolegomena*, §3). One of the essential elements in evaluating the meaning of Hume's empiricism lies precisely here: Does Hume really refer to this division, even "under another denomination"? Does he thus pave the way for criticism? The answer is essential because beyond Hume it determines more generally the status of skeptical empiricism, for the Kantian reading of Hume was influential. As the quotation from Quine at the beginning of the preceding chapter shows, it is indeed generally accepted that the opposition between analytic and synthetic propositions originated already in English empiricism, and that if it is truly a dogma, it is an empiricist dogma before becoming a rationalist dogma. Aside from the label "dogma," all Anglo-Saxon commentators share Quine's opinion. Hume is considered the "precursor of modern empiricism" precisely because he supposedly anticipated the dichotomy of propositions into analytic and synthetic.[9] Such unanimity seems suspicious: how are we to explain that contemporary empiricism agrees with a reading that places Hume in Kant's lineage?

What about Hume's demarcation between relations of ideas and matters of fact? Does it bespeak, as Kant claims, the distinction between analytic and synthetic propositions? The text most often given in favor of this thesis is Section I Part III of the first book of the *Treatise*, bearing the title "Of Knowledge." There Hume carries out, in the manner of Locke, an examination of the different types of *relationships* obtaining between two ideas. Inasmuch as judging amounts to *comparing* objects, we will have a general table of possible knowledge by examining the various kinds of relationships that can join ideas. These relationships are divided into two classes. The first "depend entirely on ideas, which we compare together"; the second "may be changed without any change in the ideas" (*T*, 69). "Proportions in quantity or number" belong to the first, which makes mathematics a science of "perfect exactness and certainty." Causality belongs to the second, which excludes the natural sciences from the field of the demonstrative. The definition of the two groups of relationships, together with its application, appears to coincide with what Kant will later distinguish as two distinct types of propositions, analytic and synthetic. Relationships of ideas seem to be "internal" relative to their terms: it seems to depend on the content of the idea of "4" that it is equal to "2 + 2," or of the idea of justice that it is the opposite of "injustice." Likewise, Kant defines analytic judgment by the inherence of the predicate in the subject (Kant's analytic judgment takes up without drastic change the propositional category that Aristotle called "essential predication"). Matters of fact appear, on the contrary, to be *external* relative to their terms, like the distance that separates two objects: I always have the same idea of the chair and the table whether they are close to or distant from one another. Examine as I may the idea I have of fire and water, I will not be able to discover in them the effects of the one on the other. Kant likewise recalls the "ampliative" character of synthetic predication, which extends our knowledge. He could take up Hume's observation:

> And as the power, by which one object produces another, is never discoverable merely from their idea, 'tis evident *cause* and *effect* are relations, of which we receive information from experience, and not from any abstract reasoning of reflexion. (*T*, 69)

This "informative" character of matters of fact seems to be the mark of their *synthetic* character. However, three kinds of questions must be answered in order to establish the value of this parallelism. First, can we ascribe to Hume the doctrine of internal relationships? Second, does mathematics (which represents one of the most interesting cases of the relationships of ideas) owe its demonstrative capacity to the fact that it is a priori, purely conceptual—in other words, without intuitive content? Finally, what role does the principle of contradiction play in the recognition of truth of the first kind (mathematical) as opposed to judgments of fact?

Hume's Doctrine of Relationships

The two kinds of relationships cannot be contrasted on the basis of being internal or external, because all relations are from Hume's point of view *external to their terms*.[10] This is easy to see in respect to relationships of things; causality, for example, brings in something that *transcends* what is *given* in the perception of external objects: "No bodies ever discover any power, which can be the original of this idea" (*Enquiries Concerning Human Understanding* . . . [hereafter, *EHU*], §50). Just because such a transcendence appears to be absent in the case of relations of ideas, one should not infer that these relations are internal. For one would have to be able to prove that the relationship of *resemblance*, for example, is given at the same time as the objects are perceived. Yet the joining of ideas is carried out by a principle of imagination, not to be conceived as an "inseparable connection" between ideas, but as a "gentle force, which commonly prevails" (*T*, 10). This means that two objects can be associated only *in* imagination (ibid., 11). To mark clearly the exteriority of the principles with respect to the ideas connected, it is enough to recall that the principles of association are for Hume the equivalent in the mind of the principle of gravitation in the physical world (ibid., 12). They are external to what they associate—simple ideas—just as the principle of gravitation is to the bodies to which it applies; they exert their effects on the mind, which, rather than governing them, is shaped by them.

Let us choose the principle of association by resemblance: this principle guides the mind from one idea to another; it forms the "natural" relationship of resemblance, which leads to a spontaneous association of similar ideas, close shades of color, and the like. But this principle also conditions the corresponding philosophical relationship that extends the use of resemblance beyond its immediate sphere of activity according to the demands of an arbitrary association linked to a "particular circumstance," for example, the prospect of systematically arranging the spectrum of colors or relating sounds to colors (*T*, I, I, 5, 13).[11]

It follows from the exteriority of the relationship of idea to its terms that the comparison of simple ideas is unproblematic, unlike what will be the case in the constitutional system of Rudolf Carnap's *Aufbau*:

> *Blue* and *green* are different simple ideas, but are more resembling than *blue* and *scarlet*; tho' their perfect simplicity excludes all possibility of sep-

aration or distinction. 'Tis the same case with particular sounds, and tastes and smells. These admit of infinite resemblances upon the general appearance and comparison, without having any common circumstance the same. (*T*, 637)

These remarks allow me to mention in passing what distinguishes Hume's doctrine of ideas from the phenomenalistic reductionism of Mach or Carnap. Hume does assert in principle that every idea is derived from an impression, but the use or "representation" of an idea can depart from its "nature" or even go beyond it. With the forming of general ideas, imagination makes its own syntheses, fabricates (or "tinkers with") concepts that will remain marked by the individual and contingent character of their genesis. We must still try to understand what Hume means when he isolates the four philosophical relationships of ideas (resemblance, contrariness, degrees of quality, and proportion in quantity or number) by saying that they "only depend on ideas." If we are not to interpret the word "depend" as referring to the doctrine of internal relations (the relation being deducible from the idea), how are we to interpret it? Following Gilles Deleuze, we could say that the way the idea is considered in each case explains the difference of the "dependence": in relationships of ideas, the idea is taken "individually," in its "own characters." Matters of fact, on the other hand, consider the idea "distributively . . . , in the determinable collection in which its manner of appearance locates it."[12] Thus, in the first case, the principles of human nature apply exclusively to given singular ideas and bring out in them relationships whose invariable character is a function of this exclusiveness. Paraphrasing Hume himself, we could say that "the understanding acts alone therein, and according to its most general principles" (*T*, I, IV, 7, 267). In the second case, however, experience is the fundamental principle that "informs me of the various conjunctions of objects." Yet experience presupposes (spatiotemporal) variation and repetition, whence arise impressions of reflections, which are novel and closely connected with respect to their content to the perceptual circumstances and to the reasoning capacity of the subject (*EHU*, §84, note 1).

To illustrate practically the type of *dependence* belonging to relationships of ideas in respect to their terms, one must consider the case of mathematics: a typical demonstrative science that owes the certainty of its propositions to this dependence. Let us reformulate our initial question with reference to this science: whence comes the "certainty" of mathematics?

Is Mathematics Analytic?

'Tis usual with mathematicians, to pretend, that those ideas, which are their objects, are of so refin'd and spiritual a nature, that they fall not under the conception of the fancy, but must be comprehended by a pure and intellectual view, of which the superior faculties of the soul are alone capable. . . . But to destroy this artifice, we need but reflect on that principle so oft insisted on, *that all our ideas are copy'd from our impressions*. (*T*, III, I, 72)

The two kinds of relationships divide the sciences into two parts. On the one hand, there are the true sciences, in which certainty is possible: arithmetic and algebra, which are *demonstrative*, as opposed to geometry, which is only intuitive and therefore an *art*. On the other hand, moral reasoning characterizes the sciences that go beyond the evidence of the senses and of memory, and bring in a "supposed link" not derived from experience, but discovered *through* experience (*EHU*, §48; *T*, 69). Between these two poles, geometry occupies the intermediate position of a nonexact science, whose certainty is nevertheless sufficient for its aim. The logical empiricists did not fail to account for the special status of mathematics in Hume's taxonomy by emphasizing the purely a priori nature of its statements. Yet, to evaluate this interpretation, one need only recall that mathematics receives its advantage over moral reasoning from a sensible feature, *perceptibility* (*EHU*, VII, 1, §48, 60). It is not the ideality of their objects that sets algebra and arithmetic apart, but on the contrary their *perceptibility*: their objects are perfectly adapted to our senses. The typical defect of our senses lies precisely in changing proportions; they "represent as minute and uncomposed what is really great and composed of a vast number of parts" (*T*, I, II, 1, 28). Against this tendency algebra and arithmetic have a remedy: "We are possest of a precise standard, by which we can judge of the equality and proportion of numbers" (*T*, I, III, 1, 71). Setting up a correspondence between two sets allows us to assert equality between numbers. The manipulation of algebraic characters according to a rule determines without equivocation the exactness of an equation. This relationship of equality, however, is no less "external" to its terms than is causality to its terms:

> Equality is a relation, it is not, strictly speaking, a property in the figures themselves, but arises merely from the comparison, which the mind makes betwixt them. (*T*, I, II, 4, 46)

Of course, the perceptibility belonging to mathematics must occur in conjunction with another property that ensures for this science the status of a demonstrative science. In the enumeration of types of relations, we notice that Hume follows Locke in admitting that one can acquire, through intuition, a certain knowledge of "degrees of quality" as well as of number, provided that the difference between the objects compared is not too small, a condition holding *in both cases*.[13] Thus, to confine ourselves to the criterion of perceptibility, other relationships of ideas, like those of resemblance or degrees of quality, equally intuitive, could be held to found different demonstrative sciences, in particular a *science of qualities*. What distinguishes mathematical statements from propositions asserting, for example, the qualitative resemblance of two objects is not the particular nature of the intuition of number as compared with the intuition of quality, but the fact that in the first case intuition can be incorporated in the proof, whereas in the second case proof is impossible, a difference explained by the *composition of the intuitive datum* in both cases:

> As the component parts of quantity and number are entirely similar, their relations become intricate and involved; and nothing can be more curious, as well as useful, than to trace, by a variety of mediums, their equality or inequality, through their different appearances. But as all other ideas are clearly distinct and different from each other, we can never advance farther, by our utmost scrutiny, than to observe this diversity, and, by an obvious reflexion, pronounce one thing not to be another. (*EHU*, XII, 3, §131, 163)

What differentiates mathematical relations from qualitative relations is that a homogeneousness of the component parts makes possible the calculation (that is, the deduction "by a variety of mediums") of equalities or inequalities between numerical or algebraic expressions. The immediate character of the distinction that qualitative relationships reveal excludes, on the contrary, any further analysis of the relationship. In other words, precisely insofar as they escape mathematization, the terms of a qualitative relationship are irreducible to one another. This red is not that orange: in the absence of a middle term, the deduction cannot be carried further.

When Hume, in the *Enquiries*, characterizes propositions expressing relations of ideas by saying that they "are discoverable by a mere operation of thought, without dependence on what is anywhere existent in the universe" (*EHU*, IV, 1, §20, 25), he cannot mean that relationships of the first kind are completely independent of the *perception* of compared objects. In the *Treatise* he adds, against the essentialist mathematicians, that "all our ideas are copied from our impressions" (*T*, I, III, 1, 72). Hume is noting thereby that our ideas depend *only* on the intuition of compared objects, whether these objects are existent or not—that is, parts of reality or results of an abstractive process.

The intuitive character of each individual step of the deductive chain in arithmetic or algebra finally explains that these sciences are "instructive," that they give true knowledge, that their derivations are "curious" or their calculations "useful." Although its terms express "the same quantity" in different forms, mathematical equality has nothing tautological about it, as opposed to strictly nominal definition and syllogistic reasoning (*EHU*, XII, 3, §131, 163). From what precedes we may infer, without having to examine the case of geometry (which depends still more obviously on "appearances"),[14] that mathematics in Hume may be called analytic only at the price of a threefold distortion of the texts: (1) relationships of ideas are external to their terms—they are established only through intuition; (2) they are demonstrative only on account of the homogeneousness of the numerical or algebraic construct—the properties of the intuitive datum forms the conditions of mathematical proof; (3) the necessity of a demonstrative series characterizes nevertheless "the act of the understanding, by which we consider and compare ideas" (*T*, I, III, 14, 166) and is not included in the mathematical datum, although it may be said in another sense that the necessity of the relationship is "given" to the mind according to the principle of association, which takes for its object numbers, algebraic expressions, and so forth.

The Role of the Principle of Contradiction

As Jean Laporte suggests,[15] perhaps Kant would have been less tempted to assimilate mathematics as Hume represents it within a body of analytic knowledge, if he had not encountered in Section IV of the *Enquiries* a reference to the principle of contradiction. Paragraph 21 (*EHU*, 25–26) clarifies for Kant the status of mathematics in Hume: the latter has mathematics depend "entirely on the principle of contradiction." From Kant's point of view, this means that it is composed of analytic judgments. It is indeed surprising that Hume speaks of "the impossibility to think otherwise" in order to characterize strictly demonstrative necessity. But what exactly does "the impossibility to think otherwise" mean? The question raised is not that of Hume's reference to the contradictory character of false judgments in mathematics, for this kind of reference can take on various "topical" functions. The problem is, rather, to determine the way in which the nature of contradiction occurs in the definition of demonstrative knowledge. Kant assumes that contradiction according to Hume is at the *source* of this knowledge. The texts, however, do not stress the *conclusive* character of noncontradiction, understood as a principle of true mathematical judgments. The true role of contradiction seems to be that of a *criterion* rather than that of a *principle*. In the case of relations of ideas, the transition from one idea to another is so natural and so immediate that understanding is forced to make it. The objective logical necessity of a mathematical proposition thus rests on a subjectively (that is, a "naturally") constraining necessity.[16]

Yet judgment implies idea, and vice versa: the status of contradiction in Hume's philosophy cannot be fully understood without attending to his conception of *judgment*. Hume is indeed following Malebranche when he believes that the three operations of the mind, which traditional logic and in particular the logicians of Port-Royal distinguish, reduce to one: "The act of the mind exceeds not a simple conception" (*T*, I, III, 7, 97). Demonstrative necessity, like causal necessity, arises from an impression. This comparison probably altered in Kant's mind the meaning of the distinction that Hume drew between relations of ideas and matters of fact. For the distinction could be understood in the following manner: when we reason demonstratively, we are conditioned by a principle, the principle of contradiction; and when we assert, for example, the equality between 2 + 2 and 4, we know that to deny the truth of this result would be to contradict our use of addition, that is, to confuse the idea of addition. On the contrary, when we examine two events, one being the cause of the other, we can very well imagine that another effect could follow from the same cause, or that the same effect could have a very different cause. Although we may have the impression of knowing the causes, and of knowing them as necessary, we have necessity in the first case, but not in the second.

In reality, Hume does not wish to preserve one kind of knowledge at the expense of another, to place mathematics beyond the reach of skeptical doubt so as to reveal the absence of a rational foundation in the natural sciences. He compares, on the contrary, the two types of necessity in order to prove that what *proof*, whose principle is a natural relationship, ensures in one case, is in the other case ensured by a belief (*T*, I, III, 14).

If proof is to escape this comparison, it must be shown that in its case at least there is an independent foundation of obviousness, an objective foundation *other than* tendency. But one would search in vain for such a foundation: demonstrative falsity reveals itself only through the indistinct and confused character of the corresponding idea, which makes the latter properly inconceivable. "What implies a contradiction cannot be conceived." *The unrepresentable is the counterproof of demonstration*, and just as there is no such counterproof for causal judgment, the impression that, as Hume says, "makes some difference," must come from elsewhere—that is, from a belief (*An Abstract of a Treatise of Human Nature* [hereafter, *AT*], 652–53).

Logical and Demonstrative Necessity

Paradoxically, it is because the feeling of demonstrative necessity accompanies the comparing of mathematical ideas but is absent from causal inferences that a logic of causal inferences is probably more useful than a logic of deduction. Formal logic indeed seems to fall under this maxim, which Hume quotes in another context: "Next to the ridicule of denying an evident truth, is that of taking pains to defend it" (*T*, I, III, 16, 176). What is trivial is not worth dwelling on. The triviality of formal logic, as Hume conceives it, is to be associated with his theory of the distinct idea: why give precepts that never have any connection with the essential questions of everyday life, that is, with causal inferences? Like Locke, Hume considers manuals on logic as collections of obvious rules in their formulation, which could end up being harmful in spite of, or on account of, their vacuousness. They can very well hide for young minds the true problems that knowledge encounters, for example, those that "experimental philosophy" (i.e., Newtonian mechanics) and especially "moral philosophy" (the Humean theory of human nature) must overcome.

However, precisely because "anything can produce anything," there can be an advantage to *extend* logic, or rather to shift it, by setting "general rules" that will determine when the relationship of causality truly applies (*T*, I, III, 15, 173). If one is to talk of *logic* and to state the rules to be followed for reasoning, let it be nontrivial precepts, as opposed to those of Scholastic logic (ibid., 175). Even thus extended to truly problematic reasoning, the true usefulness of normative logic seems rather doubtful to Hume: "Perhaps even this was not very necessary, but might have been supply'd by the natural principles of our understanding" (*T*, 175).

Like rightfulness, truth is what is actualized by virtue of natural tendencies: as Quine did later, Hume "naturalizes" logic. The science of humankind is the only possible foundation of all the other sciences, "the only one upon which they can stand with any security" (*T*, xvi).

What, then, is Hume's intention in introducing his famous distinction between *relations of ideas* and *matters of fact*? It is not, we clearly see now, to destroy all assurance with respect to the factual truths of natural sciences, which would be abandoned to the skeptics, whereas mathematics would be saved and would alone deserve the name of science. Hume intends to distinguish two types of convictions, both converging toward the unity of the human mind, which expresses itself in the total system of the sciences. The demonstrative conviction is founded on the transition between intuitions: there are immediate, proceeding without intermediaries from the distinct perception of ideas; the causal conviction, mediate, involves belief. Undoubtedly these two convictions do not have the same status. The first can be called entirely *rational*, since only the natural principles of understanding occur in it. The second is no longer such:

> Experimental reasoning . . . is nothing but a species of instinct or mechanical power, that acts in us unknown to ourselves; and in its chief operations, is not directed by any such relations or comparisons of ideas, as are the proper objects of our intellectual faculties. (*EHU*, §85, 108)

Belief plays an essential role in the experimental sciences and in everyday life, and yet it is no longer an intellectual operation; it is an archaic mental phenomenon on which the survival of living species depends.

The word "science" is, of course, not left untouched by taking into account this "supplement," which the causal conviction brings in. We do not *know* the connection between causes and effects. Instead of inferring with Locke our *ignorance* "of the several powers, efficacies, and ways of operation, whereby the effects which we daily see are produced" (*E*, IV, III, 24). Hume perceives a type of experience that is irreducible both to observation and to knowledge:

> It is allowed on all hands that there is no known connection between the sensible qualities and the secret powers; and consequently, that the mind is not led to form such a conclusion concerning their constant and regular conjunction, by anything which it knows of their nature. . . . At least, it must be acknowledged that there is here a consequence drawn by the mind; that there is a certain step taken; a process of thought, and an inference, which wants to be explained. (*EHU*, §29, 33–34)

For Locke the scientificness in matters of experimental philosophy is "out of our reach" (*E*, IV, III, 26). For Hume, on the contrary, although research pertaining to facts cannot claim to be purely demonstrative in the same manner as "the sciences properly called," it still deserves the name of science, provided that this expression is cleared of rationalist assumptions (i.e., that all interconnections be subject to verification, and in particular, that there be freedom from the assumption that causality can be regulated by the principle of sufficient reason).

This is how I construe the function of the contrast between relations of ideas and matters of fact: to show that the asymmetry between informative propositions depends on empirical genesis: thought does not rest on pure reason, but depends largely on causal inferences that are no longer rational, on natural principles that remain groundless. Hume's bifurcation does not induce us, however, to prudent silence, as would to abstention, an agnosticism like Locke's. Faced with the separation between faith and knowledge, the science of human nature is nevertheless still possible. Philosophy must in due course become experimental reasoning, and directly address, in the course of its inquiry, the exceptions that are naturally made to the universality of the principle of reason. "We can give no reason for our most general and most refined principles, besides our experience of their reality" (*T*, xviii). To observe how the propositions of science are formed and to notice disconnections, unconscious connections, and undemonstrative reasoning is not to despair of science. It is only to naturalize it, to proportion it to the human mind, which produced it.

3

Kant as a Critic of Leibniz: Character and Analyticity

This division is indispensable, as concerns the critique of human understanding, and therefore deserves to be called classical in such critical investigation, though otherwise it is of little use.

—Prolegomena (§3)

We have seen Kant alternatively asserting against Eberhard the radical novelty of his division of all judgments into analytic and synthetic, and recognizing in Locke and Hume the use of this same division. But one should not hastily conclude that Kant is freely choosing his predecessors merely to distinguish himself from the dogmatists, by favoring the empiricists against Leibniz. For if the division of all judgments into analytic and synthetic has real interest, and not merely a purely nominal Scholastic interest, it derives this interest from its association with a critique of human understanding (*Prolegomena* [hereafter, *P*], §3, 270).

In *What Real Progress Has Metaphysics Made*, Kant returns to the question of the novelty of the distinction:

> Had this distinction been clearly understood during Leibniz's or Wolff's time, we would have found every logic or metaphysics that has since appeared not only to have depended on it but also to have stressed its importance. For the first form of judgment (i.e. an analytic judgment) is always a priori and accompanied by the consciousness of its necessity. The second (i.e. a synthetic judgment) can be empirical, and logic cannot permit specification of the condition under which a synthetic judgment a priori will occur. (*WF*, 266; trans. Humphrey, 63)

Here Kant stresses the "importance" of the distinction. Does this not contradict the text of the *Prolegomena* quoted above? This would be the case if Kant

27

had not specified, already in the first of these texts, on which background opposition the importance of this distinction is to be appreciated. From the point of view of *formal logic*, the distinction is useless because in that field objects are considered in the abstract, that is, independently of the sources of knowledge about them. The distinction is essential, on the contrary, in *transcendental logic* because it is what provides this logic with the condition of its specific investigation: "How are synthetic a priori judgments possible?" It clearly follows that the aim of the distinction is to contrast the domain of proven thought, which is that of traditional logic, with an area of reason in which formal principles are of no help. The question of the (transcendental) interest of the distinction thus allows us to understand the way Kant presents the concept of analytic judgment. When Kant points out that it is "accompanied by the consciousness of its necessity," or else that it is "derived from the principle of contradiction," he is thinking of the proposition of logicians in which "the connection between subject and predicate is conceived by identity."

However, we would be conceding too much to Locke if we were to attribute to the identical connection the trivial character he gave to "trifling propositions." If purely analytic propositions are perfectly obvious, it becomes impossible to convince the dogmatists that they have not ceased to use them. The definition of analytic judgment therefore brings in, aside from the purely formal characteristic that is the predicative *decomposition* of the subject into parts, a feature that explains the fact that analytic propositions are not purely tautological. What takes place in these propositions is not an increase of knowledge, which belongs to synthetic judgments, but a progress in distinction:

> The former [analytic judgments] add nothing to the concept of the subject by means of the predicate, but merely break it up into those constituent concepts that have all along been thought in it, although confusedly. (*KRV*, III, 33)

To break up a concept allows us to "become conscious of the manifold that I always think in it" (ibid., 34). In calling "analysis" the breaking up into parts, Kant remains faithful to the terminology of his *Inaugural Dissertation* (hereafter *D*); like the word "synthesis," the word "analysis" can be taken either in the *qualitative* or in the *quantitative* sense:

> Analysis, taken in the first sense, is a regress from consequence to ground, but, in the second sense, it is a regress from a whole to its possible or mediate parts, i.e., the parts of its parts. Both terms, synthesis and analysis, we here use in the second sense. (*D*, I, §1, note)

Qualitative analysis, the method that the Greek geometers named *analusis*, consists in assuming a proposition to be true so as to discover where it comes from, and thus to arrive at a proposition already known.[17] Considered from an operating and demonstrative point of view, analysis consists in going from the conditioned back to the condition, *a rationato ad rationem*; but Kant retains only the quantitative aspect of analysis, *a toto ad partes*. This quantitative evaluation of the logical use of understanding is what makes it possible to pass from the point of view of the composition of the concept to that of its distinction; from the global concept to the subdivided concept, one proceeds from "confused" knowledge to "distinct" knowledge, a transition that represents an increase in knowledge, not *materialiter*, but *formaliter* (*Kants Logik* [hereafter *L*], §36).

Analytic propositions are true by virtue of the *identity* of concepts—of the predicate with the subject—but this does not imply that the identity is explicit; otherwise the judgment would be empty. Without falling into the purely verbal game of "occult qualities," the tautological judgment is strictly useless. If it is not absurd, *sinnleer*, it is "fruitless" (*Reflexionen* [hereafter, *R*], 3130, 3137):

> For such judgments contribute nothing to the clarification of concepts, toward which all judgments must aim, and thus are called empty. (*WF*, xx, 322–23; trans. Humphrey, 175)

An analytic judgment is an *implicitly* identical proposition, and this "implicitness" ensures its specific fruitfulness. It is "founded" on identity, "to which it can be reduced," but it is not a simple identity. The quantitative sense of analysis, which Kant appears to have chosen very early, seems inevitably to inscribe a precritical thesis in the heart of critical thought, although only under the heading of logical thought, and more precisely to be tacitly inspired by the Leibnizian idea of *resolutio*. Is this a heritage transmitted by Meier, whose *Auszug aus der Vernunftlehre* Kant commented on at length?[18] This hypothesis does not seem at first sight very tenable, for Kant energetically refuses to turn logic into "an algebra that might help us to the discovery of hidden truth" (*L*, introduction, II, 20). We have a true problem here. In order to solve it, we must compare more closely Kant's and Leibniz's respective theses on the nature and the aims of resolution.

Identity and Implicitness in Leibniz and Kant

Resolution, the Leibnizian archetype of demonstration, consists in expressing explicitly the comprehension of the predicate in the subject, a property that, according to Leibniz, characterizes every true proposition, whether it is a truth of reason or a truth of fact, although in the latter case resolution does not lie within our reach.[19] The principle of identity thus has in Leibniz the function of a fundamental operating principle. In the first place, this principle gives the *canon of truth*, which consists in the identity of the predicate with the subject. Analysis is designed to reveal the persistence of an identical content throughout substitutions of the definitions for the defined. In the second place, the principle ensures the closure of a field of calculus. In principle, this field of the identical covers the whole of the conceivable. In fact, it extends only to what is regularly reducible into irreducible elements. For the principle to apply to the *whole* of the conceivable, one must therefore resort to the expedient of a language adapted to resolution. "Universal characteristic" will be the *ars formularia* required by the principle of identity to apply only to what is comparable. Its function will be to translate into the language of calculus all the opaque meanings of ordinary language. Once an *encyclopedia* is set up, nothing will hinder the action of the principle of identity.[20] Finally, the principle of identity ensures uniformity of the field of the identical. It asserts as noncontradictory all the resolved constituents that make up the matter of partial identities.[21] Every complex term is univocally reducible to primary factors carrying basic meanings: a primordial vocabulary assumed to be not subject to change.[22]

All the properties of a legitimate principle of *calculus* are thus present in identity. In this sense, it is what founds substitution, *salva veritate*, according to the maxim that will one day be recalled by Frege: "Eadem sunt, quorum unum in alterius locum substitui potest salva veritate."[23] But the principle is not restricted to bringing the combinatory process to bear on *abstract* expressions. Not only does this principle not alter the truth, as the previous quotation ascertains, but it serves also to *found* it. In other words, the principle is not restricted to providing one of the primitive rules of the calculus, that of substitutability. What made the principle of identity an operating principle makes it likewise an ontological principle: characteristics must likewise be *real*, apply to the whole of the conceivable, and become the instrument of an invention that is not merely symbolic.

Let us deduce for our own benefit the consequence of this use of identity: in order to be a canon of truth and to work toward the closure of the thinkable, identity must call upon certain typically dogmatic assumptions. Any truth can be reduced to an identity only because human understanding is subordinated to a divine understanding in which the truths of fact coincide with the truths of reason: "If we could understand every notion as *God* does, we would see in it that the predicate is contained in the subject."[24]

The possibility of an analytic reduction of truths of fact is maintained only because of the fiction of a divine understanding. The operating incompleteness thus comes to be, indeed, metaphysically legitimated, but not conceived within its limits. The thesis of the compatibility of simple disparates constitutes another assumption, necessary for the universality of characteristics; but it amounts to asserting what is precisely to be proved: that the calculus is possible, and that no obstacle intervenes between logical possibility and real possibility. Can one, under such conditions, maintain the hypothesis of an element borrowed by Kant from Leibniz, and consider Kant's implicitness a reappearance of the Leibnizian *resolvendum*? An element revealing the adventurous character of this interpretation appears already in the *Enquiry on Obviousness*. If the idea of characteristic can hold in mathematics, in which one proceeds by *arbitrary connection* to constitute concepts, it does not belong any longer in philosophy, in which one should confine oneself to investigating an *already given* concept, with "the thing itself in front of one's eyes" (I, §1 and 2). One can no longer think here "under the signs" but only "by means of the signs." This means that symbolic construction is not freely used in philosophy, as it is in mathematics. The word becomes laden with the seriousness of a thing to be represented: "Everyone has a concept of time." Blind manipulation of abstractions retains some legitimacy only if arbitrariness is *at the source* of thinking. But just as philosophizing consists in clarifying concepts already given in words, the "considerable lightening" made possible by the symbolic procedure is obviously no longer permitted.[25]

In the *Inaugural Dissertation, contemplation* appeared as the essential part of the intuitive method of mathematics. The *Critique* enriches the analysis of this method with the idea of a *construction* of concepts in intuition. The frontier between mathematics and philosophy seems henceforth to lie here, for the latter is reduced to the exploration of concepts. The objections of 1764 and 1770 are thus at once recalled and overcome in a critical manner. On the one hand, there is no longer any *discursive arbitrariness* that could claim to be legitimate, that is, relationships between concepts having no other law than a rule stipulated by the understanding alone. In this sense, the characteristic loses its constructive prerogative. There is room only for an *intuitive* arbitrariness now: it is what is established by a nonintellectual a priori standard, in a construction only obeying pure intuition (*KRV*, A 729, 478). On the other hand, the symbolic no longer lies, as in the *Dissertation* (II, §10), in the realm of intellection:

> In algebra by means of a symbolic construction, just as in geometry by means of an ostensive construction (the geometric construction of the objects themselves), we succeed in arriving at results which discursive knowledge could never reach by means of mere concepts. (*KRV*, A 717, 471; trans. Smith, 579)

Only if it is built up *from a pure intuition* is symbolization different from an empty and gratuitous formalism; in other words, it becomes a principle of discovery. For one must go beyond the concept in order to "pass beyond it to properties which are not contained in this concept but yet belong to it" (ibid., A 718, 472; Smith trans., 580). Unlike what the universal characteristic had aimed at, it is not the discursive, as a procedure of abstract combinatory symbolization, that opens the road for discovery; it can only be intuition, alone capable of giving a *content* to knowledge. What ruins definitively, in the *Critique*, the claim of analysis to govern all that can be thought is asserted in the principle of amphibole (ibid., A 261, 215). It is only because of the *confusion of faculties* that one could have hoped to extend the calculus to all areas of reason, that one could have believed it possible to constitute an "alphabet of thoughts" in which pure concepts, empirical concepts, and a priori intuitions are indistinctly mingled. The combinatory committed the error of treating intuitions *as if* they were concepts: the imperialism of the discursive in Leibniz leads to ignoring the true site of invention—not understanding, but intuition. Far from being taken up by critical philosophy, the Leibnizian "implicitness" is dissociated by Kant into two distinct processes: that of analysis takes a different road from that of the combinatory. Later we will see how Carnap's renewal of the Leibnizian combinatory project will lead him, if not to associate again, at least to turn the two types of implicitness into formally compoundable categories (see this volume, Section 4, Chapter 4). To analyze is still for Kant to make a concept clear; but the distinction of the concept ceases to have, as with Leibniz, a *constructive* import. A definition can be made explicit, can be reached. But what more can be deduced from the definition? No *property* can spring up from the examination of the precise meaning of the concept. For demonstrating a property calls for something completely different from the identical axiom. Constructing on the other hand no longer belongs to the *discursive* use of reason: it is an intuitive operation, which becomes a combinatory technique only in the specific case of the algebraic object (*KRV*, 472–73).

   The combinatory thus loses its connection with the analytic: in a sense, it changes domain, starting henceforth from intuitions that the combination of characters has as its function to *represent*. Under such conditions, it is obvious that composition ceases to be the inverse operation of decomposition. The latter proceeds from one *concept* to other *concepts*, the former from a *concrete* a priori representation to the elaboration of a general *concept*. Each operation is now *autonomous* compared with the other. Analysis ceases to prepare synthesis. The separation between the characteristic and the encyclopedic is final.

   From the Kantian point of view, Leibniz's "implicitness" has a double meaning: a yet unknown result of a construction in the process (as when we find the formula expressing the number π without being able to encompass the series constituting it), this implicitness is *synthetic*. An indistinct content given with a concept that *can be* discursively *clarified*, implicitness is, then, of *analytic* nature. But as opposed to synthetic implicitness, the latter kind of implicitness no longer allows us to discover new properties, nor a fortiori to construct new objects. This point is worth insisting on in order to counter the continual temptation to extend analytically the field of knowledge, a temptation that, as we saw, characterizes dogmatic metaphysics (ibid., 31, B 8ff.). Encouraged by the firmness of real knowledge provided by a priori analysis of concepts, one ends up hoping that such an a priori progression will continue:

> Reason is so far misled as surreptitiously to introduce, without itself being aware of so doing, assertions of an entirely different order, in which it attaches to given concepts others completely foreign to them, and moreover attaches them *a priori*. And yet it is not known how reason can be in a position to do this. Such a question is never so much as thought of. (*KRV*, 33, B 10; trans. Smith, 48)

   From the analysis of concepts, one is imperceptibly led, owing to the confusion between types of "implicitness," to synthetic assertions that require confirming in intuition. From Kant's point of view, Leibniz is himself a victim of this "passion for enlarging" by means of analytic propositions. Because he measured the possible with the yardstick of logic, Leibniz was led to equally dangerous extremes: sometimes to the dream of universal knowledge and universal power, sometimes to exclusions contrary to common sense. "He considered as impossible what could not be made representable by simple concepts of understanding" (*WF*, 281–82).

In thus blaming Leibniz for having restricted the conceivable to the purely conceptual, Kant reminds us of the way Leibniz criticized Descartes for having restricted the conceivable to the intuitive, by suspending knowledge to the principle of obviousness. Kant is actually turning back to Cartesian intuitionism insofar as it is never from the purely discursive but from the *intuitive* that a true progress in knowledge is to be expected. Yet Kant dismisses Descartes together with Leibniz by placing them both in the context of dogmatic metaphysics. Descartes based on intuitionism a dogmatism of knowing, which assigns to the unknowable a special domain; Leibniz founds in characteristic formalism a conception of Being that deduces from the principle of contradiction an argument in favor of the real possibility of existents. Kant eradicates all dogmatism by ceasing to be interested in the existence or knowledge of *things*, but turning toward "the sensitive representation of things" (*P*, I, Remark II).[26]

General logic, therefore, cannot be the instrument used indiscriminately by either an ontological philosophy *or* a critical philosophy. It is henceforth subjected to the transcendental preliminary. The question arises again: How is one to understand the Kantian analytic, now differentiated from its Leibnizian homonym? What is the originality of Kant's solution? In order to understand better the independence of Kant's logic with respect to the Leibnizian tradition, I will question his treatment of the character. Because the analytic is the principle of *logical* thought, let us see what the material of this thought, the character (*Merkmal*), can teach us about the analytic process of subdivision.

Of Characters

For the tradition, a *character* (*nota*) is what makes an object known, or more precisely, following Seneca, what attracts one's attention to its value, as the stamp of the customs officer on a package is used as a *sign* (*iconismos*) of its contents: "Nota quibus inter se simila discriminentur."[27]

The mathematical genius of Leibniz was to interpret this iconic property of the character by making it an element of the systematic language designed to register the relationships between thoughts and to reveal new ones:

> I call character the visible note representing thoughts; the characteristic art
> is thus the art of forming and arranging characters, so that they register
> thoughts and have between them the same relationships as they have between themselves.[28]

The character will be built up following a rule of isomorphism between the compound of the idea and the compounding of the number.[29] Character being an *imaginative* auxiliary of reason, awareness of what is represented becomes unnecessary. Mechanical calculation replaces attention to the thing referred to.

What counts is less the *meaning content* of each character than the *relationships* revealed by the calculus.

Kant develops the other value of the *nota*: no longer the visible term shaped by art, but that by means of which one reaches knowledge of a content: "A character is what I become aware of in a thing" (*R*, XVI, 2276).

Character is therefore built up in the singular act of gathering evidence. More than a modification in the use of a concept, we have here a *change in orientation* of logic. The latter is, in fact, recalled from the status of a regulated interplay on abstract expressions to that of a canon of the use of understanding. *Form*, which remains its object, is no longer the *convention* of a choice of axioms and primitive terms, but the presenting of the *only* legitimate use of understanding. Logic consequently becomes both the "verifier of knowledge" (*L*, IX, 13) and the servant of transcendental logic: "according to form" now means paradoxically "from the subjective point of view" — the point of view of understanding knowing itself (ibid., 94).

This change of orientation explains the ambiguity of *Logic*, which Jean Cavaillès has emphasized.[30] This text, which in fact was written not by Kant but by his disciple Jäsche, has several levels of meaning sometimes difficult to distinguish. As a *course*, its aim is to present "classic" distinctions. The division into a "doctrine of elements" and a "doctrine of method" is perfectly suited to books of this kind, and likewise the progression from concepts to judgments to reasonings.

But this logical discourse is captured in a *critical appraisal* made possible by the transcendental aspect of logic. This critical revision consists in locating the logical meanings and possibly in showing what exceeds the purely logical sphere: it belongs, then, "to metaphysics to deal with it." Finally, certain pages of *Logic* are frankly architectonic, and call on a concept of unity of reason that the understanding knowing itself could not conceive by its means alone: see, for instance, the appendix to the introduction (ibid., 86–87).

The Question of a Twofold Use

Are all characters homogeneous? Do they make up a type? I mentioned earlier what makes the answer to this question so important: it will allow or preclude the free play of combinations within a set. The *Logic* seems to suggest that there truly exists between characters the community of an identical use: "All characters considered as grounds of cognition are of *twofold* use, either *internal* or *external*. The *internal* use consists in *derivation* in order to recognize the thing itself through characters as grounds of its cognition. The *external* use consists in *comparison*, so far as we can compare, through characters, one thing with another according to the rules of *identity* and *diversity*." Now this twofold use ascribed to *the set of characters* does not seem to me to be in harmony with the other logical texts of Kant, or especially with the requirements of transcendental analysis, to which general logic is, as we saw, always subordinated.

If we follow the other logics,[31] twofold use becomes a *principle for classifying* characters. There are those that are suited to the internal determination of knowledge of a thing, and which a fortiori can be sufficient for comparison, and there are those that, constituted *for the sake* of comparison, are not sufficient for knowing the manifold in the thing. Against Leibniz, Kant therefore asserts that, even if comparative character is more usual, it is neither the most fruitful (in reality, nothing can be derived from it) nor the most important: "The characters which serve for internal use are also good for external use, but not vice versa" (*Logik Politz*, 533).

When logic governs ontology, as in the *ars characteristica*, the homogeneousness of all characters as simple elements, or products of simple elements, forms the necessary condition of the efficiency of the calculus. Here, on the contrary, heterogeneousness constitutes an obstacle for the possibility of a formulary calculus. Indifference to the starting point of reasoning ceases to be the case. For thought is conditioned *by its relationship to the act from which it arises*: either an act of productive imagination, from which derivation starts, or an act of understanding, which sets up comparisons between occurrences. Thus what I prove for one right-angled triangle—by starting from its properties—holds for *all* right-angled triangles. What derivation starting from the ground of knowledge is capable of, comparison is quite incapable of. Its particular scope is merely illustrative.[32] So it is not enough to grant Kant with having *added* the internal use of derivation to the function of differentiation noticed by Meier;[33] one must also evaluate the change that this *scission* carries. Characters are no longer the interchangeable materials of knowledge. *Reflection* must occur in a critical way, so that their origin and thus their function may be assigned to them. The act from which they arise allows us to assess their specific cognitive role.

Let me summarize the main features of this "scission." Leibniz deemed it possible to know by means of a sufficiently dense network of comparative relationships, by the interplay of identities and differences.[34] At the time of the *False Subtlety* Kant still defines the act of judging as an act of comparison.[35] But the development of transcendental logic requires that this definition be corrected. Comparison can very well bring together representations (*Zusammenhalten*) in the unity of consciousness (*R*, 2878), but it is unable to generate a concept (*R*, 2965). Comparing and abstracting amount to revealing a *logical form* (such as gender, species), but cannot apprehend the manifold as such. The logical act is always *subsequent*: it must be preceded by an act of transcendental apperception.

Let me try to determine the nature of the bond that binds the transcendental act and the logical act. A note of the *Critique* throws light on this issue:

> The analytic unity of consciousness belongs to all general concepts, as such. If, for instance, I think red in general, I thereby represent to myself a property which (as a character) can be found in something, or can be combined with other representations; that is, only by means of a presup-

posed possible synthetic unity can I represent to myself the analytic unity. (*KRV*, B 134, 109; trans. Smith, 154)[36]

The functions of analytic unity, which Kant mentions in the note of the *Critique*, are what he calls in the *Logic* "logical acts": comparison, reflection, and abstraction (*L*, 94–95). The identity of the concept does not arise from comparison; it is comparison that *presupposes* an original identity. How would it direct itself in the manifold if it were a principle? Unless the existence of a cosmos already prepared for comparison is dogmatically assumed, one cannot explain how it can be applied. And if we insist on making all knowledge a comparison without giving ourselves this kind of dogmatic assurance, we run the risk of turning the critique of knowledge into skepticism, for universal and necessary knowledge cannot be founded if the question of the identity of what is compared is left unanswered. This is why comparison requires transcendental syntheses of apperception as a precondition; they secure meanings by virtue of the relationship to objects that are thereby determined. Thus the principle of unity, which makes comparison possible, must be discovered in the subject. This identity, which first authorizes the formation of the concept and then that of comparative relationships, is nothing other than consciousness of self across the unity of its act of transcendental apperception (*KRV*, A 108, IV, 82). The identity of contents is ultimately conditioned by the identity of consciousness in the act that synthesizes them.

From the connection between given representations (judgment) to the comparison of concepts (whence the common concept arises), there is no longer, as in Leibniz, a simple difference depending on the degree of generality (II, XI), but a *shift* in the cognitive hierarchy. Analytic unity is represented only by means of synthetic unity: "I see a pine, a willow, a lime" (*L*, 95). But these three representations, which give me the matter for working out the *conceptus communis* of tree, must *already have been grasped* (*begriffen*) in an antecedent synthetic act (*WF*, II, 274). It belongs to comparison to deploy *thereafter* its deft activity in order to join the most remote representations (*Anth*, §54).[37] Characters are thus differentiated by virtue of their *function*. If they belong to the "internal use," they contribute to the "recognition of the thing" (*R*, 2284). As "internal ground of knowledge," a character of this type is at the junction between the concept and the intuition (pure or empirical):

> How are synthetic judgments in general possible? Since, beyond my concept and outside of it, I take from the intuition that founds it something in the quality of character and I bind it to this concept. (*WF*, 339)

This character may rightfully be qualified as *the base of meaning*, for the concepts and comparative characters that belong to the "external" use will derive from it (*R*, 2883). This kind of character departs from the domain of transcendental apprehension and only takes on a narrowly logical role. Its function is only mapping and classifying among directly schematized characters. It is now, however, without value in knowledge, for it takes on the *systematization* of internal characters. This means that it receives its content from elsewhere.

Characters and Totality

Analytic unity, which results from comparison and which, as such, does not produce any cognitive content, supposes an original unity of apperception, which is synthetic. But does the analytic concept differ qualitatively, in its *internal composition*, from the synthetic concept? Do its characters bear the mark of the type of thought that produced it? Or, rather, do analytic and synthetic characters constitute an indifferent matter that a form, sometimes analytic sometimes synthetic, will take up? In his anti-Kantian controversy, Eberhard heads toward this kind of solution. Between analytic and synthetic judgments, Eberhard wants to acknowledge only the distance separating essential predication from the predication derived from the essence of the subject. In a similar manner, the only difference for Eberhard between analytic and synthetic characters is that between the primitive nature of *constitutiva* and the derived nature of *rationata*. It is only a formal difference, not a drastic contrast in content, that distinguishes the analytic from the synthetic. Kant's criticism of Eberhard bears precisely on this point: where is this difference that Eberhard claims to know already to put to use? Except for a deductive step, the *rationata* are equivalent to the *constitutiva*. They, no less than the latter, are part of the essence, and both being conceived ''now'' in the concept of the essence are likewise *analytic* in nature.

From Kant's point of view, Eberhard is guilty of an excess of presumption: *he admits from the outset the unity of characters in a solely discursive use, which presupposes that every concept is a reality given in advance.* He thus leaves aside the ''propositions in which the predicate contains more in it than is really thought in the concept of the subject''—in other words, those in which the predicate is synthetic. The second distinction that the *Logic* (viii) mentions aims at preventing this illegitimate precedence of the deductive function. Because there is an analytic derivation *and* a synthetic derivation, there are also two types of relationships between the parts and the whole within a concept. If the whole *precedes* the parts (that is, if the total concept precedes its characters), the character considered is called *analytic*. But only rational concepts have the property of being exhaustively reducible to their characters, because they are closed (at least in principle, analysis can bring out all parts of the concept) and given a priori.[38] We can make such concepts *distinct*, but we cannot form them insofar as they are given in the necessity of the a priori. Nor can we *interpret* them freely, for they already have a content determined in a transcendental condition of reason:

> If a concept is given by reason in connection with a word, then its meaning is no longer variable, for no synthesis can produce it or can change it. (*R*, 2936)

The idea of pure reason belongs to this kind of concept: without a strict equivalent in experience, it can only have a pure and a priori origin, which explains why one is compelled in its case to analysis. But the largest class of partial concepts is the one constituted by synthetic characters. These come into composition to form the whole of a concept. They are acquired through induction and directed toward the totality of the concept as a *possible* limit of the progression by successive syntheses of new characters. Why is the total concept said to be, in this case, only *possible*? Because instead of starting from it as initially given, it is only *assumed* to be completed when I refer character after character to the same subject as yet incompletely determined. If an empirical concept is involved, its limit is never sure: in most cases, I can only ascribe to it a logical sufficiency, and consider it *as if it were completed*. Thus for the word "water," under which I place sometimes fewer, sometimes more, characters (*KRV*, B 756, 477; *R*, 2914). The analytic concept, on the contrary, exists prior to its parts. It is "real" *insofar as* it is entirely in act, the condition of the unity of thought.

The previous section concerning the uses of characters allowed me to assert the precedence of knowing over comparing, of synthetic unity over analytic unity. I must add now: there is an originary analytic that is the result of no comparison and does not suppose a preliminary synthesis.[39] It is the analytic that pertains to the "pure given" — that is, the set of concepts given a priori by the nature of our understanding or our reason, such as "substance, cause, right, equity, etc." (*KRV*, B 756, 478). Although "real," this knowledge nevertheless retains a trace of its analytic origin. It is only in the collation of the representation with the object that I can judge the completeness of my analysis. But in the present case, the object is given, not constructed. And it is given a priori; consequently it is not possible to determine distinctly the conditions of its application. It will often be the case that some characters of an analytic concept are in *practice* used *implicitly*. The question of the exactness or the completeness of the analysis of the purely given is thus never apodictically resolved, but is established only by the series of examples that relate to it. Rational concepts are thus only *ideally closed*. Thought in its exploratory function is never ensured of having inventoried *everything*.

The preceding discussion enables us to fully appreciate the opposition between two interpretations of *nota*. Kantian logic develops its own conception, breaking with the formalist inspiration of Leibnizian characteristic. The concept cannot be assimilated with the unrefined result of a blind act. The Leibnizian character validates the visible sign of the idea: every instance of substitution was lawful and productive. In Kantianism, the numerous restrictions implied by the classification of characters aim at preventing the leveling that typically occurs in characteristic calculus. Priority is now given to consciousness over characteristic operation. The latter is lawful only when the former can be present. Character must therefore always be measured by the singular act from which it arises. It is from the nature of this act that we can infer the nature of the character and in turn its particular use and usefulness. No reading *technique* centered on the character allows us to dispense with this *reflection*. Therefore neither can analysis itself be restricted to an automatic technique of identification. This progress from the confused to the clear, starting with a given, results from a singular act of understanding. Conversely, to detect the analyticity of a proposition requires that one inquire into the formation of judgment, and that one ascertain that the latter is independent from intuition. To analyze is to become more aware of a content of thought. It is to learn nothing, while knowing better.

A question remains: Is the content given in advance really indifferent to the act of analysis? And under such conditions, may one not, by means of a definition, make a concept, until then possible, real—in other words, transform the synthetic into analytic? Is not the analytic, finally, what is "true by definition"? Or, in Kantian terms, can a real definition of all meanings be framed, and thereafter a nominal use be made of them? Can all meanings be reconstructed in a univocal scientific language—in Carnapian terms, can they be "constructed" so as to allow the truth-value of a statement to be determined by examining solely the rules of the language involved?

4

Definition and Analyticity in Kant

The Nominal and the Real

As I will have the opportunity to note more fully, the scope that I mean to give or to refuse to a characteristic system, understood in a broad sense, depends on the opposition between the nominal and the real. That Kant mentions the distinction between the nominal and the real is not in itself surprising, for it is traditional in logic and is taken up, for example, in the *Logic of Port-Royal*. A real definition leaves the defined with ''its ordinary idea, in which it is assumed that other ideas are contained'' (*I*, XII, 86–87). One must be attentive in this case to the reality of the idea exposed in the definition. On the other hand, a nominal definition assigns arbitrarily to a given sound the idea that one wants to signify. There is no prior usage to follow, even less is there any need to worry about the truth of what is asserted by the idea, which is not described, but only named.

But the traditional distinction and the corresponding distinction made by Kant are homonymous, and it is precisely in the understanding and use of it proposed by Kant that we will see at another level the antiformalist strategy already sketched in the treatment of character. Kant does not have in mind only the ordinary contrast between the arbitrary mode of presentation of a meaning to a word and the objective determination of a thing. The two types of definitions are for him opposed to each other both by their *use* and by the *concepts* to which they apply. The use of nominal definition is only *comparative* or diagnostic (*R*, 2994, 3001, 3003). The *definiendum* is, then, either an empirical or a rational concept (*R*, 2992–94). On the other hand, real definition is characteristic of derivation; its use is genetic. The concept that arises in this case is not already there, but is the outcome of a construction in intuition. It is a synthetic a priori concept. Nominal definition comes ''afterwards,'' whereas real definition precedes the concept as its genesis. This distinction is what now accounts for a feature of definition that

40

Locke correctly noted concerning judgments of coexistence, but which he was unable to interpret. At stake is the specific behavior determining each type of definition with respect to the completeness of characterization that it makes it possible (or not) to attain.

We saw in the preceding chapter that comparison is inexhaustible, as is the series of species that can be predicated of some genus. Insofar as it proceeds by comparison, nominal definition is as a matter of principle a *fragmentary* determination of the object. It only presents some distinctive features: "Gold is a heavy metal, yellow, soluble in aqua regia," is a nominal definition because it only has a *subjective sufficiency* for discriminating the intended object among the *universitas* of items of experience; it gives only a few indications, whose role is simply to mark rather approximately the reference.[40] Diametrically opposed to what could be called the "underdetermination" of the nominal field, construction in intuition offers the paradigm of closure on an object. The elements of the concept are lined up one by one according to an order of synthetic coordination, established by pure intuition, until they form the whole of a meaning that arises entirely from the act of its construction.

This completeness of definition is, of course, the distinctive feature of mathematical definition, a completeness connected with the *arbitrary* nature of its synthesis. "Arbitrary" is to be understood here not as "product of fantasy" or "conventionally asserted" but as the mark of a construction in which the characters to be synthesized need not be indicated from without. The freedom of the mathematician's decision concerning existence is entire. No criterion of faithfulness to an external object arises to limit from outside the completeness of the *definiens* (*KRV*, B 747, 472, 502). But this arbitrariness rests on the conditions of the pure intuition, which conditions, as opposed to the conditions of empirical intuition, are universal and necessary. The possibility that the mathematician may "forget" certain properties belonging to the concept constructed, or the possibility of an infinite dispersion of constructions, is thus excluded. *Precision*, which consists in not using more characters than necessary, is thus, in a way, the luxury of mathematical definition, for precision presupposes that completeness is already guaranteed:

> The mathematician cannot make false definitions; for that reason, he must be precise. (*R*, 2979)[41]

Real definition is therefore a complete and *objectively adequate* definition. It makes it possible not only to recognize but also to produce, in full, the concept (*R*, 29923).[42]

The nominal-real distinction and the incomplete-complete distinction thus overlap. But we must still clarify the relationship between the first of these distinctions and the general division between analytic and synthetic propositions. Insofar as it proceeds by comparison, nominal definition uses an analytic process consisting in going from the whole (given) to the parts (contained virtually in it).

Real definition, on the contrary, proceeds by synthetic adjunction of characters, and yields a concrete derivation of the concept (*R*, 29945).[43] It seems equally chancy to speak of a "real analytic definition." One must recognize on this point, however, that the obscurity of texts may lead to confusion. This type of definition, as Lewis White Beck asserts, "states the defining predicates of a given concept, known to have objective validity," this concept being given either a priori or a posteriori.[44] Although we recognize that this type of definition is analytic, it is only by forcing the text that we can suppose it is "real." Kant is satisfied with emphasizing the inappropriateness of the distinction of the nominal and the real in the particular case of concepts given by understanding: "Here nominal and real definitions come to the same thing [*fallen in eines*]" (*R*, 2995). When it comes to determining the nature of definitions of given concepts of understanding, Kant declares them always nominal (*R*, 2918) and obtained by analysis (*R*, 2929). Why, then, is the distinction between nominal and real, under certain circumstances, inappropriate? To answer this question, one must first have answered the question: Is there a path leading from the nominal to the real? In other words, can one hope to "improve" the nominal? This question determines the interpretation of the phrase "come to the same thing," and likewise the general problem of translating the synthetic into the analytic.

Once again, this question leads me to compare the respective projects of Leibniz and Kant. We know that the communicability of the nominal and the real is one of the assumptions of the characteristic, for it makes progress in knowledge possible. Moreover, the reversibility of analysis into synthesis is what founds a general combinatory. The two theses combined make up two of the central pillars of *Mathesis universalis*. It could be objected that Leibniz already contrasts the two kinds of definitions, as will Kant, according to the nature of their adequacy: subjective for the nominal definition—it only indicates the distinctive characters of the thing defined—it becomes objective when the real definition reveals a priori the possibility of the thing.[45] But from Leibniz's point of view, the distance between these two kinds of definitions is that separating the "unaccomplished" idea from the "accomplished" idea—a difference "in practice" rather than "in law."[46] To improve nominal definition, one need only continue the analysis of the reciprocal property it expresses. The reduction into simple terms, obtained from any one of the nominal definitions, gives the real definition. The latter exhibits the complete series of "ingredients" of the idea, which then appears as noncontradictory, something the nominal definition could not show because some complexity remained in it.[47] There is thus no theoretical obstacle in progressing from the distinct idea (nominal definition) to the adequate idea (real definition), even if this progress is to be expected from a deepening of our knowledge of nature. One day, from the characteristic property of gold—namely, that it is the heaviest metal—will be deduced, as in geometry, its resistance to the cupel and to nitric acid.[48] Finally, if the resolution of the reciprocal property has not yet been achieved a priori, one can consider as real (although it is not "causal") the nominal definition whose noncontradiction can be proved by the reality of the *definiendum* in experience.[49]

Why is such a passage impossible in the Kantian understanding of definition? Nominal definition is incomplete, as in Leibniz. Is it not simply still a *part* of real definition? If this hypothesis is tenable, the respective materials of nominal and real definition must be homogeneous. The first is made up of analytic characters; the second is made up of synthetic characters. Nominal incompleteness would have to be a matter of routine or ignorance. In fact, it is irreducibly linked to the fact that meaning is *given*. This is a realism of sense quite different from Leibniz's realism of essence. Kant takes into consideration the specificity of what does not allow itself to be manipulated or constructed, namely, what is given: in the diversity of empirical intuition, in the pure concepts of understanding, and in reason.[50] These different kinds of "given" make nominal definition a hazardous quest for characters without assurance of completeness. Yet they fix for definition its *invariance*:

> If a concept is given by reason in connection with a word, then its meaning is no longer variable, for no synthesis produced it or can change it. (*R*, 2936)[51]

It is thus the use itself we make of words that prevents us from confusing the two domains of definition. When a given is concerned, meanings are already present and are attributed to the word. When, on the other hand, one constructs by way of a real definition, the attribution of a name is simultaneous with the construction of a (*real*) essence. Between the two definitions there is therefore a difference not only of use and object but also of *temporality*: nominal definition is regressive. It goes back over what is already conceived so as to extract from it the attributes. But this regressive question is indefinite, in the sense that one is never sure of exhausting the meaning (*KRV*, B 756, 478, 502). Nominal definition proceeds regressively, but real definition takes place precisely during progression: it builds up the concept by coordinating the synthetic characters from concrete intuitions.

This is why the concept elaborated by real definition is called "factive" (*factitius*) or "made" (*gemacht*) and "arbitrary" (*willkürlich*): because "it is not derived from elsewhere" (than this originary act of synthesis) (ibid., B 758, 478, 502). Let us not confuse "arbitrary" in this sense with the pure convention of nominal definition of the *Logic of Port-Royal*, nor with the contingent choice between "a little more" and "a little less" of empirical meanings in Kant's own nominal definition. Once again, "arbitrary" has now the sense of that which does not have to agree with any *extrinsic* standard. The standard of definition merges with the intuitive process of construction. But if "to define" takes on such completely different senses depending on the field to which it applies, is this not the sign that the word "definition" is taken at a certain time in a derived sense? Is real definition a *kind* of definition, or is it more than this: its *paradigm*?

Definition in the Sciences: Definition, Exposition, Marking

Kant invites us to rediscover the original meaning of the term "to define" (*KRV*, B 755, 477, 501). Is it not: to limit, to mark the boundary of? To know where true definition lies, one must search for that which enables us to limit knowledge objectively to its *only* object and to *all* this object. We can exclude necessarily *incomplete* explanations, such as *diagnostic* "definitions," which serve only to mark a "Scholastic division" by means of "external" characters. Only a complete division can cover all its object; and to be complete, a definition must be canonical" (*R*, 3003)—in other words, it must justify its use.

What a priori principle can found the legitimate use of definition? A principle that, being a priori, can *present* a content; pure intuition, capable of considering universality *in concreto*, fulfills this twofold condition. The field of absolute validity of definition is thus *mathematics*. There the definition is called *genetic*, insofar as it is a construct that demonstrates the internal possibility of the defined object. But is pure intuition the only element capable of founding a definition?

Kant's position on this point seems to have evolved. He does not immediately adopt the critical classification, which consists in adding the empirical synthesis of the phenomenon to pure intuition, but considers at first that intuition is on the same level as the other powers in their a priori use. During the period when he conceives the case of the definition of rational concepts by analogy with that of mathematical definition—that is, when he makes it a *real* definition—[52] the arbitrary-given distinction disappears behind the incomplete-complete distinction. "Nominal" then becomes apparently synonymous with incomplete, which explains the Leibnizian tonality of certain *Reflexionen*.[53] But if Kant could for some time—approximately from 1764 to 1769, following the hypothetical dating of the *Reflexionen* referred to—assimilate all cases of real a priori definitions, he later commits himself to another classification. It is easy to understand that what impels him to abandon his original conception is the lack of completeness of the definitions of rational concepts, given a priori. Consequently, it is no longer true that whenever the essence is real by virtue of an a priori necessity, one may speak of real *definition*. More specifically, it is no longer true when the object cannot be exhaustively defined, which is the case when the *definiendum* is a "pure given": the concept then may be given an *exposition*, and not a definition in proper form.

During the critical period, the *given-constructed* distinction prevails over the a priori-a posteriori distinction, which yields a new classification of definitions, in which three features, given-analytic-nominal, are contrasted with three others, constructed-synthetic-real. Rational concepts have in common with given empirical concepts that they cannot be *delimited* by definition, but only called forth by certain distinctive characters. On the other hand, mathematical and physical syntheses are brought together insofar as they form their object respectively from pure intuition or given phenomena (arbitrarily in mathematics, empirically in physics).[54]

But in the natural sciences, we cannot say, as does the mathematician, "Sic volo, sic jubeo" (R, 2930). We must take experience into account to know what enters into the definition. For this reason, it is difficult to assign "final" limits to the empirically constructed concept. Future real experience can make us discover new characters of the concept (L, §103, 142). In spite of what draws together the physical phenomenon and the mathematical concept, the former is finally left out of the field of real definition.[55] Although the physical phenomenon enables properties to be derived, it cannot, strictly speaking, be *defined*, owing to what might be called its "underdetermination" with respect to total experience. It can only be exhibited from experiences (a posteriori), which determine the concept more and more completely, without ever being able to exhaust the *definiendum*.

Mathematical construction thus forms the only domain of validity of definition, insofar as it alone determines its object *omni et solo conveniendo*. The *real exposition* of physical concepts is the first retreat with respect to the paradigm. It does not supply as the latter the proof of its equivalence with the object; here the apodictic yields to the probable. A symmetrical weakening of the paradigm occurs: what Kant continues to call nominal "definition" does not deserve the name "definition" if we take the requirement of completeness seriously. For the nominal analysis of a concept has some chance of being complete only at the end of an indefinite series of examples assuring us that we have left nothing out. With respect to the paradigm of real definition, nominal definition of a priori concepts is in the same relationship as real exposition of empirically formed concepts: it cannot lead directly to completeness, but presupposes a series of nominal expositions. Finally a second weakening of the definitional requirements determines a fourth group of explanations, which we could term "verbal-nominal" as opposed to "real-nominal" definitions of the previous type. For this time, instead of starting as before from an a priori pure given, we start only from a word, whose role consists in contributing to the marking of the *empeiria*, without enlarging the sense of the concept, as was the case with the exposition of phenomena (R, 2955). The word whose use we seek to clarify teaches us nothing. To define it consists only in fixing its usual sense, without referring to any objectivity: "Nominal definition is not sufficient to result in giving an object" (R, 2916).

Dictionary definitions belong to this kind of explanation: they are only markings that are imposed on usage. Actually, to the extent that they serve only to fill in a lexicon, without leading to knowledge of objects, they are "useless" (R, 2916).

Is the Analytical the "True by Definition"?

The archetype of the series of definitions lies in the mathematical procedure of construction of concepts in intuition. In this discipline, definition finds its full justification, because the arbitrariness of the *Sic volo* coincides with the reality of the construction. But it is not the same in the natural sciences, in which the diversity of empirical intuition casts doubt on the necessity of notions built up by exposition from the matter of phenomena. Nor, a fortiori, in philosophy, in which all intuition leaves the scholar, given to the abstract universality of concepts, with no guide except a priori deductions. To what use can one hope to put definition in these two fields? In the natural sciences its role is merely that of a *hypothesis* designed to serve as a temporary base for experiments. In this sense, one resorts primarily to explanations of words:

> When we speak of water and its properties, we do not stop short at what is thought in the word "water" but proceed to experiments. The word, with the few characteristics which we attach to it, is more properly to be regarded as merely a designation than as a concept of the thing; the so-called definition is nothing more than a determining of the word. (*KRV*, B 756, 477–78, 501)

Definitions in this field will have no apodictic scope, nor especially will they exhaust the sphere of the defined, which would be the warrant of an adequacy of the theoretical with the object beyond our reach. (Kant, let me repeat, retains Locke's idea of the incomplete and indefinitely open character of the judgment of coexistence.) This indetermination of the *definiendum* bears heavily on the theory of sciences, creating a separation between mathematics, whose language is closed and homogeneous, and the natural sciences, whose language is "zetetic" and continually renewed. In philosophy, finally, definition serves only to coordinate that which, at the end of analysis, seems sufficient for the completeness of the concept to be analyzed (*R*, 2968).

We can now attempt to answer the question raised previously: is the analytical what is "true by definition"? For we see that *dependency is rather the other way around*: it is not analytic judgment that is deduced from definition; it is definition that requires *antecedently* enough analytic judgments to convince us of the sufficiency of the characters thus drawn from the concept. Just as the a priori synthetic judgment guarantees the value of real definition, likewise the analytic judgment is what makes "definition" possible in philosophy. One could therefore question the indestructibility of the synthetic and the mutual independence of the analytic and the synthetic, only on account of a misunderstanding as to the purpose of the *Critique*. If Kant made the concept the changing result of a practice, the historically determined product of a language game, and nothing more, he could conceive of giving a founding role to definition. But Kant strives, on the contrary, to undermine the empiricist assumption, illustrated, for example, by Hobbes. The empiricists wrongly believe that they can do away with absolute meanings. In fact, theoretical or moral practice turns on them without ever being able to revise them again or even to explain them (*R*, 2967). It is essential for Kant to take these meanings into account, to try to *understand* them, to capture all that can be thought in them.[56]

It may be objected here that what holds for the analysis of rational concepts no longer holds for ordinary analysis of a lexicological type: if we stick to analytic judgments that have a function of nominal clarification, should it not be said that judgment is *explanatory* precisely because it presupposes definitions of concept, which in this case are synthetic? To give an analytic judgment, is it not, in this sense, to *reread* a concept produced elsewhere synthetically? The answer to this objection lies in Kant's insistence on separating the two domains of the synthetic and the analytic (both by the distinction between two sorts of characters and by the distinction between two types of definitions). Let us recall that the concept is constituted by an act of transcendental consciousness. If the act from which the concept arises is a *production*, the concept remains synthetic — whether the production is in the process or already finished does not change anything. To reread it is to heed its nature as the *possible* end of a progression by adjunction of one character to another. If we consider on the contrary the concept as a word in the dictionary, whose mode of formation we do not question, no synthetic act having produced it, we cannot derive from it any other property of the object. Being *given*, the concept can become the matter of an analytic judgment, but it ceases to be capable of teaching us anything concerning "the thing itself." For example, the judgment "gold is a yellow metal," which Kant gives as an example of an analytic proposition (*P*, §2), is only a sentence from the dictionary, nothing more than a means of clarifying the meaning of a word, without which the concept would no longer be a "given empirical concept," but an a posteriori "formed concept."

To transform the synthetic into analytic comes down to relating to language what must retain the force of reality. The whole critical enterprise seeks to prove the illusory character of this endeavor. In its purely logical use, language extends in the limited space comprised between pure identity (simple repetition of the same thing) and analysis. In analysis, sameness is conceived *under* difference by understanding, difference being given by reason or tradition. Furthermore, sameness is the poorest category: the degree zero of thought. The "fruitlessness" of tautology is not far from the "meaninglessness" of explanation by occult qualities.[57] Both arise from an abuse of language, which in each case talks without saying anything.

Obviously, it is not possible either to raise the analytic to the synthetic, the language of identity to that of existence. Against Eberhard, and later against Maass, Kant recalls again and again the dogmatic illusion hidden under the reductionist thesis (which consists in relating to a common language the analytic-synthetic difference). Kant demands that we question then the place — nominal or real — from which we speak:

> One wants to form a judgment on a judgment; one must, however, *each time* know *beforehand* what must be conceived under the subject as well as under the predicate.[58]

I may well *ascribe* to my concept such and such a character. But will I have for that matter *extended* my knowledge? Will I not have made but a *nominal* statement? In this case I will have merely disguised as a solution that which is only the paraphrase of the problem, by reconstituting as nominal what is actually of a synthetic nature (*R*, 3130). This is precisely the vacuous proposition of know-how (*Geschicklichkeit*).[59]

Section 2
Bolzano's Renovation of Analyticity

1

Criticism of the Traditional Definition

The specifically Bolzanian concept of analyticity is brought in at an advanced stage, as the maturely formulated answer to a problem that never ceased to appear under different aspects. Only in the *Wissenschaftslehre* of 1837 does what we might call a "revolution" in analyticity occur. Earlier texts strive to adapt the Kantian definition so that it satisfies the new requirements of the anticritical mathematicians. But this definition, often revised, gives rise to growing difficulties. There were so many reasons for abandoning it, but also so many constraints working to shape the new definition. "Revolution," we said; but until the *Wissenschaftslehre*, analyticity was a marginal theme. Its main function was, as in Kant, to reveal the problematic existence of the synthetic a priori. From a theme of preliminary exposition, analyticity becomes in the work of 1837 an "integrated" concept: henceforth it is part of a philosophy and becomes inseparable from a method of identifying logical objects, *variation*. But this was a "Ptolemaic," not a "Copernican," revolution: instead of statically emphasizing the synthetic a priori, it becomes a notable property of certain propositions whose definition now requires a preliminary examination of other properties such as truth and validity. This definition, however, does not have a purely descriptive interest; the theses of Volume 3 must be taken seriously in order to portray with perfect clarity the deep *interest* that Bolzano had in his new definition of analyticity.

From the "In Itself" to the Phenomenon

The persistence in Bolzano's *Theory of Science* of certain words from transcendental philosophy strikes us all the more, for these words now serve completely different purposes. Thus the word "phenomenon" (*Erscheinung*) retains in the Bolzanian system a strategical role in that it founds the articulation of the order of

51

existence on the order of essences. It makes possible the transition from an objective set of propositions, without real existence (which it would be improper to call a "world"), and representations—called "in themselves" in order to emphasize their self-sufficiency—to the different activities of a living being: language, thought, judgment. In spite of its apparent resemblance to the Kantian *Ding an sich*, the "representation in itself" has a different status. If it is de jure independent of our knowledge, this does not mean that it is removed from human understanding; it is enough that this representation is not *the product* of understanding for its full independence to be guaranteed. Expressed differently: if it is not the consequence of knowledge, it is because this representation is, on the contrary, the origin and the condition of the possibility of knowledge. With this inversion, God and humankind are in the same position: neither of them *creates* the meanings by which they come to learn. Consequently, against Kant, Bolzano makes *Erscheinung* into a reversible relationship: the "in itself" is what founds knowledge; but inversely, it is the logician's task to return to this origin, by going through the signs that tend continually to rephenomenalize it.[1]

Bolzano defines the proposition in itself *negatively* as that which is independent of any *enunciation, consciousness*, and *judgment*. To speak of "proposition in itself" is not to add a new determination to "proposition" but to reinstate the sense of this term in its pureness. Bolzano's "in itself" plays a double function in a manner quite comparable to Frege's *Gedanke*. First, it determines the self-sufficiency of logic with respect to thought and to language. The "in itself" does not properly belong to the thinking subject, unlike representation (in the Fregean sense), which retains in it traces of the subjectivity that formed it. Hence its second function: the "in itself" allows human beings to attach the same sense to the same proposition; in this manner both communication between persons and the constitution of a common battlefield whose purpose is truth are made possible.[2] For Bolzano, statement is merely, in Scholz's terms, the "proper name" of a proposition in itself.[3] But the denomination is not without dangers: this proper name can be insufficiently explicit, a single name referring to several distinct propositions. Inversely, several statements will very often correspond to a single proposition in itself. Hence the difficulties of "translating" statements of ordinary langauge into prelinguistic concepts, which always fall short of the signs. Yet if an *Erscheinung* is possible, it is because an isomorphism is preserved in mapping the "in itself" onto language; from the diversity of expressions of natural language one can derive a class of statements in which constitutive logical elements emerge. Translation will proceed from the first to the second (see Book II, Section V). But translation has the property of being both indeterminate and infinite—indeterminate because there is no other criterion of the value of the translation except other persons' agreement, and infinite because the conditions of enunciation of every statement must be studied for a translation to be ascribed to it.

This concern for translation, as likewise the axiom stating that there are no two identical propositions in themselves,[4] is obviously inspired by the ideal of a universal logical language. Without taking up again the Leibnizian project of a universal characteristic, on account of a mistrust for formalizing symbolism, the *Wissenschaftslehre* offers a speculative equivalent of it:[5] there is an ideal set of meanings, reducible to its elements and *fixed*; it is not the symbolism that makes possible the precise and final determination of meanings, but the fact that they belong to a pure set, removed from variations attached to the individual existence and the evolution of language. But if the words of a language are in a relationship of exteriority with respect to representations and propositions in themselves, of which they are the imperfect translation, it belongs to the logician's commentary to fill in the blanks, to distinguish identities and equivalences, and to refute superficial tautologies. Thus Bolzano considers as one and the same proposition the following two statements:

The sum of the angles of a triangle is equal to two right angles.
The sum of the angles of a space bounded by three lines is equal to two right angles.

On the other hand, the two statements:

Titus is the son of Caius
Caius is the father of Titus

refer to distinct propositions because they are composed of nonintentionally identical constituents (*Wissenschaftslehre* [hereafter, *W*], §156, II, 140).[6] Let us now draw the consequence of this topical occurrence of the *Erscheinung* in the construction of the object of logic: we can no longer rely on what is "simply conceived" nor on what is said to define logical properties, in particular the analyticity of a proposition. Sources of obviousness must be sought elsewhere.

The Parts of the Proposition

What must one in general expect from a definition? It should indicate *of what parts* and *of what connection* the *explicandum* is constituted (*W*, §350, III, 399). A definition of analytic propositions must satisfy the conditions of any explanation; it should avoid "figurative manners of speech," which do not break down in a satisfactory way the concept of analytic. It should be neither narrower nor broader in its extension than the *explicandum*. Foremost among metaphorical explanations are those that use the category of states of thought to describe relationships between the constituents of a proposition. Thus Ulrich, Jakob, and Reinhold agree in defining analytic judgments as those in which "the predicate is already (implicitly) conceived in the subject." This definition, in which the influence of the *Prolegomena* is perceptible, remains extrinsic compared with the true objects of logical thought; it pertains to mental images associated with representations of the subject and the predicate, losing sight of their sense and their *objective* connection (*W*, §284, III, 61). Aside from the fact that these traditional definitions of analytic judgments miss their target, by transposing their explanation to the nonlogical domain of the psychological effects of the concept — effects whose value is after all only in the imagination (*W*, §23, I, 98) — Bolzano criticizes them for being *too large*: they break the Aristotelian rule of *soli definito conveniendo* (see *W*, the objections brought together in note 4 of §148, III, 86ff.). Let us compare the different versions of the Kantian definition of analyticity:

> "The predicate appears already there (i.e., in the subject) as a constituent" (*Critique of Pure Reason*).
> "The predicate only repeats representations of the subject" (Fries).
> "The concept of the subject is particularly determined only with respect to its parts" (Gerlach).
> "The predicate is a partial representation, or in a negative judgment a negation, of the concept of the subject" (Roesling).

These definitions have in common that they all presuppose a restrictive conception of the *constituent* of a concept (*Bestandteil*). They have meaning only if by "part of the concept" is understood a privileged representation, that is, a character directly derivable from the concept of subject. It is easy for Bolzano to give a counterexample in which a constituent of the subject reappears in predicative position without the proposition becoming analytic:

> The father of Alexander, king of Macedonia, was king of Macedonia. (*W*, §48, I, 216)

The instrument for analyzing the *concept* should be refined by distinguishing several types of connections between parts of a representation, but also of the *propositions*. Bolzano mentions elsewhere a distinction that can solve the preceding difficulty: the parts of a representation can be brought together (*verknüpft*) either in an immediate manner (*unmittelbar*) or in a mediate manner (*mittelbar*, §21). In the preceding example, the representations of "father," "Alexander," and "king of Macedonia" are all only *indirectly* connected. The statement could be translated into the proposition in itself:

> Alexander, who was king of Macedonia, had a father, who was king of Macedonia.

Reformulated in this way, the proposition appears more distinctly factual: the character "king of Macedonia," appearing as an "oblique" constituent in the concept of the subject and in that of the predicate, conveys in each case a different message. But the scope of Bolzano's criticism goes further than just confronting the traditional definition with a counterexample: it reestablishes a use lost since medieval logic, consisting in giving an equal status to all parts of speech whether they state *concreta*, properties, or relationships. *All parts of the proposition are thus promoted to the representative function*: the concept itself of representation is extended to "all that can appear as constituent in a proposition, but does not constitute in itself a proposition" (*W*, §58, I, 254).

We know that, concerning the Scholastic division of terms into *categoremata* and *syncategormata*,[7] post-Kantian logic is primarily interested in the former, reduced moreover to their purely categorematical constituents, the characters. A rightful objection to Bolzano was that he arbitrarily restricted the object of logic to the examination of predicative propositions, leading him to abandon relationships.[8] Nevertheless, I note here that the generalization of representative value to every constituent of the proposition leads to an *extension* of the object and practice of logic. Bolzano's innovation consists in conferring on syncategorematic terms precisely the property that medieval logicians denied them, that of having self-sufficient meaning. Instead of subordinating them to independent meanings that would be the true bearers of information, he gives them an equal representative status as the *categoremata*, which enables him to pass over a distinction that, we shall see, appears to him finally more problematic than truly clarifying:

> Every word in a language serves to designate a representation and some of them even designate complete propositions. (*W*, §57, I, 246)[9]

Bolzano places thus *on the same level* what Scholastic logic *separated*. But he leaves in this way — on purpose — a concomitant delimitation undetermined: the one that opposes the *matter* and the *form* of the statement. For this distinction, which Bochenski traces back to Boethius,[10] is always articulated by the logicians of the fourteenth century on the distinction between *categoremata* and *syncategoremata*. Albert of Saxony writes, for example:

> We speak here about matter and form in the sense in which the matter of a proposition or a consequence is understood, as purely categorematic terms, that is, subjects and predicates, with the exception of the syncategorematic terms which are added to them, by which they are joined, denied, or distributed, and by which a certain mode of supposition is given to them. All the rest is said, on the other hand, to belong to the form.[11]

This distinction obviously plays an essential role, for it makes it possible to define the very goal of logic, which will be to bring out the "logical constants," that is, the most notable *syncategoremata* and their rules of use (see Bochenski, *Formale Logik*, 181–82). It is therefore particularly interesting to understand what led Bolzano to give up this fundamental distinction. The indetermination or rather the disappearance of potential differences between the parts of content can be explained, of course, by the sole existence of a realistic conception of language as developed by Bolzano. If the function of language is to depict entities "in themselves," it is essential that there be an objective correlate for every linguistic unit. Syncategorematic terms like "and" and "which" can then, in spite of our linguistic intuition,[12] be explained, apart from any connection, as independent representations. Bolzano's semantic point of view is intimately bound up with the atomistic view of sense, which the syntactic approach eliminates by definition. His setting up of a semantic logic is thus inseparable from the importance he attaches to natural language and his refusal of a *Begriffsschrift*.

If we look closer, we notice that it is not only the representative nature of language, but also the exceptions to the correspondence between language and the "in itself" represented,[13] that lead Bolzano to eliminate the distinction between material and formal constituents. There are seemingly syncategorematic terms that have no significant role in the proposition, and thus must be eliminated from the actual content. Likewise, there are seemingly categorematic terms, which, aside from their function, take on also a formal role, relative to supposition or quantification. Thus the constituents "all" and "each," found in a universal proposition, are purely redundant; universal extension is actually carried by the categorematic constituent—in other words, by the concept of subject itself:

> I take it that the expression "anyone" means no more than what we think
> by the expression "person," if we do not want to limit it arbitrarily to one
> or another class of persons. (*W*, §57, I, 248)

"All" and "any" are then parts of the language that do not convey a new representation, whereas the concept of matter preeminently "is far from lacking form," following Hegel's expression (*Science of Logic*, preface). The word "some" expresses, in contrast, a genuine representation and plays its role as propositional constituent fully. The expression of quantification is thus not necessarily ensured by logical or "formal" constituents: exhibiting the essential content (*W*, §57, I, 248) of a proposition undermines any sharp distinction between material and formal constituents, or extralogical and logical constituents.

This *indetermination* attached to kinds of constituents, to their potential specialization into formal or material meanings, allows in return an extremely fruitful generalization in the expression of logical laws and at the same time makes possible the unexpected reappearance of the formal, but in an entirely different sense from what was understood by the term in the Scholastic tradition. What is the fruitfulness of this generalization? First, substitutions can be made on any constituent "one may choose," the only restriction arising from the requirement of the meaning of the whole *after* substitution, because constituents are indifferent, because they are all likewise independent of propositional context. Medieval scholars attempted such substitutions only in relation to the distinction between two kinds of constituents. Only the concepts of subject and predicate could be subjected to variation. Thus what distinguishes for them a formal consequence from a material consequence is that the former admits in subject or predicate position any categorematic term. Such a criterion highlights the role that syncategorematic constituents play in a formally valid consequence. But a constituent, taken in the Bolzanian sense, is a higher descriptive instrument, for it necessitates no particular ontological hypothesis concerning the object signified by each signifying unit. The variable is what leaves unaltered the truth of the proposition through the sequence of substitutions; the constant is what cannot be modified without changing the value of the whole. What follows from this act of variation is again a form, but in an entirely new sense.

Form as Kind

To understand the exact sense of this term in the *Theory of Science*, we must leave aside the syntactic sense of the term as it appears in the symbolic expression by means of letters. Variation reveals the *kinds* of propositions that are to be described somewhat in the way the naturalist classes animal species. A form in logic is a kind that is distinguished by a common property:

> Logic has to deal not so much with the determination of individual concepts (although it does it for some of them) than with the determination of whole kinds of concepts; that is, kinds that, owing to their particular property, ask for a particular treatment in the sciences. (*W*, §116, II, 540–41)[14]

What is said here of *concepts* applies likewise to *propositions*: the kinds are what must be brought out, such that "some of their constituents being fixed, they can be stated [*lauten*] in all others thus or otherwise" (*W*, §12, I, 48). There are in fact two acceptations of the word "form"; current logical use restricts the term to expressing a propositional structure by means of letters and signs of operators, but Bolzano does not retain this use for himself:

> If these classes of propositions are to be called general *forms* of propositions, then it is permissible to say that logic is concerned with forms rather than with individual propositions. (Actually only the written or oral expression "Some *As* are *B*," and not the class itself, should be called a form.) (Ibid., 48)

The symbolic expression of propositional kinds by means of signs does not make up in itself the *object* of logic. It is only an instrument for clarifying, for bringing back to mind, and cannot replace what it is designed to designate. On this point Bolzano accepts the Kantian criticism of Leibniz: the sign cannot be blindly manipulated; it must always be accompanied by consciousness of what it is supposed to represent. Bolzano thus rejects the interpretation of logic as indifferent to its object; this kind of interpretation, based on the symbolic writing of the syllogism, does not fit in with his semantic approach to logical kind:

> Finally I do not understand either how it can be said that we conceive in logic objects "by leaving their internal characters completely undetermined." For if we conceive an object as entirely undetermined, we could not either assert anything about it. (*W*, §7, I, 28)[15]

Signs thus give a *metalinguistic description* of propositional kinds, but do not yield a complete object. They give a fragmentary indication of the object that the logician is to examine. On the other hand, the notion of form as *logical object*, and no longer as metalinguistic instrument of description, is to be understood in the sense of kind or type (*Art*). The extensional point of view directed to sets of logical objects that have in common some notable property is emphasized (§106). Logicians bring out what I would call propositional structures, but they do not make a common form their object: their object consists in the multiplicity brought together in the kind rather than in a propositional function that would leave this or the other occurrence empty. *The refusal of formal syntax originates in a conception of the proposition as the only true object of the logician.* Everything that, by means of a symbolic notation, is substituted for the full sense of the "natural" proposition introduces a touch of confusion and virtual meaninglessness. If form is reestablished, it is solely in an extensional sense (that is, as a class of propositions) so as to preserve the diversity of individual propositions that a common property allows to be brought together under a concept.

This manner of approaching the question of the formal obviously has a direct impact on the way to define the analytic proposition. Actually, the question of demarcation between the logical and the extralogical can be posed only with respect to variation, without it being possible to derive from the latter new indications concerning the specialization or the nature of constituents. The occurrence of the distinction between the formal and the material rests not on a strictly logical difference, but on a derived difference that bears on the type of knowledge required in order to recognize the truth or falsity of propositions. As we shall see, a properly logical definition must not stress an extrinsic criterion of psychological or cognitive content. Such a distinction will therefore not be able to play a determining role in the conception of analyticity.

Can one correct failure to satisfy the rule of *soli definito conveniendo*, which is ultimately to be attributed to a restrictive conception of constituents? In order to avoid the traps of "oblique parts," Eberhard, Maass, and Krug tried to characterize analytic judgments by the *type of constituent of the subject*, which should occur in predicative position:

> This unfortunate state of affairs could be avoided if, along with Eberhard, Maass, Krug, and others, one made use of the expression that in analytic judgments the predicate is one of the essential parts of the subject or (which comes to the same thing) constitutes one of its essential characters, understanding these to be constitutive characters, that is, such as are present in the concept of the subject. (*W*, §148, II, 88)

Popularized by the controversy of the *Philosophisches Magazin*, this conception of analyticity actually goes back by way of Wolff to the Scholastic theory of essence as it appears in Suárez.[16] Wolff distinguishes three types of characters according to their relationship with the essence of the subject of predication. The *essentialia* are the necessary and sufficient characters found in the definition of essence. They are for this reason called *constitutiva*, constitutive characters. In Aristotelian terms, they are contained in the formula of the essence, ἐν τῷ λόγῳ τῷ λέγοντι τί.[17] They alone are considered by Eberhard and Maass as capable of being *analytically* predicated of the subject. For from their point of view the *at-*

tributa (that is, the properties deductible from the *constitutiva*) are the object of synthetic predication. They are not contained in the essence, though having in it their sufficient reason. They are for this reason called *rationata*, and correspond to what Aristotle calls "accidents in themselves of the first species."[18] Calling on the principle of sufficient reason—the correctness of whose application in this context, as we have seen, Kant vehemently questions—Eberhard and Maass recognize in the *attributa* characters that can be predicated in synthetic a priori judgments. Finally, the *modi*, extraessential characters of the object under consideration (i.e., characters true or false according to the case), make up the predicative material of synthetic a posteriori judgments.

Rather than taking sides in the controversy that opposed Kant and his disciples to Maass and Eberhard, Bolzano attempts to clear up the difficulties. Maass and Eberhard no doubt were wrong in believing they had exhausted the importance of the distinction between analytic and synthetic a priori propositions by reducing it to a difference between predicates (contained in the essence or derived from the essence). But the error of Maass and Eberhard may be excused on account of Kant's obscurity; Kant did not give enough precision and clarity to a distinction that *alone* makes it possible to confer on the division of propositions into analytic and synthetic the epistemological importance and scope that belongs to it.

Why did Kant not succeed, from Bolzano's point of view, in giving a "forceful proof" of the existence of synthetic a priori judgments, that is, of the existence of a nonanalytic deduction of a concept (*W*, §65, I, 296)? It is because he did not know how to extend his distinction between analytic and synthetic judgments by an equally strong contrast between two *uses of representation*, according to the type of predication—analytic and synthetic—in which they occur. Assuredly, a distinction between "analytic characters" (or "parts of a real concept") and "synthetic characters" (or "parts of a concept only possible") is found in Kant's *Logic*. But this distinction remains ambiguous so long as the character is in both cases understood as a *part* of the concept:

> Inasmuch as Kant was so concerned with the distinction between analytic and synthetic judgments, one might have expected that he would have become aware of the distinction between characters and constituents of a representation, "since the predicate of a synthetic truth can at best be a character [*Merkmal*] of the subject but not a constituent [*Bestandteil*] of the representation of the subject." (*W*, 292)

Bolzano's objection to Kantian terminology is that in the two types of predication—analytic and synthetic—the two kinds of characters pertain finally to the same logical determination in their relationship to the concept; whether the latter is real or simply possible does not change in the least the fact that relationships between the predicated characters and the subject are relationships between the parts and the whole—parts added one to the other by construction in intuition, or parts simply found in the concept already given of the subject. This is a serious confusion, which exposes the Kantian distinction to the objections of the followers of Wolff. This first objection is reinforced by the fact that the distinction made by Kant in his *Logic* between two categories of characters remains, as we saw earlier, isolated and is not followed up, either in the *Logic* or elsewhere in Kant's works. What reveals the quasi-accidental aspect of this distinction is that Kant a few pages later takes up for himself the traditional thesis of the inverse relationship between the content and the extension of a concept. But this thesis is founded on at least two confusions, the first between the character and the constituent, the second between the object and its representation.

In order to make the division between two types of *predication* absolutely clear, one must accompany the latter with the distinction between two notions that not only Kant but most traditional logicians confused: the *property* and the *constituent*. First, between these two notions there is a drastic difference, on which one can never insist too much, because it still tends to be overlooked: they do not have the same referent. The constituent is *representative*, the property is *objective*. The former is part of a representation, the latter is part of an object. A representation is something arbitrary, in the sense that it is composed of a definite number of parts. To add or to take away only one part is to form *another* representation (§64, I, 275). A part of the representation may not be "forgotten" and then "returned" to it in a so-called predication of property, because the resulting representation would already be different from the initial representation. Neither may "new constituents" be added without changing the meaning of the representation thus enriched.

Just as Locke drew from this the necessarily trivial character of nominal predication, likewise Bolzano insists that by resorting to the act of reducing a concept to its constituents, one "says nothing" of an object; one simply confines oneself to clarifying the content of a given concept. But Bolzano goes further than Locke in attempting to make clear the other pole of predication, that of "real" predication: it is the object, not the representation, that is qualified (Locke already perceived this). However, what is to be attributed to it is not a constituent but a *property*, understanding by this "what belongs to the object, or what the object has." Locke did not insist enough on this point, and Kant himself misunderstood it in his own distinction of characters.

Bolzano intends to reserve henceforth the term "character" for property, that is, for what is ascribed to a subject in synthetic predication, a predication that enhances our knowledge precisely because the character is not already included in the constitutive constituents of the subject. The conceptual parts, which Wolff called "constitutive characters," deserved the more exact denomination "constituents," because they are the parts of a total subject representation. The mistake of Maass and Eberhard can now be determined very clearly: they failed to distinguish what to include in the category of constituents of the subject. An excessive interest in what could be called the categorematic aspect of conceptual constituents made them neglect the connecting constituents, which are, as we saw, nonetheless truly representations. Failing to have grasped the difference between the concept and the object that this concept refers to, they admitted as *con-*

stitutiva properties that Kant rightly judged "external" to the concept. The existence of synthetic a priori judgment can then be demonstrated simply by emphasizing the necessity of being able to ascribe properties to an *object*: one must go out of the representation of the subject to assert that a new character suits the represented object (§64, I, 277). As far as it may be carried out, no analysis will give knowledge that alone the object makes possible.

One can, at the same time, deal with the convictions of the relativists who, starting from the same assumptions as Maass and Eberhard, believe that, according to the comprehension given to a representation (that is, according to what one "puts" in its essence), the same predication is sometimes analytic, sometimes synthetic. For example, according to the way we will define the concept of "triangle," the proposition "The sum of the angles of a triangle equals two right angles" will be sometimes analytic (if we define it as "the figure whose angles equal two right angles"), sometimes synthetic (if we define it, for example, as "the portion of a plane bounded by three intersecting lines").[19]

The advantage of the relativist hypothesis is easy to understand: if one may suspect that characters lie "in a hidden manner" in the representation of a subject, one may well admit that the predication, now believed to be synthetic, will one day appear to be analytic, as in Leibniz's conception, in which the progress of knowledge leads ultimately to the reduction of the judgment of fact to an identical truth. Against this relativist hypothesis, which rests in the final analysis on the idea that concepts can change meaning without ceasing to be "the same concept" (they would change only "for us"), Bolzano emphasizes the fully determined nature of representations.[20] The final separation that the *Wissenschaftslehre* makes between conceptual constituents, on the one hand, and objective properties, on the other, completes Kant's effort to finish with Leibnizian continuism. But in doing so, Bolzano only stresses the necessity of giving a criterion of analyticity totally free from the restrictions that everyone—Leibniz and Kant, as well as the latter's opponents—imposed on it, restricting the representational content in exclusively categorematic constituents. Owing to the imprecise character of the distinction between form and content, a properly logical definition of analyticity will have to describe the propositions concerned in terms of relationships between *any* constituents, so as to reach the full generality that one may rightfully require of such a criterion.

Two reasons, I have suggested, can explain the "obsolescence" of the Kantian concept of analyticity: the necessity of reformulating and *extending the domain of logic* and the generalization of the notion of constituent differentiated from that of *character*, as a tool for the renovation of the logical object. But a more specific negative reason also leads to an abandonment of the traditional explanations of analyticity. I cannot overestimate the relevance of this reason, to which I will return, for it is inseparable from Bolzano's innovation concerning analyticity:

In general it seems to me that all these definitions fail to place enough em-

phasis on what makes this sort of judgment really *important*. This, I believe, consists in the fact that their truth or falsity does not depend on the
particular representations of which they are constituted, but remains the
same no matter what changes are made in some of them, presupposing only
that the proposition's character is not itself destroyed. (*W*, §148, II, 88)

Let us for the moment simply note the way Bolzano presents in this passage
what constitutes the importance of analytic propositions: their *behavior with respect to truth and falsity*. The relationship of the analytic to truth is exactly reversed. In Kant, only a true proposition can be analytic. Let us go a step further:
it is because a proposition is analytic that it may be said to be *true*. Analyticity or,
what amounts to the same thing in Kant, a statement deducible from the principle
of contradiction, is the criterion itself of truth in its *logical* kind. Similarly, truth
of the intuitive kind follows from the necessity of a synthetic procedure. Recall
this definition in *Logic*: "Truth is an *objective property* of knowledge." Truth is
revealed and produced only against the backdrop of an act of judgment.

Bolzano returns to a precritical conception of truth: he looks for its definition
not in the product of a judgment but in the correspondence between a proposition
and a state of affairs. Consequently, *truth preexists the statement in which it is
expressed and the consciousness that judges it*. Bolzano coins the concept of
"truth in itself" so as to mark more clearly this independence of truth with respect to knowledge. If a proposition is thus objectively true or false, and always
in itself determined as having one or the other of these values, analyticity can be
defined only by means of a relationship between propositions of the same family
and truth-values. In this manner, not only does analyticity cease to be interchangeable with logical truth, which is only one of its kinds, but also the analytic-synthetic distinction ceases to be prolonged by a distinction in the realm of
truth between propositions of understanding and propositions of intuition. In Bolzano the analytic-synthetic distinction overlaps both the true-false distinction and
the intuitive-conceptual distinction. Henceforth there will be false analytic propositions and analytic propositions of intuition.

This reversal of perspective in respect to the notion of truth leads to a reorga-
nization of the scope of the "analytic" property. Centered until now on the proposition, analyticity appears in Bolzano only at the level of *propositional kind*.
The *importance* of analyticity lies here. It is a property of generic essence precisely because *all* propositions of the same family retain the same truth-value
when a specific constituent is varied in them. On this issue, the post-Leibnizian
critics of Kant missed as much as he what was essential. By placing the accent on
the predication of essence, they ascribe to all propositions an essentially informative function (Kant himself continues in a sense to give to analytic propositions a minimal content, in declaring them "void of content," *inhaltsleer*). Yet,
the fact that in these propositions there is an *indifferent* constituent marks, on the
contrary, their originality. Maass and Eberhard were too fascinated by the particularity of each predication of essence to discover behind each of them the com-

munity of a propositional form. The new revolution that Bolzano accomplishes in analyticity is to rely on what these propositions "do not say" rather than on what they "say." As the preceding text of Bolzano's shows, it is in order to reveal the characteristic property of analytic propositions in their relationship to truth and falsity that he allows himself "to stray from ordinary use" and give an entirely new definition:

> Suppose there is at least one [*auch nur eine*] representation in [a proposition] that can be arbitrarily varied without disturbing its truth or falsity — that is, if all the propositions produced by substituting for this representation any other representation we pleased are either true altogether or false altogether, presupposing only that they have objectivity. This property of the proposition is already sufficiently worthy of attention to differentiate it from all those propositions for which this is not the case. (*W*, §148, II, 83)

Analyticity becomes a notable property of certain propositions. To be brought out requires that the truth-values of all the propositions of the family be given beforehand. It requires, moreover, the application of a rule — understood not as a rule of construction, but as a means of classing propositions, "variation." Finally, the definition comprises a clause of "objectivity" (*Gegenständlichkeit*). To understand the criterion mentioned, we must make a long detour, examining the key concepts that appear in it: proposition, true proposition, and valid proposition.

2

Proposition, Truth, and Validity

What is a "proposition in itself"? Bolzano singles out three minimal components: a constituent that expresses a relationship (*Bindeteil*); not "to be," as in traditional thought, but "to have." The two other terms correspond respectively to the "something" that has the property in question and to the property ascribed to the subject. Every proposition thus has the general form:

A has the property b,

in which A is a representation of an object and b a representation of a property (*W*, §66, I, 297). The schema seems very simple. But several relationships are involved in it, as we shall see.

From the Subject to Its Denotation

Let us start with the representation of the subject marked by A. It forms the *Unterlage*—that is, the *base* of the proposition—or else its *Hupokeimenon*. Its importance arises from the fact that it has a privileged relationship with the object, existent or not, to which the proposition refers (§49, I, 219). If an existing or ideal object corresponds well with the representation of the subject, the proposition, as likewise the representation of the subject, is said to be *gegenständlich* (i.e., "objective").[21] But if no object corresponds to the representation of the subject, will we say that the statement does not express any proposition? This would be the case if one made *Gegenständlichkeit* a principle for excluding meaninglessness. If the principle of objectivity obviously plays the role of a minimal criterion of propositional truth, it need not apply in the case of false propositions (*W*, §127, II, 17; §225, II, 399). False propositions include propositions without any *possible* referent, such as:

A body bounded by five identical surfaces is not bounded by triangles, as well as propositions in which the reality of the referent is the object of an empirical investigation.

Among false propositions, one obviously finds propositions whose subject is realizable, but whose predicate does not "suit" the subject, such as:

$2 + 2 = 5.$

It may seem strange that Bolzano did not preclude from the outset propositions without object, as Frege will do in *Sinn und Bedeutung*. The generosity with which Bolzano accepts nondenoting propositions among false ones is due to the uncertainty in which we find ourselves concerning the reference of many propositions of experience, such as:

The inhabitants of the moon are white.

The fact that we do not know if the moon is inhabited makes the truth-value of this proposition indeterminate—for us. But in order to be able to accept or reject it one day, we must consider what it states as meaningful. The condition of objectivity regains finally its full power whenever a *property* of propositions in themselves or a *relationship* of propositions must be brought out. This criterion guarantees in this case the closure of the field of variation.

The Concrete and the Abstract

The second relationship that forms the predicative tie joins the representation of the subject with that of the predicate. But this second relationship presupposes the first one. It joins two distinct representations that are respectively a *concretum* and an *abstractum*. The *concretum* is precisely a representation compounded of the concept of "something" and an abstract that specifies its sense (*W*, §60, I, 262). The constituent "something" thus inscribes in the heart of the representation of the subject its denotative value. As for the abstract representation of property, it is "abstracted from the substance," as the Aristotelians said. Everyday life, with its emergencies and its various needs, tends to fabricate *concreta*. Language facilitates their multiplication, unlike the *abstracta*, which appear in nonsensical and cumbersome expressions (*W*, §127, II, 12).

Against the Cartesians, who consider "human being" as antecedent to and simpler than the abstract "humanity,"[22] Bolzano returns to an essentialist point of view, which makes him picture the concrete as a complex of constituents, of the type of "something that has humanity." A theory like this brings up a problem already perceived by Leibniz (who believed that the modes are not *res* but *entia*), namely, the danger of a regression to infinity:

Nam si Entitas (abstractum) Ens est, si Realitas res est, si aliquidditas aliquid est; id erit forma sui ipsius seu pars conceptus sui quod implicat.[23]

The regression will be avoided simply by making of the quality of concrete subject or that of abstract property an *internal* property of each representation that cannot arbitrarily change function in the proposition (§60, I, 250ff.). There is no reduplication of the property as a result of its substitution in subject position, as in:

Humanity has *humaniteity*

or any other such example we may choose. The representation "humanity" can in fact only appear to the right of the verb "to have." The subject of concretization, "something that has . . . ," therefore has the cathartic function of eliminating abstractions of the second degree. It allows us to preserve the functional hierarchy that makes the predicate the medium of abstract information, whereas the subject has the role of "tool" of the thing to be described.

From the Abstract to the Thing

The third relationship that determines the predication joins the abstract predicate not with the subject but with the *object* represented by the subject. This new relationship is in turn possible only by means of the operator of concretization, which, as we saw, occurs implicitly in every proposition. Predication relates ultimately the property *b* not to a representation but to the *object* that the representation of the subject denotes. This is how Bolzano characterizes this relationship:

In this case the word *relate* (*beziehen*) means nothing different from *assert* (*aussagen*). The representation *b*, or rather the property it indicates, is merely being *ascribed* to the object represented by *X* by means of this proposition. Now if it is true, then of course we can say that the object represented by *X* is *represented at the same time*, not to be sure by the *abstractum b* itself, but by its *concretum*, i.e., by the representation of "something that has the property *b*." (*W*, §66, I, 297)

The denotative value of the property therefore exists in a potential manner: once the concretization of the *abstractum* is achieved, one should be able to verify, if the proposition is true, that the extension of the *concretum* corresponding to the predicate comprises that of the *concretum* of the subject (*W*, §196, II, 330).

The Double Criterion of the Truth of a Proposition

Analyticity receives its definition from the notion of proposition and from that of truth-value, more precisely insofar as it designates a "manner" in which propositions "act with respect to truth." But what determines the truth or falsity of a proposition? The first clause a proposition must verify in order to be true is a necessary but not a sufficient condition. This clause is satisfied by a certain number of false propositions. It could be expressed thus: *in every true proposition, the representation of the subject must be "objective."* This objectivity of representation determines the objectivity of the entire proposition. Let us note that this clause is not equivalent to the rule for excluding meaninglessness. "To have objectivity'' supposes only that the representation has at least one object. This is only a purely extensional criterion, which can be ascertained only by examining the "total collection of things."[24]

To show that this clause has nothing to do with a principle for excluding meaninglessness, it is sufficient to recall that the idea of a meaningless representation is contradictory. As we have already seen, the content of a representation is made up of the set of its constituents, and from this set arises its sense (*Sinn*). The state of lacking an object pertains not to the sense but to the extension (*Umfang*) of the representation. What would a meaningless expression be? Something like "abracadabra," a combination of syllables that does not express any representation whatsoever, but is the result of a simple vocal association forming an "arbitrary word" (§70, I, 317). Far from incurring *Unsinn*, the representation without object has an operating sense, which is important in many cases, such as that of imaginary roots in mathematics.

A representation, however, can lack an object for several reasons; this allows us to distinguish several types of empty representations. First, there is a representation that lacks an object by definition, so to speak; it is the representation that the word "nothing" expresses (§67, I, 304). A second group is that of "simply empty" representations—that is, those without an empirically assignable object, which nevertheless are not contradictory. Such is the case of the representation "a mountain of gold" (ibid., 305). A third group brings together contradictory notions, such as "round square." Because these representations seem to have an object although they contain a sometimes unnoticeable contradiction, which makes their realization impossible, Bolzano calls them "imaginary" (§70, I, 322–23). Not only representations whose contradiction is conceptually demonstrable ("round square") fall in this category, but also representations whose contradiction can be brought out only with the help of empirical data. This is the case, for example, of "Alexander, father of Philip," which has no real object, "although it implies that one exists" (ibid., 323).

This classification clearly shows that in order to distinguish the various ways in which a representation can lack an object, one must start with what C. I. Lewis calls its *intension*, which in turn determines the *comprehension* of the representation. Lewis, like Bolzano, distinguishes the *denotation* of a term—defined as "the class of all actual or existing things to which the term applies"—and its *connotation*, which corresponds approximately to what Bolzano calls *Inhalt* (i.e., that which forms the definition of a term). But Lewis distinguishes yet a third signifying function, which is the *comprehension* namely, the "classification of all things consistently conceivable to which the term could apply." It follows from this definition that if there is an inconsistency between constituents, the comprehension is null, which is why the representation does not denote. Yet "round square" is not meaningless as would be, for example, "Zuke." Inversely, when there is no contradiction between the different constituents—between the various characters connoted by a term—it is still not possible to come to a decision concerning the denotation, precisely insofar as the latter differs from the comprehension. In order to do so, one must consult a list of existing things. The prerogative of organizing the rational, in Lewis as in Bolzano, belongs therefore to the extensional scope. A principle for excluding meaninglessness would be firmly set in a supposedly legislative language. But a principle for excluding nonbeing, with which we may take the Bolzanian condition of *Gegenstsandlichkeit* to be identical, refers the potential truth of speech to a world composed of individuals.

In the second part of the criterion of truth the antiformalist position of Bolzano manifests itself most clearly. What do the advocates of the formal-material truth dualism assume? They make truth into a kind of *compatibility*. According to them, one should distinguish propositions that contradict from those that do not contradict certain other propositions. This last case defines the region of "formal" truth. Bolzano does not seek to reject the advantage in examining the "behavior" of propositions when they are alternatively "compared" with distinct domains of material propositions. The larger the domain of reference, the smaller will be the set of propositions that are called "formally true." But if one wants to see in this comparison something other than a simple *relationship* between propositions (that is, their compatibility)—if one intends to make it into an *internal* property of the propositions examined—one is forced to conclude that the same proposition can be sometimes true, sometimes false. Everything depends on the propositions taken as reference points (*W*, §29, I, 141, and letter to F. Exner, November 22, 1834). Bolzano's philosophy of logic, on the contrary, rests on the idea that every proposition in itself is *true or false* in a final and invariable way, which he points out by making the truth-value a *property* of each proposition (§24, I, 108). He contrasts therefore with the formalist conception of truth a conception I would be tempted to qualify as realist:

> Whether a proposition is true or false is not at all a relationship of this proposition with others. . . . But a proposition is true when it joins to its subject a predicate that suits it. (Letter to F. Exner; *W*, §25, I, 112)

Because the vocabulary of suitability is undermined by a conceptual confusion characteristic of "pictorial" conceptions of the true proposition, in which the object is supposed to be reflected in its representation, Bolzano specifies the sense he means to give to the word "suitability" in his own explanation of truth:

> Now, if a proposition is true, then of course we can say that the object represented by *X* is *represented at the same time*, not to be sure by the *abstractum b* itself, but by its *concretum*, i.e., by the representation of "something that has the property *b*." (*W*, §66, I, 297)

With this formulation, the hypothesis of an analogy between the category of the concept and that of the object loses its purpose. The inquiry does not bear on intentions, concepts, but on referents whose extensions are to be compared. It is no longer a matter of asking ourselves if the predicate "belongs" to a concept, but if the individuals obtained from the predicate include individuals that the subject designates. This comparison presupposes the use of what I agreed earlier to call "the operator of concretization," which makes it possible to go from the property to the class of individuals that have this property. Thus, from the predicate b, the concrete "representation" of "something that has b" can be formed. After concretization of the predicate, we have two *concreta* at our disposal. A proposition is true if (but not only if) the *concreta* that arise from the predicate include the *concreta* denoted by the representation of the subject. Bolzano's criterion of truth thus can be reformulated by combining the two clauses:

> In any true proposition (of the form, A has b), there is a nonempty class of objects X of which A is the representation, and for any object Y having the property b, the class of Ys contains the class of Xs.

Unlike Leibniz, whose criterion of truth is of a *syntactic* nature (partial resolution must prove that the predicate is truly contained in the subject), Bolzano proposes a semantic and extensional criterion of truth: semantic because it presupposes that reference is made to an objective world where things can be enumerated and classed according to their properties; extensional because the models contain classes of individuals having relationships of inclusion, intersection, or disjunction. The inclusion of classes, therefore, makes it possible to explain what the "suitability" between terms is.

Bolzano's and Tarski's Semantics

Making clear the double criterion of truth in Bolzano allows us to address the question of the analogy between his semantics and Tarski's semantics, which has often been noted by commentators.[25] In his *Wahrheitsbegriff in der formalisierten Sprachen*, Tarski seeks to formulate a definition of true proposition, which, being "materially adequate and formally true," does not depart fundamentally from the one used in everyday language. Tarski quickly comes to the conclusion, however, that it is impossible to meet this double goal while staying within ordinary language, owing to the antinomies that inevitably appear in the case of a "universal" language, that is, an inconsistent one. Only in a formalized language can the levels of object-language and metalanguage be perfectly distinguished. It is clear that Bolzano did not feel the necessity of this metalinguistic perspective in semantics. There is definitely in the reference to the "collection of things" the determining of a model with which to compare the examined proposition; but this reference seems to be capable of functioning within the language that expresses the propositions to be analyzed. In his *Introduction to Semantics*, Carnap characterizes truth in a very restricted semantic system, S_2, thus:

> A proposition pr_i (in_i) is true if and only if the *designatum* of pr_i has the *designatum* of in_i (that is, if the object designated by pr_i has the property designated by pr_i)1. (24)

In spite of the analogy between this statement and the statement of the criterion given by Bolzano for the true proposition, there is an essential difference: the object in Bolzano is designated only by the representation; it is not itself introduced by independent language. What is lacking, when one is satisfied with the mere observation that there exists in the universe a (concrete) model for a given proposition, is the theoretical framework that would allow us to go from observation to proof. What is lacking is for the universe to be describable other than by means of the lexicon and the syntax of the proposition. Extensional concepts are but the incipient germ of a metalanguage; they are not yet separated from the language for which the concept of truth is formulated.

Must one draw the conclusion that Bolzano does not foreshadow in the least the semantic approach in logic? The answer to this question obviously depends on what we stress in the very idea of semantics. If this notion essentially brings to mind the recourse to a preliminary interpretation of statements, which would take precedence over syntactic considerations, one may say that Bolzano's definition of truth does truly refer to extrapropositional meanings. In this sense, a state of affairs occurs with the value of a "model" of the proposition when the latter is true, that is, "realized." Bolzano's truth is, then, very close to Tarski's concept of *satisfiability*. But if we demand in addition that a semantics, properly so called, presupposes the explicit construction of a formalized metalanguage, it must be recognized that Bolzano's enterprise falls short of semantics. His logic seems to be more directly inspired by the geographer's style than the algebraist's. If the Bolzanian criterion of truth corresponds quite closely to the property of "being satisfied by an object," one must remember that there are no variables in the strict sense in Bolzano's logic: a proposition is once and for all either true or false. Bolzano succeeds, however, in breaking from the narrowness of this logical object by constructing a concept more refined than that of truth, but presupposing it: "validity."

The Validity of a Proposition

If we confine ourselves to examining only one proposition, as most logicians did before Bolzano with the noteworthy exception of Leibniz, we will find no semantic property in it except that it is true or false. Just as the individual specimen, the only one of its kind, cannot truly give instruction in the natural sciences, neither can the proposition in itself, reduced to itself, make it possible to bring out notable logical properties. One must therefore accomplish in the logical "reign" the equivalent of Linnaeus's work in the botanical order and determine what could constitute the rationale of a propositional species, it being understood that no artificial formal construction can do away with this investigation.

Here the difficulty is as follows: how can one speak about distinct propositions without giving up the definite character of each, with respect to its own sense and its own truth-value? As today we use the concept of propositional function without perceiving in it the ontological thesis relative to the object that this logical representation makes it possible to determine, it can be difficult to understand Bolzano's reticence to pass over the diversity of propositions—the only objects of the logician—a reticence that comes out, however, everywhere in the texts (for example, W, §147, II, 78). Bolzano's solution consists in changing the inability in which the statement places us of "expressing" with faithfulness the underlying proposition into a means of classifying propositions. To accomplish this, the spontaneous disposition of ordinary language to use the same statement to designate distinct states of affairs must be transformed into a *conscious and rational procedure* allowing us first to arrange propositions into kinds, and then to identify more easily their various properties. This is the aim of the method called *variation*.

Let us start, for example, with the fact:

Wine costs ten thalers a pitcher.

If this assertion must be, as it seems, sometimes true, sometimes false, depending on the time of utterance, this is precisely because certain propositional constituents are not made explicit in the statement: those that specify the conditions of place and time that make the assertion true. Instead of considering the statement to be *incomplete*, let us consider that one or more of the constituents of the proposition are *variable*. Let us assume that in the preceding example the complete fact is expressed by the following statement:

Wine costs ten thalers a pitcher on November 13, 1835, in Prague.

We can suppose constituents indicating time and place to be variable, and substitute for them, respectively, any other day we wish and any other city where the thaler is accepted. Viewed in this manner, the initial proposition expands into a series of other propositions of the same "family," the matrix moreover being any proposition of the family. The "behavior with respect to truth and falsity" of these propositions of the same kind will be, then, exactly determinable by the ratio of truth to falsity found in them. Any of these propositions can be ascribed a "degree of validity," which expresses—as a property of a proposition—the relationship existing between all propositions of the kind. In order that an operating value be, nevertheless, retained with respect to each proposition, one must of course specify each time *which* constituents i, j . . . will be considered interchangeable.

The validity of a proposition, along with the properties derived from it, such as analyticity and derivability, is therefore defined on the basis of:

(1) the truth-value assumed to be known for each proposition of the kind;
(2) a means of classifying propositions, making it possible to delimit the kinds, the variation. The procedure of variation thus appears as the true logical innovation that makes operative the field of propositions in themselves.

The Rules of Variation

For the comparison between different propositions pertaining to the same family to be really fruitful, Bolzano perceived that it was necessary to set restrictions on the possibilities of variation. For a calculus to be possible, one must limit the infinite number of propositions that can be associated with a given matrix. A calculus of this sort can in particular have meaning only if we refuse to take into account propositions without an objective reference. Two criteria must therefore be satisfied when a constituent is varied:

(1) only variations "producing an objective proposition" should be retained;
(2) all representations *equivalent* to one of the representations already used as a substitute should be excluded from substitutions.

The first criterion leads back to the ambiguities of the criterion of *Gegenständlichkeit* already mentioned, which apply to the first degree of selection of the true proposition. This ambiguity now spreads dangerously; for application of the criterion must filter the "objective" propositions without, however, eliminating the false ones. The inadequacy of the condition that bears only on the *subject* of the proposition manifests itself sharply. This subject presumably has the value of a vehicle of denotation. But does a predicate that belongs to an irrelevant semantic category though not being inconsistent not cancel the initial denotation of the proposition? Let us follow, for example, the case of variation by which Bolzano illustrates his method. From the matrix:

The man Caius is mortal,

he develops several related propositions:

(1) The man Sempronius is mortal.
(2) The man Titus is mortal.
(3) The man rose is mortal.
(4) The man triangle is mortal.

Propositions 1 and 2 are objective, whereas propositions 3 and 4 are not. Yet nothing prevents us from applying variation to the predicate. We can substitute for p a representation that, although it may be an *eigentliche Gegenstandsvorstellung*, yields in conjunction with this subject a total proposition not without denotation (for it continues to denote what the subject represents), but perhaps, and whatever Bolzano may believe, without meaning:

(5) The man Caius is a prime number.

As we saw earlier, Bolzano takes this proposition to be false, because the predicate "is not suited" to the subject. But if proposition 5 is to be classed among false propositions, it will affect the degree of validity of each singular proposition of the family: what value must then be given to a property set on a base so far removed from the real conditions of predication? It is not out of the question to believe that Bolzano could have suspected this problem, which would explain why he gives two pages later an important modification to the exposition of the clause of objectivity with respect to variation. First, he expresses it in the following terms:

. . . whenever they have any objectivity at all, i.e., whenever the idea that forms their bases is really the representation of an object. (*W*, §147, II, 78)

Later in the text, however, he uses a much more general formulation, which suffices of course to modify completely the application of the criterion:

If we require further that only such representations can be selected as produce an objective proposition . . . (Ibid., 80)

The difficulty that Bolzano encounters here is due to the fact that his criterion of "objectivity" is of denotative, not of linguistic, nature. It originates in the ambiguous character of an enterprise such as the *Wissenschaftslehre*, which combines methods of linguistic origin (such as variation) with a realistic philosophy in which words "point to" a reality more fundamental and more definite than themselves.

The second limitation imposed on the use of variation prevents notions *equivalent* to a constituent already used in substitutions from being chosen as substitutable constituents. Whereas *synonymy* is a relationship between linguistic expressions designating *the same* representation, as *triangle* and *Dreieck*, equivalence occurs whenever two representations have the same objects. It is thus a purely extensional relationship, which applies to objective representations as well as to empty notions. This deserves to be noted, for variation can be applied to nonobjective *parts* of a total objective representation — for example, the representation of $-\sqrt{-1}$ when it is combined with $1\sqrt{-1}$ in an equation (§108, I, 515). Because all representations in themselves are distinct, the exclusions of equivalent substitutes do not get rid of "synonymous constituents," but do get rid of those that, like "equiangular triangle" and "equilateral triangle," have the same extension. This limitation makes it possible to consider the different propositions arising from variation as distinct possible "states of affairs." It ensures us that calculation of the validity of a proposition carries information not only of a purely logical nature, bearing on the relationship between true propositions and false propositions of the same sort, but also information concerning the probability of the occurrence of a certain objective situation.

In a large number of cases at least, setting restrictions makes it possible to limit sufficiently the number of substitutions, so that a numerical calculation becomes possible. Between the two extreme cases in which the substitutions will always give respectively a true or a false proposition — that is, between universal validity and countervalidity — all degrees of validity between 0 and 1 can be obtained. Thus in a lottery of ninety numbers, the proposition "Ball number 8 will be drawn next," assuming that there are five draws, has a probability of 5/90 or

1/18. This manner of calculating validity can, however, lead to paradoxical results, precisely because the degree of validity remains ascribed to the *proposition in itself*. Lukasiewicz, in a very simple example, showed how the degree of validity of a true proposition, according to the interpretation offered by Bolzano, can be equal to that of a false proposition. If in the proposition:

"6" is divisible by "3"

6 is taken as variable part, and if each number of the series from 1 to 6 is substituted for it, the degree of validity of the proposition considered becomes 2/6 or ⅓. But if the degree of validity of the false proposition:

"5" is divisible by "3"

is calculated under the same conditions, the result is still ⅓. If the initial proposition is now analyzed by considering this time 3 as the variable constituent, the relative validity becomes ⅔. We are therefore justified in questioning, with Lukasiewicz, the scope of a calculation that sometimes yields inconsistent results.

It cannot be otherwise, judges Lukasiewicz, if one confines the calculation of probability to the strict domain of the "closed" proposition: one that is entirely determinate. The solution, from his point of view, supposes giving up two things. One must stretch the too narrow frame of closed statements, so as to deal with validity at the level of "indeterminate" statements—that is, by means of propositional forms. Moreover, the strict true-false dichotomy must be abandoned in order to recognize a third truth-value, the probable. Lukasiewicz's solution implies, of course, acknowledging the importance of the concept of "logical variable." For, if one limits oneself, as does Bolzano, to dealing only with determinate objects, one can always assert that, in themselves, they fall or do not fall under a given concept. But to take into consideration the probable as such, distinguished from the real and the necessary, presupposes that the only object concerned by the language of the possible is introduced: not the individual person ("mistaken or not mistaken," as the example of Lukasiewicz goes), but *anyone, the person x*.

Lukasiewicz's criticism is directed at the shortcomings of Bolzanian validity, as a property of the proposition in itself. These shortcomings will continue to undermine the concept of relative validity—that is, of the relationship of probability. But this criticism also emphasizes that what the method of variation brings out cannot be considered purely and simply analogous to what is understood today by propositional form, although the two methods aim at dealing with sets of propositions. Even if there is an analogy between the terms "variation" and "variable," Bolzano's warning must be recalled. If one speaks of "variable constituent," it is not in the sense that the constituent itself varies, as a being that would be sometimes green, sometimes blue. One must understand by this simply that

one's attention must be directed toward every representation (or, respectively, every proposition) that differs from the first by only one constituent.

. . . There is therefore no transformation [*Veränderung*] in the proper sense of the word. (*W*, §69, I, 214)

Properly speaking, what varies is not the object itself, but the logician's "attention." Careful to actualize and to fix the meaning of logical objects, Bolzano clearly does not allow himself to call on symbolic notation to found the unity of the propositional kind. What the concept of form or propositional function requires in terms of openness and indetermination (the mark of the variable *preceding* any interpretation in terms of individuals) is incompatible with the priority of the proposition. What, then, can be the sense that Bolzano wishes to give to symbolic notation? Must one believe that the use of letters to designate propositions or terms, to which Bolzano often returns in his exposition of the laws of logic, is, in Lukasiewicz's terms, an inconsequence of which Bolzano would not have been "aware"?[26] Lukasiewicz's interpretation is acceptable only if one identifies symbols of terms and propositions with variables. Lukasiewicz had already given this interpretation concerning notations of terms in Aristotle: for him they are symbols of variables; on this notational equivalence, he will found his "quantificational" theory of the syllogism. But as Gilles Granger observed, this is an unjustified transfer of one logical technique to another of a different inspiration:

> The symbols of terms introduced by Aristotle by means of letters are not *stricto sensu* variable at the level of syllogistic calculus. They are syntactical letters, undeterminate symbols, whose identification need not be determined.[27]

This rectification is essential: the extensional meaning of Aristotelian logic reveals itself thus no longer at the level of the calculus, but at that of classes of models that satisfy a set of statements and classes of representations that satisfy a proposition. The very same concern to interpret the variable as an instrument of the calculus formulated in symbolic notation drives Lukasiewicz to suspect Bolzano of having used it, so to speak, in spite of himself. A text of Bolzano's can be found, however, that makes explicit the value he wants to give the symbols used in logic, as well as in the other sciences:

> Thus, it is obvious that the designation of magnitudes by letters, and of the different operations of addition, subtraction, etc., by the well-known signs: $+$, $-$, etc., changes absolutely nothing in the way we conceive these concepts, but only makes it easier to recall them and to keep them in mind. Such aids are already used in several other sciences, for example, in logic, chemistry, and geography, *without this inducing anyone to say that the concepts of these sciences are produced in a different manner than before*. For are these not *words* (and we use them in every science, even metaphysics) whether they are presented in ordinary notation or by the intuitive signs that designate our concepts, such as the $a + b$ of algebra? (*Einleitung in der Grössenlehre* [hereafter, *EG*], §11, 77)

Stressing thus the "intuitive" value of notation, Bolzano clearly points out the value that should be given to the letter: representative of a type of object that can be left undetermined, that is, the sign of a constant (such as any *word*) and not the free variable. The potentially operating value of the sign as such disappears completely in favor of the purely external function of memorization: it cannot be stated more clearly that signs do not have their own relevance.

3

Bolzano's Theory of the Analytic Proposition

I gave earlier the reason that leads Bolzano to reconstrue the concept of analyticity: the old definition does not emphasize enough the "importance" of this property of propositions, an importance that lies in "the independence of their truth-value with respect to the singular constituents that compose them." In explaining analyticity by generalizing extreme cases of validity, Bolzano hopes to mark this importance more clearly. A decision must be taken, however, in building up the *explicatum*: which criterion of generalization must we retain in order to go from validity to analyticity?

The Determination of a Criterion of Generalization

In validity, the constituents that can be the object of substitutions, without altering the truth-value of the proposition thus constructed, are of *any number*, although they must be specified each time, for validity is a *relative* property. The question that arises concerning the construction of the concept of analyticity is therefore that of knowing how many constituents must be variable *salva veritate vel falsitate* for the corresponding proposition to be called analytic. Once this number is determined, the property of analyticity will be an absolute property: it will not make it necessary to specify the one or several variable constituents. There are only three possibilities: one can require that *all* the constituents, or *only one*, be variable; or else one can choose an intermediate solution that would indicate the limits within which the number of interchangeable constituents should lie. Bolzano rejects from the outset the first possibility. A variation that would apply to *all* the constituents of the proposition could not, of course, preserve the truth-value:

For if we could change *all* the representations in a proposition as we pleased, then we could transform it into any other proposition whatsoever, and consequently we could surely sometimes make a true proposition out of it, sometimes a false one. (*W*, §148, II, 83)

To require the interchangeability of *all* the constituents would compromise the stability of the truth-values. What number of constituents should we choose: *a single one* or *several*? Bolzano's text appeared to certain commentators irreparably ambiguous. As they observed, the different formulations of the criterion of analyticity do not agree as to the number of variable constituents. The text of §148 itself has given rise to more than one interpretation, in order to determine the exact scope Bolzano means to give to variation when he writes: *Wenn es aber auch nur eine einzige Vorstellung in einem Satze gibt . . .* [28]

It can be affirmed with certainty, however, that Bolzano recognizes the analyticity of a proposition as soon as at least one of its constituents has proved interchangeable. Let us recall a fundamental fact for applying variation: it is not a matter of notation, but depends on the actual possibilities of obtaining different models of the element considered. For example, in the following proposition:

If *A* is bigger than *B*, then *B* is smaller than *A*

A and *B* are not the variable constituents. The signs *A* and *B* designate an undetermined constant that it would be of no interest to vary, for they refer to the collection of all the magnitudes. It would be just as irrelevant to replace in this example *A* by *X* as it would be to substitute triangle for *Dreieck*: no new proposition would result from this modification, which remains only a matter of statement.

This helps us to understand the commentary with which Bolzano accompanies one of his mathematical examples of analytic propositions:

If $a^2/2 = b$, then $a = \pm \sqrt{2b}$.

In this proposition, Bolzano explains, it is the constituent 2 that is interchangeable *salva veritate*. Expressing magnitudes, signs *a* and *b* cannot properly speaking be changed *salva veritate*. As for the more general algebraic relationship that would mark by *c* the substitutable constituent where 2 appears, it no longer contains any interchangeable occurrence in the strict sense, and consequently belongs to the synthetic proposition:

If $a^2/c = b$, then $a = \pm \sqrt{cb}$.

The fact of lowering thus to "at least one" the number of interchangeable constituents extends the class of analytic propositions. The criterion goes against what I would be tempted to call an "intuition" of analyticity. However, §148 has only given us a phenomenology of the analytic proposition in the form of a criterion of acknowledgment serving as *explicatum*. We must still try to understand what constitutes the "importance" of this new criterion, that is, to grasp the theory that the statement of the criterion presupposes.

Does Bolzano Introduce Quine?

In order to appreciate the importance of a concept, or a distinction, offered by logicians or philosophers of the past, it is always tempting to compare their concepts with today's standard, while conceding that they only announced in a hesitant manner what will be later more explicitly and more clearly recognized. Yet this reading seems to lead to what could be called a dialectical illusion, according to which the apparent familiarity of a concept, or a distinction, finally prevents us from understanding its specificity. In our relationship with the past, our current motivations work against it and discredit it from the outset. Bolzano's analytic does not escape this fate. The "substitutable constituent" is not far from the "vacuous occurrence" of Quine, who himself, when expounding his own definition, mentions Bolzano among his precursors.[29] This thesis is taken up by Bar-Hillel and presented as the only way to make sense of Bolzano's text:

> Why was "A, which is b, is b" a logical truth? Because, said Bolzano, the concept B occurred in it *vacuously*. Of course, he did not use these words, but in this convenient form, due to Quine we may render, what Bolzano would have formulated "because the concept B may be varied at will without disturbing thereby the truth of the proposition." This vacuous occurrence of a concept embodies the content-independence of the proposition, ensures its formal character, so that if the proposition is true at all, it is so formally, logically.[30]

One should not speak of "content-independence" of the analytic proposition carelessly. By *content* of a proposition, Bolzano means the sum of its constituents. To be more precise, one should say that in an analytic proposition the truth or falsity "does not depend on the particular representations that compose it." But then *on what* does it depend? It should be noted that Bolzano *does not answer* this question in §148. Precisely because Bolzano does not justify his criterion in the same text in which he presents it, Bar-Hillel believes he can fill in the blank: Bolzano understood that these propositions are true or false "by virtue of their form," meaning by "form" what a logical syntax makes it possible to build in compliance with the rules of language.

This manner of approaching the criterion of analyticity as it appears in §148 has remained dominant in later commentaries. But it presupposes that one not take into account the fundamental theses of Bolzano's logic: for example, the impossibility of founding logical activity on the distinction between formal constituents and constituents of content. This interpretation also requires that one accept the idea that Bolzano "contradicts himself" in the space of a few pages and, finally, that he gives examples that are bad illustrations of his own theory. The list of errata that this reading needs to correct in the original text appears to me to be the sign of a fundamental topical error: the text seems vague, if not contradictory, because one imposes on it foreign elements. We can assume — and this will be my hypothesis—that the commentaries have not succeeded in finding the demonstrative and explicative pivot of their corpus.

The strategy of Bar-Hillel's reading of §148 can be summed up in three interdependent theses. The first thesis consists in presenting as the aim of §148 to define a concept "which could serve as an adequate explication for what is commonly termed 'logical truth.' " Once it is admitted that this is precisely Bolzano's aim, the definition he gives can be paraphrased in the following manner (and this is the second thesis):

A proposition *p* is analytic = all the descriptive constituent concepts of *p* occur in it vacuously.

Does such a "paraphrase" conflict with other passages? A third thesis is brought in: there certainly is a contradiction between the third subsection of §148 and the two preceding ones, but this inconsistency is due to the fact that the two passages were written at different moments, the more recent one having been added too late for the necessary adjustments to be made. Finally, the best way to evaluate the relevance of this interpretive strategy is to return to the text and reread it.

Rereading the Third Subsection of §148

To understand the third subsection of §148 is essential for clarifying our problem. In this text Bar-Hillel believes he finds justification for his second thesis. All things considered, this thesis alone bears all the burden of proof. The first thesis, which assigns to Bolzano the aim of explaining the concept of "logical truth" in §148, cannot be substantiated other than by showing that this is truly the meaning to be given to the criterion he in fact provides. As for the third thesis, there is no independent reason in its favor except the task of clearing up the contradictions that the second thesis creates. Let me quote in full the crucial passage on which the "second thesis" of Bar-Hillel rests entirely:

The difference between the last mentioned analytic propositions and those under number 1 lies in the following: in order to appraise the analytic nature of the propositions under number 2, no other than logical knowledge is necessary, since the concepts which form the invariable part of these propositions all belong to logic. On the other hand, for the appraisal of the truth and falsity of propositions like those given in number 1, a wholly different kind of knowledge is required, since concepts alien to logic intrude. This distinction, I admit, is rather unstable; the whole domain of concepts belonging to logic is not circumscribed to the extent that controversies could not arise at times. Nevertheless, it might be profitable to keep this distinction in mind. Hence propositions like those in number 2 may be called *logically* analytic, or analytic in the *narrower* sense; those of number 1, analytic in the *broader* sense.

The *two series of examples*, which Bolzano alludes to and whose difficulty he comments on here, are formed, on the one hand, by a set of propositions belonging to ethics, theology, and mathematics ("a depraved person does not deserve respect," etc.), and on the other hand, by a list of propositions like "*A* is *A*," "an *A* that is a *B* is an *A*," "every object is either *B* or not *B*," and so forth.

For Bar-Hillel, this text more than elucidates what makes for the strong unity and the diversity of the examples of both series. The most original inspiration of the *Wissenschaftslehre* lies for him in this text, which is crucial and should have allowed its author, if he had had the time, to rewrite the whole book and found his logic on a different basis. Bar-Hillel sees in the text quoted a "way out" of what he presents as the dilemma in which Bolzano let himself be caught. Neither must all constituents be variable for a proposition to be analytic ("this is too much"), nor only one of them ("this is far too little"):

All *extra-logical* concepts must occur vacuously for a proposition to be "logically analytic"—what an expression!"[31]

Set in the general context of §148, the third subsection appears to have the function of an explanatory commentary on the examples of analytic propositions given. If we take Bolzano literally, the distinction he introduces here has only a clarifying value, without the least pretension, for it cannot be based on a clear-cut distinction between logical and nonlogical concepts. Consequently, in the third paragraph there is no indication of anything else but a casual remark, the equivalent of which we find again concerning derivability.[32] Bar-Hillel sees in this text, on the contrary, the sign of what at other times would be called a "rupture." But to make this thesis acceptable, he must rearrange the order of the subsections of the chapter in the following manner: he examines remark 1 *before* the third subsection which in the original precedes it. In this manner he can isolate the latter as the expression of a belated intuition, a promising remorse, which could not receive elsewhere further development. It is now time to examine the reasons that Bar-Hillel advances in favor of his second thesis.

The first argument Bar-Hillel puts forth states the incompatibility between the enlightening distinction made in the quoted text between "analytic in the broad sense" and "analytic in the narrow sense" and the text of remark 4 in which Bolzano seems to admit the ultimately inadequate character of his definition, "a little larger" than the usual definition. The value of this argument depends precisely on what remains to be proved—namely, that the third subsection presents a definition different from the former one and enclosing the field of the "logically analytic." What seems to exclude the possibility that the observation of the third subsection has any definitional value is that the distinction presented there concerns not a distinctive property of *constituents* but a characterization of the *sorts of knowledge* involved in the two series of examples. What reveals the difference between these two series is, then, not strictly logical, but pertains to an auxiliary science—in this case psychology. This distinction is therefore founded not "in itself" but with respect to our mode of acquiring knowledge.

Considered from this point of view, the two groups of examples are effectively located at different "levels of obviousness." For the propositions of the first group (e.g., "a depraved person does not deserve respect"), not only analyticity but even the truth of the proposition cannot be established without preliminary knowledge. As Bolzano remarks elsewhere, these propositions are "material," in the sense that "we leave them as they are given" (§160, II, 164). On the contrary, the propositions of the second group, "*A* is *A*," and so on, are not simple examples of ordinary propositions; they are designations of propositional kinds. Thus, because the generality of the kind is recorded in the syntactical letters, they can be called "formal" *in Bolzano's sense*. As for remark 4, I find there neither any regret for breaking with tradition nor any sense of the inadequacy of the explanation. In order to characterize the *importance* of the analytic, Bolzano writes:

> I permitted myself to give the above definition, even though I know it makes the concept of these propositions somewhat broader than it is ordinarily conceived to be, for propositions like those cited in number 1 are not ordinarily counted as analytic. (*W*, §148, II, 88)

If Bolzano had set himself the task of giving an explanation strictly equivalent to the one in use, we could attribute to him the intention of trying to correct the fact that his criterion changes the extension of the analytic. But the *Theory of Science* aims at reconstructing logic as the theory of scientific treatises on a strictly objective base. The remark quoted aims rather to warn the reader than to apologize: the reader should not miss the novelty of the concept of analyticity; *there is no reason to confine this property to propositions that possess it in an obvious manner, like those of the second group*.

In order to give some weight to thesis II, Bar-Hillel develops what I call "thesis III": it consists in defending the idea of an independent writing of the third subsection. First, he emphasizes the "inadequate" character of Bolzano's terminology in this third subsection:

> He did not change his terminology in accord with his new insight and preferred to coin the pleonastic term "logically analytic" instead of renaming his old "analytic" by, say, "universally valid" (absolutely, not in respect to some class of concepts) and using "analytic" in place of his unfortunate innovation. (12)

Once it is admitted that subsection 3 furnishes a second *definition*, one can always persist in finding in the letter of the text support for thesis II, for example, by alleging, as does Bar-Hillel, that the expression "logically analytic" is a pleonasm. Such an argument is obviously a *petitio principii*; it can carry weight only if thesis II is already established. With this assumption of inconsistency between the previous terminology and the new discovery, Bar-Hillel concludes his historical development in the fashion of "either of two things": either Bolzano *did not have time* to rewrite the whole chapter and left his text unfinished, or he *faced psychological difficulties*—perhaps hesitation, uncertainty, unconscious resistance—to come to a decision, namely, to retain in the analytic only the "logically analytic."

It is difficult to believe that Bolzano suddenly gave up the fundamental thesis of the *Wissenschaftslehre*, that is, the unity of the different levels of the "in itself": representations, propositions, truths. But then, a property that would hold of propositions written in logical symbols—according to their "kind"—would no longer hold of "material" propositions? Would there be an "analytic" for the first, whereas the second would be "only" universally valid? Such a separation goes against the spirit of Bolzano's logic, which, as we saw, always applies to *arbitrary* constituents and propositions. It is under such conditions that variation can delimit *kinds*, like "truth and falsity according to kinds," or like the synthetic.

Finally, there is Bar-Hillel's last argument in favor of thesis III, perhaps the most fragile:

Nowhere in the long annotation to §148 are the concepts defined in subsection 3 mentioned any more, nor—so far as I could find out—at some other place. (13)

Let me first express my reservations concerning the conclusive character of this argument. One can invoke the fact that the concepts of the third subsection do not occur again in the remainder of the text either to defend the thesis of a separate writing of this part or to ascertain their derived and not strictly logical character. Moreover, it is not true that these concepts do not appear later on. Jan Berg corrected on this point Bar-Hillel's assertion.[33] Thus not only can we conclude that the distinction between "material" and "logical" propositions is not essential for the definition of analyticity; comparing "logical" analyticity with "logical" derivability also makes it possible to understand that Bolzano is not thinking of a difference between *constituents*, logical or extralogical.

An "Extensional" Theory of Analyticity

Let us take up the question where we left it off: if the truth-value of analytic propositions does not depend on the particular representations that constitute them, then *on what* does it depend? Quine's answer presupposes calling on the distinction between logical and nonlogical constituents: for him logical truths are "true propositions that contain only logical words *essentially*." One of the central theses of the *Theory of Science* consists in proclaiming, on the contrary, the distinction between constituents "of form" and "of content." If there is a Bolzanian answer to the question raised, it must follow another road than that chosen by Quine. Bar-Hillel's hypothesis is founded on the conviction that Bolzano did not explicitly answer this question. This is to leave aside an essential text that, although neglected by all the commentators, fully clarifies the question, and allows us to confirm the reading of the third subsection which I just attempted.

In this text analyticity is associated with a certain structure of semantic reference to propositions of this kind, and which we can characterize temporarily as a structure of *double inclusion*, for true analytic propositions, and of inclusion on exclusion, for false ones. Analyticity, as likewise the particular property of the interchangeable constituent, depends therefore on a *restriction* imposed by the proposition on a truth holding for a set of objects. Let us take the example of a true analytic proposition given in §148:

> This triangle has the property that the sum of its angles is equal to two right angles.

We already know that there is a constituent variable *salva veritate* in this proposition. How can we know which one, except by trial and error—in other words, by trying to vary in turn all the constituents? Bolzano tells in §197 the way to identify it:

> The particularity of the proposition considered lies in the fact that its representation of the subject, "this triangle," contains a constituent (the representation *this*) that is connected with the rest of the proposition in such a way that the different objects it represents when this constituent is considered arbitrary and interchanged with any other representations, all belong to a certain kind of thing (here, to triangles in general), of which the property expressed in the representation of the predicate holds universally. (II, 333)

The variable constituent is thus determined by virtue of an extensional property, which explains at once the role it plays and the analyticity of the proposition. Indeed, it imposes a *restriction* on the universal extension of a concept, which functions with respect to the proposition, like a datum that limits the possibilities of variation. In order to clarify this property, let us call v the interchangeable constituent, $p(v)$ the analytic proposition, g the generic concept in which v takes on different values, and $p(g)$ the universally true proposition that bears on the maximum extension g. If we eliminate in the previous example the restriction to "this triangle," we obtain a truth that holds for any kind of triangle:

> Any triangle has the property that the sum of its angles equals two right angles.

Let us recall that Bolzano considers that every representation is to be taken universally whenever it occurs without a determinant. Thus by eliminating the demonstrative pronoun, we obtain a universal proposition. If this proposition is true, as in our example, the collection of *concreta* denoted by the representation of the subject is included in that of the *concreta* obtained from the predicate by concretization. This inclusion is the sign of the truth of the universal proposition, and from this truth the truth of the proposition restricted by the variation of v is determined. We could first of all represent the case of the proposition by the following schema (for clarity, I represent the extension of the predicate, but it is obvious that the two extensions can also be exactly identical):

Figure 1

The constituent *v* has this in particular that each one of its variants is inscribed inside the total extension of the subject *S* of *p(g)*. The analytic proposition thus states concerning an individual or a subset what already holds for the kind. The variable constituent is what makes it possible to apply a restriction to the kind. An analytic proposition can therefore be represented by a double inclusion, the first describing *p(g)*, the second *p(v)* itself:

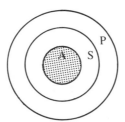

Figure 2

In an analytically true proposition, not all the variations on a particular constituent can be carried out outside the kind of objects that, being included in the *concreta* of the predicate, make up the subject of a true proposition. The complementary action of the clause of objectivity prevents any uncontrolled straying from the boundaries marked by the total extension of the subject *g*, which I will call, on account of this role, the "dominant kind." I can illustrate this analysis with a second example. In

A depraved man does not deserve respect

it is the constituent "man" that secures the restriction of the extension of the dominant kind, "every depraved being." There are as many analytic variants as there are individuals and subsets in the total extension of depraved beings. We notice again how the clause of objectivity secures the closure of the variation within the kind.

We can now without difficulty account for the analyticity of the principle of the excluded middle: "Every A is *B* or not-*B*." The difference that distinguishes this case from the previous ones lies only in the fact that there are here two variable constituents that each impose a restriction on the maximum extension of "the collection of all objects." Indeed, the constituents substituted for A denote a series of objects of this total collection without being able to go beyond this extension, which by definition is maximum. As for the disjunction "B or not-B," which makes up the predicate of the proposition, it is clear that the corresponding *concreta* coincide with the extension of all objects, once it is granted that "not-blue" is a "remote character of Pythagoras's theorem" (*Paradoxien des Unendlichen* [hereafter, *PU*], §26, 97). It should be noted, however, as opposed to what was established earlier in the case of mathematical analytic propositions, that the use of syntactical letters *authorizes* variation. If we consider the syntactical letters as nonvariable insofar as they already designate the collection of all their represented, the principle of the excluded middle becomes a synthetic truth or simple inclusion.

Although Bolzano does not develop specifically their mode of functioning, analytically false propositions can receive an analogous extensional treatment. In this case, there is, of course, no longer double inclusion, but inclusion on exclusion. The restriction on the complete extension of a kind continues to characterize the function of the variable constituent. Here again no substitution makes it possible to go beyond the kind and give rise to an inclusion of the subject in the predicate, that is, to a truth. Thus, in the example:

A depraved man nevertheless enjoys eternal happiness,

it is the constituent "man" that designates the place of the variants within the dominant genus: "being." Figures 3 and 4 illustrate variation in the case of false analytic propositions, according to whether they apply to the subject or to the predicate.

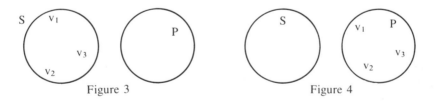

Figure 3   Figure 4

Figure 3 corresponds to the case of variation we just analyzed on Bolzano's example. The different objective variations belong all to the same kind, which is strictly disjoint from the kind that appears in the predicate: "What has the property of enjoying eternal happiness." No inclusion can therefore arise in the course of variations: substitution will always give rise to falsity. Figure 4 presents a similar case, although not mentioned in Bolzano's examples, of a variation bearing on the predicate of a false proposition. We can give for an example:

Any A that has b has not-b.

The class of *b* and of not-*b*, being disjoint and complementary, it is certain that no substitution for *b* will modify the characteristic of "false by virtue of kind."

If one had to attempt to give the status of synthetic proposition by means of this schematic representation, the definition would be purely negative: in a synthetic proposition there is no constituent that can be varied without altering the truth-value of the proposition. In other words, nothing prevents certain variations from denoting new individuals and from causing, because of this, "an escape from the kind" of such a nature as to reverse the truth-value of the initial proposition. Thus in the example of a "true" synthetic proposition:

God is omniscient,

which states of God an essential and exclusive attribute, we cannot vary the representation "God" without the proposition becoming false. As for substitutions for "omniscience," they will of course give sometimes true propositions, if what is substituted represents a divine property, and sometimes false ones, in the opposite case. Figure 5 illustrates this case of the true synthetic proposition: the shaded part represents the set of true variants that includes the initial proposition. But it is clear that, for either the subject or the predicate, other variants are possible for which no inclusion will obtain.

Reciprocally, a false synthetic proposition occurs when some of the variations performed on the subject or the predicate give rise to an inclusion of the extension of the subject in that of the predicate, whereas others give rise to an exclusion. Bolzano gives the example:

A triangle has two right angles.

Variation for the constituent "triangle" makes it possible to encounter some true propositions and a large number of false ones. Another example in which variation applies to the predicate is given by:

A right-angled triangle has two right angles,

in which the constituent "two" can be varied so as to make the proposition true.

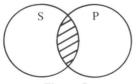

Figure 5

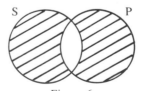

Figure 6

Figure 6 represents the way in which exclusion can become, after variation, an inclusion between extensions of the subject and the predicate. Here the shaded part represents the set of objects to which the subject and the predicate refer through substitutions giving rise to a false proposition. The nonempty intersection of the subject and the predicate in their "maximum" extension shows that some substitutions will give rise to truth.

Should the approach to analyticity appearing in §197, which could be called "submodelizing," be understood as a kind of "second definition"? This would be to return quite needlessly to historical hypotheses à la Bar-Hillel. The explanation I attempted to develop using the allusive text of §197 seems to me to explain rather the semantic "functioning" of a property, which was stated in its systematic generality in §148. Viewing the first text in the light of the second enables us to perceive better what a *kind* or a *form* of propositions is. For we now possess extensional guidelines for understanding the relationship between propositions. An analytic proposition is one we could call "ectypically" true, in which the variable constituent imposes a restriction within the kind of the subject in which a predicate holds universally (or inversely within a predicative kind holding universally of the subject). This "dominant kind" constitutes the preliminary datum that analyticity presupposes. It is then itself the subject (or the predicate) of a synthetic truth. This synthetic datum is not to be understood in a subjective manner: it is not "given to a subject," as was the case of the Kantian analytic. It is an "objective" datum that the analytic proposition is restricted to exploring by sectors and which it exemplifies for some individual or some species belonging to the genus. The synthetic is the property of propositions that cannot be grounded on a preliminary datum with respect to their truth-value. Bringing out the preliminary datum in the interpretation of the analyticity of a proposition allows me to clarify the third subsection of which I have thus far offered a purely corrective reading. For this preliminary datum is what occurs in "extralogical knowledge." In the first series of examples, the variable constituent is hidden; to discover it, we must recognize the universal truth—or the universally false proposition—to which it owes its own truth-value. In the second series, this semantic functioning does not have to be discovered in the datum; it is explicitly described. Later, in the chapter dealing with analyticity in logic, we will encounter again the problem of "purely logical knowledge."

4

Epistemology of Analyticity

In what respect does the clarification of the true sense of the definition of analytic propositions by Bolzano make it possible to understand the role of these propositions in the expositions of a science that is "founded and convincing," an exposition whose rules it is the logician's task to point out, according to Bolzano? Because the properly *theoretical* import of a proposition depends on its status in a *deductive series*, our investigation turns immediately to the exact relationship that ties analyticity to *derivability*. On the elucidation of this relationship hinges the position of an analytic proposition in deductive reasoning: Can it be a principle or a theorem, a premise or a conclusion?

Analyticity and Derivability

Can we characterize the relationship between the property of analyticity and the relationship of derivability by saying with Ursula Neemann that derivability in Bolzano is "an enlarged version of his definition of analytic proposition"?[34] It all depends on the way we understand the *enlargment* in question. Whereas analyticity is one of the *internal properties* of propositions, derivability is a *relationship* between propositions. Nevertheless, they present an analogy: both are "extreme cases." Analyticity, as we saw, is an extreme case of validity; derivability in turn is an extreme case of the relationship of *probability* (§61, No. 3, II, 172). Indeed, the propositions $M, N, O \ldots$ are said to be derivable (*ableitbar*) from the propositions $A, B, C, D \ldots$ with respect to the constituents $i, j \ldots$ when *all* the representations that, substituted for the occurrences $i, j \ldots$, make the propositions $A, B, C, D \ldots$ true, also make the propositions $M, N, O \ldots$ true (§155, no. 2, II, 113). When the "comparative validity" of the proposition M with respect to $A, B, C, D \ldots$ is less than 1, there is no longer any relationship of derivability, but a relationship of probability. As for the extreme case, similar to that of universal countervalidity, it is that of absolute nonderivability, which is realized by the relationship of *exclusion* (*Ausschliessung*) (§159, II, 147). In Tarski's terms, we could sum up the analogy between analyticity and derivability by saying that a proposition is analytic if every series of objects is either always or never a model of the propositional species. For derivability to occur, every model of the premises must also be a model of the conclusions.

Although instructive, this structural analogy between analyticity and derivability cannot yet inform us about "functional" exchanges between the one and the other. Is there any relationship of logical preeminence or anteriority between them? In order to answer this question, it is essential to recall my extensional interpretation of the criterion of analyticity. I brought out the existence of a certain relationship between constituents, which determines the analyticity of a proposition. I called $p(g)$ the proposition that arises from the extensionally maximum variation of the variable constituent $p(g)$, and verified that $p(v_1)$, $p(v_2)$, *and so forth, form different propositional variants produced by restriction on $p(g)$.* We saw in $p(g)$ the vehicle of latent information that the analytic proposition presupposes, because it is confined to actualizing, ectypically, one of the submodels of $p(g)$. It is now possible to characterize this proposition $p(g)$ as the *premise* of a derivation that every analytic proposition involves necessarily although implicitly—a derivation that is, in this case, of a particular type. It so happens that, without relating it to the problem that concerns us now, Bolzano nevertheless studies this case of derivation, whose relevance for the analytically true is obvious:

> If a pair of propositions, "*A* has *x*," "*B* has *x*," have the same predicate, which is the only representation in them to be considered variable, then the second is derivable from the first if the subject representation of the first, *A*, stands in the relationship of inclusion to the subject representation of the second, *B*. If this is not the case, the relationship of derivability does not apply. (*W*, §155, II, 127, no. 35)

Bolzano examines immediately thereafter the similar case in which variation applies to the subject:

> When a pair of propositions, "*X* has *a*," "*X* has *b*," have the same subject, which is the only representation supposed to be considered variable in them, the second is derivable from the first if representation *B* (the *concretum* corresponding to *b*) includes representation *A*; and if this is not the case, there is no relationship of derivability. (Ibid., no. 36)

Our extensional schema allows us to understand that analytic propositions have a behavior similar to that of the *conclusion* of a deduction, when the latter is not reversible. The conclusions have two correlations with their premises: they "say less," but their validity is higher. What is meant by "saying less"? The following remark suggests the answer:

It is absolutely true that the premises all together *enclose more in them* [*mehr in sich schliessen*] than their conclusions, when one understands by this that in general more can be deduced from them than can be from their conclusions. (§155, II, 132–33)

Is this deductive potentiality belonging to the premises not the corollary of an attribution bearing on the totality of a kind? Such a property makes especially *synthetic* propositions appear as the premises of a deduction. We cannot infer that the conclusions of all reasonings are, generally speaking, analytic propositions. We can assert, however, that every analytic proposition can be the conclusion of a definite deductive schema. The second property of conclusions is bound up with the first, although this property may at first appear paradoxical:

However, it is no less true that the relationship between premises and conclusions can be compared with the relationships between included representations and comprehensive representations, and that there are usually a larger number of representations that will make the conclusions true than there are that will make the premises true; or, what comes to the same thing, the degree of validity of the conclusions is usually higher and always at least as high as the degree of validity of the premises. (Ibid., 133)

What constitutes the paradox of this assertion is that Bolzano applies to the premises and conclusions of a deduction a relationship of comprehension (*Umfassen*) in a sense *opposed* to the one we would expect. An ordinary example of derivation like:

All *A*s are *B*s
Some *A*s are *B*s

indeed tends to show that the subject of the conclusion is *comprised* in the subject of the premise. But if we do not consider any longer the extension *taken absolutely*, that is, with reference to the number of individuals *objectively* denoted, but in respect to the cases in which the proposition is false when we carry out variations on the constituents *i, j* . . . , the stipulation that "says less" sets less harsh conditions for its truth, and consequently is satisfied by a larger number of models. If we qualify this extension as "formal," in contrast with the preceding one, which we could call "material" because it designates what the proposition taken in isolation denotes, we see that the preceding paradox, of which Bolzano is perfectly conscious, is due to the fact that the larger extension of the conclusions from the formal point of view can go along with a lesser extension from the material point of view.

Yet analytic propositions especially enable us to understand this inverse relationship between the material and the formal extension of validity: a true analytic proposition, like "this triangle has angles equal to two right angles," materially denotes *a single* individual; but, by variation on this, it extends to the whole genus "triangle." To be, in some way, unfalsifiable by construction—that is, sheltered by a synthetic truth that on the contrary is exposed to the "formal" falsification of variation — is what accounts for the universal validity of a true analytic proposition. The two properties just mentioned form the germ of a semantic theory of the informative content of propositions.

Analyticity in Logic

The previous discussion allows us to assign the role of analytic propositions in deduction: they are well suited for the role of conclusions, but they are excluded from the role of premises. How do they occur in particular sciences? Carried away by his controversy with the advocates of a *purely analytic* logic (Fries, Hoffbauer, Twesten — on this issue, all faithful to Kant), Bolzano even ventures to say a little rashly:

> I can share these views even less, for I believe, on the contrary, that there
> is not a single theorem worth presenting in logic or any other science that
> is a purely analytic truth. (§12, I, 52)

"Any other science": we will not take Bolzano literally, for in mathematics the decisive importance of certain analytic theorems of the science of quantity must be recognized. It remains nevertheless true that, in opposition to the Kantian idea of logic, this science contains for Bolzano a "large number of synthetic propositions" (§315, III, 240). In the meantime, the criterion of analyticity has changed considerably. But let us not miss what is at stake in Bolzano's assertion: it is possible to produce knowledge by pure concepts (without any intuitive involvement). Logic gives a particularly convincing example of the possibility of framing rules independently of a "given" — the hypothesis of a "pure given" having moreover become unattractive with the disappearance of the transcendental subject:

> Who could define as analytic the propositions "there are representations,
> intuitions, and concepts," "a proposition divides into at least three parts,"
> "truths are governed by a relationship of fundament to consequence," and
> a hundred others of the same kind? (Ibid., 240)

Following up these first examples, whose determinative or informative value appears obvious, Bolzano analyzes the most difficult case, namely, the rules of syllogisms:

> Even the rules of the syllogism are wrongly considered analytic truths. One
> can well say that the proposition "If all men are mortal, and if Caius is a
> man, then Caius is mortal" is analytic in the broad sense indicated in §148.
> But the rule itself that from two propositions of the form A is B and B is C
> follows a third of the form A is C is a synthetic truth.

This distinction does not surprise us in the least. It is enough to recall that the constituents "man," "mortal," "Caius" — which are variable *salva veritate* in the first case — are in the second case designated by syntactical letters to which a new variation cannot be applied. In terms of our interpretation, the first case appears as an *application* of the rule stated by the second proposition. It owes its universal validity to the restriction that it applies to the total extension of the rule: it is its submodel, an analytic exemplification. The rule states on the contrary a relationship of deduction, which accompanies an extensional increment: from the existence of two sorts of propositions—namely, "*A* is *B*" and "*B* is *C*"—the existence of a third sort of proposition is inferred, distinct from the first two with respect both to subject and predicate: "*A* is *C*." The logical rule thus maps out the extensional relationship that makes of a deduction a discursive progress. It is, therefore, considered as a rule, a synthetic truth, whereas each syllogism gives rise to an analytically true proposition insofar as it applies the rule in an illustration in which this synthetic universality disappears.

Let us now return to the difficult problem encountered earlier, pertaining to the status of "logical knowledge" mentioned in the third subsection of §148. If the rules of syllogism, as founding structures of any particular instance of reasoning, are analytic propositions, what can be the status of those other propositions of logic, such as "*A* is *A*," "an *A* that is a *B* is an *A*," "A or not-A," and so on? We know that Bolzano already partially answered this question by pointing out in the same subsection that these are analytic "in the strict sense." Yet his remark quoted earlier urges us to be careful: if "no theorem in logic is analytic," must one not search *below* analytic propositions "in the strict sense" for founding synthetic truths of which the former would only be instances? In this manner the meaning of this "logical knowledge," which, according to Bolzano, should be sufficient for ensuring recognition of the analyticity of "logically analytic" propositions, becomes clear. They would be general principles that establish the conditions of possibility of the predication and the reduction of concepts.

Let us examine, for example, the identical proposition "*A* is *A*," temporarily tolerating the noncanonical form of this statement. We recognize the analyticity of this proposition from the presence of a vacuous occurrence on either side of the copula—at least in the predicative schema with "to be," which Bolzano rejects. We have here a "formula without content" to which Trorler ascribes the power of founding the activity of the knowing mind, "its absolute spontaneousness." But this proposition is for Bolzano an analytic truth and therefore derived from a more general synthetic proposition that governs the relationship of parts to whole in the concept:

> The characters constituting a concept, taken together, are not *equal* to it, but are the same thing as it [*einerlei*]; they are itself. (§45, I, 209)

This truth is part of the set of rules that specify the reduction of a representation to its characters or a proposition to its constituent parts. The operation of *Zerlegung* is governed by synthetic truths, but its *applications*, considered as submodels of the rule, are analytic propositions. If in logic the distance that separates a synthetic model from its analytic instances is never considerable, the case is completely different in mathematics.

Analyticity in Mathematics

The new definition of analyticity disrupts the traditional division between analytic sciences and synthetic sciences: not only, as we saw, is logic essentially synthetic; mathematics—typically the domain of the synthetic in the Kantian conception—is now to be attributed to the analytic, and even "is in the most suitable position to be called a purely analytic science," for "if not all, at least most of its theorems appear to me purely analytic" (§315, III, 241). Because the role of the analytic in mathematics appears remarkable enough to Bolzano, the distinction between the analytic and the synthetic in that field deserves to be clarified.

Let us take, for example, a treatise of analysis. A mistake concerning the analytic nature of a theorem would immediately result in a mathematical error. For that would amount to falsely attributing to it the character of a ground of truth without seeing that it is *deduced* from a synthetic truth of a much larger scope (*W*, §583, IV, 403; see also §447, 117). Let us return, for example, to the Kantian paradigm of synthetic truth: $7 + 5 = 12$. This proposition is deducible from the proposition expressing the associative function of addition: $a + (b + c) = (a + b) + c$, a proposition that is itself analytic, for it can be derived from the definition of the concept of *sum* in the very broad sense in which Bolzano takes this term:

> A sum is a class of objects where the order of parts is not taken into account, and where the parts of parts are considered parts of the whole. (*W*, §305, III, 186; see also §84, I, and *EG*, III, §92, 131r, 153)

A concept as general as that of "sum" has applications in very different domains: in logic, for example, where the constituents of a representation or a property make up a collection that has the property of being a sum; in mathematics also and obviously, for among other things the commutation and association having to do with addition are deduced from the identification of any set (eventually infinite) of numbers with a sum. Thus these two properties, expressed for example in algebraic form, give rise to analytic propositions in which the sign of addition (+) must be considered as variable *salva veritate* (considering a, b, and c, as designating objects having the specified property—namely, of being parts of a sum).

This example enables us to understand that it is not always easy to identify the analyticity of a mathematical proposition if one fails to perceive which constituent occurs "vacuously." It seems characteristic of progress in mathematics to enlarge the domain of the analytic, but in a quite different sense from what the relativists meant thereby. This gradual enlargement of the analytic does not arise properly speaking from an *enrichment* of concepts causing a continual transfer of synthetic discursive productions leading toward knowledge "crystallized" in analytic propositions. Once the *concept* is distinguished from the *word* that expresses it, we can interpret this supposed change of concept as representation of different concepts under the same term. Mathematical progress is to be conceived not as an adjunction of meaning but as a deepening of meaning. If there is progress in mathematical knowledge, it is because the true composition of a concept, until now manipulated naively as a simple representation, is discovered. What is gained, then, by revealing the internal structure of a mathematical concept? On the one hand, this makes it possible to learn the objective dependence of the theorems in which this concept appears relative to a more fundamental truth serving as their "objective foundation." On the other hand, this brings out the strictly analytic character of the theorems, insofar as they are derived from a synthetic truth that founds them.

However, not every truth more general than a given theorem is on this account the objective foundation of the latter. It must satisfy a condition not yet mentioned: it must be also *simpler* than the particular truth. When both conditions are met, the synthetic proposition may legitimately precede its analytic applications. For example, the analytic proposition:

The surfaces of similar triangles are correlative to the squares of respectively similar rectangles,

can be preceded by the simpler and more general synthetic proposition:

The surfaces of similar figures are correlative to the squares of respectively similar rectangles. (§602, IV, 438)

The first of these propositions owes its analyticity to the vacuous occurrence of the constituent "triangle." In what way can it be called "more composite" than the second one? Because the constituents of the second proposition "only make up one part of the constituents of which the first truth consists." To the representation "figures" must be added the three constituents *"which are triangles"* in order to pass from the second to the first truth. Nevertheless, according to the deductive principle already mentioned, the first proposition "says less" than the second, for it states a truth only partially, by specifying only part of its actual extension. It is easy to understand that a reader possessing only analytic truth would be led to the mistake that Aristotle illustrates in this way:

One could believe that this triangle, because it is an isoceles triangle, has angles equal to two right angles.[35]

If the authors of mathematical treatises do not want "what is actually a part of the whole" to be taken in the demonstration "for the whole," they, more than any others, must make it their golden rule always to mention explicitly the analytic or synthetic character of the theorems they introduce. A second example will show what prevents a proposition that, while being more general, is also more composite than another from serving as the objective foundation of the latter. A quick allusion of the *Wissenschaftslehre* tells us that "at least according to a particular conception" of this theorem, the binominal theorem can be considered as an analytic proposition (§315, III, 241). The introduction to the *Science of Quantity* is more explicit and clarifies the status of this theorem relative to the objective consequence, thus informing us indirectly on what makes it analytic:

The well-known proposition stating that

$$(1 + x)^n = 1 + nx + n \cdot \frac{n - 1}{2} x^2 + n \cdot \frac{n \cdot 1}{2} \cdot \frac{n - 2}{3} x^3 + \ldots$$

where *n* designates any number—positive, negative, fractional, irrational, or even complex—provided that $x < 1$, is obviously much more general than the proposition stating this equality only for a positive and integral exponent. However, the second truth should not indeed be considered an objective consequence of the first; therefore one also cannot require that the first proposition be presented before the second. For although the first is really much wider [*weiter*] than the second, it is not as such simpler, but considerably more composite; for the concept of a power of which the exponent can be a *representation of any degree* is much more composite than that of a power of an integral exponent. (§4, 70r, 94)

The ''second'' proposition states the formula of the binomial for a positive integral exponent; this is the formula Newton gave in 1663, before expanding it to fractional and negative exponents. The ''first'' proposition is the result of the effort of various mathematicians to prove the formula of the binomial for any exponent. Bolzano himself gives in 1816 a demonstration for a rational and irrational negative integral exponent (later Cauchy gives the demonstration for a complex exponent; Bolzano's text suggests that he already knew Cauchy's demonstration: he read and annotated the *Course in Analysis* in the German translation that appeared in 1828).

In the ''second'' proposition, which is historically the first, a constituent can *still* be varied without altering the truth of the formula, which means that in Newton's original version the binomial formula is analytic. But—a quite exceptional fact—we cannot infer that its objective foundation lies in the corresponding synthetic proposition, which is the same formula, ''for any *n*'' in which no new substitution is possible. The reason Bolzano gives may today appear spurious: any exponent ''whatsoever'' is a concept too complex to found the more simple concept of positive integral exponent. This exception should not, however, be surprising if one remembers Bolzano's insistence on rejecting the presumed ''law of covariation of the comprehension and the extension'' of notions. The comparison between the two concepts—''positive integral exponent'' and ''any exponent''—shows that if the first is subordinated to the second and consequently extensionally larger, it is also equally *simpler*. For the demonstration of the formula comprising the positive integral exponent belongs only to algebraic combinatories. To prove the general formula, on the contrary, requires a theory of convergence and of limits.

This example shows that simple extensional subordination between truths is not the uniform order that we could have expected to encounter and would have made possible a hierarchy of theorems directly corresponding to their degree of generality. *There is a second dimension of classing truth* whose conflict with the preceding dimension (following the synthetic-analytic axis) was foreshadowed by the failure of the law of covariation between the extension and the comprehension of concepts. It is a relationship of principle to consequence, as is required by a rigorously scientific presentation of truths. The relationship of *Abfolge* calls for more than mere *deducibility*. The objective consequence that it reveals requires that demonstration follow *first* the progression from simple to complex and *only after*, and if possible, that from general to particular. The criterion of extensional subordination is consequently a secondary principle in hierarchizing mathematical theorems.

What we learned from the role of analytic propositions in mathematics can be summed up in three points:

(1) This science proves that analytic propositions can be *theorems*, and, on account of the extreme compositeness of its concepts, that they even constitute by their capacity to submodelize and to "say less" the indispensable demonstrative relay between very general principles and the resolution of a highly composite particular problem.

(2) In spite of the frequency of analytic theorems, mathematics shows examples of conflict between the ideal order of subordination of particular truths (analytic) to general truths (synthetic) and the order that the relationship of objective consequence imposes. This conflict is obviously to be related to what in retrospect appears a gamble: the project of expressing the theory of science in the context of natural language.

(3) In spite of its exactness and rigorousness, the mathematical expression does not always reveal the true composition of concepts. This third remark prompts me to clarify the question of the *statement*: if there is a *problem of analyticity*, not only in mathematics, but also in the other sciences and in the ordinary use of language, is it not most often due to the traps of language? Directing our attention now to the conditions of the expression, insofar as they give again to analyticity significance and usefulness according to the rhetorical aspect of the *Treatise* taken as *Darstellung*, I turn to a new problem: the object of the investigation is no longer the property of propositions in themselves, but the distortions that arise when the difference between the statement and the proposition is forgotten.

5

Analyticity and the Rhetoric of Science

Bolzano identifies two kinds of illusory statements that can prevent recognition of the analyticity of a proposition (*W*, §148). Sometimes the statement exceeds what is required: the variety of terms it contains conceals the analyticity or even the identity of the proposition. Sometimes it falls short: an apparent tautology dissimulates a synthetic proposition. In this, Bolzano settles the dispute that opposed Leibniz and Locke in their *Essays Concerning Human Understanding*. Bolzano defends Locke: if identical propositions exist, it is always only a matter of nominal explication. These propositions carry no "instructive" knowledge. Whenever some usefulness is given to identical propositions, it is because one relies wrongly on the identical form *of the statement* in order to infer the identical content of the proposition. Moreover, the two methods that Bolzano points out to debunk unquestioning belief in a statement are part of the anti-Leibnizian store of arguments. If it is a matter of showing that there are identities hidden under the appearance of syntheses, then it is to deny that they have an intrinsic operating scope. If, on the contrary, it is a matter of showing the actual syntheticity of propositions disguised as tautologies, it is again to deny that an identical proposition could not have claimed any usefulness. This passage calls for a second remark: the relationship Bolzano establishes between analyticity and identity is precisely an inversion of the relationship that Leibniz saw. The fact itself that identity is treated in the notes shows that it has become a question subordinated to that of analyticity.

The First Case of Illusion: "The Synthetic Effect"

The same phenomenon accounts for two aspects of analyticity that may seem, at first sight, unrelated. I mean, on the one hand, the occasional difficulty we may encounter in recognizing the analyticity of a proposition and, on the other, the advantage of resorting to analytic propositions when we want to convince readers of the demonstrative rigor of the treatise we submit to them. Because the statement plays imperfectly its role by expressing a proposition either incompletely or emphatically, it becomes necessary in both cases to reveal the true nature of the truth expressed, especially if it is synthetic. Any mistake of this nature entails a misconception of the demonstrative function of the proposition concerned.

Should one look for what makes these imperfections of the statement possible in the original incapacity of language to translate adequately the ideas that precede it? It would be then a Cartesian thesis that would place the *Theory of Science* in the tradition of logic manuals, going two centuries back, and would prompt the authors to add a chapter on the explanation of "cryptic or exponible" propositions, in which they would try to clarify "verbal expressions that, owing to their obscureness, need explanation" (§169, II, 211). But an explanation that consists in trying to restore in each case the full meaning that figures of speech sometimes hide is finally for Bolzano only a lazy and superficial approach barred from reaching the true reason of the phenomenon in question. Not that an interpretation of statements, appealing to the *intention* of communication, trying to go beyond a literal statement toward a fuller meaning, is not valid or even fruitful. But such an interpretation falls short of any psychological, linguistic, or rhetorical explanation. One must look for it in the property that representations, propositions, linguistic or mathematical signs have in common: they are organized like a *sum* in which the parts of the parts are the parts of the whole. For two contents (which have this property of being sums) to be *the same*, their *reduced* constituents need only be the same in the same order. Whence the diversity of statements for one and the same proposition: it is possible to cut differently in the fabric of constituents, provided the order of composition is preserved (§56, I, 244).

This double criterion of synonymy—same content, same order of constituents, excepting the formulation—gives a glimpse of the function that Bolzano assigns to mathematical signs as well as to the words of language: they cannot claim to reflect the objective internal composition of the representations they designate. They have essentially an *abbreviative* value. They project in a linear order (*eine gewisse Folge*) concepts that are not hierarchized in one dimension. Thus they function as indexes for complex meanings, which only an active interpretation makes it possible to reach through them. This general characteristic of signs, along with the association property of constituents, explains the frequency of statements actually expressing an identical proposition while appearing to have a cognitive content. This is obviously true of the following statement:

A bachelor is an unmarried man,

which represents a proposition of the form:

Any *A* having *b*, has *b*

Acknowledging identity, however, presupposes, as Locke noted, linguistic knowledge or knowledge of abbreviations already introduced, in the case of mathematical statements.

Explanation and Identity

What is meant by "linguistic knowledge"? The propositions whose role is to make explicit the meaning of a concept—*explanations*—belong in fact to three different categories.

(1) *Determination* (*Bestimmung*) indicates which exclusive properties belong to an object. The role of determination is obviously to found the possibility of speaking about a simple representation. It ascribes a property without requiring for that matter a division of the subject concept in the predication (§509, IV, 226ff.).

Because such a property is determinative only insofar as it characterizes exclusively its object, between the representation of the subject and that of the predicate (after concretization) there is a relationship of equivalence, which requires demonstration. The identity occurring here is no other than what the tradition called "numerical identity." A true identical proposition is not what is stated in a determination: as Aristotle noted, an identical proposition would be unsuited for determining an essence.[36] Determination belongs to the realm of real and not strictly nominal knowledge.

(2) The second type of explanation—*division*—remains within the limits of the subject concept. It breaks down a representation into its constituents with equal success in the case of empirical representations as in that of pure concepts. Against Kant and under the influence of the disqualification of transcendental logic, Bolzano considers both types of representation as equally open to univocal resolution: a closed and final definition (§559, IV, 346). Because this definition by *Zerlegung* specifies "from which constituents and following which connection a concept is formed," it is not enough to consider, as do "almost all logicians," that the relationship between *definiendum* and *definiens* is a relationship of equivalence. There is actually only one and the same representation, which appears here in its abridged form in one word, there in its "developed" version (ibid., 340). This type of explanation serves to reveal a sort of "natural" synonymy that is at the origin of all communication by means of signs. If explanatory propositions of this sort can have some usefulness, although they are identical, it is because an acquisition of language must again cover the distance separating the simplified expression from the intrinsic complexity of meaning (Bolzano is following Locke here). Whence a paradox: Should these intensionally identical propositions not be demonstrated? I will return later to this problem, which Frege also encounters in his theory of definition.

(3) The third type of explanation resembles the nominal definition of Port-Royal: *explication* (*Verständigung*). It "explains the meaning authors choose to give arbitrarily (i.e., at their own convenience) to any sign." From such an explanation, one obviously cannot derive anything concerning the thing itself. The

only truth that can be deduced is of a linguistic nature, "a truth concerning the words or the symbols" (§515, IV, 244). This third type seems at first sight to be equivalent to the second type: in both cases the same representation is stated. Nevertheless, the object of the predication is no longer immediately the concept with its constituents, but a *sign*, which in subject position receives a certain representational content (in predicate position).

Verständigung, then, occurs at a metalinguistic level, in a way that recalls determination. Just as the latter states a property of a thing, explication ascribes to a word the ability to represent an object of a different type, namely, the representation in itself. Division proceeds from concept to constituent—so to speak, horizontally, whereas the two other types of explanation work vertically to join the object to the concept, the meaning to the sound. The establishment of a connection between the term and the representation does not have to be demonstrated (which as Locke noticed does not prevent it from having to be *learned*). What could be called the "strictly" nominal synonymy of explication is therefore quite different from the "natural" synonymy of division. This "symbolic" or "metalinguistic" synonymy arises from the failure of natural synonymy. It is because we recognize ourselves as unable to exhibit the objective composition of a given representation that we are obliged to form one arbitrarily. The internal relationship between *definiens* and *definiendum* is then superseded by an external relationship of decision or convention. These extra details make it possible to evaluate how Bolzano reflected on Locke, without seeking to let the nominal cover almost entirely the field of scientific discourse. The division of a concept into its constituents is not conceived as entirely subjected to the arbitrariness of a linguistic decision; unlike Locke, Bolzano believes our representations of things to be objectively founded. Whence the distinction he makes against Locke between a fruitful and a gratuitous synonymy. Only the second truly belongs to the nominal.

Equations differ from explanations in the sense that they do not follow a predicative model, which allows them to have a symmetrical structure governed by the relationship of equality. The distinction between explanations of the first type and those of the third type, between determination and explication, makes it nevertheless possible to understand by analogy what differentiates two kinds of equations. Just as the determinative definition asserts the equivalence of two representations, most equations state the equivalence of two distinct representations, such as:

$$\sin 45° = \tfrac{1}{2}.$$

But there are equations analogous to explication:

> When two (or more) representations whose equivalence is stated in an equation are representations of the form "the meaning of the sign A" (i.e., the representation we wish to express by this sign), I will allow myself to call this equation "symbolic." (*EG*, §53, 108r, 131–32)

Symbolic equations assert, as do explications, propositions designed to make linguistic communication possible, but about the symbols of a similar representation assumed to be interchangeable. Bolzano seems to admit the validity of the equation "$A = A$" only in this metalinguistic sense (ibid., §54, 109r, 132).

The Second Case of Illusion: The Tautological Effect

Can it be said of those who talk without wanting to be understood that they are *really speaking*, that they are "giving signs of themselves"? If we hold with Bolzano that the linguistic expression is *doubly* controlled—by a single source of rationality, which is the meaning "in itself," and by a personal will singularized in a specific intention of communication—then the answer to the question is negative. This makes it possible to state this fundamental truth, which in Bolzano plays approximately the role of a conversational postulate à la Grice: "Every speaker wants to be understood" (§387, III, 555). Yet, tautological statements are an example of messages in which "nothing" seems to be said: an empty message, which lays on speakers the suspicion that they could well be insincere. Here it is no longer the complexity of the statement that makes us think that they are trying to deceive, but, on the contrary, the *absolute obviousness* of the message, its emptiness, that gives the warning. Locke makes this type of statement a kind of *game*—a hardly human game if we take seriously the metaphor of the monkey who passes an oyster from one paw to the other—gaining by such shifting nothing other than amusement. To form mechanically a truth by simply redoubling the subject, like "oyster is oyster," belongs to the same rather primitive "triflingness." The latter makes language the material outcome of a functional game, without taking into account what constitutes its true dignity and finality: the means of communicating an "instruction" "useful for the conduct of life."

Bolzano follows Locke, whose acuteness he praises (*W*, §148, II, 87). Every properly named tautology is vacuous and useless, and whoever would state a tautology would say nothing in reality. But one must always grant that the speaker meant something, and inquire whether what appears tautological does not appear so owing to an ellipsis. Following up this criticism of the tautological *proposition* by questioning the tautological *statement*, Bolzano does not confine himself to extending the field of meaningful statements, by dissociating what we would call today the sentence's meaning—its literal meaning—and the speaker's meaning. This interpretation allows him to defend Locke's thesis, which was threatened by Leibniz's series of counterexamples, leading to prove that tautologies or "semi-identicals" could well be of "some usefulness."[37] "*A wise man is still a man*, which teaches that he is not infallible, that he is mortal, and so forth."

If a tautological or semi-identical proposition can be useful, it is, from Leibniz's point of view, because it makes deductions possible, either from the subject or from one of its parts. Once one recalls what the essential and the derived properties of the concept of "human being" are, it becomes "instructive" to contrast one of the attributes by which a human being tends toward the divine and the immortal with those that characterize the human being as an "animal" or a "finite being." Bolzano offers, on the other hand, a very different explanation of the usefulness of the preceding statement. The identity of words simply conceals a difference of meaning, so that the proposition expressed in this apparent tautology is in fact: "Even a wise man is fallible."[38] Because this proposition is *not* analytic, it takes on a significance for communication. Leibniz's argument is thus rejected.

Bolzano uses a second conversational postulate to restore apparent tautologies to their real syntheticity: "A speaker cannot *wish* to state a tautology." To call on such a postulate opens the road for a branch of rhetoric specializing in the identification and interpretation of false tautologies. Two types of situations should be distinguished: sometimes the tautology actually uttered will be a purely erroneous enunciation, a simple error of expression, which will be immediately brought to light by an inquiry. Sometimes it will be intended as spoken by the speaker, with a semantic intention to be deciphered. To restore the meaningful value of a tautological statement, such as one that entails ellipsis, presupposes that one goes beyond the aridity of its expression. "What is evil, is evil" should be able to be completed according to the intention the speaker could have had in using an ellipsis. We enter thus into the domain of singularities of expression. It is not possible to describe them exhaustively, but I will cite two examples:

I cannot resolve to present evil other than as evil.
The effort to embellish evil is a useless one, for sooner or later one will discover it for what it is.

Knowledge of the context of the expression makes it generally possible to understand the intention of communication that prompts a tautological expression. But genuine tautology is not consciously stated to express indirectly another proposition; it is spoken unintentionally, making speakers embarrassed when they come to realize it. Thus the advantage of using the tautological reduction of the statement in a refutation to prove that a supposed "demonstration" reduces to the unproductive repetition of the same proposition.[39] The examination of these "statement effects"—false tautologies, apparent syntheses—allows us to reconsider the problem of the epistemological significance of analytic propositions. For if presenting a true tautology is "inexcusable" in a treatise, it may become appropriate, or even necessary, to point out an identity that the complexity of a statement may make us miss. Tautology is an extreme case. Analytic propositions have many other possible uses.

The Analytic at Work

How is a scientific treatise written? The fundamental aim of the *Theory of Science* is to answer this question by showing both the foundational and the architectonic role of logic as a general theory of systems of truths. To answer this question presupposes that one calls on two series of rules.[40] The first series depends on the objective nature of logical objects. From this point of view analytic propositions are always derived truths, of restricted extensional scope. But although they may attract the interest of the logician as extreme cases of validity, they do not have intrinsic theoretical significance. However, the cognitive process to which every treatise must lead does not directly deal with truths in themselves, but with statements. The knowing subject is a real person, with preknowledge that hinders the recognition of truth, as well as the specific objectives that selectively guide one's capacities of attention. A second series of rules specifies the conditions of *written transmission* of the truths composing a science. This second part of Bolzano's logical research could be called "pure rhetoric," provided this word is taken to mean the rules that govern a convincing written theoretical presentation.

What distinguishes significantly "pure rhetoric" conceived in this way from any pure or applied pedagogy is that the latter discipline can offer only a linear disposition linking statements, with the important restrictions that the limits of memory or the attention of an audience impose. Only the "scope of the book" allows a systematic order to be deployed. Like the "in itself" that it is modeled on, the book is made up of a hierarchy of propositions that no extraneous consideration of time, audience, or tutorial limitation can water down. The book is thus on the order of being what is furthest from existence and nearest the mode of being "in itself." The whole body of partial reasons from which a theorem is deduced can be developed only in the spacious "patience of the book." The ability of a book to transmit scientific knowledge must not lead us to believe that the *whole* of a science can be, as it were, photographically reproduced in it, and that for two reasons. First, the body of truths belonging to any science is infinite: logic as the theory of science must teach us to *choose*, among the infinitely many truths composing a science, which ones *deserve* to appear in a corresponding treatise. Second, a treatise that would be confined to expounding *essential truths* — that is, those strictly constitutive of a science — would be strictly *unreadable*, at least for the majority of readers (§436, IV, 100). For a treatise to fulfill its double aim to present the truths of science in a *founded and convincing* manner, it must mention, in addition to the essential truths, two other classes of true propositions: *auxiliary truths*, borrowed from other sciences to complete demonstrations, and *occasional truths*, which are the examples, the practical applications, the stylistic observations — in a word, all propositions whose goal is to retain the attention of the reader.

The "pure rhetoric" that Bolzano creates in the treatise of treatises, which the *Wissenschaftslehre* represents, is thus itself an intermediary discipline. As such, it cannot claim the dignity of a science, but pertains to an *art*, on account of its temporary nature. This art could be characterized as the technique of scientific writing (*W*, §393, IV, 11ff., 14; §395, IV, 24; §11, I, 44). The book reflects only the unfinished state of the science studied as a timeless totality. Moreover, it is always directed toward a *definite* public, to whose needs and culture it must be adapted. "Pure rhetoric" develops thus in a constant to-and-fro between the objective hierarchy of truths in themselves (as it is imperfectly apprehended at a particular period) and the particular capacities of knowledge, collectively identifiable in the *types of readers*: the scientist, the technician, and the layperson (§429 and 430, IV, 87ff.). The treatise cannot hope to give more than a glimpse: a patently awkward, provisional, changeable copy of science as it is in itself.

The Pragmatics of Analyticity

As one may guess, the twofold obligation imposed on the scientific treatise— peremptory order of the internal constitution of truth, constraints from the finite point of view from which its recognition arises—determines the usefulness of analytic propositions. If the realm of truth was the only relevant one, these propositions would disappear behind the universal truths from which they receive their own validity. But in the realm of knowledge, it is not possible to be satisfied with universal statements; a delicate balance has to be found between impenetrable generality and redundant detail (§372, III, 471), a balance in which analytic propositions constitute an essential element. The freedom with which they are used depends on three factors, which today could be termed "pragmatic."

The first factor lies in the specific nature of the discipline under study. If it is a "very composite" science, the analyticity—or even identity—of propositions does not follow immediately; it is less easily identifiable. Deductions are less immediate, to such a degree that analytic propositions may have to be demonstrated (as in analysis). The second factor lies in the *capacity* of the subject: subjects trained to reason, with a good memory and an independent faculty of deduction, will be more able to deduce for themselves an analytic truth from a synthetic truth, without it being necessary to devote to this deduction a special development in a treatise. If the treatise is aimed at a large public, it will be necessary to sustain the deductive faculties of readers by explicitly mentioning some particular consequences of the general truth (§444, IV, 112–13).[41]

Finally, the sense of analytic propositions depends on the objective of the authors of treatises. Are they concerned with reinforcing or increasing the knowing of readers already versed in the science studied, with initiating young people to reasoning, or with enabling technicians to master the practical applications that a theory can explain? Analytic truths will have a corresponding role in the treatise. We already know their importance in application or illustration (*W*, §544, IV, 315ff.). In a strictly scientific treatise, however, they will be set aside, owing to their relative informational poverty.[42] The search for the delicate balance between the analytic and the synthetic in each particular treatise shows ultimately whence analyticity gets its usefulness: from a *tension* between the theoretical pole and the practical pole of knowledge. Although this contrast does not at all concern truths in themselves, it acquires in the elaboration of treatises an importance that, theoretically, was not to be expected. This tension is nevertheless founded. It is accounted for by the fundamental ethical principle to which all human activity is subordinated, and which governs thus a fortiori an activity that involves as seriously human responsibility as the writing of treatises: the "supreme principle of all theory of science":

> In dividing the whole domain of truth into particular sciences and in presenting these sciences in their own scholarly treatises, our procedure must always be as the laws of morality demand and consequently so that the greatest possible sum total of goods (the greatest possible advancement of the general welfare) is produced by it. (§395, IV, 26)

This advancement of the general welfare presupposes that one *classes* difficulties, that one takes into consideration the real needs, that one attempts to give readers the "knowledge" they ask for. The aim to increase the number of readers is what motivates the particularization of truth into submodels. The analytic is the instrument of a rhetorical strategy that seeks to combine the advantages of the example with the rigor of "saying less."

If I now attempt a general view of the various maxims gathered for using analytic propositions, these propositions appear to have three functions. The role of analytic propositions is not, generally speaking—with the exception of mathematics—to expound a *definite* thesis concerning the object whose theory is being worked out. Of importance, rather, is to capture by means of these propositions knowledge already formed, at a *critical moment* of its use: at the point where law and experience meet, or that where rule and life conflict, or finally that where language is contrasted with the immediate presentation of meaning. "Experimental" propositions are illustrated by the example already analyzed: "This triangle has angles equal to the sum of two right angles."

Unlike clinical statements, which convey a new observation and are synthetic, experimental analytic propositions apply to singular cases a synthetic truth established elsewhere. Very close to this use, analytic propositions of the second type are distinguished only because they derive a rule of action from a principle. Instead of being demonstrative, they are *practical*. To this type belongs the example already studied: "A depraved man does not deserve respect."

Finally, the analytic propositions of the third type would be essentially *explicative* (in the second or third sense of the term; see the earlier discussion). The following would be an example: "Every triangle is a figure."[43]

The Bolzanian Strategy of Analyticity

The Bolzanian definition of analytic propositions presents synthetic truths as forming the final authority of the truth of a theory. Recalling Plato's metaphor of weaving, one could consider the syntheses as the *warp* that holds the fabric, whereas analytic propositions would be the *woof*—filling threads that adhere to other threads: simple deductive intermediaries, "interstitial" auxiliaries. The other aspect of the analytic also has its equivalent in the same metaphor. Just as the woof gives to the fabric its fine quality, the "saying less" of these propositions is what makes communication in its pragmatic dimension possible. For submodels are *necessary*. Their "inferiority" and their value as intermediaries qualify them for presenting the objective order of science in the dimension of finitude. They occur in the realm of speech and of knowledge under the cover of synthetic truths. And one must submodelize all the more, because the language one uses goes against the transparent complexity of concepts in themselves—all the more, finally, because the assumed knowledge of the reader-student is modest.

Does this division of labor, which excludes the analytic from "determining" functions while reserving for it roles that belong to cognitive finitude (intermediary, example, application), not ultimately amount to resting all philosophy of logic on a new dualism? I was able to credit Bolzano with having gone beyond certain dualities of traditional rationalist philosophy, such as "form-content," "intuition-concept," "given-constructed." But what are we to say of the division that has persisted since Kant set it forth—following up perhaps Locke's conception of substance—between the "in itself" and its *Erscheinung*? If representations, propositions, truths "in themselves" are the source of meaning on which language will draw, how can the statement under certain circumstances *intervene* between the meaning intended by the speaker and that understood by the hearer? How are we to explain that the composition of mathematical meanings requires a long intermediary chain of analytic propositions? Would there not be a virtue characteristic of mathematical symbolism? Is the problem we encountered concerning explanation, relative to the necessity of proving from which constituents a concept is constituted, not evidence of a vicious circle? What would constitute such a demonstration: would it compare the *definiens* to the model "set in itself" or would it justify the definition by satisfying the standard that it represents itself? Hegel's criticism of Kant's "thing-in-itself" seems to apply as relevantly to the "in itself" of Bolzano: "[Kant assumes] the existence of a *thing-in-itself* foreign and external to thought, although it is easy to see that an abstraction like the *thing-in-itself* is not anything other than a product of thought, of abstractive thought, that is." Whatever value we give to this kind of objection, it seems to neglect the topical specificity of Bolzano's "in itself" with respect to Kant's "thing-in-itself." The author of the *Theory of Science* is concerned with accounting for the conditions of possibility of the recognition of truth and of its transmission through the *medium* of the *treatise*. The "in itself" acquires there the function of justifying the necessity and the universality of the organization of propositions. I suggest calling "ontotranscendental" this function of the Bolzanian "in itself": "transcendental" because Bolzano continues, in my opinion, to formulate in Kantian terms the question of the possibility of knowledge; "Ontotranscendental" because knowledge cannot be founded by itself—in the pureness of an act of intuition or of understanding—but can only be founded by resorting to an independent domain, subsisting in the Being, or rather "objective." This separation between the "full" sense, in which truth becomes "cosmos," and the linguistic and cognitive expression, which is given in the *pathos* of finitude, is what circumscribes the field of analyticity.

We will understand better this topical change if we compare Bolzano's analytic with the nominal of Locke and the analytic of Kant. Locke contents himself with indicating the edge of knowledge, without being able to *delimit* it, because the "in itself" is always "beyond" our cognitive capacities. Of substance, we know nothing, and no path leads from primary qualities to secondary ones. Nominal discourse only expresses our inability to give to substances a real definition. Under such conditions, the only sure discourse is discourse without scope; only "trifling" propositions are sheltered from refutation. Kant is less far from Locke than is often thought: if he believes against empiricism that it is possible to found the legitimacy of natural sciences, he does so by contrasting with an empty analytic — formal product of understanding — a productive synthetic. The aesthetic and the transcendental deduction allow him to circumscribe the limits within which a science of phenomenon is deployed.

Locke's substance and Kant's thing-in-itself remain "external to thought," according to the expression of Hegel. Bolzano turns Hegel's argument around: to say that the "in itself" is the product of abstractive thought is to prevent oneself from understanding how a thought can ever be true. Truth is not a process but an objective being that does not need to be produced. It only needs to be discovered again. Far from being "produced" by thought, it is because the "in itself" *gives* itself to thought that the latter is possible. The "in itself" determines the architectonic of the system, that is, the limits of each science. Consequently, it is what forms the model that the writers of treatises follow. Leibniz's analyticity was triumphant: key of all rationality and end of all demonstration. Kant's analyticity was imprisoned in the formal repetition of thought. Bolzano's analyticity is the modest messenger of higher truths.

Section 3
Frege and the Hypothesis of Analyticity

1

Analyticity and the Language of the System

The concept of "analytic proposition" appears very rarely in Frege's writings. Aside from the seven paragraphs that *The Foundations of Arithmetic* devotes to the concept, there is practically no other explicit trace of it. Does this mean that the concept lacks true importance for Frege? The opposite is perhaps true. Frege does not mention this concept for the purpose of giving a new explanation or, as Bolzano, a purely logical explanation of a traditional concept with a laden past. For the significance of analyticity is now attached to a concrete project: it must be the mortar for building up the system of arithmetic. Analyticity is linked to the bet Frege makes, to demonstrate that all the concepts of arithmetic can be defined and all the theorems of arithmetic can be derived by means of a small number of basic concepts and purely logical fundamental truths. This accounts for the fact that Frege expounds once and for all what he understands by an "analytic truth," and does not return to it. He never ceases to refer the legitimacy of the system he is building to this concept. The way in which *The Foundations* presents the question of the analyticity or syntheticity of a truth confirms this. What constitutes the meaning of the question of the analyticity of a truth, for Frege, is the actual possibility of deducing mathematical truths from primitive logical truths, a possibility whose only proof lies in the actual construction of a system of arithmetic:

> The question is removed from the sphere of psychology, and assigned, if the truth concerned is a mathematical one, to the sphere of mathematics. The problem becomes, in fact, that of finding the proof of the proposition, and of following it up right back to the primitive truths. If, in carrying out this process, we come only on general logical laws and on definitions, then the truth is an analytic one, bearing in mind that we must take account also of all propositions on which the admissibility of any of the definitions depends. (*Der Grundlagen der Arithmetik* [hereafter, *GA*], §3, 3–4)

With this introductory text it is already clear that the analyticity of *logical* propositions is not itself in question but is rather presupposed by the problem Frege has to solve: he is not concerned with knowing what an analytic truth is; it is a logical truth, that is, as we shall see, a truth belonging to the system of logic. But he is concerned with knowing whether the truths of a science can be clearly identified as analytic or synthetic: as logical or not. What is at stake in the concept of analytic truth, then, depends on the possibility of carrying out the logicist reduction and deduction of mathematical truths (or the truths of another science, if the question of analyticity or syntheticity arises). At the time of *The Foundations*, the system is only sketched, and the object of the book is to throw some light on the conditions that foretell its accomplishment in the near future. Analyticity is an important concept for Frege, not for its explanatory interest, but for its foundational value. A logical proposition or one derived from logical truths is analytic: the concept of "analytic truth" is from the outset conceived by Frege in its *metasystematic* scope, insofar as it makes it possible to characterize the membership of a proposition to a "purely logical" system. The "criterion" of analyticity that Frege uses consists simply in enumerating the cases in which a truth will be recognized as logical: either it is a "general logical law," or it is a definition or ensures "the use of a definition," or else it is deduced from preceding ones. These cases exhaust the various roles a truth can play in a system. But then, we may ask, how can we explain what constitutes for Frege the importance of the *system*?

Systematicity and Analyticity

It is worthwhile to compare two texts thirty years apart; they correspond to two phases of Frege's logicist program—the one optimistic, the other disenchanted. The first text dating from 1884 begins *The Foundations*:

> After deserting for a time the old Euclidean standards of rigour, mathematics is now returning to them, and even making efforts to go beyond them.

The other text, dating from 1914, is subsequent to the failure of the logicist hypothesis. The tone is bitter; it is no longer time for optimism. In spite of that, Frege shows that he has not lost in the least his initial conviction concerning the necessity of working toward a systematization of mathematics:

> Euclid had an inkling of this idea of a *system*; but he failed to realize it and it almost seems as if at the present time we were further from this goal than ever. We see mathematicians each pursuing his own work on some fragment of the subject, but these fragments do not fit together into a system; indeed the idea of a system seems almost to have been lost. And yet the striving after a system is a justified one. We cannot long remain content with the fragmentation that prevails at present. (*N*, I, 221; trans. Long and White, 205)

What makes this *Streben nach dem System* a "legitimate quest"? The question seems unnecessary: since Wolff has the system not been scientific? Let us recall the second preface to the *Critique of Pure Reason* and the tribute paid to the "strict method of the celebrated Wolff," or the architectonic of pure reason, which expounds the rules of this method. We find already in these texts the main features that Frege acknowledges as "rigorously scientific" knowledge. For the "rhapsody" of partial and scattered knowledge the system substitutes an *articulation* of truths that allows an *organic* development of knowledge. From this development by internal differentiation arise two essential properties of systematic knowledge: it is *exhaustive*—in the sense that it generates "from inside" all possible deductive consequences of principles—but it is at the same time *closed* to the extent that no external adjunction is tolerated once the principles are laid down.[1]

To describe the system in this manner is still not to produce the foundation of its legitimacy. One could distinguish a transcendental use and a formal use of the system, according to the interpretation that is given of the demonstrative continuity through which the science acquires its unity. In the *Critique* the progression of the transcendental deduction depends on the authority of the architect. Pure reason, in its critical function, exhibits by deduction what it constituted itself in its transcendental function. The question of continuity is then resolved in a purely negative manner, by the absence of an obstacle on the road leading from the faculties of the subject to the transcendental object. As we remarked in respect to Bolzano, the systematic philosophers of the nineteenth century raise the constraints guaranteeing demonstrative continuity—in other words, the condition of the development of the system. Bolzano dismisses metaphysics from its architectonic function to promote instead logic as a science of truths in themselves. There is more than a methodological requirement here: the theory of systems breaks with the philosophy of the subject, which made the system the instrument of reason in its quest for unity. Systematicity, henceforth characterizing knowledge only in a secondary manner, becomes the property of objective truths independent of any subject.

Like Bolzano, Frege conceives the system as an objective model of which every science must yield a copy as exact as possible. But Frege encounters the question of continuity, not only as the objective condition of the existence of a body of truths, but also as a test to which the logician's enterprise of reconstruction must be *concretely* submitted. This topical difference is more clearly understood when we evaluate what distinguishes Bolzano's and Frege's projects. The *Theory of Science*, on the one hand, portrays the logical organization of truths in general. Systematic continuity is presupposed rather than tested by the *Wissenschaftslehre*. Frege's project, on the other hand, is no less general than Bolzano's in its ultimate ambition, for he is concerned with expounding "the laws of the laws of reason," but this must at the same time be carried out in a concrete manner, failing which it would lose any credibility. Continuity must now be verified in detail in the connections of a body of truths. For a truth to be called analytic or synthetic—logically demonstrable or empirical in the terminology of the *Be-*

griffsschrift—the condition of this identification must be given, *the absence of a hiatus (Lückenlosigkeit)*, that is, the absolute continuity of demonstration.

It is on this point that Frege perceives the inadequacy of the Euclidean axiomatic. The effort to specify all the propositions on which the *Aufbau* actually rests neglects the rules of deduction and of consequence.[2] Yet what source can be ascribed to nonformed transitions of the type "it is easy to see that . . . "? Logical continuity between propositions ensures that the nature of deduced propositions be determined, understanding by "nature" not only the gnoseological kind to which propositions pertain but also an independent objective property of the knowing subject. Demonstrative continuity is therefore more than a methodological requirement: it is the touchstone of the "natural" continuity by which a system develops from the core (*Kern*) of primitive truths into an organic whole. This biological metaphor determines in Frege, as in Kant, the way the development of a system is grasped. However, the topical shift from the subjective transcendental to the objective transcendental changes the meaning of the metaphor. In the *Critique*, it refers to the aim of the underlying work of reason, which seeks to emphasize its goal by a particular schema. For Frege, on the contrary, it recalls the extraordinary deductive capacity "contained" in the original truths. Just as the embryo "contains" the fully developed individual, so these primitive truths of logic "bear within them" the developed system:

> The properties that belong to these foundation stones of science contain as if in germ its entire content. (*Kleine Schriften* [hereafter, *KS*], 104)[3]

The organic simile thus unexpectedly restores the Kantian determination of the analytic predicate as "what is contained" in the concept of subject. What constitutes, then, these *Urwahrheiten* that are "in themselves" the whole system? For the system of arithmetic, it is only "logical" laws, that is, the "laws of being true." We can now answer the question raised previously: What makes the "quest for the system" legitimate and necessary is the existence, beyond the theorems of arithmetic, of an absolutely true body of thoughts whose combination makes it possible to generate all the truths of mathematical science. Analyticity is to ensure the continuous diffusion of these outstanding truths up to their most remote consequences.

Understanding the mode of topical insertion of the concept of analytic truth in Frege's writing implies examining not how this concept is *introduced* or *defined*, but rather how it is *applied*—that is, how continuity from basic laws to the theorems of arithmetic is ensured, and then how these primitive laws come to form the basis of the system. To reveal the analyticity of arithmetic propositions therefore presupposes a particular technique of concept construction, and more generally a new formula notation.

Analyticity and Formula Language

The rigorous continuity that makes it possible to reveal the true premises of the system of arithmetic imposes particular conditions to be laid on the expression of truths and their relationships: from the outset natural language seems to Frege unable to satisfy the requirements of a systematic notation. Shaped for the ear, designed to convey quickly orders or practical advice, it ceases to be suited when some precision, some univocity, and some rigor are demanded, because it does not reveal the internal organization of the concepts stated in the expressive structure, as is shown by the variety of relationships that the same grammatical forms make it possible to express: *Berggipfel* means "mountain summit," whereas *Baumriese* means "giant tree"; or because it conveys a concept by some inessential characters or by some metaphorical expression, which hinders in both cases rigorously clarifying the systematic role of each expression (*Nachgelassene Schriften* [hereafter, *N*], I, 113). Thus, already in 1879 the *Begriffsschrift* appears as a notational technique inseparable from the systematic program. Frege's "characteristic," as he himself will sometimes call it, continues similar attempts by Boole, Schröder, Grassmann, and even Wundt, among the most recent. But it is distinguished both by its *method* and by its *ambition*. The ideography does not aim only at solving problems, it will not be only a *calculus ratiocinator*. It aims at elucidating by means of the notation all the *content*, thus achieving a notational unity for what was formerly called "form"—the rules of formation and deduction of propositions—and for the "content" of functional expressions. Frege takes up with much more refined ideographic means Leibniz's objective: the *character* of concepts will have to appear in the notation, but they may be formed by using, in place of the traditional *compositio*, all the resources of "generality" (quantification), negation, and implication.

By opening for the logical notation the field of conceptual "contents," Frege is conscious of bringing about a revolution that he compares to the discovery of the internal structure of the atom, whose indivisibility had been maintained for centuries. One of the consequences of this revolution was the complete overturning of the traditional relationship between "form" and "content." *Now the concept takes on both a categorematic and a syncategorematic function.* It is no longer possible to be satisfied with conceiving logic as "simply formal" or "indifferent to content." Analyticity having become constructive, logic can acquire again an essential role in a new *Mathesis universalis*.

If logic may have appeared to be an unnecessary science, Frege believes that the cause lies in the fascination produced by natural language. In particular the tripartition "subject-copula-predicate" leads the logician to innumerable complications, without solutions having any properly logical interest. If analyticity could have appeared to be a simple repetition of something given, if the development of content could resemble a clarifying of something "already thought," it is because the traditional theories of the proposition could only reinforce the two main obstacles that hinder perceiving "conceptual contents." The first obstacle, arising from ordinary language and reinforced by traditional logicians, consists in masking propositional identities with the statement. For Frege to accept with Bolzano a general isomorphy between statement and meaning would be to concede too much. Two statements do not have to have the same subject and the same predicate to have the same meaning. The active or the passive voice is a matter of "lighting," not of meaning. A logical analysis of natural language should distinguish three levels:

(1) The statement has a sense insofar as it expresses a thought (*Gedanke*).
(2) It has a denotation (which is not, as Bolzano thought, the "object" to which it ascribes a property, but truth or falsity).
(3) Finally, the statement comprises also "associated representations," which make up its "style" or its "lighting." We have here a parameter foreign to logic, precisely on account of the intersubjective variations that affect it (*KS*, 247).

To neglect the lighting is to recognize the multiplicity of possible "subjects" or "predicates" for the same thought. The sentence

Caesar conquered the Gauls

can be analyzed in different ways, distinguished simply by the number of units that argumentation can fill—that is, by the proportion of "saturated" and "unsaturated" constituents:

Caesar conquered . . .

. . . conquered the Gauls

. . . conquered . . .

The identity of statements of the same thought, which the tripartite analysis masks, will thus be revealed by an analysis, simply bipartite but not exclusive, any bipartition being acceptable within the limits of the argumentation units available. Any sentence can be divided in various ways in terms of a function sign (unsaturated) and an argument sign (saturated). This is a mode of analysis applying to natural language, yet having a more adequate expression in formula language. But because they did not manage to identify identical thought "under its different garments," traditional logicians were unable to grasp the structural relationship between the propositions of ordinary language and the equations and analytic expressions of mathematics (we saw in Bolzano the difficulties involved in analyzing mathematical propositions in terms of "having a property"); the idea of a simply bipartite articulation thrusts itself on Frege as early as the *Begriffsschrift*: "In this I strictly follow the example of the formula language of mathematics, in which, also, one can distinguish subject and predicate only by doing violence (to the language)" (§3, 3; Bynuum trans., 113). The functional bipartition of the proposition into a "complete" part and a part "requiring a complement" appears in this new analysis as the fundamental logical articulation of all thought, more fundamental in particular than the relationship of subject to predicate, which represents only an example of it. Thus understood, the concept can be identified with a *function* whose value is always a truth-value (*N*, I, 203).

To achieve this result, Frege modifies the concept of function so as to extend its application to equalities and inequalities. He accepts as arguments "any objects whatsoever" (*Gegenstände überhaupt*)—among them, truth and falsity. Hence the concept is distinguished from other functions only in that it relates a truth-value to each argument that completes it. Its course of values (*Wertverlauf*) produces a bipartition between the objects it subsumes and those it does not subsume, the extension of the concept being made up of all the arguments for which the corresponding proposition has taken on the value "true."

A second disadvantage of the predicative interpretation of the proposition also explains why analyticity was identified for so long with the unproductiveness of logic. Natural language, indeed, conceals under the same term "to be" a fundamental difference from the point of view of logic. "To be" designates sometimes *subsumption of an object under a concept*, sometimes *subordination* indicating the dependence of a lower concept on a higher concept. The proposition "Caesar is a man" and the proposition "a man is a rational animal" allow of the same analysis, according to the tradition. The singular term "Caesar" can be analyzed as if it were the subject of a universal proposition—that is, in taking the concept in its full extension.[4] In both cases, the proposition was declared true for the same reason: because the idea of the subject contained the idea of the predicate, or, in extensional terms, because the extension of the predicate contained the extension of the subject. Frege forbids henceforth any "comparison" of this kind. For subsumption, which is the fundamental relationship, joins two *heterogeneous* parts: *the unsaturated part denotes a concept, the saturated part denotes an object* (one of the consequences of this analysis is to make convertibility impossible). Subordination should not in turn be confused with "inherence." The latter relationship joins the concept to its property (for example, a first-order concept to a second-order concept). We will say, then, that the first falls not "under" but "within" the second (*Grundgesetze* [hereafter, *G*], I, §13, 24). Finally, subordination simply states an implication between two concepts of the same order.

What natural language confuses, formula language will distinguish. The advantage does not lie only in greater distinction, in the more accurate analysis of the relationships between concepts. What we gain is to be able to derive in a purely analytic way what appeared until now as belonging to synthesis, namely, to derive a property from the "horizontal" structure of concepts. By thus making the derivation of properties from concepts possible, formula language circumvents the difficulty created by Bolzano's distinction between predication of property and predication of constituent. Predication of property is no longer excluded from logical derivation, and predication of object is set, at the very base of the whole system, in functional unsaturation. Associated with the three constructional means—implication, quantification, and negation—subsumption becomes a very flexible descriptive instrument at the logician's disposal, so flexible that it permits concepts *without object* to be treated.[5]

Formula Language and Its Referent: Frege's Realism

A late work of Frege's, *Gedankengefüge* (1923), reveals the conjunction of theses by means of which he continued to conceive the nature of concept, and more generally of language as a means of knowledge and exchange. "It is astonishing what language can do": How is it possible with so few syllables to express an infinite number of thoughts? This remark on the *productiveness* of language (*was die Sprache leistet*) leads him to question the relationship between thought and its expression, which can account for this fruitfulness of language. What must be presupposed for this fruitfulness of language to be possible? It must be isomorphic with thought—in other words, the parts of the thought must correspond to the parts of the statement. The construction of the sentence serves as an image (*Bild*) of the construction of the thought. It remains to be seen how the *Aufbau* of thought is formulated, what the notion of unsaturated part explains. As usual, Frege argues in this text in terms of conditions of possibility. There is no productiveness of natural language without the latter holding as an image. There is no image without isomorphic construction. All logical analysis should follow this isomorphy in which natural language finds the condition of its productive dynamism. The unity of sense of thought therefore cannot be understood without analyzing it into two complementary parts, one unsaturated, the other saturated.

But if we were to remain at the level of sense, the question of truth would be left unanswered. Yet the question of the respective denotations of the constituents of the thought is obviously crucial for our comprehension of the function of the system of logical truths and of the meaning to be given to analyticity: Does the system only have an operating value, or does it also have a descriptive scope? In other words, is Frege a realist?[6] What complicated the issue for a long time was the impossibility in which commentators found themselves before the publication of the *Nachlass*, of resolving the enigma raised by the article "Sinn und Bedeutung," in which the study of denotation is confined to proper names. Certainly the article "Begriff und Gegenstand" shows that the sense-denotation distinction applies equally to predicates. Nevertheless, the impossibility recognized by Frege of speaking about a concept without designating it by an object name led to the belief that it was not a *concept* that the corresponding predicative expression denoted.[7] The confusion reaches its height with what we could call, giving to the expression its full value, "Church's historical misinterpretation," a misinterpretation popularized by Carnap in *Meaning and Necessity*:

> With respect to predicators, Frege does not seem to have explained how his concepts are to be applied; however, I think that Church is in accord with Frege's intentions when he regards a class as the (ordinary) nominatum of a predicator (of degree one)—for instance, a common noun—and a property as its (ordinary) sense. (§29, 125)

Frege would have undoubtedly attributed such a text to those whom he called "the logicians of extension." The commentary contains a kernel of truth: with respect to identity, it is the extensions that are relevant. But the commentary nonetheless passes over in silence the fundamental difference between a concept name, which is unsaturated, and a sign of extension or course of values, which is saturated. Moreover, although unpublished at the time Carnap wrote, Frege's explanation had been formulated. That he set the examination of the sense and the denotation of concepts aside for a separate article, entitled "Developments on Sense and Denotation," shows well enough that he was conscious of the flaws in his first article. This new text enables us to understand the scope of the thesis of unsaturation, and has in addition the interest of pointing out what may have led Frege to develop this new propositional analysis. A brief note of the "Developments" adds indeed:

> The words "unsaturated" and "predicative" seem more suited to the sense than to denotation; *still there must be something on the part of the denotation which corresponds to this*, and I know of no better words. Cf. Wundt's *Logik*. (*N*, I, 129, note 2, trans. Long and White, 119)

The allusion to Wundt allows us to mark out Frege's progress toward the idea of conceptual unsaturation. Frege probably owes the idea of a propositional bipartition to Wundt. For according to Wundt, the copula should not be understood as a *third* constituent of judgment. It belongs to the predicate: "It is what indicates that the concept joined to it must be conceived *in a predicative sense*," writes Wundt in his *Logik*.[8] If Frege refers to Wundt in the notes, it can only be for the idea of a *semantic* category of the predicative or the unsaturated. The conceptual expression, as Wundt well perceived, is unsaturated *in its meaning*. But we must go further and accept a similar unsaturation in the *denotation* of the predicate:

> The denotation of a proper name is the object it designates or names. A concept-word denotes a concept, if the word is used as is appropriate for logic. (*N*, I, 128; trans. Long and White, 118)[9]

A proper name has a denotation if there is an object designated by this name. A similar requirement must be laid on the names of function so that conceptual notation will not be a pure combination of formulas: the property of "strict delimitation" (*scharfe Begrenzung*) states that a predicate denotes a concept provided that, after saturation by any name of object, the resulting expression denotes a truth-value (we will return later to this principle and to its relationship with the principle of contextuality). This interpretation of the denotation of the predicate as being *the concept itself* overthrows what could be called the "realism of common sense," which is inclined to recognize as existent (in the objective sense of *es gibt*) only the individuals and the classes conceived distributively. The fact that Frege insists, nevertheless, that the conceptual terms have for reference a concept, and not an extension, and that this thesis is for him the condition of the objectivity of ideography, appears still more clearly in a letter in which he presents his thesis to Husserl, whose own conception in the matter is close to that ascribed by Carnap to Frege:[10]

> All I should like to say about it now is that there seems to be a difference of opinion between us on how a concept word (common name) is related to objects. The following schema should make my view clear:

Proposition	Proper name	Concept-word	
↓	↓	↓	
sense of the proposition (thought)	sense of the proper name	sense of the concept-word	
↓	↓	↓	object falling
denotation of the proposition (truth-value)	denotation of the proper name (object)	denotation of the concept-word (concept)	→ under the concept

Frege, quite intentionally, sets in the lower right corner of his table objects falling under the concept. It is not essential for the concept that it actually subsume objects, for a concept has a sense and a denotation insofar as it is unsaturated. On the contrary, the analogy the schema stresses is one that holds between the propositions, the objects, and the concepts from the point of view of *objectivity*; they are indeed *of the same objectivity* (*dieselbe Objektivität*; *N*, II, 96). Frege recalls that this idea was already present in *The Foundations* (§47), but could not have received there sufficient expression, owing to the absence of the sense-denotation distinction. This identity of the various propositional constituents with respect to objectivity ensures the *fruitfulness* of the ideography. As long as the formulas are well formed, the proper names and the names of functions have a denotation. The deductions thus yield an objective state, the state of truth, and do not reduce to an arbitrary combination of formulas.

The Problem of the Schein-Begriffe

Frege's schema specifies, moreover, the status to be ascribed to the sense of a predicate. At each level of analysis (proposition, proper name, predicate), the sense furnishes the mediation between the symbolic expression and its denotation (respectively, truth-value, object, concept). For a concept-expression or a function-expression to have a *sense* depends only on following the rules of construction, that is, the device of notation that keeps one or several argument places open. One can write, for example, "half of something" to designate a function, the expression "something" being designed to keep the place of the argument open. For the expression to have a sense, it is sufficient that the *Darstellung* that suggests a possible relating of arguments to values of the function occurs. But the denotation of the predicate asks for more than this simple operating possibility. It must be "strictly delimited": for every argument, one must be able to say whether or not it falls under the concept. If we return to the preceding example, taking for argument name the object name ''moon'' (or any object that is not a numerical extension), we obtain a sentence in which the law of the excluded middle does not apply:

Half of the moon is smaller than 1.

The search for the correct—that is, ''strictly delimited''—concept thus presupposes that the sense of the predicate is enriched enough so as to obtain a precise extension, for example, by restricting the variation of arguments to a particular domain of objects. In his controversy with the formalists, which among other things bears on the conditions that definitions must satisfy, Frege views the proof that the symbol really introduces a definite denotation as the essential stage of the construction of a function symbol. The sense of a function is thus a specific unsaturation whose referential value must still be established. There is therefore no reason to consider, as does William Marshall,[11] that ''function-expressions do not have a sense.'' For the sense appears, in a negative manner, as what remains when the denotation is lacking. That one can still speak *about* this expression is enough to show that a function-expression has a sense even when it fails to denote. This is what Frege does, for example, in his criticism of the theory of irrational numbers; it is also what the historian of mythology does (*G*, II, 76). The number of ''possible'' concepts whose name can be written in the ideography is greater than the number of ''objective'' concepts: those that give rise to true or false propositions. A symbol retained in the expression of the system must thus satisfy a double criterion:

> Logic must demand not only of proper names but of concept-words as well that the step from the word to the sense and from the sense to the denotation be determinate beyond any doubt. Otherwise we should not be entitled to speak of a denotation at all. Of course this holds for all signs and combinations of signs with the same function as proper names or concept-words. (*N*, I, 135–36; trans. Long and White, 125)

The *first* criterion belongs to the realm of sense: notation must bring out the saturation, the unsaturation, and all the particular relationships that determine thought. The *second* one goes from the sense to the denotation. The function must be everywhere determined; the concept must offer a strict partition of the universe of objects into two classes. As we shall see, this second-denotative requirement is applied to all the symbols of *The Basic Laws*: the thought of the system will not be a ''blind'' thought in the sense that it will ascertain the denotation of all its expressions. At this cost analyticity can be constructive.

2

How the Definition Becomes Analytic

An initial examination of the Fregean concept of definition reveals two features that may seem contradictory. On the one hand, from the *Begriffsschrift* until the last texts of *Logik in der Mathematik*, Frege defends constantly the purely *symbolic* character of the act of defining. To define is only to stipulate by convention the identity of sense between a complex expression, the *explicans*, and a short, easily manipulated sign placed to the right of the definitional equation, the *explicatum*. This stipulation being introduced only for the purpose of expressive convenience, it follows that it is not at all essential for the deduction: "Nothing follows from it that would not also be inferred without it" (§24, 56). We find the reminiscence of this idea thirty-five years later:

> Of course the sentence is really only a tautology and does not add to our knowledge. It contains a truth which is so self-evident that it appears devoid of content, and yet, in setting up a system it is apparently used as a premise. I say apparently, for what is thus presented in the form of a conclusion makes no addition to our knowledge; all it does in fact is to effect an alteration of expression, and we might dispense with this if the resultant simplification of expression did not strike us as desirable. (*N*, I, 224–25; trans. Long and White, 208)

How are we to reconcile this purely conventional origin, this strictly stipulative function, which governs the syntax of the definition, with the other requisite that Frege sets for true definitions, namely, that they be *fruitful*? Is there not here, according to the expression of Reinhardt Grossmann, a "tension" between the "abbreviative" conception of definition and the epistemological criteria that preclude any arbitrariness: "Frege describes definitions as being fruitful, as capable of proving their value as acceptable or not, etc."[12] Diametrically opposed to the stipulative presentation of definition, a second series of requirements concerns its

theoretical efficiency and its own logical importance. This epistemological requisite pertaining to the definition is mentioned in the introduction to the *Foundations*:

> Most mathematicians rest content, in enquiries of this kind, when they
> have satisfied their immediate needs. If a definition shows itself tractable
> when used in proofs, if no contradictions are anywhere encountered, and if
> connexions are revealed between matters apparently remote from one an-
> other, this leading to an advance in order the regularity, it is usual to regard
> the definition as sufficiently established, and few questions are asked as to
> its logical justification. This procedure has at least the advantage that it
> makes it difficult to miss the mark altogether. Even I agree that definitions
> must show their worth by their fruitfulness: it must be possible to use them
> for constructing proofs. Yet it must still be borne in mind that the rigour of
> the proof remains our illusion, even though no link be missing in the chain
> of our deductions, so long as the definitions are justified only as an after-
> thought, by our failing to come across any contradiction. (*GA*, ix; trans.
> Austin, xxi)

This text shows that the fruitfulness of a definition *results* from its agreement
with two series of rules ("definitions *show their worth*" but cannot be *legitimated* by their fruitfulness). First, it must satisfy a requirement of *systematicity*.
One should not merely form a definition "according to needs," that is, piecemeal, without any formal precaution, or as Frege puts it without "logical justification." Here one must clearly distinguish the role of the axioms and that of the
definitions, and specify which rules are to be followed in order to guarantee a
denotation for the definition. Second, the definition is subjected to a requirement
of *operationality*. Frege requests that no definition be introduced if it is not actually used in the demonstration, in other words, that one refrain from cluttering
up the system with purely "ornamental" definitions. But if we recall that definition, in its first acceptation, is a simple abbreviative stipulation of which Frege
says repeatedly that it is logically unnecessary, this requirement is not unques-
tionable. Is such a definition not naturally destined for the role of ornament, understanding by this not an *adjunction* affecting the style of demonstrative presentation but, on the contrary, a supposed elegant *economy* of expressive means? If
definition is restricted to replacing a group of signs by a simple sign, without the
sense or a fortiori the denotation being altered, how are we to rest epistemological requirements on it, to prefer one definition to another, or even to consider a
definition false? Do the requirements of systematicity not exceed the law of *Sic
volo* characteristic of stipulation? Instead of seeing here a *tension* between rival
conceptions of definition between which Frege would in a sense be torn, as Reinhardt Grossmann suggests in his *Reflections*, can we not attempt to understand
this duality of the Fregean theory as topically founded? A text of the *Nachlass*[13]
confirms the necessity of distinguishing two possible points of view on the question of definition.

The "technical" works like the *Begriffsschrift* or the *Grundgesetze* treat definition as "part of the system of science." According to this point of view, which we will call "intrasystematic," definition appears as a simple tautology that, by the identity it states between two expressions, does not increase at all the information contained in the deductive series in which it occurs. But this intrasystematic point of view that concedes to definition only the formal status of tautology refers to the *objective* order of meanings, not to the *subjective* order of their acquisition. Should we be astonished by this taking into account of the subjective, of the "activity of the mind" that leads to definition, on the part of a philosopher who asserts as the first principle of his *Grundlagen* "the separation of the subjective and the objective"? That would amount to missing the true purpose of those remarks. Their aim is neither to bring representation up to the level of an object of logic nor to analyze definition as a specific mental activity of division or construction, but on the contrary to locate this action preliminary to building up the system as an intuitive manner of approaching logical structure (*die Einsicht in den logischen Bau, die sie gewärt . . .*).

These remarks on the genesis and the acquisition of definition have another motivation. Frege is obliged to explain the system, to clarify its structure, to justify its definitions — in other words, to show that the formalization he offers does indeed give rise to arithmetic. This activity, both critical and metasystematic, initiated in the *Grundlagen*, amplified in numerous texts of the *Nachlass* (in particular those brought together under the title *Ueber die Grundlagen der Geometrie*), consists essentially in evaluating, both in their method and their content, the other approaches to definition. Thus the series of requirements placed on the truth, the fruitfulness, and the usefulness of definition become clear. To say that a definition is false is not to retract the conventional nature of the stipulation that initiated it; rather, it is to challenge both the sense and the denotation of a sign taken as *explicatum*, to deny, for example, that number is a series of units. Frege criticizes ornamental, implicit, conditional, or fractional definitions, by showing that these are only *apparent* definitions, and he attacks the definitions of number given in treatises on arithmetic, according to the same critical or metasystematic necessity. There is here a characteristic *importance* of definition, which belongs less to its *logical* status *in* the system than to the *comprehension* of the system:

> The real importance [*Bedeutsamkeit*] of a definition lies in its logical construction out of primitive elements. . . . The insight it permits into the logical structure is not only valuable in itself, but also is a condition for insight into the logical linkage of truths. (*KS*, 302)

This assertion contradicts the texts in which Frege qualifies definition as "logically inessential" only if one confines oneself to a superficial reading. The choice of terms — "insight" into logical structure, "insight" into the logical linkage of truths — indicates that the true relevance of the definition is *epistemological* and not *logical*. We find again here a distinction familiar to Bolzano, and one that seems to be inseparable from the double value of the propositions of a treatise. A parallel could be drawn between the status of analytic propositions in the *Theory of Science* and that of definitions in Frege's works. For Bolzano, analytic propositions are objectively less rich in content than the corresponding synthetic propositions, and yet they have a role to play in a scientific treatise. The system of science, as an objective body of truths bearing among themselves objective relations of deduction and consequence, is one thing; the apprehension we may have of the system, which designates the specific function of the treatise, is another. Frege suggests the same distinction here, when he mentions the "insight" into the concepts with the help of definition. The latter necessarily has a different meaning (in the double sense of *Bedeutsamkeit*: "meaning" and "relevance"), according to whether the point of view of the system or that of research and justification of the system is adopted. We must now try to grasp the consequences of this twofold and unequal treatment of definition.

Frege recalls that the activity preliminary to the introduction of a definition can be of two sorts. Either it consists in breaking down a concept already given, used, for example, in the natural theory of arithmetic; or it appears as a construction, that is, like a new combination of known elements, an example of which Dedekind gives with his concept of the cut. Let us recall the radicalization brought by Kant to the contrast between the two types of activities attributed by him to different faculties and giving rise to definitions distinct in their methods and in their results. The constructive definition of the mathematician can determine effectively and completely its object. In decomposition, on the other hand (e.g., in philosophical definition), completeness is not guaranteed, and it is not an object that is determined but a meaning. It is interesting to note how Frege transposes these elements of critical philosophy into his own realistic philosophy: he places all that concerns the given-constructed distinction in what we will call the sphere of the "presystematic":

> Thus it is all the same for the system of mathematics, whether the preceding activity was of an analytic or a synthetic kind; whether the *definiendum* had already somehow been given before, or whether it was newly derived. For in the system, no sign (word) appears prior to the definition that introduces it. Therefore so far as the system is concerned, every definition is the given of a name, regardless of the manner in which we arrived at it. (*KS*, 302)

The rejection of the distinction *Zerlegend-Aufbauend* from the system goes along with the dissolution of the contrast between the nominal and the real on the part of the system. The system proceeds by manipulation of signs, *in abstracto*, but the concepts it gives rise to are nonetheless *effective* (*wirklich*). This reconciliation between a purely operating procedure and the genuine constructive scope of the definition precisely constitutes the condition of possibility of the realistic interpretation of the system. But all heterogeneousness between constituents must be eliminated, whether they are obtained by decomposing concepts that are wrongly taken to be elementary by natural theories, or they come into composition in formulas with other concepts "newly" derived from the system. The problem every reductionist must solve in the first place is precisely to verify that construction coincides with reduction, without any epistemological precedence of the one over the other in case, as in Frege, reduction is carried out in a "realist" spirit.

Beyond definition, we see that it is the conception of the *symbol* that is directly affected by the reconciliation of the nominal with the real, which gives to the nominal the power of the real and which submits the real to the realm of the symbol. If mathematical definition was real in Kant's sense, that is, if it formed its object *in concreto*, it would have, according to Frege's expression, "the prerogative of introducing the object." We could, consequently, assume that "it can only be given in a single way" (*GA*, §67, 78). But the possibility of a systematic development presupposes that the definition only gives one of the approaches to denotation, without closing the other possible channels to the same referent. Behind the refusal to separate the nominal and the real, there is the base of the theory of identity and the distinction between sense and denotation, which is the essential part of this theory (see my Chapter 3). We may ask then under what conditions *definition is entitled to act in both categories, that is, to produce an object and to compose symbols*. What enables Fregean definition to associate the arbitrariness of *Namengebung* with the effectiveness of the construction of a denotation? It is clear that the answer to this question must associate formal rules that will guarantee the grammaticality of the formulas constructed and semantic rules making it possible to interpret well-formed expressions. The originality of the Fregean solution lies in asserting as a fundamental metasystematic thesis the indissociable character of the syntactical elaboration and of the semantic interpretation. "The superior principle of definitions" is formulated thus:

Correctly-formed names must always denote something [*Rechtmässig gebildete Namen müssen immer etwas bedeuten*]. (*G*, I, §28, 45; trans. Furth, 83)

It remains to understand the sense of this *müssen*. We perceive, of course, the value of a condition of possibility of the *Aufbau*. If the systematic presentation of science has some value, it is on the condition that the deductive series are not simply a free combination of signs, but refer to an objective realm of truths and concepts. To understand the necessity that this principle acquires in Frege, one must mention his criticism of formal arithmetic in the *Grundgesetze*. Let us assume the hypothesis of a system conceived as a set of figures governed by rules, such that of E. Heine or that of J. Thomae (*G*, II, §86 to 137, 96– 139). The rules are conceived as simple arbitrary stipulations. No requirement to refer to previously given objects is laid on the symbols. In such a system, "the signs are everything"; they do not represent anything and, consequently, do not have reference in Frege's sense of the term. If their content must be qualified, one could say that it consists in "their behavior with respect to rules." If it proved effective such a fiction would have the interest its authors ascribed to it, that of developing methods of calculus that avoid the "metaphysical difficulties" associated with the assumption of the existence of numbers. But from a Fregean point of view this enterprise encounters three insuperable difficulties.

Let us first examine the *simplicity* and the *economy* that one hopes to achieve by transposing arithmetic into a formal game. Things quickly appear to lack the expected clarity. The refusal to interpret the signs already makes the task of demonstrating, which in its progress does not have the support of thoughts, rather arduous and ungratifying. The calculus progresses only by configurations of signs and rules of transformation. Moreover, a careful analysis of the functioning of this formal game makes it necessary to distinguish the *signs of the game* from their mention in the *theory of the game*. The pieces of the game acquire a double role, according to whether they are apprehended in a given configuration of the game (in which case they lack reference) or in the metalanguage (in which case they refer to the elements of the game). But the rules can also have a double role; they can appear in the game as arbitrary stipulations, allowing certain transformations and forbidding others, while in the theory of the game the notions of valid deduction and of theorem reappear. This double inscription so complicates the structure of the system that one can believe that it was invented in order to carry the confusion to its height. Formal arithmetic does not represent at all a simplification or a lightning of the work of the arithmetician.

A second obstacle lies in the possibilities of *expansion* of a purely formal system of arithmetic. How can we formulate criteria of identity, without granting reference to the manipulated elements? Not only will an object or a function not be recognizable in different formulations, but it will be even theoretically impossible to identify a sign as the same in two distinct presentations or occurrences. On the contrary, the existence of a definite reference is what guarantees the possibility of recognizing the *identity* of signs and the entities they denote, and the *unicity* of reference for equivalent expressions.

Finally, the purely synctactic treatment of a formal system raises the problem of its *application*. Chess, for example, has no application, because the various configurations of the game have no reference. How can we account, following up this analogy, for the fact that arithmetic is not a game but a science, in other words, that it is applicable? The only possible answer to this question is to consider arithmetic as a system of thoughts, expressed by its formulas and its theorems: whence its universality. All of the propositions of this science denote a truth-value: whence its necessity. These three types of problems, which cannot be solved in a formalist conception, reveal *a contrario* the triple role of a simultaneous construction of names and references: *cognitive*, insofar as the mathematician's intuition rests on the existence of a content of thought; *demonstrative*, insofar as the expansion of axioms rests on bringing out the identity of references; and *foundational*, insofar as it would have been impossible to found the universal applicability of arithmetic if the signs were not backed up by denotations, if the propositions were not backed up by truth.

Thus, the superior principle of definitions holds first as an a priori requirement imposed on the entire system. But it must be accompanied by *rules* guaranteeing the requested correspondence between correct construction and denotation. These rules are in turn of two sorts. It must be proved that once denoting simple names are available, they can be used in a construction that will form new denoting names. These rules pertain to what could be called the *formal* derivation of denotations. But it must also be proved that there are denoting simple names. This belongs to the equivalent of Kant's *transcendental* deduction. Formal derivation is undertaken by Frege in paragraph 29 of the *Grundgesetze*. It consists in stating the rules of formation of well-formed expressions from previously derived expressions, and simultaneously in giving the proof that the new expression has an interpretation: either it denotes a truth-value or it enters into the expression of a truth-value. There are in fact two procedures for introducing a denoting expression. Names of denoting functions can be obtained from proper names already recognized as denoting. It is enough in this case to saturate the functional expression to be tested by means of denoting proper names. If the proper name obtained in turn denotes in each case, then the functional expression has itself a denotation. This "first approach" consists in proceding from the denotation of the argument and that of the complete proposition to the denotation of the functional part. The predicate is thus constructed by means of saturated denotations, that is, by anticipated saturation.

A "second approach" consists, on the contrary, in acquiring names of denoting functions by desaturation of compounded proper names. An argument place in which a constant occurred is thus spared. But, just as one can use a proper name either for saturating a name of function to be tested or as the crucible of a function-expression obtained by eliminating a constituent of a proper name, likewise one can combine these procedures to construct reciprocally denoting proper names from denoting names of function. Whether the function, saturated by the proper name to be tested, gives a denoting proper name again, or whether it is taken as the argument of a second-order function to be tested, the latter will be denoting if the whole into which it enters is still denoting. Thus these rules make conceptual notation an *effective* procedure of construction on the condition that one follows the clauses governing the connection between the various constituents, and in particular on the condition that one notes the specificity of the argument place markers with Gothic or Latin letters (indicating the bound variables or the free variables), and that one does not confuse the function-expression with the names of objects.

It remains to be proved, that there are denoting simple expressions, which can serve as *Bausteine*; that is, one must rest formal derivation on a transcendental deduction. This is what Frege does: after expounding the principle of the compositionality of denotations, along with the corresponding rules in paragraph 29, he sets about to derive the semantic content of the basic vocabulary in paragraph 31. What remains to be done is to show that the preceding rules apply *also* to *elementary function*-names on which the system is built. The foundation stones of the building, as the condition of possibility of all future semantic derivation, are asserted and not demonstrated:

> We start from the fact that the names of truth-values denote something, namely, either the True or the False. (*G*, I, §31, 48; trans. Furth, 86)

The True and the False are thus the two objects that make up the referential base of the system. The second step is taken by testing the function $-\xi$ and its complement $\rightarrow\xi$. For if the basic objects are taken as value of argument of these two functions, it is clear that the result is each time definite: it is one of the two truth-values. The two functional expressions are therefore denoting. The same operation is repeated afterward for function-names of condition, of equality (by again taking truth-values as arguments), and of generality. Finally, Frege turns to the "less simple" problem of the semantic derivation of the expression of course of values "$\acute{\epsilon}\, \varphi\, (\epsilon)$":

> The matter is less simple with "$\acute{\epsilon}\, \varphi\, (\epsilon)$"; for with this we are introducing not merely a new function-name, but simultaneously answering to every name of a first-level function of one argument, a new proper name (course-of-values-name); in fact not just for those (function-names) known already, but in advance for all such that may be introduced in the future. (*G*, I, §31, 49; trans. Furth, 88)

We know how crucial the deduction of this object is for Frege's purpose, since the definition of number implies that the denotation of this expression is established. Frege splits the difficulty into two stages. First, it must be proved that a "true course-of-values-name," taken as argument of function-expressions already known to be denoting, $-\xi$ and $\rightarrow\xi$, yields again a denoting proper name. Then, placed in argument position for functions of condition and of equality already tested, it forms with each of them a first-level function-name of one argument—a crucial deduction, but one which is the Achilles' heel of the system. For although the inference:

> [$f(x)$ denoting well-formed expression $\Rightarrow \acute{\epsilon}f\,(\epsilon)$ denoting well-formed proper name]

is valid in most cases, it ceases to be valid when the course of value is taken itself as argument of the function that served in its construction. This procedure, named "impredicative" by Russell, is considered by Frege, at the time of the writing of the first volume of the *Grundegesetze*, to be guaranteed by its conformity with the general rules of semantic derivation presented previously; it is, nevertheless, obvious that these rules and not merely the object "course of values" demand revision.[14]

The existence of this deduction of denotations allows Frege to justify what makes the definitions of the system *effective*. It is not the definition as an abbreviation that accounts for this aspect, but rather the logical architecture that, with the help of the principle of compositionality of denotations, forms expressions that a priori have reference. We understand thus that there is no contradiction in exposing a stipulative theory of definition and requiring simultaneously that every definition should express a denotation. This last requisite corresponds to a general constructive principle, which holds well beyond the particular case in which definition condenses a given formulary sequence into a single sign. These remarks now make it possible to establish a second "functional ambivalence" of definition. In the preceding pages, we saw what makes definition the instrument of a finite cognitive capacity, which rests on external marks, unable to capture the totality of thoughts and their relations with unfailing precision. Now, the first principle of definition requires that definition *always* determine whether or not each object falls under the concept defined. This principle of "complete determination," which in Frege's mind "corresponds" to the more general requirement of denotation of well-formed expressions, goes beyond the finitude of our knowledge:

> Thus there must not be any object as regards which the definition leaves in doubt whether it falls under the concept; though for us men, with our defective knowledge, the question may not always be decidable. (*G*, II, §56, 69)

The effectiveness of definition that determines the descriptive, "realist" interpretation of analyticity as a "transformulary" property of the objective system of science depends on an ontological rather than strictly semantic regulating principle. The principle of complete determination requires the *Aufbauer* to model his constructions on the extensions and the functions "in themselves." True, the unconditioned application of variation remains out of our reach. What is in one's reach, on the contrary, is to adapt the status of definition in the system to its role of registering the objective organization of mathematical entities, functions, and objects. This explains Frege's objections to the mathematicians of his time in their use of definitions. We could sum them up by saying that those mathematicians did not grasp the referential scope of the analyticity of the system, and consequently they neglected three types of requirements designed to preserve it. The principle of *completeness* led Frege to refuse *conditional* definitions; the principle of *formular continuity* (with which piecemeal definitions conflict) must verify both the correction and the intrinsic organization of the denoted concept. Finally, postulate definitions cast doubt on the principle of *simplicity*. Effectiveness, continuity, and absolute legitimacy — these three features characterize precisely the formulates of the system as analytic: let us examine more closely what happens when a definition contradicts one or another of these principles.

The Incompleteness of Conditional Definitions

A definition that would only follow syntactical rules of construction would retain only a nominal scope. This is the case of Peano's "conditional" definitions, which fail to determine a denotation because they do not hold absolutely:

> Now I reject conditional definitions, which you frequently give [writes Frege to Peano] because they are incomplete, because they only state for certain cases, not for all, that the new expression is to mean the same as the explaining one. And so they miss their aim of giving a denotation to a sign. (*N*, II, 182; trans. Kaal, 114)

This refusal to use the restriction of the domain of variation of definitional functions has for its counterpart the freedom—which Frege, like Bolzano, never thought to question—to accept as false, unlike Peano (*N*,II, 192), propositions that could just as well be set aside as meaningless (*N*, I, 262). Peano may not be wrong when he considers that the quarrel with Frege concerning conditional definitions "reduces to a simple question of notation," if one adds that the question of notation is not without philosophical significance. This marks the difference between constructing a closed formal system, restricted to the treatment of a partial domain, and building up in a universal language an interpreted system, conceived as if it were modeled on an "absolute" frame of reference.

The Uncertainty of Piecemeal Definitions

In paragraph 4 of the first part of Peano's *Formulaire de mathématiques*, one reads the following definition of equality of classes:

$$a, b, \quad \in K \quad \supset : a = b. \; = . \; a \quad \supset b. \; b \quad \supset a \; (\text{Def}) \; (\text{p. 5})$$

This definition implies the existence of other domains of variation. Thus, the definition of equality must be reformulated for integers, rationals, irrationals, imaginaries, etc. "Piecemeal definition" (*stückweise Definieren*) seems thus to be the natural complement of conditional definition and to meet, in an appropriate manner, the requirements of a developing science.[15] But from Frege's point of view, the equivalence between definitions with "absolute" or "partial" frames of reference presupposes that three requisites, which one rarely sees simultaneously fulfilled, are satisfied: first, that the successive hypotheses actually exhaust the cases of possible values for the variable; second, that the areas of specification considered by each partial definition are strictly disjoint;[16] and third, that no symbol to be defined is used in the theorems as if it were defined *before* the series of specifications is completed. Yet, in the mathematician's eyes this possibility constitutes the advantage of the procedure of partial definition. Because he is sensitive to this operating and heuristic character of the symbol, Peano does not deny a "diversity of opinions" concerning what the signs denote in fact. "Monstrous assertion," comments Frege (*ein grosses Wort*): the sense must be determined from the start for science to be possible. Without a preliminary agreement concerning what the signs denote, there is no possible comprehension among mathematicians, no possible truth for the statements. Let us examine what a piecemeal definition is made of: if the first element of the series that constitutes it does not furnish a complete definition, it is not even a definition. But if this definition truly defines its object, then either of two things occurs: either it "draws the same boundaries" as the following definitions (but then the discontinuous succession of definitions compromises the *demonstrative continuity* of the systematic construction, that is, the analyticity of the system), or it does not denote the same object as the following definitions, and in this case contradicts them, although the contradiction is rarely patent, owing to the division of the explanation.[17] The formalist does not share Frege's concern, for he does not expect from his system the objective determination the logician expects. For the latter, building up the system presupposes that analyticity is established as near as possible to the "organic" constitution of mathematical beings: it admits of no compromise, of no constructional artifact.

"Postulate-Definitions"

The third principle, called the "principle of simplicity," is typically transgressed by the formalists. This principle asserts:

> The name defined must be simple; that is, it may not be composed of any familiar names or names that are yet to be defined; for otherwise it would remain in doubt whether the definitions of the names were consistent with one another." (*G*, I, §33, 51; trans. Furth, 90–91)[18]

A definition for Frege must appear as an equation of one unknown accompanied by its solution: one should no longer have to demonstrate the existence or uniqueness of the solution, since the rules of construction of denoting formulas already guarantee them. But the function of *indication* (*Andeutung*) should not be misunderstood: its role is to represent concepts or objects, not to determine them. We already know the rules of representation: if the *definiendum* is an expression of function, (at least) one argument place must be left open in the expression of the *definiens*; if a proper name is concerned, the Latin letter appears in the definition with the purpose of representing the proper name. As long as the replacement of this indication by a denoting proper name has not been carried out, the definitional equation has, properly speaking, no sense, but it is the schema of a possible true thought. It is completely different if, in the formalist spirit, the indication that the symbol ensures has for its function to circumscribe a *range* within which the sense of the defined expression should be located. Thus, in Hilbert's procedure, the axioms are considered as so many characters that concur to define the primitive notions: this definition, named "implicit," following Gergonne's term,[19] consists in stating the relations or the essential properties of the object to be defined. As it is the totality of axioms that compose the Hilbertian "definition," the objection pertaining to piecemealing applies here. But another reason for refusing to give definitional value to this procedure has to do with the absence of referential determination: instead of *fixing a denotation*, this procedure allows what is in question to be guessed and admits of an infinite number of solutions.[20] Finally, for Frege the axioms are noncontradictory because they are true; to carry out Hilbertian definition presupposes that one reverses this relation. To make truth a result, for Frege, is to prevent oneself from ever reading it: it is the truth of axioms that founds *a parte ante* the possibility itself of the system; this truth gives its full sense to the requirement of analyticity. There is no blind definitional procedure.

Let us sum up the points established.

1. Considered from the point of view of the system, definition is a simple *stipulation* that summarizes a construction of concepts or extensions by a sign taken to be identical in sense and denotation with the complex expression. The syntax of definition perfectly preserves the *continuity* of the construction. No jump is made, which makes definition definitely eliminable. In other words, the substitution of the *definiens* for the *definiendum* is always possible.

2. This syntactical continuity cannot, however, suffice. It rests on a semantic deduction of the "building blocks" of the systematic construction, so that one can ascertain a priori the denotation of a definition by subjecting it to the three requirements of completeness, univocity, and simplicity.

3. If the definition is effective in the system, it is because it remains always subordinated to antecedent truths, whose recognition is independent of definition. This means that definition is noncreative. It must not make possible a deduction that would be impossible without it. Conversely, no demonstration needs to be necessary for justifying the occurrence of a definition, which does not mean that all philosophical (that is, epistemological) or, better still, presystematic legitimation should also be banished. Discourse concerning definition constitutes, on the contrary, the connection between the formal, intrasystematic construction and the presystematic, "intuitive" grasp of objects and concepts. In discourse the decomposing process of the first stage of research is reconciled with the construction proper. But one must keep in mind that such a discourse is on the border between logic and epistemology, understood as "psychology" of knowledge.

3

Objectual Identity and Analyticity of the System

To understand the mutation that Frege subjects definition to, one must clarify the relation joining the *definiens* to the *definiendum*. Frege asserts that this relation does not reduce to a simple *equivalence*, but expresses a genuine *identity*, conceived as the coincidence of an object with itself. Such an interpretation of identity ensures the possibility of a reduction understood as bringing out the logical essence of arithmetic, and consequently is closely dependent, from the topical point of view, on the value of analyticity as a systematic mortar. If the purpose of the reduction had been more modest, other solutions could have been chosen. Frege could have distinguished, like Russell and Peano, the equal sign of definition from the equal sign that appears in mathematical equations. But then it would have been necessary to give up the "recognition" of identity that arises in "good" definitions, and only see there an arbitrary stipulation, which is what Russell does in a letter in which he answers Frege on this issue.[21] If we keep in mind the restrictions Frege imposes on definition, we understand that the only possibility open to him was to call on the undefinability of identity. To recognize that the identity of definition constitutes a case different from that of identities of the theory would lead us to choose between two possibilities equally inadmissible for Frege: either to admit the constitutional equivocity of the equal sign—which Peano, on the contrary, can accept without difficulty, since he is not concerned with securing his construction on an objective frame of reference; or to undermine the descriptive claims of the system, by declaring that the system is purely arbitrary; but if the system ceases to have the property of an organic development and begins to resemble the discontinuous product of a *technè*, it also loses any foundational interest. To characterize the manner in which Frege conceives the relation between the elements of the system, one must recall the contrast made by Trendelenburg in his *Logical Investigations*:

In the organic realm everything is development (*Entwicklung*), only in craftsman's work is there juxtaposition [*Zusammensetzung*]. (*Logische Untersuchungen* [Berlin, 1840], II, 71)

The system is either organic or it is not. Analyticity loses all its effectiveness if it is established by a mechanical composition, that is, by means of *contrivances* of construction. Fregean identity is thus linked with the hypothesis of analyticity in that it must succeed in canceling any distinction—disastrous for a project whose reductionism is of a realistic inspiration—between *metalinguistic* identity, which asserts equivalences between formulations, and the *intratheoretical* identity, which governs numerical equalities, for example. We know how Frege manages to adapt identity to this double role so as to justify a homogeneous treatment to the equal sign. He has the function duality ensured, not by a distinction between specific relations of identity, but by a distinction bearing on the fundamental dimensions of any sign. Each name has a *sense* and a *denotation*. A "metalinguistic" identity is not a particular category of *Gleichheit* but a relation of equality between names appearing within quotation marks. It is the usual sense of these names then that is denoted. Conversely, an "introtheoretical" identity asserts simply the coincidence of denotation between two expressions whose sense can be different. There is therefore only *one* identity, of "absolute" or "objectual"[22] scope, since it expresses the complete coincidence of denotation between the signs to the right and those to the left of the equal sign. It is precisely the univocity of identity understood in this way that founds the *descriptive* value of the system and removes the suspicions of contrivance that could throw some uncertainty on the value of the reconstruction.

But identity occurs for yet another reason in Frege's use of analyticity as a metasystematic concept. With the distinction between the sense and the denotation of a sign, Frege *shifts* the Kantian criterion of analyticity—and its correlate, syntheticity: "an increase in knowledge" ceases to constitute the specificity of the synthetic and is now interpreted as the passage from one *sense* to another, without anticipating the nature (analytic or synthetic) of this passage. A more precise investigation into the conditions of discovery of the identity of denotation is necessary for us to decide on the nature of the identity in question. If the truth of an identical judgment can be demonstrated a priori from only logical laws, the identity will be analytic; it will not, as such, always be given with immediate obviousness in nontrivial cases in which the sense of the two terms is different. If, on the contrary, the proof of the identity of denotation requires resorting to observation, the identity will be synthetic. Thus, the *epistemological* difference that in Kant played the role of a fundamental criterion of the analyticity and the syntheticity of a proposition must be interpreted as a *semantic* difference. But the criterion finally retained by Frege is neither epistemological nor even semantic. It is logical or "metasystematic" (in the sense specified in Chapter 1 of this section) in that it rests on the type of demonstrative validity that founds the truth of identity.

It did not appear immediately to Frege that the contribution of identity to the success of what I have called "the hypothesis of analyticity" of arithmetic must thus be *twofold*, under the form of the semantic distinction between sense and denotation *and* under the complementary aspect of the "objectual" interpretation of the relation of identity (as coincidence of denotation between signs). We will see that the conjunction of these theses, and not, as is generally believed, the demonstration of the first among them, constitutes the radical novelty of the article "On Sense and Denotation."

The abundance of commentaries on the first page of "On Sense and Denotation" is evidence of the problem that interests us here.[23] Frege declares that he has given up the thesis he held at the time of the *Begriffsschrift*, namely, that identity is a relation "between signs of object." He thus breaks off with an "extrinsic" conception of identity, and it is on this issue that he himself sees the real conceptual revolution of the 1892 article. It is, of course, tempting to retain a completely different lesson from this article and to interpret as alone truly decisive the introduction of the henceforth classical distinction between *Sinn* and *Bedeutung*. A parallel drawn between the famous article and paragraph 8 of the *Begriffsschrift*, however, proves that it is not the distinction in question that is new, but another thesis that, in truth, transforms both the distinction as it was sketched in the *Begriffsschrift* and the status of identity.

Which "illusion" is Frege trying to dispel in the 1879 text? It is the false impression that identity, as a relation between names of the same "content," can only concern *expression* and not *thought*, so that one may ultimately dispense with it in conceptual notation. The way the problem is formulated shows that Frege seeks to conciliate a "metalinguistic" interpretation of identity with the fact that an identity judgment may "concern the thing itself," that is, not reduce to a "pure matter of form." How does he manage to dispel this "illusion"? Very clearly by the same means as those that will be used in "On Sense and Denotation." If we pass over a terminological difference, we easily find again under the terms "ways of determining a content" and "what is given," what will be distinguished later as constituting the sense or "the way in which an object is given," and the denotation. Moreover, the geometry example of 1879 announces the similar example that appears in the text of 1892: let a fixed point A lie on the circumference of a circle, and let a series of straight lines rotate around this point. Then let us call the point of intersection of each of these lines and the circumference point B. If we consider the tangent at A, point B coincides with point A. The name A and the name B thus have in this case the same "content," "and yet we could not have used only one name from the beginning since the justification for doing so is first given by our answer." The existence of two names for the same referent is thus founded on the objective difference between "ways of determining" the same object. The interpretation of the example complies completely with the subsequent distinction: the difference between ways of determining the referent—to which corresponds the difference between names—explains the cognitive value of judgments of identity and implies that they concern "the essence of thing itself.'' Here, however, the analogy between the two texts is incomplete. For, carried away by his proof concerning the objective difference between the two *Bestimmungsweisen*, Frege makes a concession to Kantianism that he will necessarily regret:

> "In this case, the judgment as to identity of content is, in Kant's sense, synthetic. (*B*, §8, 15; trans. Bynuum, 126)

This is a major concession, since it leads to giving mathematical identities the status of synthetic propositions in the same way as the propositions of geometry, as soon as their significance for knowledge is acknowledged. Does Frege not implicitly accept here that the propositions of arithmetic (whose logical and a priori character he pointed out in the preface) are in fact a priori synthetic — by substituting, more exactly, logical laws for Kant's pure intuition in the constructive role? The text of 1879 presents a transitory state of Frege's thought concerning the theoretical scope of the concept of analyticity. The use Frege makes of Kant's expression ''are not a pure matter of form'' shows that the Kantian set of problems penetrates even into a conception of logic opposed to that of Kant. We remember that for Kant logic is a ''pure matter of form.'' He deduces the barrenness of analytic judgments from this feature. It is therefore difficult to maintain, as does Frege in 1879, that the property of synthetic judgments is to convey knowledge, while trying to free logic from the blind alley of ''form indifferent to content.'' The *Grundlagen* will break with the Kantian criterion (which Frege will persist in recognizing as identical with his own, but, as we shall see, in conformity with specific topical contraints), on the one hand, by identifying the analytic-synthetic contrast with the one with which the *Begriffsschrift* opens (between propositions deducible from logical truths and truths of fact), and, on the other hand, by distinguishing in a complementary way between general laws of logic and axioms (eventually a priori, but nonlogical) of particular sciences. Only then will logic see its fruitfulness recognized. The identities will become at once and rightfully analytic and informative.

But the thesis of the syntheticity of ''cognitive'' identities has yet a second guarantee, in paragraph 8 of the *Begriffsschrift*: it is tied to the thesis of the twofold role of signs, a thesis that in turn goes along with a ''metalinguistic'' conception of identity. On this issue, ''On Sense and Denotation'' causes an upheaval essential for the destiny of the hypothesis of analyticity.

The Thesis of the ''Disappearance of Signs''

Identity is presented in 1879 as a relation between *names*. To justify this exception in conceptual notation, Frege must build without preparation a theory of the twofold use of signs, sometimes representing a content, sometimes representing themselves:

> Although symbols are usually only representatives of their contents — so

that each combination (of symbols usually) expresses only a relation between their contents—they at once appear *in propria persona* as soon as
they are combined by the symbol for identity of content. (*B*, §8, 13–14;
trans. Bynuum, 124)

If relations of identity pertain to *signs*, it is self-evident that a theory of identity must take on one or another form: either one claims an objectual scope of
identity, conceived as material coincidence, but then only two occurrences of the
same sign will be able to make up the terms of a true identity, which excludes
nontrivial identities, which are precisely the only interesting ones. This interpretation, which, for example, prevents us from understanding the fundamental fact
that ½ and 3/6 are equal, will not be retained (*KS*, 108). Another solution remains: by "identity" is understood a relation between signs that have the same
"content" (*Inhalt*). But one gives up at the same time understanding identity as
complete coincidence, since the signs on which identity bears do not *coincide*.
The discovery of identity presupposes that one examines the relation of each of
the signs with what it designates (that is, its content). But this relation is only a
perfectly contingent linguistic fact. As Frege notes in "On Sense and Denotation":

> Nobody can be forbidden to use any arbitrary producible event or object as
> a sign for something." (*KS*, 143; trans. Black, *57)*

How to understand, then, that from the same premises Frege deduces in 1892
a conclusion that seems to contradict word for word that of 1879:

> In that case the sentence $a = b$ would no longer refer to the subject
> matter, but only to its mode of designation." (Ibid.)

There is a contradiction only if it is assumed that the premises remain the
same. But in the meantime Frege gave up the thesis of metalinguistic identity. We
already know what obliges him to give it up: if identity is a relation between
signs, one must limit the scope of the construction. The system aims at arranging
a domain of meanings, but the channels toward the designated entities are cut off.
Moreover, the unicity of the object of mathematics depends on the languages
used. To restore the constructive power of "objectual" identity interpreted as a
complete coincidence, the *conception of the sign* must be modified drastically, so
as to prevent the possible reversal of the representative function of symbols, becoming themselves mathematical objects in the equalities. "On Sense and Denotation" exposes this new conception with clarity:

> If words are used in the ordinary way, what one intends to speak of is their
> reference." (*KS*, 144; trans. Black, 58)

This new thesis allows Frege to ground his whole system in "the thing itself."
The symbolic is an external preliminary to the grasping of the meanings. Its
function is to *express* a sense and to *designate* a denotation. But it is never
opaque, in the sense that a sign cannot mention itself: it is always designated by

another sign, and in this case, its sense is the denotation of this new symbol. This thesis is the indispensable ingredient of the analyticity of mathematical identities: an identity pertaining to the symbols would have required an empirical learning of meanings and would therefore have taken on a synthetic value. But if identity "cuts across" the signs and concerns an objective "state of affairs" (namely, the relation of a reference to its senses), the a priori demonstration of identity acquires a foundation *independent of speech*.

The preceding reflections allow us to bring to light the fundamental theses on which Frege builds the concept of identity:

(1) The thesis of the objectual scope of identity: identity must be understood as a complete coincidence.

(2) The thesis of the use of signs (or the thesis of the disappearance of signs): signs never occur in a proposition in order to represent themselves, but serve to designate a denotation.

(3) The thesis of the unicity of use of identity: there will be no relation of metalinguistic identity distinct from that of identity occurring in the system.

We have seen how these theses converge to make the hypothesis of analyticity possible. It remains to be understood how they inspire what could be called the "grammar of identity."

If we list the passages in which Frege introduces the concept of identity, we notice that he mentions four features. On the one hand, he takes identity to be what mathematicians conceive under the concept of equality. On the other hand, he grounds identity on an *essential property* of any *object*, that of being "*sich selbst gleich*," a relation whose strictly logical character must be revealed. But this purely logical principle should not be confused with its ontological version: every object is identical with *nothing but* itself. It is the principle of indiscernibles that sustains the latter thesis, whose strictly logical nature is debatable. Finally, Frege presents identity as a property of certain formulas of the system, and thus clarifies it from the angle of syntax: "It is actually the case that in universal substitutability all the laws of identity are contained" (*GA*, §65, 77).

Equality as Identity

The reduction of equality to identity is an essential step in the logicization of arithmetic, both to finish with the diversity of opinions that prevails in arithmetic concerning the equal sign and to prove concerning this key concept the significance of the logicist project. The transition, one may say, is sufficiently prepared by the numerous logicians who, well before Frege, accepted the coincidence between mathematical equality and logical identity. But it belongs to Frege to have gone about this reduction systematically, that is, to have conceived its primitive terms and its fundamental laws so as to make such a reduction effectual. If mathematical equality, interpreted as identity, becomes a relation general enough to apply to numbers, to the terms of a definition as well as to empirical descriptions, it is because a preliminary extension of the concept of *function* as well as the complementary easing of the notion of argument prepared the way for such a generalization.

Identity is then a function of first order, whose arguments are necessarily *objects*. An equality between functions cannot be directly constructed in conceptual notation. Nevertheless, the "corresponding" relation can easily be obtained by applying two procedures. The Basic Law V, on the one hand, justifies changing the generality of an identity between functions into an identity of course of values and, reciprocally, makes it possible to deduce the identity of the corresponding functions from the equality of the extensions. On the other hand, the possibility of reducing a second-order function to a course of values by means of the following definition

$$\vdash \backslash\dot{\alpha} \left(\begin{matrix} g \\ \hline u = \dot{\varepsilon}g(\varepsilon) \end{matrix} g(a) = \alpha \right) = \alpha \cap u$$

(G, I, §34, 53)

guarantees the duality between objects and functions of any order from the point of view of identity — or its "correlate" of order n.

That identity is a function of first order is not without consequences: this motivates in particular interpreting propositions as proper names of truth-values that must be treated semantically as *objects*. If propositions did not name objects, the relation that joins them in logical equivalence could not be assimilated with mathematical equality. Thus we see how Frege avoids the proliferation of relations of identity according to the hierarchy of functional orders. His reduction of functions of higher order to objects, by means of the arch and the concept of extension, plays the role of Russell's principle of reducibility, but by assuming, unlike the authors of the *Principia*, the existence of classes.[24]

From Reflexivity of Identity to Indiscernibility

Are there things that do not coincide and yet do not differ in any way? Certainly: those natureless things!'' (Die Zahlen des Herrn H. Schubert, *KS*, 257)

To conceive identity as the property that every object has of being identical with itself — as Frege does in the preface of the *Grundgesetze* — or as the result of "the impossibility of recognizing an object as different from itself," conveys a logical determination of identity indispensable for the purpose of logicism, mentioned also during the controversy concerning the excesses of the abstractionists.[25] But two quite different aspects of identity must be distinguished here; on the one hand, the purely logical property of reflexivity, according to which any object whatsoever is in a relation of identity with itself; on the other hand, a property that is no longer formally reducible to simple reflexivity, according to which an object is identical *with nothing but itself.*

Although the purely logical property of reflexivity is used by Frege (during the construction of the number 0), he must also, even if implicitly, call on a stronger property, stating that a thing is identical with nothing but itself, this property being, as we shall see, necessary for ensuring the descriptive determination of the system. The identity of the thing, governed by the principle of the indiscernibility of identicals, will be taken for an obvious truth that, in combination with the principle of indiscernibles, sustains all approaches to identity: the systematic approach as well as the substitutive and the operating approaches. What does the principle of the indiscernibility of identicals state?

> Sequitur etiam hinc non dari posse in natura duas res singulares solo numero differentes: utique enim opportet rationem reddi posse cur sint diversae, quae ex aliqua in ipsis differentia petenda est.[26]

This principle asserts that two things cannot be different in an exclusively numerical way (*solo numero*); they must differ by some quality or property, such that "their difference can be accounted for." It can be symbolized thus:

(1) $(\forall x)(\forall y)[(x = y) \supset (\forall \varphi)(\varphi x \equiv \varphi y)]$.

This principle can be understood only in its relation with two other of Leibniz's axioms. The theory of individual substances asserts, on the one hand, that there cannot be any extrinsic denomination of substances. All the relations in which they occur must have a foundation in their individual essence. A sufficient cognitive difference must, on the other hand, correspond to this determination of the essence. The principle of sufficient reason guarantees that the diversity between two substances can be accounted for:

(2) Si $a \neq b$, $(\exists P)(P(a) \wedge \sim P(b))$.

This second principle states the possibility of specifying the character that founds the separate existence of substances.

Nevertheless, the combination of these two theses, concerning internal relations and sufficient reason, does not yet suffice for demonstrating reciprocally the logical impossibility of the existence of two indiscernible things. It shows that different singular things have distinct predicates (at least one, which can be characterized), but not that things having the same predicate cannot coexist. As Locke writes to Clarke, such a supposition "is possible in abstract terms." A second principle must therefore be accepted, the principle of indiscernibles proper, according to which it would be incompatible with divine wisdom to create two perfectly indiscernible things—in other words, that two things that have their predicates in common are identical (and no longer, as in (1), that two things that are identical have their predicates in common:

(3) $(\forall x)(\forall y)[(\forall \varphi)(\varphi x \equiv \varphi y) \supset (x = y)]$.

The conjunction of (1) and of (3) makes it possible to obtain an equivalence, called "Leibniz's law":

(4) $(\forall x)(\forall y)[(x = y) \equiv (\forall \varphi)(\varphi x \equiv \varphi y)]$.

This law, based as we saw on the assumption of a wise and thrifty God, acquires in the characteristic system an essential function: that of guaranteeing the *real scope* of the characteristic. Like Frege, Leibniz expects that his notation will suitably describe the universe. The principle of continuity combined with Leibniz's law founds the correspondence between the formulary constructions and the universe, ensuring for infinitesimal calculus, for example, a physical application. Frege too uses implicitly the principle of indiscernibles to ensure acknowledgment of the *unicity of denotation* between expressions of different sense. Without such a principle, nothing authorizes our asserting that the evening star is identical with the morning star. For even a set of common properties, verified for the former and the latter, could not justify our inferring the existence of a single object having these properties. The principle of indiscernibles therefore functions ultimately as an organizing principle of the cosmos and of possible knowledge of it. It replaces a principle of the synthetic unity of apperception. In Frege, the principle of indiscernibles founds a possible knowledge as *a determined relation of predicates with an object.*[27] Whereas in Kant the identity of an *act* founds the identity of the object of knowledge under the diversity of representations, in Frege the identity of denotation is guaranteed by a thesis that remains implicit: "Every object is identical with nothing but itself."

We can understand now how this principle adds a complement to the requisites of the first two "theses concerning identity" presented earlier. Identity can be conceived as a complete coincidence; the signs can denote a specific entity *only* if one has at one's disposal a principle of identification of the object of knowledge. The principle thus makes it possible to designate as *the* object of an investigation the class of equivalence of its own *Bestimmungsweisen.* Without it, "what a chaos of numbers we should have!" (*N*, II, 195). There would not be, for example, a single number that could be characterized as "the first prime number after 5, but infinitely many: 7, 8 − 1, (8 + 6)/2, etc." The justification of the use of the definite article thus has its foundation in Leibniz's law. This means that the comprehension of identity as "identity of an object with itself and itself alone" plays first of all the role of condition of possibility of the conceptual notation as a scientific instrument, as likewise the objective realm of sense plays the role of condition of possibility of a thought and communication in general.

Identity as "Substitutability without Restriction"

The substitutive approach to identity occurs in the texts of Frege sometimes as an "explanation," a "definition," or a "principle expressing the essence" of identity, sometimes as the consequence of the logical principle of the identity of an object with itself. Thus Frege first asserts that he takes up Leibniz's "definition" of identity (*GA*, §65, 76– 77). However, the legitimacy of substitutions is presented in 1903 as depending on the unicity of denotation between two expressions (*G*, II, §104, 111). This change should be associated with the objections Husserl raises in his *Philosophie der Arithmetik* against Frege's presentation of identity.

In his review of Husserl's book, Frege begins to retract his thesis of the "explanation" of identity, as this confused account evidences:

> I agree with the author that Leibniz's explanation *eadem sunt quorum unum potest substitui alteri salva veritate* does not deserve to be called a definition; my reasons, however, are different. . . . This explanation of Leibniz's could be called an axiom that brings out the nature of the relation of identity (*Gleichheit*); as such, it is fundamentally important. (*KS*, 180; trans. Jourdain and Stachelroth, 80–81)

It seems at first that faithfulness to Leibniz does not in the least require considering his formula of substitutivity as a *definition* of identity. Another Leibnizian formula, *omnis autem substitutio nascitur ex aequipollentia quadam*, makes it possible to interpret substitution as a rule of the use of signs derived from the axiom of identity properly so called.[28] In the second place, whether it goes back to Leibniz or is due to Frege, the intention of defining identity by the substitutability does not seem to escape the vicious circle that Husserl points out. Let us assume that we have demonstrated the substitutability *salva veritate* of two contents. It is still legitimate to ask the question *quid juris*; what makes it possible to substitute one content for another in some or in all true judgments? For Husserl, the answer is obvious: it is the identity of contents that founds their substitutability and not the opposite. But this identity of content requires an intensional criterion stronger than mere equivalence, namely, an identical composition of identical characters, in agreement with Bolzano's criterion of propositional identity. Husserl's criticism deepens further the analysis, by showing that any *application* of a substitution leads us inevitably to acknowledge an identity:

> If the foundation of the knowledge of equality of two contents lay in interchangeability, it would be necessary in each case to place our recognition of interchangeability before that of equality. But the latter act does not itself consist of no other than a certain number, even an infinite number of acts each of which implies acknowledgment of an identity, that is of the equality of a true judgment which refers to the first content, and of the "same" judgment which refers to the second content. But, to acknowledge all these equalities, one will need knowledge of what, relative to each of these pairs of judgments, holds as the "same" true judgments, etc.[29]

This relevant objection according to which the definition of identity by substitutivity contains a vicious circle deserves more than the contemptuous reply given by Frege. For if there is a Fregean way out of the circle, it does not avoid new difficulties. Frege has a retort to Husserl's objection, which explicitly rests on an atomistic theory of sense: "Equal characters taken one by one are what found the equality of judgments, and not the same judgments that found the identity of characters."

Frege starts from the opposite hypothesis: "Only in composition do words mean something." Husserl's objection then loses all its force: it is the comparison of the *true instances* of judgments in which the constituents to be tested occur that provide the criterion of their identity, and not the *intensional* examination of the identity of content of these judgments. Consequently, substitution can account for identity, as a property of the substitutable, because substitution requires only correlating each proposition with the truth-value it *names*. But by giving this answer to Husserl's objection, Frege is, as we shall see, faced with the new difficulty of preserving an intensional acceptation for his logic.

Extensional Identity and Identity "of the Content"

Frege's reply to Husserl raises a new doubt. If one takes identity as the property of the "substitutable *salva veritate*," has one not simply defined a purely extensional criterion of equivalence, in itself insufficient for determining the coincidence of content that pertains to an intensional criterion? The fact that sense represents here, in a way, a "supplement," following Frege's expression, is not in itself problematic. It is the natural consequence of the interpretation of identity as a relation between denotations, whose cognitive value arises precisely from the difference between the *sense* of proper names. However, the attribution of a strictly referential domain to identity leaves pending the question of what constitutes for the senses (*Sinne*, the meanings) the property of being "the same" or "identical with one another."

So that the solution of this problem is independent of extensional coincidence, Bolzano distinguished two relations: *equivalence* is the relation that joins interchangeable constituents *salva veritate*. But identity of sense holds only between *expressions* that designate the same constituent. Synonymy therefore calls on a stronger criterion than equivalence. Unlike the latter, it applies to statements (and not to "propositions in themselves"). Thus ultimately it is the concept of "proposition in itself" that, in Bolzano's logic, makes it possible to clarify what the synonymous statements have in common. In Frege's philosophy, thought acquires a comparable function. It is the content that "is recognizably the same in the translation too" (N, I, 222; 206). However, unlike Bolzano, Frege does not directly infer the semantic structure, that is, thought, from the structure of the statement. By refusing propositional congruency (*Satz* in Frege's works means "statement") as a criterion of synonymy, he must produce an objective criterion for the identity of thoughts, so that "we are given free rein to pursue proper logical analyses" (*N*, II, 102). The letter to Husserl on November 1, 1906, represents a first stage of this investigation of the logical objectification of thought. Frege mentions the latter as that which a "standard proposition," representing "a system of equipollent propositions" (although different on account of style or coloration), expresses as essential from the logical angle. The letter of December 9 of the same year again takes up the question with the intention of producing a more precise criterion. Leaving aside propositions that contain "a logically self-evident constituent," Frege suggests the following criterion: two propositions A and B express the same thought if one cannot be taken to be true and the other false — and reciprocally — without yielding a logical contradiction (detectable solely by means of logical laws). But the strict application of the criterion leads us to consider as "the same thought" commutative statements such as "3 + 4" and "4 + 3," which Frege actually wishes to consider as distinct in sense (KS, 226). Moreover, the restriction bearing on the "logically self-evident constituents" renders the concept designated to serve as the cornerstone of logical exercise barely effectual. Extended to logical objects, the criterion would result in confusing all the theses of propositional calculus as having the same sense (since one cannot be denied without the others being contradicted), a result Ajdukiewicz will later oppose to the theory of sense of Carnap's *Logical Syntax*. Probably aware of these difficulties, Frege modifies slightly the criterion in a text of the same year. Two propositions express the same thought if A cannot be acknowledged as true without *acknowledging immediately* the truth of B, and reciprocally (N, I, 213). As the previous one, this new formulation excludes from the outset the case of propositions containing logical constituents, which would make acknowledging the truth of A or B trivial. What this second criterion brings to the fore does not seem enough to make it an "objective" criterion. Assuredly, reference to the "immediate acknowledgment" of truth, which replaces setting up "purely logical" laws, has the advantage of restricting the field of propositions that will hold as synonyms.[30] But it seems that this "acknowledgment" depends in turn on the prior grasp of the sense. An immediate acknowledgment would be possible in the case in which the sense of judgment A accounts for the proper formulation of judgment B. For example, commutativity is part of the sense of the operator of composition, so that "A and B" is immediately acknowledged as equivalent to "B and A." It is this last criterion that is mentioned in one of the later articles called "Gedankengefüge." In contradiction of certain earlier texts,[31] Frege defends here the synonymy of the following pairs of propositions:

"A and B" *and* "B and A."
"Not [(not A) and (not B)]" *and* "A or B."
"If B, then A" *and* "not (not A and B)."

The transition from the first of each of these propositions to the second is *analytic* in a sense slightly different from the one that was formerly understood by this concept. Logical laws are not, properly speaking, what justify deriving the second formula but simply "awareness of the sense" of the operators. Both notations are equivalent here in the intensional sense, the differences being simply a matter of style or lighting. It remains to know whether the intensional *identity* of "A" and "not not A" can be convincingly defended. By retaining as "thought" only what is logically relevant, Frege bars the possibility of explaining the particular cognitive effect of propositions of the kind:

$(A \wedge B) = [(A \vee B)$ and not $(B \supset \text{not } A)]$.

On account of this, a good part of logical activity takes place in what Frege would call the "accessory." This difficult quest for a criterion of the identity of thought shows that the interpretation of identity, as indissociably an intensional relation of coincidence and an extensional property of what can be substituted *salva veritate*, can only partially correspond to the practice of the system. We saw that the "objectual" interpretation is indispensable for the *Aufbau* to be at the same time a construction *and* a description. What is defined (the number 1, for example) must be the only object to which the numerical expressions 1^2, $1/1$, cos 0, etc.) refer. But in fact nothing prevents conceiving the system as a calculus progressing only by equivalences, without granting the freedom of identifying objects. It is sufficient to give up identity in order to improve, so to speak, the system. But we saw that the logical matter itself, thought, is taken in the objectual interpretation of the result of equivalences.

4

On the Status of Axioms: Analyticity in Germ

Until now we have examined the means Frege has allowed himself in order to found the *expansion* of the fundamental truths of logic into the system of arithmetic. We have seen how his conceptual notation lends itself to a genuine logical practice while remaining regulated by the general requirement of denotation. We must now consider what forms the starting point of the system, namely, the set of truths the calculus has for its goals to develop in its deductive consequences. It would be a mistake to interpret these axioms as a set of arbitrary hypotheses for future manipulations, in the sense in which the formalists use them. The axioms are, for Frege, the authority that confers on the system its *truth*; with them originates the referential value of the system as a whole. This truth must then be "diffused" over all the propositions deducible from the axioms, provided the requisite of *Lückenlosigkeit* is strictly respected. The purely formal truth of the consequences is accompanied by a truth in a way "material," namely, that of the fundamental logical properties and relations registered in the *Grundgesetze*. These are *given* truths, without which the project of building a system would be not only doomed to failure, but entirely impossible. The value of the system lies in its being firmly set in the primitive body of "absolutely" true propositions.

This characteristic of axioms as a preliminary "given" of analyticity incites us, of course, to return to the Kantian definition of analytic judgment. As the analytic proposition, for Kant, is restricted to developing in the predicate a character already given in the concept of subject, likewise analytic truths, for Frege, are propositions derivable from *given true principles*, namely, the fundamental logical laws.[32] On the basis of this analogy, we could be tempted to infer that Frege takes up the Kantian conception of analyticity.

Three sorts of arguments seem to justify this comparison. In the first place, Frege himself appeals to the Kantian distinction: he "does not mean to assign a new sense to these terms" of analytic and synthetic, "but only to state accurately what earlier writers, Kant in particular, have meant by them'' (*GA*, §3, 3n). In the second place, one should be sensitive to the "cognitive" characteristic of Frege's axioms: they are unprovable propositions, guaranteed by their *obviousness*. Finally, one remarks that Frege, curiously enough, remained silent concerning a question that seems unavoidable: why and by what right are the laws of logic granted as true? Does Frege's silence not constitute the tacit proof that he takes up the Kantian solution? These three sorts of arguments lead us to place Frege's logicism within the sphere of Kantian epistemology—a very "psychological" epistemology (in the usual sense of the term),[33] since the demonstrative authority is supposed to be founded on the exhibition of processes of inference viewed as producing *belief*. Thus inquiry bearing on the "given" truth of the axioms leads one finally to express one's opinion concerning the distinction Kant and Frege draw between analytic and synthetic propositions. A "cognitive" reading suggests that Frege does not at all intend to innovate with respect to the Kantian conception, but only wishes to complete it in places where it appears insufficient.[34]

We see how this interpretation conditions comprehension of analyticity as an expression of the organicity of the system of arithmetic. Is Frege simply a Kantian logician who would have perceived better than Kant a possible extension of the sphere of analytic propositions until it encloses a whole portion of the synthetic a priori? Or should one understand his concepts in a completely different way and mark ruptures where Frege does not detect any? Three questions should enable us to clear up this problem. First, should the logical axioms be conceived according to the Kantian schema, namely, as a type of privileged knowledge owing to the *cognitive source* that produced them? Second, is the logicist enterprise "above all" epistemological? Finally, is the distinction between analytic and synthetic propositions, developed by Frege, an appendix to the Kantian distinction? The meaning to be assigned to Frege's reduction of arithmetic to logic depends on one's answer to these three interdependent questions. A positive answer to all three questions would imply that Fregean logicism must be interpreted as the attempt to refer the whole of arithmetic, and even the whole of mathematics, to an understanding that produces rules. The foundation of mathematics is then to be understood in the framework of transcendental philosophy. If, on the contrary, one answers these questions negatively, logicism appears as a novel theoretical requirement, which it will be our task to determine.

The Axioms of Logic and the Source of Knowledge

We recall the essential role played by the axioms of logic in defining analytic truths. Let us quote more fully the relevant passage of the *Grundlagen* in order to emphasize the division, drawn there, between two types of axioms:

> If . . . we come only on general logical laws and on definitions, then the truth is an analytic one, bearing in mind that we must take account also of

all propositions upon which the admissibility of any of the definitions depends. If however, it is impossible to give the proof without making use of
truths that are not of a general logical nature, *but belong to the sphere of
some special science*, then the proposition is a synthetic one. For a truth to
be *a posteriori*, it must be impossible to construct a proof of it without including an appeal to facts, i.e., to truths which *cannot be proved* and *are
not general*, since they contain assertions about *particular objects*. But if,
on the contrary, its proof can be derived exclusively from general laws,
which themselves neither need nor admit of proof, then the truth is *a
priori*. (*GA*, §3, 4, trans. Austin)

The difficulty of this text lies in the conjunction of two criteria that seem to
coincide perfectly. An analytic truth being necessarily a priori, the temptation is
strong to consider all synthetic judgments as a posteriori. But as closer scrutiny
reveals, this coincidence is illusory: the contrast between a priori truths and a
posteriori truths is established through the notion of *demonstration*. A posteriori
truths "cannot be proved" in that they cannot be reduced to axioms (to "general
laws, which themselves neither need nor admit of proof"). The error here would
be to identify too quickly these axioms with the logical laws proper. We know
that Frege accepts with Kant the synthetic a priori nature of the truths of geometry. These are propositions endowed with "generality," which can be proved
from given axioms (by a priori intuition of space). On the other hand, the analytic-synthetic contrast brings in a division *within the provable*. This distinction
requires only that analytic truths be derivable from general axioms, but that the
axioms from which they are derivable be propositions of "a general logical
nature" and not axioms "belonging to the sphere of some special science." Thus
at this stage of Frege's thought, geometry is classed among the special sciences.

The two distinctions (analytic-synthetic and a priori-a posteriori) rest on two
very different concepts of *generality*, which necessarily creates confusion. There
is, on the one hand, the "relative" generality of the axioms of geometry, whose
principles are general in that they do not concern "definite objects." They form
a transcendental framework for every object position in space. Nevertheless, they
lack "absolute" generality to the extent that they hold only in a *particular* area.
The axioms of geometry are necessary only as regards conceiving a spatial or a
physical object. But they do not cover the whole field of the thinkable by their
determinations. Thus, these synthetic axioms are quite *general* in the sense that
they are transcendental truths, but they are also *definite* truths to the extent that
they are not *universal conditions of thought in general*, which is exclusively the
case of logical truths. The correct distinction between analytic and synthetic
truths presupposes then that it is possible to discriminate the logical laws from the
axioms of the special sciences. Logical truths have in the definition of analyticity
a highly privileged position: independent of any deductive process since they do
not need to be proved (and actually could not be, insofar as they are, in a sense to
be qualified, "irreducible"), they also do not await any legitimation from the

fruitfulness of the deductions they make possible. Attentive to this privileged position of the axioms, commentators have been surprised to observe that Frege did not seek at all to derive this privilege from any *origin*, in a genealogy that would take on the value of a legitimation:

> The question why and with what right we acknowledge a law of logic to be true, logic can answer only by reducing it to another law of logic. Where that is not possible, logic can give no answer. (*GI*, XVIII, trans. Furth, 15)

Should one see in this sentence an "avowal of inability," as Michael Resnik suggests? Or does this sentence actually state Frege's answer to the question of the foundation of the legitimacy of logic? What does Frege say? Only by *departing from logic* can we answer the question: what makes a logical axiom true? If we *accept* this question, we are inevitably led to call on a feeling of obviousness. This means that in abstaining from answering this question Frege is motivated by a strict observance of the concept of *limit of logic*:

> I shall neither dispute nor support this view; I shall merely remark that what we have here is not a logical consequence. (Ibid.)

To the extent that an appeal to obviousness, or any mental constraint imposing acknowledgment, can concern only the reason of holding-for-true (*Fürwahrhalten*) and not that of the *truth* of axioms, a "justification" of this type would be empirical; that is, it would be confined to putting forth propositions of fact without "generality." It follows from this that it cannot be *on account of their evidence* that the axioms are true. A psychological reason actually can be criticized by an anthropological reasoning: at this level of analysis, nothing prevents imagining that another being, differently constituted, would reject what appears obvious to us. However, by discrediting the obviousness of any founding status, Frege does not intend to deny himself the value of *symptom* that belongs to it. Obviousness is evidence for the existence of true logical axioms. Assuredly, nothing prevents imagining a being who would be insensitive to obviousness as we perceive it. *But* it is impossible for us to deny the truth of these logical laws once we have acknowledged it. Acknowledgment of the law "prevents us from doubting which of the two, the law or us, is right" (*G.*, Einleitung). In other words, the necessity of the law appears in the apodictic nature of the judgment by which we assert its truth. Because the law is *objectively* true, contrary to the suggestions of the skeptics inclined to see in it only the effect of a habit of thought, we are unable to conceive what a thought that could free itself from it would be like. The objective nature of the law, which makes it a *description of the being-true*, explains its *prescriptive* and *universal* nature (*wo immer, wann immer und von wem immer geurteilt werden mag*).

The law functions then as a *condition of possibility*, not only of judgment, but of holding-for-true, of thinking and of deduction. It is consequently excluded that *judgment* could account for what makes a proposition an axiom. This act of judgment is secondary to the set of logical laws that found its legitimacy and authorize its development. Judgment consists in the transition from a thought (antecedently "grasped") to its denotation.[35] But the fact that a definite thought has a certain truth-value is not the *product* of judgment. It is an objective property of thought: "So with every property of a thing there is tied up a property of a thought, namely truth" (*Der Gedanke, KS*, 345; trans. Geach and Stoothoff, 6)..

What holds for all true thoughts holds also for these universally (and a priori) true thoughts that are the axioms of logic. It appears then that the quest for the "sources of knowledge" of the axioms cannot cast any light on the logical cornerstones of thought.

What Makes a Proposition an Axiom?

The question of the distinctive characters of logical axioms must be reformulated in nonpsychologistic terms: what entitles a proposition to be an axiom, and what distinguishes intrinsically a logical axiom from a "special" one (understanding thereby an axiom of a particular science)? Axioms are truths that *cannot* be proved. Frege develops a conception of the axiom different from that of Leibniz, in whose eyes the axioms must *prove* their truth by reduction to the principle of identity. This conception differs also from that of Kant, for whom the axioms get their validity from the obviousness inherent in construction in a pure intuition (but then mathematical or physical axioms are concerned; logic, precisely because it is not developed in intuition, only comprises rules). For Frege, the axioms *cannot* be demonstrated because they are the *constitutive authority* of the very idea of demonstration (in the case of logical laws) or the irreducible truths constitutive of a definite object of science (in the case of particular sciences). But they also *should not* be given a proof. Axiomatic truths generally do not need to be proved. What constitutes this self-sufficiency of axioms, which makes them the incipient germs of the system? If the axioms can be said to be true without resorting to their deductive consequences, it is because they have a particular structure whereby their *presentation* can coincide with the *acknowledgment* of their truth. This is the argument Frege opposes to the formalistic comprehension of axioms:

> So long as I understand the words "straight line," "parallel," and "intersect," as I do, I cannot but accept the parallel axiom. If someone else does not accept it, I can only assume that he understands these words differently. Their sense is indissolubly bound up with the axiom of parallels. (*N*, I, 266; trans. Long and White, 247)

The last sentence of this quotation dispels a confusion possibly created by the first. It is not the *isolated* comprehension of the expressions "point," "straight line," "parallel," and so on, that imposes acknowledgment of the axiom. But, on the contrary, in agreement with the second principle of the *Grundlagen*, it is in the context of the axiom that the constituents find their "essential" use. Thus, the truth of the axioms can be understood only in this realistic philosophy of propositional sense. The axiom is true because it exhibits an objective relation between a function (understood as *that which is denoted* by the functional expression) and the objects constructed as extensions of concepts. The obviousness of the truth of the axiom is thus only an effect of this "essential occurrence" of the constituent in its determining context. We will note here that if, in the order of *acknowledgment*, one passes from the sense of the constituents, given in the context of the axiom, to the denotation of the latter, in the order of *being*, it is the objective relation between denotations that founds the truth of the axiom.

Consequently, what legitimates in Frege's eyes the potential fruitfulness of fundamental truths is not their "obviousness" but their "determining" nature, that is, the property of circumscribing the essence of the object of science. What entitles a truth to hold as an axiom is thus not of the same nature as a "criterion." As the order of knowing is always second relative to the order of being, nothing guarantees that our construction of the axiom, the relation we discover between its constituents, actually corresponds to the objective state of the relations sought. A constituent considered simple can subsequently prove to be reducible. Moreover, when one comes up against simple constituents, one comes up against the limits of language. Being unable to reduce, one also cannot *define* the constituents of the axioms. A procedure of substitution can be used, but it is not part of the system. "Elucidation" (*Erläuterung*) belongs only to the pedagogy of the system. It is doubly informal since it uses ordinary language to "point to" (*winken*) the denotations of simple constituents and since it remains in general implicit, resting on the reader's ability to catch on. These obstacles to bringing out what would be the *criterion* of axioms, and which are a result of their general function as conditions of possibility, explain the occasional reappearance of the vocabulary of the "sources of knowledge" in Frege's texts. The epistemological distinction between types of knowledge, specified by their relation with intuition, with reason, or with the senses, makes it possible to characterize positively not only what allows us to acknowledge the truths of axioms of logic but also what distinguishes the axioms of logic from those of geometry.

Are the sparse remarks concerning the epistemological characterization of axioms in Frege's works enough to cast doubt on the realistic interpretation being defended here? A more careful analysis seems to prove the contrary. First, the texts called on in favor of an essentially epistemological approach to axioms reduce to two. The first text is a letter to Hilbert of December 27, 1899, in which the passage concerning our problem is contained in one sentence:

> I call axioms propositions that are true but are not proved because our knowledge of them flows from a source very different from the logical source, a source which might be called spatial intuition. (*N*, II, 48; trans. Kaal, 37)

We find this "logical source" mentioned again only twenty-five years later, in a text that belongs to Frege's postlogicist period. Are these two texts capable of threatening the doctrine exposed in the preface of the *Grundgesetze*? The letter to

Hilbert must be placed in the context of the controversy opposing Frege and Hilbert concerning the nature of axioms. Concerned with showing that it is the truth of axioms that entitles them to hold as principles, Frege takes up an argument that is undeniably of a Kantian type. Nevertheless, this reference to Kant pertains to an elliptical argumentation that does not allow us to infer that Frege presents his "theory" of axioms here. As for the text of 1925, the occurrence of sources of knowledge must clearly be referred to its goal. Frege aims first of all in this text to explain why Russell's contradiction was able to ruin his construction, even though the basic laws should have presented the conditions of all rational thought and therefore be pure of any extraneous adjunction coming from experience. It is a matter of accounting for the error that led to the paradoxes of the theory. Yet, in this later text Frege remains typically a realist, and in this respect is far from Kant:

> The connection of a thought with one particular sentence is not a necessary one; but that a thought of which we are conscious is connected in our mind with some sentence or other is for us men necessary. But that does not lie in the nature of the thought but in our own nature. (*N*, I, 288; trans. Long and White, 269)

The error is explained by this hiatus between the essence of thought and our human essence. The "logical aptitude" of human beings uses the same language in which other competing aptitudes, such as the poetic aptitude, are expressed. Thus the concept "source of knowledge" is called on in this text only to account for *Verunreinigungen* that hampered the progression of axiomatics: the illusions of the sense, the inadequacy of the language, and so on. If one cannot explain then what distinguishes the axioms of the special sciences from the fundamental laws of logic in a directly "epistemological" manner (that is, in terms of a "cognitive source"), does an objective characteristic allowing us to justify this distinction exist? Such a characterization can effectively be obtained from a definition of logic as a science of the "most general laws of the being-true" (*N*, I, 139). We discern in this definition three distinctive features not only of logic but also of its axioms.

(1) The *normativity* of logic distinguishes it from any other discipline. The other sciences conceive the *rule* as a regularity and not as a prescription. As for ethics, although it is also part of the normative "sciences" it cannot prevent an action from transgressing its interdictions. Logic, on the contrary, states requisites to which one must submit in order to be *able to think*. The logical axioms therefore have the value of conditions of possibility as well as of standards of thought.

(2) Logic treats of *truth*; this is its object or, as Frege says, its "goal." Truth is to logic as predicates like "heavy" and "hot" are to physics or "acid" is to chemistry. It is its "specific" object (*in ganz besonderer Weise*). There is, however, a fundamental difference between this object of logic and the particular predicates of the natural sciences: truth determines in itself and completely the

essence of logic, whereas physics and chemistry have other objects than "heavy," "acid," and so forth.

(3) As the particular sciences also claim to say the truth, it should be added that when logic makes truth its object, it aims not at a particular content of true judgment but at the most "general" conditions of true thought—a universality closely tied with the fact that the laws of logic are a priori and thus do not depend on any empirical particularity. However, as we have seen, their universality goes beyond pure apriority.

Are these features enough to found the separation between logical axioms and "special" premises? They correspond to a systematic description; that is, they state the status that, in the system of the sciences, is that of logic. But if it is a matter of extracting the axioms of logic from the body of premises in the formal construction of a science, they are not sufficient for obtaining the demarcation sought. This is why Frege acknowledges the still *undetermined* character of this characterization.[36] One could think that the "formal" nature of logical axioms make it possible to reduce the undetermination of the distinction. Yet, what does "formal" mean exactly? This word applies to certain *uses* of logic, in particular to schemata of deduction, insofar as they regulate the practice of *substitutions*. In this sense of the word "formal," logic cannot, according to Frege's phrase, be called "formal without limit." Frege encounters Bolzano here by claiming a *content* for logic, a content that circumscribes it as a science: "Toward what is proper to it, its relation is not at all formal" (*KS*, 338). There are specific concepts that form the irreducible content of logic. These are precisely the "foundation stones" from which Frege works out the system of the *Grundgesetze*: "There is something which . . . ," truth, extension of a concept, negation, implication, etc. These strictly logical concepts or objects are, however, not identifiable other than as the residue of substitutions. As Kambartel remarks in his preface to the *Nachlass*, nothing arises to fill the gap between logic as a science of the *general* laws of truth, a pure, a priori, and universal science, on the one hand, and the purely factual manner in which its constituents are identified, by means of an analysis of definite propositions of common language and scientific discourse, on the other hand.[37] One may prefer to see here a *disadvantage* of Frege's doctrine, but it is impossible to diagnose an incoherence. Indeed, the realist option assumes that the basic matter from which we build a science is *given*. The logical objects are part of this matter that we must grasp without being able to produce. The mediocre effectiveness of the boundary between what is formal and what is not is the unavoidable consequence of a realist philosophy of logic.

Is the Logicist Enterprise above all Epistemological?

In his investigations into the foundations of mathematics, Frege was engaged in an enterprise which was, at bottom, epistemological, and which presupposed assumptions about knowledge which he inherited from his predecessors and never questioned. (Kitcher, 236)

The inquiry into the final foundation of the axioms of logic proves to be decisive for the opinion we will form of the nature of Frege's logicism. Do the axioms receive in the final analysis a "cognitive" legitimacy? Frege's work would then have to be interpreted as an epistemology derived from Kant, although in actual fact a Kantianism distorted by the psychologism of Herbart or Wundt. If, on the contrary, the axioms are true "before" being obvious, if consequently the characteristics of our knowledge of axiomatics are without foundational relevance, the logicist program cannot be confined in an epistemological framework. From what precedes it may be inferred that only the second of these possibilities is open. We are then faced with the question of what the "debt" that Frege admits to owe Kant really amounts to. The previous discussion makes it possible to assert that Frege does not "take up" purely and simply Kantian concepts: he makes the activity of thought depend on the existence of an objective and independent reign of *Gedanken* and denotations. Whereas in Kant understanding produces its own rules, without any other criterion of objectivity than the agreement between various syntheses, Frege introduces, like Bolzano, a radical separation between that which pertains to truth and that which depends on the *Fürwahrhalten*: the rational subject consequently ceases to produce the intelligibility of its own knowledge to become only its *effect*. Rational activity in Bolzano and in Frege pertains to the acknowledgment of truth, the two authors disagreeing, however, as to the means of obtaining this acknowledgment (Frege sees in conceptual notation an instrument superior to language, while Bolzano believes that ordinary language is the vehicle of the theory). Kant's understanding produces the categories, Frege's understanding *is produced* by thoughts.

Is it not pure conformism on the part of Frege to place his thought in the wake of Kant? Such a judgment would not make justice of the subtle filiation that continues to exert its force from Kant to Frege. Frege's "debt" lies in posing the problem of objective knowledge in terms of *conditions of possibility*. What path must one follow in order to reveal the legitimacy of a science, in order to exhibit its universal and necessary character? Kant's answer consists in showing that necessity and universality are two interdependent features and signs of an a priori power of knowledge.[38] Frege does not challenge this thesis, but he seeks *beyond* the power of knowledge for the system of truths that founds it. If Frege were strictly Kantian, he would add that mathematics, reduced to logic, is a science of understanding. But he does not think to do so, because he locates elsewhere than in a power the conditions of possibility of the development of logical truths into a system of arithmetic. There is thus at the same time a dependence of Frege's philosophy with respect to Kant and a significant modification of the idea of condition of possibility. In Kant, to present a condition of possibility amounts to deducing from a transcendental power types of syntheses for the representations, namely, forms of knowledge insofar as they determine a priori the configuration of sciences. For Frege, the condition of possibility occurs in a different inquiry and rhetoric. The problem will not take on the form of a question in the Kantian manner: what legitimate hopes do the combined powers of sensibility and understanding allow us to have? Rather, it assumes the form of an assertion: objective science exists, effective thought exists, logic that is not only rigorous, but efficient and creative exists. This fruitfulness *must* not rest on the mental constitution of an individual person nor on that of a species nor even on some "power" of the transcendental subject; it must rest on the independent nature of truth that is at the origin of the human mind itself as reason. Without this organized domain of truths, with their hierarchy between fundamental laws, particular axioms of a science, theorems, we would be unable to think.

From transcendental philosophy to Frege's realism, the relationship between *understanding* and the *given* is what undergoes the most characteristic topical inversion. The problem the *Critique* had to resolve was to reconcile the idea of an a priori knowledge with the fact that knowledge must conform to what the objects of the senses given by the intuition are "in themselves."[39] Frege shifts the conditions from the knowing subject to the object known, following a movement I have already qualified, concerning Bolzano, as *dogmatic*. Here the objective characteristics of the given (that is, thoughts) allow us to conceive them in a uniform and, consequently, universal manner. As for this *medium* that the "source of knowledge" constitutes in the matter, it is not the task of logic to carry its exploration any further. The task of logic, that is, of philosophy,[40] is limited to asserting the objective, independent, and constituting character of the reign of *Gedanken*.

We can now answer the question that gives the title to this discussion. When Frege mentions the necessity of a reconstruction of arithmetic, it is not in order to have a sure knowledge of the discipline; it is in order to bring out the essence of this science, an essence that is "contained, as a germ, in the original truths." Thus the aim of the reduction is foremost not "epistemological" in the sense of being primarily a question of restoring to the proofs a power they would not have otherwise, but "ontological," so to speak, in the sense of being primarily a question of describing in its essence the nature of the science of arithmetic. This implies that the ultimate goal of reduction is to take up the challenge of Kantianism. There exists an a priori knowledge without preliminary intuition, made possible by a set of fundamental logical truths that are *given*. From their network results the entire body of mathematics, and by their intermediary our mind becomes reason (*GA*, §105, 115). I suggested earlier calling this new theme of conditions of possibility, of which Bolzano's philosophy is a first instance, "ontotranscendental." Instead of founding science on a theory of knowledge, it sets an objective domain of truths holding as an absolute frame of reference whose modes of presentation (thoughts) are absolutely determined. It is this "reservoir of thoughts," always available and unaffected by change, which accounts for every cognitive activity. Frege's ontotranscendental is consequently to be understood as a means of making epistemology superfluous as I elsewhere showed that it does away with the necessity of a *philosophy of language*.[41]

Frege, Kant, and the Question of "Cognitive Sources"

The relationship between Kant and Frege is not simply one of "influence." Frege uses in a secondary manner the language of "cognitive sources," but in order to subordinate knowledge to a truly constituting objective reign. From the point of view of a comparative topics, the difficulty consists then in understanding what Frege meant when he mentions in a note of the third paragraph of the *Grundlagen*:

> I do not, of course, mean to assign a new sense to these terms, but only to state accurately what earlier writers, Kant in particular, have meant by them. (3 note)

Or else, when he sums up the content of his book, writing in the last paragraph:

> From all the preceding it thus emerged as a very probable conclusion that the truths of arithmetic are analytic and a priori; and we achieved an improvement on the view of Kant. (118)

To achieve "an improvement on the view of Kant," Frege must have conceived his own work as dependent on Kant's approach. How can one continue to defend Fregean orthodoxy against an "epistemological" distortion, when Frege seems to refuse the role of an innovator?

The Legitimacy of the Act of Judging

What is peculiar about the note quoted is that it is embedded in a sentence in which Frege undeniably exposes a criterion of analyticity that no longer concides on an essential point, with Kant's criterion:

> These distinctions between a priori and a posteriori, synthetic and analytic, concern, as I see it, not the content of the judgment but the justification for making the judgment. Where there is no such justification, the possibility of drawing the distinctions vanishes. (3)

If Kant's distinction started from the "content of the judgment," the one Frege proposes starts rather from *that which legitimates* the act of judging. The set of premises and deductive laws of the system, of which the proposition to be judged is a part, is what gives its validity to this "shift." The criterion of analyticity can therefore only be applied in a systematic framework. This restriction of the domain of validity of the distinction by means of the notion of system or demonstration yields, as we know, the key to the enumeration given in the following paragraph: "If . . . we come only on general logical laws," "definitions," "propositions upon which the admissibility of any of the definitions depends," and so on, "then the truth is an analytic one." It is certainly not by inquiring into our grounds, in each case, for "believing" (a proposition) that we would dispel the impression of the arbitrary nature of this classification. On the other hand, we have a clue that guides us between these different categories as soon as we have identified in them the parts of a deductive system.

The way Frege reinterprets Kant's definition does not leave the extension of the analytic untouched. Since the possibility of applying the distinction *vanishes* when a judgment is made without justification (that is, outside of any demonstration), a large number of propositions that Kant held to be analytic cease to be characterizable as analytic or synthetic. This is true in particular of the informal assertions of everyday language from which Kant drew his examples, that is, when they cannot be reconstructed as propositions of a definite deductive series, and likewise of a certain number of philosophical propositions insofar as their content does not allow a systematic reconstruction ("the universe is infinite" and "the mind is without extension" are neither analytic nor synthetic; the positivists will soon say that they are meaningless). Although his own definition of the analytic reduces its extension, Frege remarks elsewhere that Kant's definition is "too narrow" (*GA*, §88, 99ff.). He means that Kant's definition is *not exhaustive* — not merely because it only deals with the particular case in which a concept forms the subject of the proposition (taking thus the affirmative universal judgment for the type of judgment to which the others reduce), but also because Kant's analysis of the concept as a conjunction of characters only exploits one and the less fruitful of the possible relations between propositional constituents. If we try to judge the extent of change that Frege's criterion imposes on Kant's definition of analyticity, we see that the former: (1) reinterprets the content of Kantian judgment in terms of a deductive system; (2) modifies the extension of analytic propositions; and (3) changes the essential properties connected with analyticity; for the barrenness of Kant's analytic, Frege substitutes, as we have seen, the fruitfulness of the analytic. As a result of substituting the system for the point of view of the clarifying consciousness of the subject, the subject loses in Frege the direct control of its own productions. And it is the system, insofar as it objectively reproduces the essence of logic, and not the consciousness that judges it, that proves "fruitful."

These three features of his analyticity undoubtedly constitute the corrections Frege held to be essential. It is in this sense that he believed himself to have "achieved an improvement on the view of Kant." We are now able to understand what motivated the note to the third paragraph of the *Grundlagen*. A debate on this subject is possible precisely because Kant and Frege "meant" *the same concept*. Topically, the note belongs to the same metalogical philosophy as that which inspires the whole book. Of course the *sense* of Frege's definition does not coincide with the sense Kant gave to it. But the *same concept* is "meant" in both cases, just as Cantor, Schröder, Baumann, Mill, Lipschitz, and others sought to define the same concept of number by different channels. No more than the various entities objectively denoted by the expression of "number" can be said to exist, is it legitimate to view the property "is analytic" as varying from one writer to another: there must be some correct description of this property that gives it its genuine logical dimension. "It seems that Kant did have some inkling of the wider sense in which I have used the term of analytic judgments" Frege again says (*GA*, §88, 99–100), because, without yet having the logical instruments of the *Begriffsschrift*, he already was aware of the metasystematic scope of the concept. In our interpretation Frege's note is understood not as an avowal of the influence of the Kantian theory of knowledge on his own research, but, on the contrary, as the expression of a realist standpoint that he takes concerning the objects of the theory (truth, falsity, "condition," etc.), as well as their properties (analyticity, continuity, etc.).

From the A Priori of Kant to That of Frege

The hypothesis of analyticity formulated by Frege in 1884 occurs in the wake of a recurrence of optimism during the nineteenth century brought about by the philosophy of systems. If we may speak of a return to Kant, it is in the sense that it was then believed possible to answer positively the critical question. The initial question of the *Critique of Pure Reason*—"How can we make progress in metaphysics?"—results in the examination of the power of reason in relation to a pure a priori knowledge. The possibility of asserting synthetic a priori judgments then founds the possibility of metaphysics as a science. This distinction between analytic and synthetic propositions still plays a founding role in Frege's philosophy. Just as synthetic a priori judgments guarantee in Kant the objectivity of a science of principles, so here the possibility of developing a priori a system of logic raises mathematics to the rank of a genuine science of principles.

This analogy must now, however, conceal the difference of status between the a priori of Kant and that of Frege. The analysis of the a priori conditions of possibility of knowledge leads Kant to the deduction of a transcendental power of constitution and organization of the forms of knowledge. Frege's a priori is still the mark of a universal and necessary knowledge, but this transcendental breaks away from the medium of a *subject*. It remains a condition of objectivity, but remains pure only if it proves to be independent of any process of knowledge. The act of a subject is, thus, no longer founding; the primacy of the a priori is that of an absolute origin of which the subject (insofar as it is rational) is the product. In this sense, we can speak of optimism: rationality is that of the *thing itself*. The system in itself of truths, as well as the originary organization of meanings into thoughts, forms a cosmos for reason. Moreover, the representation of the essence in an adequate symbolic reconstruction marks the beginning of an era of scientific progress and of faith in final results, since it is the core of the science that was finally discovered. Frege's Kantian rhetoric, therefore, should not mislead us. The transcendental approach certainly persists, but *without* a critical backdrop—a fundamental rupture, which implies other divergences.

"Ontotranscendentalism"

The question Frege addresses is still of a Kantian type: "How is a pure and a priori science of mathematics possible?" But the answer he gives to this question is undeniably precritical. He does not intend to examine in detail the instruments for generating knowledge that we can legitimately use; formula language, for example, is not associated with the foundational value of an a priori intuition operating *in concreto*. Frege seeks a foundation *prior* to all knowledge: the objectivity of the reign of *Gedanken* and *Bedeuteungen* precedes every activity of thought and knowledge. It is not only what *directs* discursive activity; it is also what forms the latter's *condition of possibility*. I called "ontotranscendentalism" this philosophical theme, which consists in placing in the independent existence of essences and senses the conditions of possibility of a subject's knowledge.

The Fruitfulness of the Analytic

A dogmatic approach such as this is typically accompanied by a setting aside of the contrast that, in Kantianism serves, on the contrary, as a guideline for deductions. Intuition is no longer as radically contrasted with understanding, because the faculty of knowing no longer determines the objectivity of the known.

It is striking to note here that Frege does not consider that the formula characters call on intuition. He puts an end to the division of roles between simple decomposition (which in Kant was the specific function of understanding in its formal use) and the production of a priori contents that pure intuition could generate in mathematical activity. But to say that fresh knowledge can be acquired without intuition is to imply that the analytic is not that barren and desolate territory Kant's *Logic* described. The logical form properly speaking is powerful enough to generate all the truths of arithmetic.

Finitude

With this liberalization with respect to Kantian dualism between production of new forms and reproduction (which is complementary to the fundamental division between producing and receiving), it is the whole locus of finitude that is modified. In Kant, the figure of the thing-in-itself marks the limit of possible knowledge, while on the other hand, analyticity marks the location of what is only recognized. The "already conceived" constitutes in a way the inner border of knowledge. Frege gets rid of these two landmarks of the limits of knowledge. Knowledge becomes absolute again as during the heyday of metaphysics. All knowledge reflects the Being of the thing, all subjective marks being erased from the object of knowledge (whence the cathartic function of formula language). Analyticity in turn undergoes a mutation since what until now was the model of nonknowledge, knowledge of understanding, becomes what reproduces in thought the genesis in itself of the system of logic.

Since knowledge is knowledge of the essence, it is on the side of the representation that, in a more insidious manner, finitude comes to bear. There is, in fact, a *distance* between the model and its copy that can be exploited in a realist philosophy to account for error (as for evil and ugliness). Is the object known such as in itself? Does the depth of the mental, historical, and especially the linguistic not tend constantly to lead research away from its ideal goal? Was the essence correctly grasped by the representation the system gives of it or was it only fleetingly, incompletely perceived? Such is the constitutional uncertainty that essentialism casts on the hypothesis of analyticity. The latter is, actually, at the beginning just a hypothesis because the logician must test concretely the operating possibilities of the system in order to assure himself that he is indeed exhibiting the essence of the mathematical and not some artifact foreign to the essence of number.

Logicism after the Antinomy

Frege's logicist program hinges on two theses that are intimately bound up in his conception of the *system*: (1) mathematical notions are in fact reducible to purely logical notions, and mathematical truths are deducible from the axioms of logic;[42] and (2) *all* the truths of arithmetic and, consequently, the whole of mathematics are deducible from logical laws. The first of these theses is most directly endangered by Russell's antinomy,[43] first of all by the uncertainty it reveals about the extension of the *logical*, and second, by the limits it imposes on the enterprise of reducing mathematics to logic. Let us examine the case of logic first. Foundation stone of the analytic, mortar of deductions, logic should constitute a sure material that would play without errors the double role of foundation and construction. The antinomy suddenly reveals that one of the most fundamental notions of the system, that of "course of values," is perhaps not logical after all, since it is responsible for an inconsistency in the system of fundamental laws. The poison is at work: every foundational enterprise will come up against the value of the sign of membership—is it a "strictly mathematical" notion? Hence one should give the word a meaning independently of logic, for example, by assuming an independent source of mathematical knowledge, as the intuitionist school and Gödel will do in different ways.[44] And if one wishes at all costs to maintain the unity of the logical and the mathematical, one will continue to append to logic the grammar of the sign " $\in$." But will such a feat make it possible to cast light on the true nature of membership and logic, or will it, on the contrary, laden both with an extra confusion?

Logic appears afterward as a denomination that would have become trivial by necessity. The *logical* is what logicians must consider as such, what for them is an element of manipulation. The antinomy reveals an old use, rather than creating a new trivialness in the use of the term "logic." Frege isolates at the beginning of the *Grundlagen* the logical from the empirical only by resorting to a circular argument: fundamental truths are logical because universal, universal because a priori, and a priori because logical—a circle that seems inseparable from an essentialist argumentation, powerless to specify positively the origin of the pure given. Whence the temptation to emphasize a source of knowledge that would account for this given. But if one begins to suspect the hidden contrivance the use of the term "logic" would conceal, the idea of "reduction" becomes in turn an object of suspicion. Frege had the ambition to exhibit the essence of number. The failure of his attempt leads us to doubt the existence of such a core, unique and absolute, of the science of number. The idea of the formalization of arithmetic is not what is challenged here. New attempts will be made, stimulated by the antinomies. The first of these reconstructions is the theory of types formulated in the appendix of the *Principles*, which will be developed in the *Principia*. The various formulations of set theory, from Zermelo-Fraenkel to Von Neumann, will exhibit for the same object, the number as well as rival and incompatible representations. The idea of reduction then loses its plausibility. How can one believe in the thesis of revealing the essence, when instead of a single and final elucidation, one has a heterogeneous plurality of formal representations? It seems therefore more appropriate to interpret each construction not as yielding a *reduction* of arithmetic to logic but, following the suggestion of Hao Wang, as simply constituting a *translation* of the one into the other.[45] More precisely, each formalization seems to demonstrate that arithmetic and set theory are equivalent theories, in the sense that to each true proposition of the one corresponds an equally true translation in the other. But the proliferation of formal incompatible (that is, not intertranslatable) representations disqualifies any one among them in its claim to express the essence of number. The theme of reduction disappears behind that of the multiplicity of language games.

We discover at the same time that the foundational theme is not left untouched by this change of vocabulary. If a formalization of arithmetic through set theory only offers each time a translation of the one into the other, why should we continue to think that arithmetic needs this foundation? Is it not just as certain as the formal constructions that serve to translate it? Why can we not just retain from these systems what they have to offer, namely, local models of intelligibility, without seeking to promote by their means a foundation for arithmetic that for centuries has been supported by its sole practice?

The first thesis of Frege's logicism thus received two setbacks because of the antinomy. But the second thesis will not wait long for an even more radical contradiction. This second component of logicism, let us recall, lies in the conviction according to which "the" system of arithmetic is *complete*: all the truths of arithmetic are actually deducible from the axioms of the formal theory. Yet, Gödel proves in 1930 the impossibility of deducing all the truths of arithmetic from the axioms of set theory. In the formulation Tarski later proposes, this amounts to saying that the class of truths of the elementary theory of numbers is not *recursively enumerable*.[46] The results are even more serious for the logical program than were the antinomies. For if the meaning of the latter can practically be minimized by a realist philosophy, as the technical inadequacy of a first attempt, the theorems of incompleteness state properties holding for any formalization of arithmetic. It is now perfectly clear that the limitations stated by the first theorem of incompleteness and by Church's theorem[47] shut out definitively any hope of obtaining an exhaustive representation of the truths of arithmetic in an entirely "logical" system.

The philosophy of logic, thus, discovers in the practice of formalisms reasons for giving up essentialism. The way is paved for a new thesis, which will come into vogue during the twentieth century: the laws of logic are of a purely linguistic nature. The secularization of analyticity takes place at the same time as its retrieval by an officially "empiricist" philosophy, which, however, as we shall see, pays slight attention to the essentialist origin of the heritage.

Section 4
The Foundational Strategies
of Rudolf Carnap

1

From One Venture to Another

There is a profound analogy between Frege's work, *The Foundations of Arithmetic*, and Carnap's first work, *The Logical Structure of the World*. Carnap resumes the attack on synthetic a priori judgments just where Frege left it off. Granted that the propositions of arithmetic are actually reducible to purely logical theorems (which was Frege's venture), and granted that the propositions of geometry are, *qua* parts of a mathematical (and not a physical) theory, purely analytical propositions (following Russell's result), it is now possible to prove that the empirical concepts of the natural sciences can be entirely derived from the elementary data of observation with the help of purely logical constructions. Thus, the help of "a priori syntheses" is definitively set aside, insofar as such propositions lack any usefulness and even any meaning. The analyticity of mathematics was established by Frege by means of a redefinition of the concepts of arithmetic in purely logical terms. For Carnap, this is a final result that Russell's paradox does not revoke. This first result should now be put to use, by showing that a similar reduction can be obtained outside mathematics, not, of course, by proving the purely logical character of the whole of science, but by proving accurately the *portion of logic* in the composition of its concepts. Like Frege, who "succeeded" in founding mathematics by showing that their statements are translatable into purely logical terms and, furthermore, could be deduced solely from logical laws, Carnap plans to found the unity of science by translating all its terms into clearly logical *or* empirical ones (that is, into terms of basic experiences). It is thus the idea of analyticity worked out in the *Foundations* that inspires *The Logical Structure of the World*, the sharp distinction between logical and factual terms being the main assumption that the system has as its task to apply to the reality of science and whose legitimacy it must simultaneously prove. The system of empirical concepts combines four features that mark its originality amid the systematic tradition of which Kant's deduction and Frege's system constitute the essential stages:

(1) *Setting up series* of *empirical* concepts shows, against Kant's opinion, that these concepts can be rigorously and exhaustively *defined*, and that they can be *deduced* from a common base.

(2) Each concept receives its epistemological and rational status from its place in the system. The idea of a hierarchy among the sciences is replaced by the clearer notion of implication between the concepts of science.

(3) The concrete edification of the system of constitution makes it possible to bring out the discursive continuity between the propositions of sciences of various levels. This *Lückenlosigkeit* is not accompanied, however, by the interdeducibility of the propositions of the sciences, as was true of mathematical theorems from the laws of logic in the *Basic Laws*. By the reduction is concerned only the material of the sciences, their "objects." The purport of systematic continuity consists mainly in setting aside "usurpated concepts" (an advantage already noted by Kant). Once constituted, the system allows us to raise with respect to each concept the question *"quid juris?"* Upon completion of the system, the answer to this question can in a way be "calculated." Every ill-formed concept will be singled out, thus making it possible to refute the metaphysicists, instigators of "false problems."

(4) Last but not least, the concrete edifications of the system make it possible each time to prove its possibility and to confirm its objectivity. The fact of generating from a single principle all the elements of the realm is represented as the guarantee of the objectivity of its mode of development. It is this feature of the system that makes Fregean analyticity the indisputable criterion of the *logical* essence of number. Carnap derives the same benefit from having gone through with his reconstruction of the world, with nevertheless an essential difference.

Both Kant and Frege conceived systematic development as the flowering of what is contained in the germ. We find nothing of the sort in Carnap. The system does not show at all how the "basic" sciences bear higher truths, but only a *translation* of the former in terms of the latter is always possible. Reduction has thus lost its claim to exhibit the essence of the reduced object. It must now assign respectively to the formal and to the empirical their congruous portions in the language of unified science. This observation can lead one to believe that reduction is henceforth part of an *empiricist* strategy that consists in limiting the field of the knowable to what experience itself makes it possible to justify. This is precisely how it is understood by the members of the Vienna Circle, who call the new current of thought that they represent "logical empiricism." We will see, however, that one must introduce some essential distinctions here. The antispeculative orientation of Schlick's circle prompts its members — who for the most part are not professional philosophers — to call themselves "empiricists" and to dissociate logic from an essentialist realist philosophy. But the label "empiricist" has here a polemical value rather than a technical sense. One must therefore examine the argumentative procedures as well as the very project of the young Carnap in order to discern the real function of the theory of constitution.

The Secularization of Logic

The very expression "logical empiricism" manifests clearly what is perceived by the members of the Vienna Circle as constituting the spearhead of their movement: the substituting of a clear-cut dualism—analytic (logical) propositions and synthetic (empirical) propositions—for Kant's threefold schema (analytic, synthetic a priori, and synthetic a posteriori propositions). The specificity of this new dualism cannot be appreciated if one does not grasp how it leads back again to the Kantian goal of founding the sciences: what makes it possible to abandon the synthetic a priori category is precisely the capacity of the new logic to take on functions previously reputed to be transcendental. *The architectonic and constitutive function of the a priori forms of intuition and of pure concepts is thus taken up de facto by logic.*

But one must agree on the term "logic." Unlike what Bolzano or Frege thought, logic does not have for Carnap its own object; it lacks content. Without this, the very intelligibility of the unity of science, under the apparent dualism conveyed by the expression "logical empiricism," would be compromised. Frege's logic *must* be secularized, riven from any ontological foundation and daringly set under the pure nominal, that is, the conventional institution of signs:

> *Logic (including mathematics) consists solely of conventions* concerning the use of symbols, *and of tautologies* on the basis of these conventions. (*Der logische Aufbau der Welt* [herafter, *A*], §107, 150)

This "secularization" of logic, which makes it possible to extend considerably its domain, although it minimizes the graveness of ad hoc constructions is also the only way to save logicism from the difficulties engendered by the paradoxes.[1]

Russell and Logical Constructions

It is actually Russell, not Carnap, who first had the idea of applying to physical statements the Frege-Russell criterion of systematic reconstruction. For the theoretical statements of physics to receive an experimental *confirmation*, there *must* exist some way of correlating the objects that appear in physical theories (electrons, molecules, etc.) with sense-data. But this correlation cannot be established if one is not able to identify in experience the relationship of a term with its correlate. Yet, only one of the terms of the correlation is given: nothing allows us then to verify the correlation of the theoretical object with the experience that illustrates it. There is in experimental demonstration a *gap* that affects the validity of the natural sciences *in the same way* the demonstrative discontinuities of the natural theories of arithmetic endangered the validity of this science. Russell reasons thus as early as 1914, in his article "The Relation of Sense-Data to Physics." He suggests using the same method in physics as was employed in arithmetic: replacing the inferred entity by a *logical construction*, retaining of the initial object only the properties relevant for the truth of the proposition in which it is described. What shows that such a construction is possible in physics is that an experimental prediction *already occurs there*:

> and in so far as the physical state of affairs is inferred from sense-data, it must be capable of expression as a function of sense-data.

The course of naive epistemology must then be reversed: instead of going from the theoretical object to the experimental prediction, one must try to reconstruct the theoretical object in terms of sense-data. In other words, Russell suggests undertaking the "empirical deduction" of physical concepts. The advantage is above all that of a clarification for physics, and Russell alludes to the specifically logical interest of such an undertaking only in passing:

> The problem of accomplishing this expression (of the physical state of affairs as a function of sense-data) leads to much interesting logico-mathematical work.[2]

In his own copy of Russell's text, Carnap jots down in the margin: "That will be my task." For in such an empirical deduction, Carnap sees first of all the *logical* interest, namely, an essential recentering, which is enough to change the direction of Russell's initial project toward a new type of rationalism. *Thus one must judge the success of the Aufbau above all according to its formal procedures*. Even if Carnap exhibits these procedures *in concreto*, and does more than outline what the system of concepts of science would be, it is not on the basis of the exhaustive accomplishment of the derivations that we will evaluate constitution. The formal procedures are what form the *theses* of constitution, and not a particular chain of definitions by which these procedures are illustrated. Whereas Frege's venture could be won only on the condition that mathematical truths be derived from logical truths, Carnap's requires only that the suggested outline be probative, that is, that it prove the possibility of the enterprise of unifying the sciences.

The Idea of Reduction

To build a system of constitution presupposes that one knows how to "reduce" the concepts of natural theories, in other words, that one manages to express them by means of a more limited vocabulary. Carnap's reduction is usually taken to be an application of Russell's principle of parsimony: reduction would allow us to dissolve useless "entities" and to clarify the store of concepts truly necessary to scientific reasoning. If this is one of its consequences, the system does not, however, bring about an ontological purification. For the objects near the sensorial base are, nevertheless, already abstract: what is at stake in reduction is not to *return to an originary bedrock* (which is the approach of traditional empiricism rather than that of the logical empiricists) but to exhibit the exact importance of "form constituents" (*Formungskomponenten*) in knowledge (*A*, §183, 260) by applying in a novel way the logic of the *Principia*:

> *a* is said to be *reducible* to *b, c* . . . [means that one produces] a rule of translation which gives a general indication how any propositional function in which *a* occurs may be transformed into a coextensive propositional function in which *a* no longer occurs, but only *b* and *c*. (*A*, §35, 47; trans. George, 60–61).

This "general indication" will take the form of a definition called a "constructional definition," since while making it possible to *eliminate* the concept *a* in favor of the concepts *b* and *c*, it furnishes an *order* between the concepts.[3]

The adequate instrument for the stratification of spheres, characteristic of a genuine system of concepts, is *definition in use*: it makes it possible to stratify the system, that is, to build up concepts belonging to different spheres. It thus exploits the properly constructive dimension of definition and saves the construction from the triviality of an elementary combinatory between elements of the same type. Definition in use consists in stating the predicates the objects must have in order to belong to the class that one seeks to build. The concept of "prime number," for example, could be given a definition in use:

> *x* is a prime number = df *x* is a natural number and has only 1 and *x* as divisors

To give a definition in use of a class or a course of values (what Carnap calls a "relation extension") does not consist in explaining the meaning of the new symbol in a traditional way, by specifying the characters of the concept taken in isolation. For the substitution allowed by definition in use only takes place in complete sentences (*A*, §39, 51–52). The criterion of validity of this definition is purely extensional: the *explicandum* and the *explicans* will be said to be of the "same meaning" if they are substitutable *salva veritate* in all propositions in which they may occur (*A*, §40, 53).

The Idea of a Factual Criterion of Reducibility

To hierarchize concepts, one must, of course, have something more than a mere ordinal scale on which to arrange them. One must also be able to differentiate between two concepts, *the order in which* the reducibility takes place and *the concepts between which* the relation holds. How can such a comparison between the presystematic concepts be reached, and how can one be sure of being *exhaustive* in the construction? The problem Carnap faces here is a classical one of characteristic systems that Leibniz formulated thus:

> The knowledge of language will advance along with the knowledge of things and will help it greatly, and a thing will be able to have as many

names as properties; *but there will be only one that will be the key to all the others*, although one cannot always reach it in matters that depend on experiences.[4]

In other words, the question of essential reference must be settled; that is, it must always be possible to discover a name "that will be the key to all the others" for a given systematic object. However, reduction must not bring in an ontological hypothesis, as was the case in Leibniz's philosophy. One must obtain a purely analytic demonstration of the universal possibility not only of logical but also of factual reduction. Carnap shows, first of all, that there is a *factual* criterion of reducibility that satisfies the formal requisite I mentioned earlier. In "realist" language, it can be stated thus:

> We call an object *a* "reducible to the objects *b, c, . . .* " if, for any state of affairs whatever, relative to the objects, *a, b, c, . . . ,* a *necessary and sufficient condition* can be indicated that depends only on objects *b, c.* (*A*, §47, 65, trans. George)

In spite of the fact that a "factual" criterion is concerned, the proof of the *equivalence* of the two criteria (logical and factual) is carried out in a purely formal manner. The logical criterion requires the equivalence of the *definiendum* and the *definiens*; the factual criterion states a necessary and sufficient condition, which will be logically expressed by an equivalence. This first step is purely analytic, since it just asserts that the two criteria are logically equivalent.

But we have not shown yet what is implied by the phrase "for any state of affairs whatever." If the factual criterion demanded that one examine every state of affairs in which the object to be reduced appears, then the criterion would be inapplicable, for there is no a priori means of knowing if *every* state of affairs has been examined (no more in fact than there is a procedure of determining if the number of these states of affairs is *finite*). Carnap's solution consists in substituting for an indeterminate empirical procedure a determinate linguistic procedure, that is, in solving this problem in a manner that is still purely analytic. It is enough to indicate a character capable of *representing* the object:

> It turns out, however, that for each object there is a *basic state of affairs.* It occurs in any other state of affairs only in connection with this basic one. (*A*, §48, 66, trans. George)

This may give the impression that an empirical fact is concerned here. But this is not the case, as one will understand by reading the paraphrase of this "fact of system" in constructional language:

> For every object, there is a *fundamental propositional function* such that all occurrences of the object can be expressed with the aid of this fundamental propositional function. (Ibid.)

The basic state of affairs is nothing else than the standard minimal statement in which the object receives both a scientific or sensorial characterization (in terms of property or relation) and a name. In the *Aufbau*, the basic state of affairs plays the role of the name, which, in the Leibnizian characteristic, is "the key to all the others": the propositional function makes it possible to symbolize univocally each concept. Let us assume that the object to be constructed is "temperature equilibrium"; to say that there is a propositional function that enables us to express all the occurrences of this relation is simply to construct an elementary proposition in which the object is referred to:

X stands to Y in the relation of temperature equilibrium.

Temperature equilibrium should be treated throughout as a relation between two terms. The basic state of affairs thus merely designates the connection of the thing with its state of affairs by means of the relationship between the symbol and the minimal statement in which the latter occurs. This second stage of the proof of adequacy is thus still purely "formal." It rests on the possibility, exhibited by Wittgenstein in his *Tractatus*,[5] of conceiving the space of things as the dual of the space of states of affairs.

By correlating each object to a fundamental state of affairs, Carnap answers one of the difficulties noted by Gilles Granger, concerning the treatment of *internal properties* of things. The characterization of each object by its basic state of affairs yields the a priori grammar governing the manipulation of its symbol, so that every empirical description of facts relative to the object can only be carried out in the formal setting designated by this grammar. On this account the notational rule and the essential constituent of the thing correspond to one another, following the requirement set by Leibniz. The thesis of the existence of a basic state of affairs therefore ultimately has for its consequences: (1) to make possible the articulation of the logical and the empirical in the system of constitution; and (2) to guarantee a semantic interpretation for the system of descriptions. If they are well formed, definitions must refer to a universe of possible facts.

Definition and Empirical Identification

The adequacy of the criterion supposes finally that the mortgage indicated by Leibniz is paid off; in other words, for every basic state of affairs corresponding to an object to be defined it is shown that there is a necessary and sufficient condition (and only one). Let us take the *definiendum*: "X stands to Y in the relation of temperature equilibrium." How are we to determine the *definiens*? Carnap answers this question by calling on the principle of verifiability: even if an indicator (*Kennzeichen*)—that is, a condition permitting identification of a state of affairs—is not explicitly invoked by a science to characterize a given concept, it *can* always be discovered. The principle of verifiability demands that every concept of science arise from a testable observation. As this principle constitutes a condition of possibility of science, it is established a priori that to each expression of a natural theory corresponds a fact of observation (eventually complex) that contains in its atoms the necessary and sufficient conditions of the basic state of affairs to be defined. In the example chosen, the necessary and sufficient condition will be:

> If bodies X and Y are brought into spatial contact (either directly or through the mediation of other bodies), then they show neither increase nor decrease in temperature.[6]

From the *existence* of science, Carnap deduces *the necessity* of having for each concept a definite description serving as an "infallible" indicator of the corresponding state of affairs. This thesis, arising from the principle of verifiability, is an analytic truth deducible from the concept of science, which is *given*. That an indicator exists in an analytic truth, which will guarantee the factual possibility of reductions. As for knowing which indicator to use for each concept, it is not for the *Aufbauer* to decide. He must confine himself to borrowing the indicators used in each field: the validity of the descriptions cannot be given an a priori answer, and it is not up to the philosopher to evaluate their relevance.[7] The transition from the logical principle of reduction to its application to empirical concepts is thus itself ensured by the conjunction of analytic operations and of the assumption of the existence of science. It now remains for us to single out the major principles that regulate, in the *Aufbau*, the relations between science and data and that make the enterprise of constitution possible.

Extensionalism

> The reductive force of a constructional system consists not in showing that a given entity is identical with a complex of other entities but in showing that no commitment to the contrary is necessary. (Goodman, *The Structure of Appearance*, 26)

From Carnap's point of view, resorting to definitions in use amounts to choosing a linguistic procedure allowing us to speak of certain extensions. Two propositional functions are said to have the same denotation (*Bedeutung*) if and only if they have the same extension, that is, if the same argument-values give them the same truth-values. Carnap takes up here the *thesis of extensionality*, expounded in the *Tractatus*, according to which "in every statement pertaining to a propositional function, the latter can be replaced by its symbol of extension." Following Wittgenstein, Carnap radicalizes the application of the principle as employed by the first logicists. One thing is to consider this thesis as yielding the criterion of logical equivalence between concepts; another is the thesis Carnap defends: one can always *replace* the propositional function by its extension. For the concept then loses its "determination."[8] The realist pretension of reconstruction is thereby displaced. Undoubtedly the system must describe reality in a structural way (as it appears in ordinary experience and in scientific observation, both being fundamentally homogeneous), but there will be no term-to-term correspondence of the constructions with presystematic objects. The system refers only *globally* back to the absolute frame of reference that experience constitutes.

The immediate consequence of the thesis of extensionality in this radical version is a new grammar and semantics of the concept. Since the agent of determination is now extension, the concept becomes capable of representing logically all those that are coextensive with it:

> A propositional function that is expressed with the aid of the new symbol is not associated with just a single, determinate, previously introduced propositional function f, but with all propositional functions that are coextensive with f; in other words, the new propositional function is associated with the extension of f. (*A*, §40, 53)

The grammar of the concept is simplified since it is no longer necessary to account, as did Frege, for an equal sign between concepts "corresponding" to the equal sign between functions. The terms of a concept and of an extension are equivalent variants of a same logical reality. However, recourse to the thesis of extensionality presupposes three theses preliminary to the constitutional process.

The Paradox of the Criterion of Extensional Identity

From the standpoint of the completed system, the equivalence of the *definiens* and the *definiendum* is a trivial result. Definition appears as a mere abbreviative stipulation whose expression is necessarily tautological. As we saw concerning Frege's definition, this intrasystematic point of view does not enable us to understand the explanatory scope of definition. Carnap and Goodman in turn make the remark.[9] Yet, if the equivalence of the *definiens* and the *definiendum* creates no difficulty within the system, it is precisely the crucial problem of constitution to ascertain the validity of the equivalence of equation of the former concept, taken from the lexicon of science, and the new concept, belonging to the language of the system. One needs a criterion by which to *judge the system*. The thesis of extensionality seems capable of furnishing this criterion. It is sufficient to substitute for the "previous" expression an expression of the system that preserves in the translation the truth-value of the propositions of ordinary language (and of the natural theory) in which the expression occurs. But the application of the extensional criterion encounters a difficulty that Goodman tries to elucidate. To what will we apply the test of substitution? If we should, for example, replace the presystematic expression "unconscious thought" by a formal analogue of the system written "Sup C," what truth-value should be given to the equation:

> Unconscious thought of X = Sup C (X)?

The statement will be tautological only if all the extensional tests are completed. Yet, a number of the sentences to be tested presuppose that the logical equivalence under consideration is *already established*. In his own system Goodman suggests replacing the strong criterion of identity of extension by a relaxed criterion, more in tune with the real possibilities of reduction. It will be demanded of an *accurate* system of definitions—without yet assuming its adequacy—that the set of *definientia* be *isomorphic* to the set of *definienda*. The extensions belonging to the system and to its presystematic model no longer have to be identical. It is enough that they be *of the same structure*.[10] Carnap also contemplates the possibility of constructing several isomorphic systems. But he conceives this possibility as what must constitute the operative potential of constitution, and not at all as an internal limitation of his formalism in its ability to identify an extension from one world to another. He ascertains, on the contrary, at a later stage of the system the unicity of the model for the formalized system of the *Aufbau*.

What is then the clue that makes it possible to compare the extensions belonging to different systems? For Carnap, it lies in the unicity of the semantic principle that governs the acquisition of knowledge in the presystematic as well as their reformulation in the system. The principle of extensionality can be applied only because, *whatever the language considered*, the conditions required for an expression to be meaningful are the same; that is, *all* languages have, following the words of Goodman, the same "ultimate factors," namely, the same logical and the same empirical constituents. It can then be assumed that, in whatever way the fabric of immediate data is cut, the various descriptions are isomorphic. What stands here in place of a principle (in conjunction with the principles of verifiability and of structuralism, to which we will return) is the *fact of the unicity of sensorial organization*. This fact plays here the role typically held elsewhere by the transcendental conditions of the unity of apperception. Whatever the instrument of expression by means of which experience is symbolized, the same intuitive genesis is represented there. Within the limits of this genesis, the overlapping of extensions is in a way predetermined by the universal application of these three principles.

Sense, Denotation, and Extensionality

The requisites of the thesis of extensionality, in its radical acceptation, exert in return a force on the Fregean notion of sense. Although Carnap claims to maintain Fregean orthodoxy on this issue, the use he makes of the distinction between *Sinn* and *Bedeutung* is quite different from what Frege conceived. Two shifts take place.

First, as the extension replaces the concept, Frege's distinction between *concept* and *object*, primary as it was, becomes a mere matter of words. The concern to found "ontologically" the articulation of symbols in the proposition prompts only suspicion on Carnap's part. "Logically it makes no difference to say that a given sign denotes an object or a concept," as long as one does not confuse the object that "corresponds" to the concept (i.e., its extension) with the *objects* that fall under it (i.e., the elements that belong to its extension). If there is a difference between the object and the concept, it is only from the psychological point of view, on account of the fact that the "mental imagery" accompanying each manner of speech differs (*A*, §5, 5).

The terminological clarification equally touches the proper name, which in Frege designated every term representing a saturated denotation and, therefore, among others, the extensions of the concepts and the courses of value of the functions. Carnap now reserves the possibility of receiving a proper name for the sole ostensive data. All the other supposed "proper names of object" are definite descriptions that bring in functional expressions and relations; these cease at the same time to have an independent reference. The extensions will on this account be qualified as *quasi objects*: Carnap follows here the Russell of the *Principia* against Frege.

In the second place, the *sense-denotation* distinction is subjected to a reshaping similar to that which affected the distinction between concept and object. Only *denotation* retains a logical relevance in the process of constitution. Sense is now reinterpreted as belonging to the psychological domain. The referent of a sign is then globally considered as being the "object" that the sign designates, while the sense is "that which the intensional object, i.e., representations, thoughts, etc., which the sign is to evoke, have in common" (*A*, §44, 61). This is an important piece of information: being what the representations mentioned by the sign *have in common*, the sense is associated with the linguistic mode used, while the referent being what the symbol designates, is independent of the natural language.

This duality of function (world representation) leads us to distinguish two types of "values": the sense is what accounts for the cognitive value of the system of constitution. But only the logical value, which takes into account only the denotations and the extensional facts, has a foundational value. The question of the *informative* nature of the system can thus be resolved in *psychological* terms; this extends in a typical manner what we called the *secularization* of analyticity. Whereas Frege accounted for the significance of derivations by emphasizing the diversity of "ways of giving the denotation," *objectively* distinct ways, Carnap explicitly identifies the effect of knowledge with various intuitive representations (*A*, §50, 69). But it is no less obvious that he does not wish for that matter to give up the cognitive effect of definitions to arbitrary associations between representations. The empiricist flavor of the new interpretation of sense must not endanger the univocal comprehension of the system. Hence the importance of the phrase stressed earlier, in the definition of the sense of the sign (what the representations it brings about *have in common*): that common representations may be presented by the sign indicates that its acquisition causes a *definite* sequence of representations. In Carnap, as later in Quine,[11] a behaviorist theory of language acquisition is what accounts for the actual regularity of the process of meaning. But unlike Quine, Carnap keeps psychology under the authority of reason, the association of ideas apart from denotation: the prerogative given to denotation and the capacity of identifying the latter in an extensional manner counterbalance the potential empiricism of the theory of sense. It is not only by challenging the possibility of this identification of reference that Quine corrects Carnap in an empiricist sense; it is also, as paradoxical as it may seem, by rejecting the phenomenalist thesis.

Phenomenalism

> Misgivings over the notion of analyticity are warranted also at a deeper level, where a sincere attempt has been made to guess the unspoken *Weltanschauung* from which the motivation and plausibility of a division of statements into analytic and synthetic arise. My guess is that *Weltanschauung* is a more or less attenuated holdover of phenomenalistic reductionism (Quine, *The Ways of Paradox and Other Essays*, 138)

Extensionalism, in a more or less "radical" version, imposes itself as one of the necessary conditions of the edification of a system of constitution. *Phenomenalism*, on the other hand, is a philosophical decision[12] concerning the nature of the base chosen for this construction. Other choices are possible. The *physicalist* choice takes for basic data the minimal *objects* of perception, and reconstructs the universe from atoms. What Goodman calls a "realist" system starts from *qualia*, the sensitive qualities being taken as undefinable. The "particularist" phenomenalism of Carnap consists in taking as a base elementary experiences, considered as totalities, prior to any separation into objects or qualities. As a philosophical option, phenomenalism involves three theses that regulate one another.

The first thesis is a version of the principle of verifiability that states the closure of sense on the actually perceived. Experience is an immediate given (with the restriction that the third thesis will impose on this "immediacy," the content of experience being logically prior to the relation of experience). The gaps in the stream of experience can be compensated by a constitutional procedure allowing us to restore the empirical continuity, without these "compensations" interfering with systematicity. This first thesis conflicts on at least two points with Hume's empiricism. On the one hand, the role ascribed to the principle of verifiability presupposes the existence of a science capable of being *rationally* legitimated. On the other hand, the constructive "compensations" replace the activity of belief and make it possible to rationalize inferences (causality, identity through time, etc.).

The second thesis has to do with a subject's ability to retrieve what served as the experiential origin for each concept. It is of little importance that Carnap presents as a necessary "fiction" the possibility that a subject should remember the whole stream of prior experience and should be able to establish the relevant relations. What is important is that the system presupposes that the reversibility of the cognitive process leads us back to the bare facts, without any adjunction other than logic. What could be called Carnap's "optimism" lies in considering here that all the relations other than the basic relation are logical and add nothing to the content of experience. But this "optimism" is founded on a rationalism that, starting from science, leads the analytic-synthetic dichotomy revealed by the system of knowledge back to its origin.

Finally, experience is not an indistinct terrain in which the subject could carry out occasional and haphazard sampling. The given is the domain of an undefinable empirical relation, not that the individual experiences (*Erlebnisse*) are already compounded or harmonized by a natural principle. Being indivisible, they are "in point form, without properties" (*A*, §69–70, 94–95). Yet what qualifies these *concreta* to become building blocks is that they are governed by what Hume would have called an "impression of reflexion," the relation of recollection of similarity, *Rs*. However, whereas in Hume the impressions of sensation and the impressions of reflection are two disjoint classes, in Carnap *experiences are pre-arranged by the relation*. In Kantian terms, the "manifold" is always already subject to it.

The three features explain how, despite the empiricist appearance of phenomenalism, this thesis is given in the system an essentially rationalist function. Of course what appears is not yet the object reconstructed by science but its sensorial counterpart—extensions of experiences over which the relation of recollection of similarity ranges—preparing the possibility of this object. What Quine denounces in this thesis is precisely that it functions as an *artifact* and establishes science only by denying the discontinuity in which the latter actually evolves.

Structuralism

Phenomenalism represents only a constructional option; structuralism serves a more fundamental necessity. It is not only a proposition of theory of knowledge; it is an "architectonic" thesis that defines the *object* of science as well as its *development* while it simultaneously founds the objectivity of the system.

Structuralism and Information: Structural Description

The structuralist thesis asserts in principle the possibility of translating any statement about contents (i.e., definite empirical objects) into a purely structural statement, that is, one in which occurs only relations between elements that are determined solely by the latter (*A*, §15, 19). Thus formulated, this thesis is clearly linked to two propositions we encountered earlier: (1) only the logical meaning is relevant in the translation under consideration. The description given by a railroad map or a botanical classification can be replaced by a diagram or a list of pairs (*A*, §14, 17); (2) relations are always prior to their terms. Thus, the term does not contain excess information compared to the relations in which it occurs.

The *proof* of the structural thesis cannot, however, be carried out in an entirely formal manner, for it brings in an empirical proposition we encountered while examining the notion of *reduction*, namely, that "for any domain of objects, a univocal system of descriptions can be given, without resorting to ostensive definitions" (*A*, §13, 16). Guaranteed by the existence of *Realwissenschaften*, this regulative principle justifies the closure of the set of synthetic statements objectively sufficient for exhaustively describing a specific domain of experience.

This closure of the synthetic has a strategic role. Where one knows that a finite series of descriptions makes it possible to code all the relevant information of the domain, one also knows, on the one hand, that ostensive definitions are no longer necessary for fixing the reference of a concept and, on the other hand, that any synthetic statement about the elements of the domain will not bring in any element other than those that belong to the current list of descriptions defining this domain. In other words, the closure of information with respect to the system of descriptions authorizes transforming this system into a "structural description" (*Strukturbeschreibung*; A, §12, 14). Instead of pointing out the property of each term, one characterizes each of them as the nodes of a network. This is what is required if one is to bring out the purely formal relations that hold between the points of this network, and thus prepare the "analytic" or rather "quasi-analytic" treatment of these elements.

To understand better the originality of the analytic procedure of the *Aufbau*, it is worthwhile to compare Hilbert's implicit definition with Carnap's structurally definite description. Hilbert proposes to "define" the terms of the system of geometry only by the network of relations that the axioms set as undefinable. The only requisite of such a system lies in its noncontradiction. It is therefore in a purely analytic manner that one calculates the properties of one of the objects mentioned by the axioms, as a sequence logically deducible from the axioms of geometry by means of purely a priori procedures. In fact, Hilbert's axioms "define" not a *definite empirical field* — geometry — but a formal schema capable of various applications. Here the relation between the analytic and the synthetic is then that between an abstract structure and various interpretations. The search for an interpretation appears moreover as an approach different from the elaboration of a system of axioms. Carnap's procedure of formalization follows the opposite path. Instead of beginning with a purely abstract structure, he allows a given system of descriptions to be the starting point. In this way are satisfied the requirements connected with the interpretation and thereby with the noncontradiction of the system. There are objects that, before being "set up as a structure," are subjected to a semantic reference. The problem of the *agreement* between the formal schema and the objects of an empirical domain is thus solved *prior* to formalization. For the formalization to be accomplished, one must already know (at the end of an a posteriori investigation carried out in the natural science under consideration, but which it is not for the philosopher to undertake) the denotation of a description and the truth-value of the proposition in which it occurs. For this reason, the theorems, pertaining no longer to the *object* of an empirical domain but to the *formal properties* of the relations between the elements of this domain, are *empirical* to the extent that they express confirmed states of affairs (A, §106, 147–48, 268). They are, however, equally *formal* and as such authorize purely *analytic* derivations. Finally, the theorems characterize not an indeterminate class of empirical objects (that is, an empty structure with multiple interpretations) but determinate objects of experience. Carnap intends to make this *categoricity* of his formalized system a *logical* axiom, ensuring a priori for the completed system a univocal anchoring in the empirical universe.

From Complete Formalization to the Anchoring of the System

If this complete formalization can be accomplished, it is, among other things, because "the objects that are constructed (from original basic relations) in a certain way show a certain empirical behavior" (*A*, §153, 205)—that is, because the formal properties of the relations are capable of conveying all the necessary scientific information about the terms. It must therefore be possible, in particular, to formulate a description of the basic relation that was taken as indefinable, by using the constructions that were set up with its help. One thus obtains *the conversion of the synthetic into the analytic*, since the basic relation is defined in purely formal terms, although its origins are experiential and the information coded by means of it is synthetic.

The final stage of formalization consists in continuing the reduction by carrying the completed system back to its own base. Forming a closed structure, the data of the system make it possible to cover up any intuitive trace and to close it on itself as an adequate and cognitively sufficient formal architecture. One must nevertheless ascertain that this formalization will not cut the system off from its initial empirical anchoring. The idea of a founded relation (*fundierte Relation*) is what guarantees a unique frame of reference for the system, even though the empirical content of the basic relation is expelled from it. It ensures, indeed, the possibility of a univocal recurrence of the formalized definitions of the system toward the empirical experiences that were their original model. This idea yields a fundamental metasystematic axiom:

> *Rs* (or any other basic relation which can serve to build up a system of constitution) is the only founded relation extension from which we can construct in a given way a certain sufficiently high-level object, still to be chosen, which shows certain empirical characteristics. (*A*, §155, 208)

With the help of this axiom, *Rs* can be reduced to a purely formal relation, defined by its structural properties in the system:

$$Rs \ = \ \mathrm{Df} \ \iota \ \{\mathrm{fund} \cap \hat{R} \ [T \ (R)]\}$$

Here *T* is any empirical theorem of a sufficiently high order. *Rs* indeed is the only relation that can satisfy, "in a natural manner, in an experience," the abstract constitutional conditions of the derivation of the empirical theorem *T*.

This guarantee is far from being a trivial consequence of construction. For, from a purely formal standpoint, one can imagine that the system could be satisfied by instances of empirical relations other than those that were actually employed. One would then have the case of a Hilbertian axiomatic whose propositions characterize not a definite system of objects but a potentially infinite class of such systems, one model being as good as another once it is proved that it satisfies the axioms. The ultimate success of the systematic construction depends then on the validity of the concept of "founded relation." It is this concept that alone ensures the univocal to-and-fro between experience and its formalization. If the dimension of formalization (and thus the analytic realm) is essential for the accessibility of empirical concepts to a discursive treatment, the dimension of recourse to experience (the synthetic realm) is capital if the system is to be operative. If a *calculemus* is ever practiced in this new language, it can only be for the purpose of interpreting in a realist language the eventual discoveries of "blind" manipulation. The unicity of the model is indeed an imperative in the context of this "realist formalism." One understands then why Carnap is determined to make the concept of founded relation a *purely logical* notion. For this concept obviously arises from the wish to guarantee a priori the empirical determination of the formal theory. It is limited to dictating by an ad hoc convention, that alone the relation of origin can ultimately furnish the system with an interpretation that makes all its concepts "denoting." Since experience is extralogical, the relation between logic and the domain of interpretation must itself be logical: it is on this condition that the theoretician of constitution can ground in reason the application of forms to a content.

Structuralism and Unified Science

Structuralism, finally, has a greater import insofar as it enables us to answer the traditional question: "What guarantees the scientificity of knowledge?" Or, "what makes science an *objective* knowledge?" Carnap rejected the transcendental thesis that emphasizes the constituting power of the subject of knowledge concerning its own objects. He also rejects the inquiry I have called "ontotranscendental," which takes into account an independent realm of meanings. One notices, however, that Carnap poses the problem of the objectivity of knowledge in a manner similar to Frege. Just as communication is possible in Frege only by being firmly set in the independent objectivity of logical truths and in the universality of thoughts, so science in Carnap furnishes the firm point that makes an agreement possible between the subjects of knowledge. Because science only deals with *forms*, it can go beyond the contingency of individual perception. Being by definition private and incomparable to that of another subject, a sensation is incapable of furnishing a medium for intersubjective communication. *One must therefore* locate the possibility of an intersubjective agreement in the universality of the formal relations that unite the contents (as such opaque and intransmissible).

On an essential point, nevertheless, Carnap's treatment of objectivity seems to depart from Frege's: if relations, unlike their terms, are public, it is not because they are endowed with a constituting objectivity, after the manner of Frege's logical laws; it is because they pertain to linguisitic forms. When language expresses relations, it is, in a way, perfectly suited to its object. The contents, on the other hand, are controllable, that is, "accessible to conceptual anlaysis" (*A*, §15, 19), only to the extent that they occur in networks of relations. Taken as a general condition of objectivity, the structuralist thesis seems then to lead to a paradoxical result: scientific analysis seems to dissolve content in favor of forms. As Carnap writes:

> Our thesis, namely, that scientific statements relate only to structural properties, amounts to the assertion that scientific statements speak only of forms without stating what the elements and the relations of these forms are. Superficially, this seems to be a paradoxical assertion. (*A*, §12, 15)

Does taking into consideration the sole forms not amount to confusing scientificity and analyticity? If analyticity, as Frege and Russell showed, represents the final state of mathematics, is it not paradoxical to seek to extend to the empirical sciences what could succeed only in a purely a priori science? Does a purely *formal* foundation of science not end up masking the firm setting of knowledge in the factual? Carnap now believes he is able to answer this skeptical objection of the nonlogically minded empiricist. The discourse of science cannot be founded other than by exhibiting the way in which the constitutive elements of this discourse can be rationally reconstructed, that is, by working out a system of constitution. That one may ignore the importance of the role of constituents of form in the acquisition and the systematization of knowledge should not be astonishing, since the formal element occurs spontaneously and unconsciously in knowledge. Whence precisely the necessity of going back to the formal conditions of possibility of acquiring knowledge: logic can found experimental knowledge; it alone allows us to spell out the conditions of scientificity.

The system of constitution rests on a set of theses designed to make the setting up of structures compatible with an empirical anchoring. Five theses, which we need only recall as they have already been discussed, seem relevant here:

(1) The thesis of the unity of the domain of objects (and, correlatively, the principle of verifiability).
(2) The thesis deduced from the existence of sciences: it is always possible in principle to describe each theoretical domain by a unique network of descriptions.
(3) The thesis concerning the relational nature of any information.
(4) A logical thesis: the theory of types of the *Principia* makes it possible to build up extensions of different types, that is, to differentiate levels in the system.
(5) The "logical" axiom of the founded relation: the completely formalized system is categorical.

In this manner the reciprocal relation joining the *Logical Structure of the World* and the project of a unified science takes shape. As an ideal already partially achieved, the unity of science furnishes the *Aufbau* with some of its fundamental theses (theses 1 and 2). But by making operative a complete formalization of knowledge, the *Aufbau* in return supplies evidence of the fruitfulness of the program of unification. This reciprocity gives to the constitution enterprise its properly utopian dimension.

2

The Procedure of Quasi Analysis

The Fundamental Problem of Constitution

As we saw in the preceding chapter, the true interest of the *Aufbau* lies not in the example of a constitution system if offers but in the set of formal procedures that it is the function of the example to illustrate. These procedures must combine two properties traditionally associated with two independent "faculties": they must be purely *formal* (i.e., logical) so as to preserve the analytic-synthetic division on which the organicity and the objectivity of science are founded. But they must also be *constructive*. The procedures in question must make it possible to work out chains of derivation from an indivisible basic given, the indivisibility of the base being obviously an a priori requirement that applies to every constitution system (*A*, §68, 93–94). However, the indivisibility of the base places the *Aufbauer* before a difficulty Bolzano already presented very clearly (*W*, I, §64). One could characterize it by saying that the requisite of indivisibility of the base raises a contradiction between what might be called the *form* and the *project* of the constitution system. For, on the one hand, the system seeks to integrate into its chains of definitions the concepts of clinical and experimental psychology, for example, those of "sensation," "visual quality," "touch," and "emotion." These objects are usually conceived as characteristics of experiences.

But, on the other hand, experiences are taken as the indivisible basic elements. How then can they be analyzed without at the same time jeopardizing the a priori requirement that makes the system possible? We may note here that, as the requirement of indivisibility, the difficulty we are speaking about is likewise a priori: one cannot hope to sidestep it by choosing fundamental elements that would avoid the paradox. The primitive relation, that of recollection of similarity, already seems to conflict with the indivisibility of its own terms, since it is a relation of ''part'' similarity, and thus presupposes, at least apparently, the existence of distinct parts in experiences.

The inadequacy of the *intensional* (*inhaltlich* or ''in comprehension'') or ''absolute'' conception of analysis (that is, an analytic that would proceed by breaking down a concept into its parts) is not only perceptible in constitution theory. It is also emphasized by the research of psychologists of perception. Köhler noted in 1922:

> What is produced in the whole cannot be deduced from the characteristics of separate parts. But conversely, what is produced in a part of the whole is determined by the laws governing the structure of the whole.[13]

From their research the Gestalt theoreticians inferred the necessity of developing a new epistemology that would break with the convenient symmetry established by mechanistic thought between analysis and synthesis, the division into parts and the reconstitution of the whole. In a lecture given in the 1920s, Wertheimer looked forward to the new logic that would be capable of expressing the particular relation a given configuration might entertain with its elements, whenever these are irreducible to ''constituent parts.''[14] Carnap makes use of the work of the Gestaltists not only by adopting as undefinables irreducible totalities, experiences ''taken in point form,'' but also by taking up the taste of inventing a formal procedure capable of accounting for the relations that such a configuration has with its ''elements.'' Since the difficulty arises from an intensional conception of analysis, Carnap develops an *extensional* analysis of experiences: an analysis using only classes of objects and relation extensions. Carnap calls this new analytic tool *quasi analysis*. To understand how this procedure solves the paradox of the indivisibility of the base, one must go back to an unpublished manuscript from 1923, *Die Quasizerlegung*, a study preliminary to the *Aufbau*.

The Idea of an ''Immanent Analysis''

In *Die Quasizerlegung* Carnap examines how the theory of relations renews the conception of conceptual analysis. Traditional logic employs what he suggests calling ''absolute'' analysis: one predicates of a particular concept the characters belonging to the objects that fall under this concept. These characters are then held to be the constituent parts of the concept. This type of analysis owes its popularity to its ''tractability.'' It makes it possible to characterize a singular element without having to go through the other elements of the domain. But this tractability is obtained at a cost: it obliges us constantly to enlarge the descriptive resources of language, without enabling us to set in advance a limit to the extension required by an exhaustive analysis.

There is another kind of analysis, ''relational'' analysis, which does not have this disadvantage. It consists in characterizing the objects of the whole under scrutiny by their reciprocal relations. This analysis can therefore take place within the bounds of the domain of objects, offering the possibility of an ''immanent treatment of its domain'' (*eine immanente Gebietsbehandlung*). But this advantage is partly neutralized by the clumsiness of the relational technique that must be called in when the goal is simply to characterize an individual element of the domain.

Carnap had the idea of developing a new procedure that would combine the advantages of absolute analysis with those of relational analysis. Like the latter, it would provide an immanent treatment of the totality of objects submitted to it. Like the former, it would furnish an individual characterization of the elements of the domain. This procedure consists in ''transforming the given relations of description so that they preserve the property of the immanent treatment of the domain, while acquiring the formal aspect of a division so as to make the individual treatment of elements possible'' (2).

Called at the time ''quasi division,'' this new method of analysis consists in *converting* the extensions of relation into *characters* common to several elements. Assuming that it is logically feasible, we see how the new method answers the formal problem raised by the Gestaltists. The initial given being made up of a closed set of relations, the ''constituents'' obtained through this procedure obviously depend on the total configuration of the domain to which they belong. To emphasize this relational aspect, we will call them ''quasi constituents.'' But we understand also why quasi division answers at the same time the paradoxes of the base of the system. For the elements that are related by the relational descriptions can be *simple* without this irreducibility hindering the application of quasi division. What the latter brings out is not a ''part'' but an ''aspect'' of the object. The fact that an object falls under several concepts does not imply that this object is composed.[15] What was believed to depend on an intensional analysis can be done in a purely extensional manner, by proceeding to a logically higher level (the class). At the same time the intensional paradox of indivisibility disappears.

Analysis and Quasi Analysis: The Limits of the Analogy

When he writes up the text of the *Aufbau*, Carnap borrows from the earlier manuscript what appears to him likely to throw some light on the formal status of the new analytic procedure that he renames ''quasi analysis.'' He then has a tendency to stress that ''the procedure of quasi analysis . . . stands in exact formal analogy to the indicated procedure of proper analysis'' (*A*, §71, 97), at the risk of preventing the reader from perceiving the specific characteristics of quasi analysis. It is probably this pedagogic intention that strangely enough will be responsible for the major misunderstanding the *Aufbau* met with. The 1923 manuscript nevertheless makes it possible to shed some light on the corresponding developments, even if it must not be excluded that Carnap might have modified some of his ideas on the issue at the time of the final writing.

The ''procedure of proper analysis'' Carnap mentions in the preceding quotation obviously refers to the relational analysis. The ''analogy'' between this type of analysis and quasi analysis is due to the fact that they both start from the same type of data: what is required is the extension of a relation ranging over the domain to be analyzed. In both cases this relation must have two minimal formal characteristics: it must be *symmetrical* and *reflexive*, so that every pair of elements that are joined by this relation can at the end of the analysis process be ascribed a common constituent (or quasi constituent).

Let us note that analysis and quasi analysis alike *can* start from a relation that is not only reflexive and symmetrical but *transitive* (without this being for either one a necessary condition). Such a relation determines disjoint classes of equivalence, whose common property can be directly derived. The application of the principle of abstraction to the construction of numbers is carried out with the help of such a relation, which Carnap calls an ''identity'' (*Gleichheit*) (*A*, §11, 13). In this case the recognition of (quasi) constituents is remarkably easy. But from the constitutional point of view, it is, as the manuscript notes, a ''degenerate'' (*Ausgearteter*) relation because it does not allow new constructions to be derived.[16]

It is therefore best in analysis and quasi analysis to start from a symmetrical, reflexive, and nontransitive relation—that is, a *similarity*. But the greater amount of information conveyed by a similarity is obtained at the cost of the particular difficulties encountered in analyzing it. For by definition a similarity between the objects x and y implies that they resemble one another two by two, but not always in the same aspects. It is therefore not possible to derive directly the common (quasi) constituent from the similarity classes, because similarity is not transitive, whereas the relation ''to have a certain (quasi) constituent in common'' is. The formal problem raised by the transition from the one to the other occurs *in the usual procedure of analysis as well as in quasi analysis*. To illustrate this problem, let us examine the example of quasi analysis that Carnap gives in the 1923 manuscript and takes up again in the *Aufbau* (§71, 98). Let us assume that a musical chord, perceived as an irreducible totality of sound, is obtained by striking on a piano the keys C, E, G of a given octave (this fact is hidden from the agent). To be able to carry out the quasi analysis, one must have a set of other chords and isolated notes, as well as a similarity relation ranging over the whole domain. The examination of the extension of this relation makes it possible to construct classes, defined in the following manner: (1) each pair of elements of the class stands in a relation of kinship K; (2) there is no element outside the class that stands in the relation K with all the elements of the class.

These classes, called in the *Aufbau* ''similarity circles'' (*Aehnlichkeitskreise*), *represent* what their elements have in common. Whether (relational) analysis or quasi analysis is concerned, the (quasi) ''constituents'' obtained are not of the same type as the objects they qualify, as opposed to the characteristic isogeny between the parts and the whole. Until now we have not encountered any formal difference between the procedure of relational analysis and quasi analysis. There is, however, a formally essential difference between them that appears more clearly in the manuscript than in the *Aufbau* and that consists in their respective relation with the *represented object*. The constituents brought out by analysis have their own "existence," independent of analysis. For example, when one makes a relational analysis of colors in the game of "Mastermind," one obtains a result that should be comparable term for term with the series of colors of the opponent. Likewise, in an analysis the composition of the object must always be recognizable by means independent of the analysis itself. On the other hand, quasi analysis has the specificity of producing quasi constituents, without being capable of discovering them. In quasi analysis there is no tribunal to appeal to. One might say that analysis is realist by definition, whereas quasi analysis is constructive by definition, in the sense that it cannot confront the quasi objects that it constructs with the facts. More exactly, the facts revealed by quasi analysis are precisely those that spontaneous knowledge would give us, if it were to start from the same data. For knowledge has *no other formal means* except those that quasi analysis makes use of in order to abstract classes of qualities from undecomposable experiences. This manner of producing the represented is not without formal consequences. However, these consequences will become apparent only in cases in which analysis and quasi analysis diverge in their principles, that is, as a function of the corrigibility of their results. For this reason the respective *application* of analysis and quasi analysis must be examined.

"Unfavorable Circumstances"

As a method originating from the theory of relations, quasi analysis, after the manner of analysis, must remain in its use a purely logical procedure. One of the gravest objections that could be leveled at the *Aufbau*—and which, as we shall see later, *was* leveled against it—is that it fails to separate clearly, in its application of quasi analysis, the strictly logical procedures from the empirical postulates concerning the state of the observational datum. In this respect, we must single out the three most common cases in quasi analysis, for each one implies a different relation between the formal and its range of application. The incidence of extralogical recourse to observational data shows up increasingly as one moves from the simplest and least problematic case of quasi analysis using a relation of *identity* to corresponding procedures using *part identity* or, finally, *part similarity*. With the first type, quasi analysis works from an identity, which determines, as we know, classes of equivalence. What makes this case relatively easier to deal with is that every nonempty class of elements related to a given element generally satisfies the conditions required for determining a quasi constituent (except if certain unfavorable circumstances occur, to which we will later return). This type of construction makes it possible, for example, to construct various sensorial areas, which are so many abstraction classes from the chains of qualities (visual, auditory, tactile, etc.). A more commonly used relation in quasi analysis is that of part identity (*Teilgleichheit*), which is a reflexive and symmetrical relation without transitivity. Two experiences are in this relation when there is a quality class to which they both belong. But this quality class can differ from one pair of experiences to another, the same element generally belonging to a large number of different-quality classes. Finally, the relation of part similarity (*Teilähnlichkeit*) makes it possible to construct qualitative orders. It is indeed a symmetrical and reflexive relation, but one that requires that related elements should have only a *similar* feature (and not, as previously, a *common* feature). Two blue objects are in this relation, for example.

We shall temporarily pass over the general problems involved in the specification of *dimension* as a distinctive criterion of sensorial classes, retaining only the difficulties that concern the formal consequences arising from the choice of one of these types of relations with respect to quasi analysis. It is generally granted that quasi analysis on a transitive relation does not pose any special problem. Actually, quasi analysis can be vitiated by the existence of systematic relations between the elements of the domain, just as the two other kinds of quasi analysis I singled out.

With Carnap, I shall call the following difficulty "the problem of *constitution completeness*." One can conceive of certain characteristics of the extensional data required by quasi analysis that would prevent the latter from arriving at "exact" results. Sometimes the circumstances will be such that they will prevent the derivation of a quasi constituent. This unfavorable situation, called "companion" (Carnap) or "companionship" (Goodman), occurs whenever one of the constituents appears only in conjunction with another. Let us therefore admit that any experience comprising a given constituent also comprises another, which in turn occurs in other experiences. Thus what quasi analysis brings out is the constituent that is, so to speak, the most "social": the one represented in the most diverse experiences. The "accompanying" constituent, on the other hand, will not have an extensionally distinctive criterion and thus will be confused with the constituent it accompanies. Let us remark here that the companionship difficulty is not the prerogative of nontransitive relations; it can also occur in the case of a quasi analysis by identities. The second problem, on the other hand, only arises with quasi analyses on nontransitive relations.

This second variety of circumstances unfavorable to the application of quasi analysis (on part identity) lies in the possibility of achieving, under certain circumstances, the construction of *superfluous* quasi constituents, that is, not corresponding to any "objective" similarity class. This occurs whenever each element of the datum is in a part relation exclusively with itself and another element (if the set has three elements). Termed by Goodman "imperfect community," this case brings out one similarity class too many, since all the elements bear a relation with one another and seem to have a definite common constituent, whereas they are only related in groups of twos or threes, and so forth.

We can see now how these difficulties could threaten the logical integrity of reconstruction. It suffices that the agent of constitution should *be obliged* to dismiss one of the hypotheses unfavorable to the success of quasi analysis for an empirical postulate to slip into the "logical" reconstruction. The full force of Goodman's argumentation stems from the fact that he interprets as "dismissals" these few lines of §70 of the *Aufbau*:

If there are no systematic connections between the distributions of the different colors, then this unfavorable case, namely, that the second property is missing in a color class, becomes the less likely the smaller the average number of colors of the thing and the larger the total number of the things is. (*A*, §70, 96)

Yet this text in no way aims at establishing the possibility of quasi analysis, since it appears in the course of a presentation of *analysis proper*. The quoted text is therefore not a solution seeking to elude the difficulty of the companion, but a mere stipulation allowing one to follow up the derivation of the constituents in the example proposed, as the remainder of the text shows: "Let us assume that in our case the unfavorable conditions are not fulfilled . . . " If Carnap is not guilty here of the coup denounced by Goodman, according to whom he imposes trivially the condition of possibility of the success of quasi analysis, what then is his solution to the extensional obstacles we have just outlined? Two series of unpublished texts allow us to cast a little light on the way in which Carnap evaluated this difficulty and thought that he might solve it.

The Formal Solution of 1923

The comparison between analysis and quasi analysis, developed in the 1923 manuscript, *Die Quasizerlegung*, is of the greatest relevance here. What distinguishes the two, we may recall, is that a test independent from the results is possible only in the case of analysis. Now, if there is no possibility of a test independent from the results, there also can be no failure of quasi analysis. The characteristic incompleteness of companionship can therefore vitiate an analysis, but not a quasi analysis. This difference must be brought out in a purely formal way; the manuscript sets out to accomplish this by building up an axiomatic of quasi analysis. The first three axioms are shared by analysis and quasi analysis. They correspond to the definition of a similarity circle in the *Aufbau* (§71, 97):

I. If two elements are related, they have at least one quasi-constituent part in common.
II. If two elements are not related, they do not have any quasi-constituent part in common.
III. If two elements *a* and *b* have the same kinship (that is to say if *a* is related to all the relatives of *b*, and only to them), they have the same quasi-constituent parts.

But a *fourth principle* allows us, in the case of quasi analysis, to exclude a priori the formation of quasi constituents that might not be strictly necessary in accordance with the initial extensional data:

IV. There is no one quasi-constituent part whose omission leaves the fulfillment of requisites I, II, and III unchanged.

This principle then functions as a *principle of economy*, from which theorem 7 is derived, especially designed to avoid those quasi constituents that cannot be detected through the extensional means at one's disposal:

7. If the fundamental requisites are met, no quasi-constituent part is the companion of another. That is a consequence of principle IV, for such a part could be omitted without violating I and II.

The manuscript thus presents a formally clear and satisfying solution to the question of companionship. The question that naturally comes to mind is why the *Aufbau* does not mention it. I remarked earlier that the difficulty of companionship is mentioned only in connection with analysis. Why not simply include the formal solution of the manuscript, thus dissipating possible objections that were bound to be leveled against quasi analysis? Carnap's letters explain what motivated this silence in the *Aufbau*.

In a letter to Nelson Goodman on January 28, 1938, Carnap explains his decision to limit himself in the *Aufbau* to a "simpler method" of quasi analysis. I will quote a long passage from his letter, which also informs us that the question of completeness had been widely debated at the Thursday gatherings of the Vienna Circle around 1925:

The reason for choosing the simpler method for the *Aufbau* was, first, the greater simplicity and, second, just the fact that even a more complicated method could not reach the aim mentioned. I discussed the latter point in detail with my friends. To their objection that then the method of *Quasizerlegung* was not appropriate for the purpose intended, I replied that the construction intends only to give a "rational reconstruction" of what really happens in the development of our knowledge by perceptions, and that if certain unfortunate configurations of the experiences happened to occur, the person in question would also in reality come to so-called wrong results, that is, to systems of qualities different from the normal ones.

How are we to interpret this answer? Is it an acknowledgment of failure that recognizes shortcomings in the axiomatic of *Quasizerlegung*? A cursory reading might suggest that this is the case, and attribute to the discovery of the difficulty of imperfect community, for example, this verdict on the incapacity of the method to guarantee completeness. But a more careful examination of Carnap's answer shows that a *logical shortcoming* is not in question. No method *can* or *should* be set up to compensate for the supposed imperfections of the "simple" version of quasi analysis precisely because the validity of purely extensional derivations is irrefutable. What causes a false diagnosis of the shortcomings of quasi analysis is the substitution of a realist point of view for that of rational reconstruction. The realist point of view consists in abandoning the constraints connected with the application of quasi analysis, while supposing some test is possible, *laterally* so to speak. Goodman's objections, for example, unwittingly reestablish the fiction of an omniscient God capable of testing through originary intuition, that is *without construction*, what constitution derives from its extensional given. But if one takes the reconstructional project seriously, one must be ready to draw all the consequences. If the perceiving subject has *no other means* of arriving at his concepts than through a quasi analysis of his own experiences, his concepts will retain the trace of their experiential origin. It is not impossible that for him "things may go wrong," so to speak, that the subject might construct for himself a system of qualities without any possible objective counterpart, failing to be intersubjectively valid.

The selection of a "good" picture of the world does not, however, come within the responsibility of quasi analysis. Rather, one should turn Goodman's objection around: it is because quasi analysis makes no empirical claim concerning the organization of the given that it need not assess the "normal" or "abnormal" character of its results. At a later stage of constitution, one will be able to rectify some of the elementary constructs according to other people and with the help of mathematicized concepts of experience. But some bases will turn out to be extensionally too poor: the perceiving subject can empirically be placed in a state of sensory deprivation; it is his experience, and not his logic, that will suffer. The very idea of rational reconstruction would be of only trifling interest if it were not closely connected to the existence of positive sciences. An endeavor of reconstruction has some meaning because these sciences have already developed their concepts. For by starting from a *subject*, one cannot bet on the necessity and the universality of the constructions. But the *existence of sciences* guarantees *a parte post* the possibility of an extensionally diversified experience. Quasi analysis awaits nothing more than this guarantee offered a priori by the system it founds.

The Problem of Essential Overlapping

As we have already mentioned, it is with the third relation, the relation of part similarity, that the real difficulties begin and that our doubt increases concerning the formal purity of the derivations.[17] Two experiences are "part similar" if they have parts that *resemble* each other, like the light blue of the sky and the dark blue of a piece of cloth. However, to construct the similarity circles, we must overcome a specific difficulty, that of so-called accidental overlapping. An example will make this clearer: Let us assume that three elementary experiences A, B, and C each have an approximately red spot and an approximately blue one. When we come to set up similarity circles, we will assemble all the red experiences in one class, and all the blue ones in another. But experiences A, B, and C will be at the intersection of these two classes. Yet this intersection is not relevant for the construction of the order of colors, for red is not blue's neighbor. One must therefore find a criterion that lets one distinguish this *fortuitous* intersection of part-similarity classes from an *essential* intersection, one that occurs when the classes in question are actually classes of elements of neighboring colors.

Is there a *formal* criterion that would allow the *Aufbauer* to distinguish between the two kinds of overlapping? Would this criterion, provided there is one, fulfill the condition of *Lückenlosigkeit*, systematic continuity, or would it fraudulously bring back an empirical content?

Against all the commentators who unanimously stress the shift of constitution on this issue toward an empirical claim, I would like, if not to plead not guilty, at least to present the facts of the case in a more favorable light. What Carnap is being reproached for here is that he proposed a criterion of essential overlapping that cannot be justified a priori. Stated in the language of "fictitious operations" (i.e., in the form of an instruction given to the agent of constitution), the criterion is the following:

> *Fictitious operation* (of quality classes): for each pair of similarity circles that have a considerable part (at least half of one of them) in common, *A* forms the intersection and the two remainder classes. The resulting classes, if they have a considerable part in common with any other similarity circle, are again divided, etc., until classes are reached that are not divided through any similarity circles in the indicated way. These are the desired quality classes. (*A*, §112)

What one finds objectionable in this "criterion" is obviously this unfounded numerical statement: Why should the intersection cover at least *half* of one of the classes? What allows one to arrive at that proportion? One could answer here that this instruction should be taken not as a *criterion* for essential overlapping, but as a metrical illustration of a purely logical criterion. But the argument breaks down on its own, since Carnap takes up an analogous formulation in the very "language of constitution":

> A class *k* of elementary experiences is called a quality class if *k* is totally contained in each similarity circle that contains at least half of it, and if, for each elementary experience *x* that does not belong to *k*, there is a similarity circle in which *k* is contained, but to which *x* does not belong. (§112, 153)

By providing this numerical criterion, Carnap sends us back to §81 on the theoretical problems of the construction of quality classes:

> In essential overlapping any piece of similarity circle that is split off includes at least an entire quality class (i.e., a not inconsiderable fraction of the similarity circle or of one of its parts). (§81)

In accidental overlapping, on the other hand:

> The part which is split off is generally very small relative to the quality class as a whole and especially relative to the similarity circle.

We will concede that the "considerable-inconsiderable" contrast, as likewise the adverb "generally," can lead us to suspect the illicit occurrence of nonlogical contents in the construction. We notice here, however, that these contents are no less "logical" than the general contrast between analytic and empirical propositions on which the entire construction rests. To understand this, let us return to the example studied by Carnap in §81. Let us examine the two locations in the visual field, which we shall call A and B, respectively, and which for the sake of simplicity we will conceive as composed of a multiplicity of discrete colored points. Let us assume that A is occupied by a bluish body and B by a reddish one. Five points of A will be neighboring in color so that the various corresponding experiences are gathered in the similarity circle of blue; likewise five points of B will justify the gathering of correlating experiences in the similarity circle of red. However, these two similarity circles will be disjoint only on the following condition: A and B must not appear conjointly in several elementary experiences in the same visual locations. Actually, this condition is too severe: it supposes that a systematic variation should affect all the elements of the visual field from one experience to the next. The problem is, therefore, to know how to distinguish cases where similarity circles intersect, because they contain qualitatively or intrinsically related elements (like two similarity circles of the neighboring colors blue and indigo), from cases where they intersect, because some of their elements happen to be fortuitously joined at the same locations. If one takes a "realist" point of view, one "knows" that these elements are not related: red and blue are not similar. Is there a nonrealist means of separating the two kinds of overlapping? The only means at our disposal is to compare the sections of the similarity circles that intersect: with essential overlapping, the intersection is very large; with accidental overlapping, it concerns only an insignificant portion of the experiences belonging to a similarity circle.

On what then does this comparison rest? On a property of the world? It would have to be this sort of property, if the success of the constitution depended on a particular order among experiences. The fundamental hypothesis of constitution theory consists rather in denying that an a posteriori order could emerge from an accidental series of experiences. That is not to demand that the world should have such and such a property. It is simply to take up in the extensions the initial distinction between empirically and formally true propositions; experience does not allow us to encounter invariable relations that only appear with scientific objectification, with the bringing out of formal relations between quasi objects. This difference in the way experiences relate to one another according to whether their relation conforms to a rule can be anticipated in the system as long as it is a question of a *difference of form between propositions*, a difference without which the very idea of science would lose its condition of possibility. If "analytic hypotheses" are possible in the case of colored experiences allowing us, for example, to project the properties of the intersections of color spheres onto the similarity circles uniting the experiences, it is due to a property of the color space that might be called "grammatical." As it was frequently put at the time, the similarity of red and crimson is an *internal* relation between the colors. On the other hand, nothing in the grammar allows us to predict that this green object will be scented, or will be lying on a red surface. Such matters concern empirical propositions.

Thus the difference Carnap's criterion strives to exploit is one opposing two categories of propositions, which he will later call quasi-syntactic and synthetic. The former seem to say something about the world, whereas they actually reflect a formal aspect of the descriptive language used. In this sense, the distinction is founded on the contrast that can be made in the system between analytic propositions and empirical ones. To this second distinction must correspond an extensional image. Hence the possibility of finding one's way in the construction of qualities.

The preceding developments do not strive to prove that reconstruction was a *feasible* task. Carnap himself recognized the *anticipated* character of his own outline. Rather, these developments appear to us to stress the *philosophical coherence* of the rules and of the project of constitution. Such insistence is perhaps not superfluous; indeed, it is because they raised questions that were secondary with respect to the project that some commentators believed that they had found fault with the *Aufbau* or even refuted it. Perhaps the weaknesses of the work stem from the fact that Carnap wanted the book to be accessible. First the title: it was on the advice of Schlick that Carnap opted for the definitive title in November 1925. If he had stuck to the unappealing and quasi-medical title of *Konstitutionstheorie*, instead of the false promise implied in the title *Der logische Aufbau der Welt*, Carnap would have avoided undue attention to the *content* of his definitions, to the detriment of the general constitution theory.

A second aspect of the book worked against it: the fourth part serves as an illustration of the first three. Carnap realized too late that the reader would never take seriously the distinction he himself drew with great care and even scrupulousness between the *thesis* and the *example* of constitution. It is this dualism that gives substance to the objections leveled against quasi analysis.

> When I think about my present view concerning the *Aufbau* [wrote Carnap in 1939], or rather the differences between my opinion at that time and the present ones, I should not include at all the details of the construction of the system of symbolized definitions. Even at the time of writing the *Aufbau* I did not mean the definitions as an expression of my opinion or as belonging to the assertions made by the book. As you know, I said in so many words that they are not meant in this way, but merely as an illustration to explain the method.

It is not the inadequate character of this or another derivation that eventually leads Carnap to give up the method of quasi analysis. Even when he turns away in *Testability and Meaning* from a "molecular" approach to language — in accordance with the principle of verifiability in the strict sense — Carnap maintains that such a language *can* be chosen, preference for this or another type of language being purely a matter of convention.

The Portion of Forms

The continuity of the construction, that is, the quality of the system called by Frege *Lückenlosigkeit*, no longer has in the *Aufbau* the function of revealing the analytic character of mathematics that it had in the *Grundgesetze*. However, this continuity makes it possible to bring out the respective portion of form and empirical given in knowledge. The given reduces to extensions of the primitive relation. The constituents of form obviously appear as that which makes up the true vehicle of empirical information. They are both conditions for *acquiring* knowledge and for *calculating* new forms.

Is it legitimate to speak of "calculating"? Should one not resort to knowledge accumulated by the *Realwissenschaften* in order to build up the forms of the quasi objects? Consequently, is the formal description not guided by empirical observations, and thus deprived of the purely deductive recourse precisely furnished by a calculation? To answer this question, one must be sensitive to what might be called the "dynamics" of analyticity in the project of constitution. One may thus understand that the system of constitution leads, on account of its very logic, to the idea of a purely deductive calculation of forms of objects.

How Is an Analytic Synthesis Possible?

"Quasi analysis is a synthesis that wears the linguistic garb of an analysis" (*A*, §74, 104). The use of quasi analysis, a purely analytic formal discipline, in the synthetic construction of quasi objects leads one to dissociate two series of contrasts: analysis and synthesis on the one hand, and analytic and synthetic propositions on the other. The distinction between *analysis* and *synthesis* can no longer be drawn by means of the *formal procedures* used. For, from the point of view of formal reality, quasi analysis is only slightly different from analysis; in the metaphor of the *Aufbau*, the former "wears the garb" of the latter. And yet, quasi analysis produces a *synthesis*. It proceeds "by forming classes of elements and, furthermore, relation extensions of these classes" (*A*, §74, 104) — by producing the synthesis of basic experiences. The distinction between analysis and synthesis must therefore be made in accordance with the finished system. To analyze is to "go down to" the base of the system; to synthesize is to go up from the base toward the most abstract forms, in the direction of constitution:

> Since every object of science is constructed from the basic elements, to analyze it means to trace back [*zurückverfolgen*] the procedure of construction from the object itself to those elements that are required for its construction. (*A*, §74, 103)

It follows from this that "analytic" should no longer be contrasted with "synthetic." "Synthetic" is, indeed, the adjective that qualifies the constructive nature of the process of quasi analysis (ibid., 104). As the latter is, moreover, purely formal and analytic, the association of the formal criterion and the epistemological criterion would lead to a contradiction. "Analytic" must therefore be contrasted with "empirical." This second distinction should be understood in terms of Frege's' criterion, whose application is considerably extended by the theory of constitution. The *analytic* axioms are those that "can be deduced from the definitions alone (presupposing the axioms of logic, without which no deduction is possible at all)" (*A*, §106, 147). *Empirical* axioms reveal, on the other hand, "a relation between constituted objects that can only be established on the basis of experience" (ibid.). For example, axiom 2 of the *Aufbau*, which states the symmetry of the relation of part similarity, ascribes to this relation a property that is logically constitutive of it that follows from the definition of this relation. It is therefore analytic. On the other hand, axiom 1, which states the asymmetry of the relation of recollection of similarity, is founded on the observation of relations between experiences and is therefore empirical.

The preceding organization of axioms and propositions of the system into *analytic* and *empirical* ones makes it possible to locate unambiguously the procedures used by the system of constitution, such as the rules governing quasi analysis or, more generally, the rules of the theory of relations (*A*, §104, 144–45). These procedures do not depend on a certain state of the world. They are therefore not established a posteriori; they are consequently *analytic* principles.

The whole theory of constitution (i.e., logic) is thus made up of rules of formation and transformation that could very well be called a priori because "the construction and the knowledge of objects logically depend on them," but which should not as such be assimilated with *elements of knowledge*. They are only *conventions*. As we saw, the final contribution of the *Aufbau* is not to be sought in the "material" assertions, that is, in the concrete schemata for reducing empirical concepts. The analytic axioms and, along with them, the formal procedures used in the derivations, are what constitute the original and final contribution of the outline. Since the importance of the *Aufbau* lies in its formal procedures, no harm is done to constitution by emptying it of any relation to the empirical. It might be said that by separating the formal features from their realization in an empirical construction, one accomplishes the process already started. One passes then from the intrasystematic use of the contrast between the analytic and the empirical to a metasystematic use that characterizes the point of view of the theory of constitution (*Konstitutionstheorie*, as opposed to *Konstitutionssystem*; see, for example, *A*, §179, 252). The aim of constitution theory is not to build up a system of constitution but rather to work out a system of formal rules from which a pure theory of object forms can be derived (*A*, §105, 146). The various rules of derivation used in the outline can then serve as a clue in the search for more general rules. For example, the statement of the legitimate transformations that make the relations accessible to quasi analysis (rules 2–7) seems to apply a single, more general rule:

A homogeneous relation is to be transformed in as simple a way as possible, so that quasi analysis becomes applicable to it. (*A*, §105, 146)

Constitution theory thus singles out *formal schemata* by proceeding according to a strictly "technical" mode: the advancement of constitution does not yet make it possible to reach the true *architectonic* unity toward which it tends.[18] Carnap does not, however, give up the idea of such a unity. The schemata under which the various formal rules come together must in turn admit of deduction from a single principle: the highest principle of constitution occupies the position Kant set at the summit of his system of pure reason. So far we know very little about such a principle, except that it is possible that it will be discovered one day. It would be general enough so that all the formal rules used in the various systems of constitution would be deducible from it. Thus the idea of a complete formalization would be reached, which would make constitution theory a purely deductive science.

The Extension of the Analytic: From the Transcendental to the Formal

So far only a program of research has been offered for constitution theory. But this program allows us to perceive better the contribution brought by the division between the purely analytic field and the empirical field to the delimitation of the respective domains of constitution theory, that is, philosophy or logic (these three terms being henceforth equivalent), and unified science. The task of the first is to set *conventions (Festsetzungen)*. For logic determines conventionally the rules according to which the procedures for bringing together and for organizing the data as well as the legitimate transformations of statements. To take up a metaphor Carnap often uses, one might say that constitution theory shows how a system of coordinates is formed, what the various systems of axes that can be chosen are, and what the calculations permitted by each of them are. Science consists simply in *applying* this system. First, by choosing a system of axes and by fixing a point of origin: it is the moment of constitution that produces an "absolute frame of reference" of scientific activity. Then begins the possibility of a nonanalytic predication, that is, properties and relations not registered in the definitions can be sought in order to enrich the knowledge of the objects of the system.[19]

When one changes the field of inquiry, passing from intrasystematic comprehension to metasystematic considerations, one notices that the importance of the analytic is increased. The entire system of definitions is now considered as a set of propositions true by convention, serving only to explain the meaning of the words science uses. It is true that these conventions are established on the basis of observation data. But once the system is completed, they cease to be revisable through experience, having now merely a tautological value. The system of concepts is in fact only designed to serve in turn as a base (*Unterlage*) for empirical predications. Not only is the whole of logic, including its most important branch—constitution theory—purely analytic, but science in its first stage of clarifying references is also an applied logic (applied to science itself in its determinate historical state) and, on account of this, again analytic.[20] One is not able to understand what motivates this extension of analyticity if one does not discern therein the effect of the formal reflection Carnap practices on the transcendental concepts. The analytic takes on a constitutive value and governs not only the constitution of objects of a possible knowledge, but also more generally the relation of a concept with an intuition: the possibility of *applying the forms.*

The idea that Carnap can substitute the formal for the Kantian transcendental subject in the constitutive function that Kant ascribes to the latter goes against the conception one generally has of logical empiricism. It must be added that we do not intend to make Carnap a disciple of Kant, but simply to bring out a topical relationship designed to correct what the name of "empiricist" tends to suggest. As early as 1925 conventions become compatible with empiricism, and it is enough to emphasize that these conventions are without content and, consequently, are tautological (i.e., logical) in nature. They continue, therefore, to be conceived as a priori, and, consequently, make it possible to transfer all the synthetic a priori to the side of the analytic. We easily see how this transition is supposed to mark a sharp rupture with one of the essential claims of Kantianism. But this rupture is less deep than one would be led to believe, for, at bottom, the questions judged to be relevant and the acceptable kinds of solutions have not changed. In what sense does Carnap remain an empiricist?

Let us take as an example the capital problem of delimiting our ability to know. Traditionally empiricism is, in Kant's phrase, "the censor of reason." Hobbes and Hume, for example, infer from the experiential origin of knowledge the existence of bounds of knowledge. There are indeed objects that are not "proportionate" to our cognitive ability, such as the infiniteness of space and time. Kant calls this type of obstacle to knowledge *technical.* If our means of knowledge were improved, if new instruments could extend our perception beyond the actual thresholds, we would have access to a larger portion of reality. Beyond the bounds, there is always, from the standpoint of classical empiricism, something to be known. Thus, the determination of the bounds of what we can know rests on a *conjecture.* Starting from the current state of knowledge, and estimating the eventual improvements of the techniques of measurement and observation, the empiricist marks out the field of possible questions. He draws the boundary right where the possibility of an empirical test ceases.

We know Kant's objection to the language of bounds: the empiricists strive to restrict the activity of understanding without this restriction being established according to a *definite* principle. Hence this regressive recourse to an obscure realm of forever insoluble questions. Once it is understood that only knowledge of phenomena exists, nothing alien to reason remains. All questions are soluble, all dialectical departures themselves pertaining to a foundation, perhaps not in experience, but in the idea.[21] Like Kant, Carnap thinks it is possible to delimit a priori the realm of the knowable. Although he employs indifferently the words "limit" (*Grenze*), "bounds" (*Schranke*) and "frontier" (*Randpunkt*), it is clear that the principle of verifiability is what circumscribes the realm of rational activity. The field of action of science is thus truly *delimited*, and so delimited a priori since the principle of verifiability is an *analytic* one, given by constitution theory simultaneously with the concept of science. Within the limits determined by the requisite of verifiability, namely, that the propositions of science employ exclusively constituted or constitutable concepts, science can be said to have no bounds. Nothing escapes the jurisdiction of science; science extends to all the thinkable (*A*, §180, 253– 55).

What marks unambiguously this a priori character of the assertion is that the nonlimitation of science (*Unbegrenzheit der wissenschaftlichen Erkenntnis*) does not need to be submitted to the facts. If unanswered questions still exist today, they will be said to be unsolvable "practically, but not in principle." The "technical" obstacle of the empiricists is thus restored, yet with a new certainty — which is no longer empiricist — that such an obstacle cannot constitute an essential hindrance. Constitution theory allows us to anticipate a priori the development of the system of concepts and to assert that, sooner or later, the concepts concerned will find their proper place in the system.[22]

If there is no thought outside the system of concepts of unified science, what becomes of metaphysical questions? The outline of the *Aufbau* allows us to give this question an answer that, lacking a constitution system, classical positivism did not have the theoretical means of clarifying. It is true that Comte considered metaphysical propositions to be meaningless and showed how they belong to a historically obsolete type of inquiry. However, as Jürgen Habermas observes,[23] this is a nonradical criticism, an exclusion that the absence of "reflection" dooms to inefficiency. One can indeed show that the concepts of metaphysics that Comte believed to have rejected in fact continue to affect implicitly the discourse of positive legitimation. It might be said, paraphrasing Habermas, that the reflection Comte did not know how to go about, Carnap was able to undertake. For constitution makes it possible, as we saw, to reevaluate all the traditional notions involved in metaphysical discourse. If some of these notions prove to be untranslatable, they will be excluded from the domain of meaningful concepts, without as such escaping a rational treatment (insofar as historicocultural objects, etc. are concerned; cf. *A*, §181, 256ff., and §183, 260–61). But some of the metaphysical concepts can thus receive a *positive substitute*; such is the case of the notions of reality and appearance, identity, and individual. The concept Comte took to be typically metaphysical, that of causality, finds in the world of perception a sphere of legitimacy and can receive therein a strictly formal definition. Once again here Carnap's approach repeats that of Kant. Metaphysics should not provoke a sterile skepticism. One still must understand what made its concepts possible, and why they failed to produce unanimously recognized theses.

For Carnap, the two major kinds of error into which the metaphysicians fall arise from their misunderstanding of the rules that govern a meaningful language. The first error consists in using notions in themselves legitimate without worrying about their domains of application. Thus, in the best of cases, the properties that properly belong to a category of elements of the statement are transferred to the objects. Such is the case, for example, of the illicit employment of *identity* in the ordinary use of this term. In the worst of cases, one has made a statement that is meaningless because it violates the conditions of employment of the notion (when one says, for example, "the one is identical"). The second and more general error of metaphysics consists in thinking that philosophy as such escapes the jurisdiction of science. A good illustration of this illusion could be found in the division Bergson establishes between two regions of experience, the mind belonging to the metaphysical approach and matter belonging to the scientific one.[24] Kant himself fell into this error, by making synthetic a priori propositions a subject matter for philosophical inquiry and one that conditions its legitimacy. For what "formal reflection" on metaphysical and transcendental concepts indeed proves is that the philosopher does not have a vocation for contents. He never works directly on experience. By becoming a constitution theory, philosophy discovers that its mission is always and solely a pacifying one. It does not prompt debates; it dissolves them. Rather, it promotes discussions concerning the usefulness, the opportuneness, the fruitfulness of the various modes of presentation (*Darstellung*) of a given axiomatic. Being purely analytic, philosophy evolves only in the realm of *convention*. It lacks the dimension of *truth*. For example, it is not a matter of *choosing* between realism, phenomenalism, and idealism. These are only various means of reconstructing experience, each of which can present advantages for exposition that the others lack.

Since the time of the *Aufbau* Carnap strove to reconcile the seemingly contradictory positions on the stage of "scientific" philosophy. Already the *pax philosophica* consists in exhibiting the extensional equivalence of the two theses at stake in the controversy, both appearing then as variant formulations depending on a different linguistic decision. We will soon see what mediating role Carnap tries to play between the advocates of logicism and those of formalism. Leibnizian *Calculemus* finally replaces the dogmatist's debate. Such at least is the hope that the institution of the Vienna Circle materializes. Philosophy engages in a new type of activity, both remote from any proper content and near that which science proposes to it. From a simple extreme-concept, the analytic has become the criterion of the legitimacy of the whole of philosophy. After the *Aufbau* there is no longer any philosophy except one about language.

3

The New Foundational Project

The concept of *analyticity* in the *Aufbau* was presupposed rather than fully worked out. Adapted to a conventionalist interpretation, the logicist conception constituted one of the conditions for the relevance of the project. For without the assurance of the complete vacuity of the formal, without the reduction of all the mathematical to the purely logical, the backbone of constitution would be missing. Logicism being largely presupposed, the question of the logic of science is posed, in the *Aufbau*, in terms of the extension of analytic procedures to the treatment of empirical concepts. The second phase of Carnap's work, corresponding to the period during which he wrote the *Logical Syntax* (1931–35), may resemble an abandonment easily explained by both the "formal" and the "material" difficulties of the project. The principle of verifiability comes up against dispositional concepts; phenomenalism proves to be incompatible with the theory of observation that gradually prevails in the discussions of the Vienna Circle. But what might be taken for a retreat appears to us rather to correspond to a radicalization of the same project. Once the properly logico-philosophical task of constitution elucidated by the *Aufbau*, the *Logical Syntax* addresses the problem that was still incipient in the former work. It sets out to develop in a fully explicit manner the formal rules that govern no longer a particular system of the concepts of science but any system, whether it is a formal or an interpreted axiomatic.

It is then illusory to see in the *Syntax* a sort of narrowing of the philosophical inquiry. For an elucidation of the rules of a general grammar of scientific language must simultaneously specify the *general* conditions of the application of a formal system to experience—conditions that will not only be *shown* by concretely setting up a system of constitution, but will also be *described* by a set of recursive rules—and unambiguously fix the purely analytic character of the propositions of philosophy, in other words, of what might henceforth be called the metalanguage of science. One could characterize this second phase by saying that the "foundation circle" acquires a more precise shape and, so to speak, is claimed in this metalanguage. The analytic-synthetic distinction is no longer, as previously, *exploited* as a property already functioning in natural theories and simply revealed in its pureness by the system. It is now the object of a formal treatment; it receives in the — analytic — metalanguage a definition that guarantees its applicability to any language. The aim of the *Logical Syntax* is to prove the legitimacy of this kind of circularity.

The tautological character of mathematics is the first article of the theoretical creed accepted by the members of the Vienna Circle. All members and "sympathizers" of the Circle adopt enthusiastically what seems to be the final solution to the issue that constitutes for them the weak spot of traditional empiricism: What are the origin and the nature of mathematical truths? If they derive from experience, whence comes their universal validity? If they do not derive from experience, do they come from a rational or intuitive *synthetic* a priori principle? Tautology has for the members of the Circle a clearly defined function: it must save empiricism from the blind alley into which Kant and, later, several conventionalists led it by developing a theory of the mathematical founded on synthetic a priori principles.

Tautology as a Weapon against "Apriorism"

What Carnap calls "empiricism," in the 1930s, is defined by a single thesis that is actually most often presented in a negative manner: "It is the position according to which there is no synthetic a priori knowledge." One could attempt to reformulate this thesis in a positive way, by resorting to the version of the principle of verifiability contemporary with the *Aufbau*: any content of knowledge is reducible to (purely formal, quasi-analytic) relations between immediately given experiences. By challenging the notion of a synthetic a priori proposition, "logical empiricists" seek of course to forbid the very possibility of metaphysics, which in their eyes is defined as the attempt to explore a cognitive content that would belong to it proper, since it would not be directly accessible in experience nor reducible to logico-mathematical relations. However, they also have another opponent in view, who is closer to their theses and was for many among them the intermediary who led them to their current conception of "empiricism": I mean the conventionalists who, like Poincaré, inspired the antiempiricist tonality of this early text of Carnap's:

> Philosophy has proclaimed for some time now that the construction of physics cannot rest on the mere results of experimentation, but must also apply principles that do not come from experience.[25]

What then appears for Carnap to form the radically antiempiricist feature of contemporary science is the presence of axiomatic systems that he interprets as synthetic a priori propositions, not in the strictly Kantian sense of "necessary conditions of the object of knowledge,'' but as conventions posited as principles in accordance with considerations of method (as the methodological principle of simplicity). Conventions, for Poincaré, are synthetic a priori principles because they are neither arbitrary and purely nominal, nor empirically given.

The shift from the synthetic a priori to the conventional prepares for the final retrieval of the conventional in the analytic. The decisive step is taken when the conventional is reinterpreted as that whose validity rests on a linguistic rule — in other words, what is tautologically true. The concept of tautology has the advantage of furnishing an *explicatum* of the concept of convention compatible with the principle of verifiability: instead of saying that logic and mathematics are conventions (which leaves the status of such principles undetermined and may make the principle of verifiability ineffective, not only in its application, but even in its own legitimacy), one will say that they constitute, following Hahn's phrase, an "immense tautology" so as to annex the conventional in its entirety to the purely formal, empty of content.

Once tautology is endowed with this function, one must still define it to make it coextensive with the logico-mathematical and to explain why until now mathematics was truly believed to have content. Curiously enough, "tautology" thus understood regains the full value of the logicist venture. One could say that it makes it possible to renew, as it were, the content of this venture since it is no longer a matter of bringing out the naturally and organically logical essence of number, but of showing that in logic and mathematics, only linguistic forms are concerned. Redefined as a "true proposition by virtue of its sole form," tautology has above all a heuristic value: it designates, under the proviso of "certain conditions being fulfilled," not only, as Wittgenstein would have it, the formulas of propositional calculus that remain true whatever the truth-value of their sub-formulas, but any mathematical proposition (insofar as Frege's venture seems likely to be won) and even any mathematical proof as a series of formulary transformations carried out in accordance with certain conventions. As Hans Hahn says, "What we mean after the transformation is always the same as what we meant before it."[26] One can therefore speak of tautology when confronted with any symbolic practice regulated by linguistic conventions. Even if we do not actually calculate each member of an equality so as to be able to exhibit the final identity step by step, such a proof always seems possible. Tautology appears explicitly then as a putative property, a heuristic principle, that, although in the process of being validated, must be "essentially correct."[27]

During the years 1930–31, the logicists continue to come up against the three axioms of the *Principia* that, as Russell confessed, can with difficulty pass for analytic. The axiom of reducibility, which the ramified theory of types renders necessary, is not "logically valid." The axiom of choice and the axiom of infinity make existential assertions concerning the constituents of the universe. How can Carnap hope to overcome these three obstacles to the logicist solution?

The Axiom of Infinity

Every proposition of logic is a tautology; therefore the same is true from the point of view of logicism for every proposition of mathematics. Yet the axiom of infinity is not valid on the basis of its sole form. If it is nevertheless valid, it is so only contingently. For certain domains of objects, it is valid; for others not. (Carnap, "Die Mathematik als Zweig der Logik," 306)

The logicists disagree among themselves concerning which axiom creates the most difficulties. For Russell, it is undoubtedly the axiom of infinity. As he remarks in his lecture before the Mathematical Society of France, what distinguishes precisely the multiplicative axiom from the axiom of infinity is that the first "has the form and the character of the axioms of logic: we do not know how to prove it from empirical data"; the second, on the other hand, does not even have the appearance of an axiom of logic, asserting, as it does, that *there are* an infinite number of objects in the universe. Without such an axiom, nothing would guarantee that, beyond a certain number, all cardinal numbers might not be equivalent to the null class.[28] The axiom of infinity is therefore necessary in order to prove that infinite series exist. This means that it is indispensable for the construction of real numbers and, concerning analysis in general, for the definition of transfinite cardinals and so forth.[29] To preserve the "logical," that is, the "tautological," character of the axiom, Russell offers a solution that, as he admits, although it does not solve the difficulty, nevertheless has the advantage of exhibiting the implicative structure that, according to him, characterizes mathematical propositions.[30] Instead then of postulating the axiom of infinity I to prove a proposition S deduced with its help, one simply asserts the implication $I \supset S$. In other words, one no longer asserts unconditionally the existence of an infinite number of objects; one merely asserts that, *if* certain structures exist, *then* there are some other structures whose existence follows logically from the former.

At first Carnap gives a favorable account of what seems to him to constitute an acceptable solution from the logicist standpoint.[31] The success is, however, precarious: truly "mathematics has been deduced from logic," but logic in turn reveals the antecedence of synthesis over analysis, to the extent that its constructions are valid only if certain states of affairs are given. Mathematical reasoning will be possible only in certain worlds—a situation logic can easily describe as an implication, but cannot produce purely a priori.[32] The durable solution will appear later. This solution uses one of the possibilities of *interpretation* of the axiom of infinity that is obviously inspired by the construction of the *Aufbau*. For instead of considering the objects of the world as those a "language of things" denotes, one can interpret them as being fourfolds of real numbers defined by a Minkowski coordinate system. These individuals can be specified purely a priori. Consequently this frame of possible experience, necessary for the construction of infinite series, can retrieve the logical domain. But will these individuals admit of being interpreted without a vicious circle as forming the domain required by the axiom of infinity in order to guarantee the existence of infinite series? In the final analysis, the validity of Carnap's interpretation is defendable only if, at least implicitly, one considers the construction of coordinates as independent from their being filled in and the construction of an infinite series of classes as always possible. Logic must include the notion of infinity prior to any construction of this concept, which the *Logical Syntax* will in a way officialize by founding the claims of the language on the rules of the metalanguage.

The Axiom of Choice

The axiom of choice (or "multiplicative" axiom), too, is a necessary axiom: it serves, for instance, to prove that a product is null only if one of its factors is null. It states that

> any class of mutually exclusive classes being given, there is at least one class which has exactly one common term with each of the given classes.[33]

This axiom was taken as evident by Zermelo and was used to prove that every set can be well ordered.[34] Russell shows, on the contrary, that if the axiom is indeed "evident" for finite classes, such is no longer the case when it is applied to infinite sets.[35] The axiom has this in particular that it "ceases to be evident from the moment that we realize what it signifies."[36] The axiom is required when the enumerability of the members of a class *ceases to apply*, namely, in the case of infinite sets.

The axiom of choice, whose strictly "logical aspect" Russell emphasized, carries nonetheless an assumption concerning a class of selection, which is aimed at remedying the absence of a corresponding demonstration. In his article of 1931, Carnap mentions the nonanalytic character of the axiom, but he hastens to restore the tautological value of his statement by again resorting to the resource of conditionalization. Embedding the axiom of choice in an implication, of the form $C \supset S$, again makes it possible to get rid of its "content," by retaining only the formal features of the implication of which it is the premise.[37] Undoubtedly, the procedure of conditionalization may appear unduly ad hoc to a Fregean foundationalist. But it prefigures the interdependence that the *Logical Syntax* will attempt to reveal between the validity of a proposition and the resources of the corresponding metalanguage. The mistake of conditionalization lies not in postulating what it belongs to logic to prove a priori, but in giving to one and the same language the dual task of proving the logical validity of the proposition and making use of it in the inferences.

The Axiom of Reducibility and the Question of Impredicativity

A greater difficulty, perhaps the greatest difficulty, in the construction of mathematics has to do with another axiom posited by Russell, the so-called *axiom of reducibility*, which has justly become the main bone of contention

for the critics of the system of *Principia Mathematica*. (Carnap, "Die logizistische Grundlegung der Arithmetik", trans. Putnam and Massey, 45)

In the article of 1931 just quoted, it is neither the axiom of infinity nor the axiom
of choice but the axiom of reducibility that seems truly problematic to Carnap.
Only for this axiom does he seek to give an original logicist interpretation.

Frege could not get used to the idea of calling on the theory of types; it con-
flicted with the idea of simplicity, the naturalness that a credible logicist reconstruction should have. Carnap turns Frege's impression around: in favor of the
theory of types is its "naturalness." In building a system of constitution, "it is
so to speak, a matter of course."[38] This is no longer the case with the ramified
theory of types, and of its indispensable complement, the axiom of reducibility.

Unlike the "simple" theory of types, the ramified theory does not merely sub-
divide the functions into distinct "types" according to the sort of arguments they
can legitimately receive. It further subdivides the properties of a same type into
orders, in accordance with the form of the definition that introduces them. The
axiom of reducibility gets rid of the inextricable difficulties raised by the differences of order for the expression of mathematical theorems (in particular for the
theory of real numbers) by stipulating simply, by "brute force" (as Carnap
says),[39] that the different orders of a same type can be reduced to the lowest order
of the type. Russell is the first to acknowledge that if the axiom of reducibility is
true, it is true, in Wittgenstein's words, only because of a "fortunate acci-
dent."[40] But how can one dispense with this axiom, if one wishes to avoid the
antinomies and the vicious circle principle? Carnap considers that, from the
standpoint of logicism, the cure is worse than the illness. It is better to confront
directly the risk of antinomies and delimit exactly the problem raised by the vicious circle, without ramified types and the axiom of reducibility, than it is to
laden the construction of mathematics with this cumbersome and too obviously
"ad hoc" procedure. He undertakes then, during the period 1930–31, to reexamine the difficulty that the theory of ramified types was supposed to solve. His
own strategy is to separate two questions that the axiom of reducibility and the
theory of ramified types deal with in a global way. *On the one hand*, one will
show that the simple theory of types suffices to avoid the antinomies. *On the
other hand*, one will remove from the ramified theory its second motivation by
presenting an inoffensive version of the principle of vicious circle.

We will not exhibit in detail the first part of this program, which takes up without any changes the solution presented by Ramsey in his article of 1925, "The
Foundations of Mathematics."[41] The main idea is to separate two categories of
antinomies. Antinomies that can be expressed in a "purely logical" language,
such as that of "impredicable" property (i.e., "which does not belong to itself"), are called logical. These do not demand calling on a ramified theory,
since the simple theory suffices to prevent their appearance. What are left are
antinomies that are not expressible in a purely logical manner. These are the "semantic" antinomies, whose "psychological or epistemological" character Ram-

sey emphasizes. They do not then call for a "purely logical or mathematical solution."[42]

However, for Russell, the semantic paradoxes arise from a violation of the vicious circle principle; whence the second part of Carnap's program. The principle states that "no whole may contain parts that are definable only in terms of that whole, or in terms of parts that call for it or presuppose it"; whence the preventive role of the ramified theory, a theory Russell proposed because he sought to get rid of impredicative definitions, diagnosed as the cause of the antinomies. Ramsey and then Carnap reconsider the diagnostic. One can remedy the logical antinomies with the simple theory of types. As for the antinomies of natural language, they simply reflect the imperfections of a nonlogical language. The real question is therefore no longer *how* can one avoid impredicativity, but *why* exactly should one avoid at all cost impredicative definitions? Do they truly present a danger for construction?

The way Ramsey unravels the mystery of impredicativity has the advantage of pointing out a possible road, without yet reaching a true constructivist solution. Ramsey rests his proof on the idea that it is fully admissible to assume the existence of the totality of properties. In Ramsey's view, Russell's error is to have not carried extensionalism far enough, and he considered that every class, even infinite, should be definable.[43] For Ramsey the equicardinality as Cantor defines it is not a real relation. For two classes to be called equicardinal, it is not necessary that a one-one relation mapping them term to term actually be *produced*. It is enough that there *may* be one.

Ramsey therefore represents the "absolutist" version of logicism. He introduces again into post-Fregean logicism the dualist approach of nineteenth-century systems of science by contrasting the necessary characters of mathematical entities (here: classes) with the empirical (and therefore contingent) limitation of the art of the system, understood as a set of formulas reproducing more or less adequately the a priori relations between intemporal logical truths. It is characteristic of realist logicism not to limit mathematical identities to those that are already known. Carnap finds that Ramsey carries realism a little too far. In his logicist zeal Ramsey forgets the Fregean requisite without which any reduction loses its exactness and its acuteness. Every expression of the system should have a denotation guaranteed by construction. Ramsey's nonconstructible classes open the way for arbitrary fiats of a "theological mathematics."[44]

How can the circularity of impredicative definitions be rendered nonvicious, once recourse to a transcendental logic is put aside? Carnap follows Ramsey on one point: Russell is afraid of impredicativity because he has a too narrow conception of the notion of class. Not that there is any room in logic for nondefinable classes; but there are two ways of conceiving universality.[45] What is concerned in the *Principia* is a *numerical* universality. It is in this case, and only in this case, that one cannot refer to the "totality of properties" without having constructed it by enumerating all the individual properties that compose the set. There is, however, another universality called "specific" universality. The latter is established not by enumeration but by logical derivation from other properties, that is, by proof.[46] The impredicative definitions are therefore legitimate if one uses a demonstrative procedure that does not call for an examination of all the arguments of the function. The *tautological* character of the statement suffices to justify the validity of the statement for any function taken as argument. It matters little how this tautological character will be brought out or that this tautology will not be provable "if there is no solution to the problem of decision in this logical system." What counts is that *impredicativity is not what makes this kind of a decision in principle impossible in every case*. The type of solution merely outlined here will be, as we shall soon see, taken up and expanded in the *Logical Syntax*.

The Question of the Denotation of Logical Expressions and Its Significance

The previous discussion shows what separates Carnap's logicism from Frege's. Carnap, unlike Frege, sees the decisive contribution of logicism in the "first thesis" of reductionism. This thesis concerns the definition of mathematical concepts in purely logical terms. It satisfies the constructivist requirements insofar as they apply to mathematical concepts.[47] The second thesis, which states that *all* mathematical theorems are derivable from purely logical axioms, constitutes a field of research. The difficulties encountered do not cast doubt on the possibility of their being one day overcome. For Frege and Russell, the fundamental question was that of the *essence* of the mathematical. The existence of purely logical denotations having been demonstrated, the symbolism had for its purpose the *reproduction* of an intemporally valid hierarchy between logical truths. On the contrary, Carnap's reductionism no longer has a descriptive intent. The crucial problem for him is the possibility of *applying* mathematics. A logical system of mathematics should thus above all strive to provide a solution for the gap between *formal science* and the *application of forms*. The epistemological import of the first thesis is what justifies the work still to be accomplished to prove the second thesis. It is indeed by means of this logical definition of mathematical concepts that one can justify even the most elementary transformations of the propositions of applied arithmetic. For example, from the proposition:

(1) "The only persons in this room are Hans and Peter,"

we can deduce the proposition:

(2) There are only two persons in this room,"

only on the condition that we have an *interpretation*, in the mathematical calculus, of the sign *two*, enabling us to recognize that "the persons Hans and Peter" fall under this concept. Carnap is very close here to the antiformalist Frege: the limit of the formalist conception of mathematics lies for him in the inability of this conception to legitimate a transformation of this nature, any more, for that matter, than it can account for any deduction involving an application of mathematics. To apply mathematics presupposes that one knows how to *interpret* its symbols. Logicists alone are able to give such an interpretation. Once number is defined as a property of a concept, it is possible to derive the numerical property that belongs to the concept "the persons Hans and Peter," namely, "a concept whose extension comprises two individuals." To apply mathematics is thus *to use the logical denotation* of the arithmetical sign so as to reason numerically with propositions that are not yet put in numerical form. But what exactly should be understood by the term "logical denotation"? It is well known what Frege understands thereby: not the operative sense conferred on a sign by its occurrence in an axiomatic structure, but that which makes this occurrence possible. The sign refers to an entity independent and antecedent with respect to the system, which it is supposed to denote. As we have seen, the realism of the construction guarantees, in both Frege's and Russell's system, the determination of logical denotation. But what more can conventionalism add to the strictly operative conception of the denotation of formal signs, that is, to the most ordinary formalism? Carnap returns emphatically to the question of the *Deutung* of logical and mathematical concepts during 1930–31, because he believes he has a *criterion* of logical denotation. Not that one can dream of reaching the extrasystematic reference of logical terms: "They do not have an independent denotation."[48] But concepts such as "function," "variable," "negation," or "disjunction" define a purely structural field of operations and provide the corresponding sign of the symbolism with what could be called a "formal sense." Thus, the question of the denotation of logical signs is reformulated in a way that makes it possible to reconcile Frege's requirement with formalism. But, at the same time, the question of the foundations of mathematics becomes a matter not of returning to logical essences but of *inserting mathematics in a total language*.

Logical Denotation and the Problem of Foundations

In order to illustrate the interdependence of the question of denotation and that of foundation, let us quote the following manuscript notes in which Carnap summarizes the substances of a speech given in Berlin for a symposium organized by Reichenbach:

> The problem of the foundations of *mathematics*: not only metamathematics (semantics of the formal mathematical system), but also insertion of mathematics in a universal language! (Thus Frege's requisite is satisfied: signs must have a denotation, *that is*, be applicable in synthetic propositions! But the requisite is satisfied by formalist means.) *Solution to the logicism-formalism conflict.* (Carnap Collection, University of Pittsburgh Libraries, notes, July 1, 1932, Archives 110–07–23)

That Carnap presents in Berlin a thesis that we will find again in the *Logical Syntax* is not in the least surprising, since this work is being composed at the time. What is less well known is that as early as 1929–30, in an unpublished manuscript, "Untersuchungen zur allgemeinen Axiomatik," Carnap seeks to solve the problem of the foundations of mathematics by *inserting this discipline in a unitary language*. However, in contrast to what he will undertake from 1931 on, in the *Logical Syntax*, the unitary language in question is "flat," if one understands by this that it does not include metalinguistic descriptions. Nevertheless, this language has two parts, corresponding respectively to the *formalist* and *logicist* phases of the foundational process.

The first phase is that of mathematical insertion, in the formalist style: a system of axioms is established, without worrying yet about the denotation of the symbols. These axioms will, however, be supplemented by synthetic axioms, making it possible to apply the formulas to a domain of objects. The second phase, which coincides with the setting up of the universal-mathematical axiomatic, is that of "retrospective [*nachträglich*] logical analysis: the logician seeks to give a "logical" denotation to the purely formal signs of the mathematical axiomatic. Carnap calls principles (*Grundsätze*) the propositions designed to supply the formalist signs with a logical denotation (their denotation being until now indeterminate), in order not to confuse this "fundamental" axiomatic phase with the particular formalist axiomatics of the antecedent stage:

> Let us choose as an example of an axiomatic system of arithmetic Peano's axiomatic system for natural numbers. The concept of number and individual numbers 0, 1, 2, etc., also occurs in this system. We distinguish, *qua Peanian numbers*, Peano's 0, etc., from *logical numbers*, the "logical zero," etc. *Qua* logical concepts, the latter have a completely determinate denotation; the former, on the other hand, have an indeterminate denotation, *qua* concepts of an axiomatic system, and are thus applicable to very different domains. (*"Untersuchungen,"* Carnap Collection, University of Pittsburgh Libraries 080–34–03, 7; cf. "Eigentliche und uneigentliche Begriffe," 361)

From this insertion of axiomatic theories in a universal axiomatic, Carnap expects three results, which he summarizes thus:

> (1) Every mathematical sign receives one or more denotations; and, more exactly, purely logical denotations. (2) If the system of axioms is noncontradictory, each mathematical formula becomes a tautology. . . . (3) If the system of axioms is complete (in Hilbert's sense), the denotative analysis becomes univocal; each sign receives exactly one denotation; thus the formalist construction would become a logicist construction.[49]

This project of a universal axiomatic constitutes the final attempt to reveal the *tautological* character of mathematics. Let us note that the concept of tautology already signifies an important concession to formalism: it is no longer considered necessary for the logicist hypothesis that the general axiomatic should contain only logical laws. Carnap even suggests calling by the neutral term "fundamental discipline" (*Grunddisziplin*) this universal language, which along with logic includes arithmetic and set theory. The logicist hypothesis nevertheless retains a heuristic value, and Carnap applies himself to the logicist salvaging of the so-called empirical axioms of the *Principia*.[50] What is essential then is that the hard core of logicism ceases to be a question of doctrine. It will be possible to conceive arithmetic and set theory as distinct from logic without having to deny them a "fundamental position (and a foundational one)" in the construction as a whole. This shift in emphasis is a consequence of the transition, already mentioned, from the *essentialist foundation* to the *integrating foundation*. As the unique language that becomes the reference point of the tautological character of mathematics, the concept of "analytic" can supersede that of "logical" truth. As we shall soon see, it is precisely *because* universal axiomatic relaxes the logicist hypothesis that Gödel's discovery will not deal it a fatal blow.

Taking up Wittgenstein's concept of tautology, Carnap modifies it by extending its application to equalities. Tautology retains for the most part the characters ascribed to it by Wittgenstein: it says nothing because it does not exclude truth cases (being universally valid). But once reduced to its logical structure, mathematics is supposed to become openly tautological, which it already was in a sense. It is not at all necessary to interpret this *Sinnlosigkeit* as that which could show, but could not express, the logic of the world. One might say that tautology is made commonplace by logical empiricism, in the sense that it is fully a proposition, whose vacuity is sufficiently explained by the necessity every language faces of positing certain conventions regulating the use of words and the transformation of statements. There is nothing to hinder one any more from seeking to express the relations between forms and from deriving mathematics from logic. The two disciplines are homogeneous with respect to one another, insofar as formal (nonrepresentative) techniques are concerned. Being more secure in its procedures, however, logic makes it possible both to guarantee the rectitude of the mathematical operation and to cast light on its applicability. In 1930–31, the concept of tautology is at its peak: it still appears to be the only concept capable of founding the unicity of the logical and the mathematical. The difficulties raised by the nonlogical axioms of the *Principia* seem to be overcome or about to be overcome. There is not yet a "crisis" of analyticity. The turning point is not far off, however: in October 1930, Hans Hahn presents before the Vienna Academy of Sciences a short summary of two of Gödel's main results, which will be published the following year.[51] The happy days of tautology are over. If mathematics is analytic, it will not be in the sense of being tautological. But logicism is hard to kill. The *Logical Syntax* will attempt to save analyticity from the blind alley into which the theorems of incompleteness led it.

Analyticity, Descriptivity, and Arithmetization

In a letter from von Neumann to Carnap dated July 7, 1931, one can read this evaluation of the impact of Gödel's discovery on what could be called the "Königsberg spirit":

> I am presently of the opinion that Gödel has proved the unrealizable character of Hilbert's program ["I have known this since September 7, 1930," he adds in a footnote]. . . . I therefore consider the point of view that we adopted at Königsberg, concerning the question of the foundations, to be completely outdated, owing to the fact that the fundamental discoveries of Gödel have set the question at an entirely different level. (I know that Gödel is much more cautious about the value of his results, but he does not see, in my opinion, the true relations that they have with this problem.[52]

Hilbert's goal was to prove by finite means the noncontradictory character of classical mathematics.[53] Yet Gödel's results suggest that the predicate "to be provable" is not recursive (i.e., not finitist) for a system comprising Peano's axioms and the logic of the *Principia* (with natural numbers taken as individuals). The theorems of incompleteness seem to destroy any hope of giving a *proof* of consistency by *employing finitist means*. No recursive system of axioms, which is noncontradictory, is complete relative to the propositions of arithmetic. We may note here that completeness is a *relative* property: a formal system is complete when every proposition that *can be expressed* in its symbolism in accordance with the formation rules is formally decidable. A system is thus complete *relative* to a set of propositions. Each proposition of the set must be decidable for the system to be complete relative to that set. If the axioms of Peano completed by the logic of the *Principia* are chosen then as the system of reference, one can bring to light arithmetical propositions that, although "well formed," can be neither proved nor refuted *within* the system. This result not only affects Hilbert's program; it also casts doubt on the tautological character of the most elementary part of mathematics, namely, the theory of natural integers; hence the ruin of the Königsberg theses. As von Neumann puts it, the problems, among others that of the status of logic and mathematics, must not be taken up again, "at an entirely different level." The *Logical Syntax* represents the effort to raise logicism to this new "level." The concept of analyticity that is redefined there takes into account Gödel's results and even takes on the aspect of a generalization of the methods used in Gödel's proofs (methods, it must be added, already in use in the Polish School).

Three aspects of the construction of the concept of analytic should be emphasized here. Inaugurating the syntactic nature of this type of research, the distinction between language and metalanguage forms the frame of reference for any definition of "analytic." Analyticity becomes once and for all a *metalogical* notion. In this syntactic process, *arithmetization* occurs in an essential way in order to guarantee the universality of the results and, at the same time, the representability of the metalanguage in the language, which allows the syntax itself to be interpreted as a set of analytic propositions. Finally, the concept of analytic is an openly *indefinite*, ineffective concept, which is to make a virtue of necessity and to reform logicism once again so as to liberalize a little more the criteria of validity.

From the "Fundamental Discipline" to the "Metadiscipline"

That analyticity is taken to be a "metalogical" property is not in itself a novelty; we saw that such was the point of view taken on this concept by the Fregean definition. If the *Logical Syntax* innovates, it is not simply because the metalogical level is recognized and exploited. It is because the relations between object language and metalanguage—*Hilfssprache* in Frege's terminology—are on their own the object of a formal activity depending on the object language chosen. The analytic ceases at the same time to hold as an absolute property of certain propositions, as was the case in the *Grundgesetze* and even in the *Aufbau*. What we have now is a concept whose definition may vary according to the type of object language, and especially according to the resources the metalanguage possesses.

Carnap in a letter to Neurath dated December 23, 1933, comments thus on the contribution of Tarski, in whose work he locates one of the "historical roots" of his *Syntax*:

> It becomes clearer and clearer: all our problems are syntactic problems. This goes to strengthen the thesis of unified science. Not everything being solved, but a set of new tasks to be taken up.[54]

Tarski's concept of metadiscipline has the highly original feature of rendering a *unitary* vision of science compatible with a *pluralist* interpretation of the analysis of forms. And Carnap insists precisely on this bivalence in his letter to Neurath. He locates here the simultaneously doctrinal (unitary) and programmatic aspect of the metalogical approach. Tarski's metamathematics is pluralist to the extent that each formal system calls for a particular metalinguistic treatment. In other words, the investigation of a deductive formalized discipline requires setting up a "special metadiscipline."[55] Yet general remarks need to be made, in order to specify "the meaning of a series of important metamathematical concepts, common to special metadisciplines," and "to determine the fundamental properties of these concepts."

Rule and Formal Thought

In the famous text in which he exposes his conception of the object of arithmetic, Hilbert states the originary character of the sign—"in the beginning is the sign"—only by setting aside the "particular circumstances of presentation" that could hinder recognition of universal forms.[56] Likewise for Carnap, logic is *formal* not only insofar as it turns away from nonlogical denotation, from "judgment content" (*Gedanken oder Gedankeninhalt*); it is formal also to the extent that it retains from the symbolic expressions only what manifests the universality of the rules (*LS*, §1). The formalness is that of the rule, rather than that of the written sign, the latter simply holding as an empirical representation of *Gesetzmässigkeit*. To subject the sentences of a language to formal treatment is therefore to refuse to see in them anything other than a series of signs as well as to reduce these signs to purely singular configurations (*Gestalten*). The sign always refers to a *type* of expression *by virtue of a rule*. All the effectiveness of the formal rests on the possibility of this reference. The extralogical connection of the word and the denotation is therefore destroyed only by strengthening the grammatical connection of the sign and the rule that governs it, the rule being the real object of pure syntax. In order to mark this difference between the outer appearance of the sign and the relevant differential element, Carnap proposes distinguishing the *syntactic* form of a symbol from its "figurative" from (*figurelle Gestalt*) (*LS*, §4, 15). The syntactic form is to the figurative form what the rook, as an abstract element, structurally determined by the rules of the game of chess, is to the concrete piece of wood or ivory of a more or less suggestive form. In order to be able to determine the identity of the syntactic form of two signs, one cannot go by the figurative form. The rules of language are what authorize this recognition. In other words, the rule takes on the status, belonging in Frege to the logical law, of a condition of possibility of formal thought in general.

Such an idea of the formal requires that the pure syntax designed to exhibit it fulfill two conditions. The rule must, first of all, be recognizable effectively by the sole form of the symbols of the metalanguage used. In addition, the syntax being constructed must clearly pertain to the formal structure of the expressions, and not to the physical signs taken as pure empirical events. Let us suppose a "special syntax" that uses some descriptive predicates in order to characterize the elements of the object language. For example, the predicate "to be a variable" will be expressed by "*Var*," and that of "logical numerical sign" by "log *Zz*." One can express in such a syntax the property "to lack an effectively written proof of S_1"; but one cannot assert that such a proof of S_1 is impossible. In other words, a merely descriptive syntax would at best yield a *geography* of symbolic forms. Pure syntax has, however, a much higher ambition: not only to describe the rules of a language, but also to elucidate the foundations of logicomathematical discourse in general—consequently, to go beyond the limits of the represented language so as to single out the universal rules holding for every possible language. The project of a logical syntax therefore calls for a method making the transition from a *geography* to a *geometry* of forms of language.[57] There is a method that will make it possible to satisfy both requirements, and Hilbert was the first to set forth the idea.[58] As early as 1904 he suggested considering logic as a branch of the theory of arithmetic. Yet Carnap mentions, in his personal notes, an encounter with Gödel in August 1930, during which the latter presented to him his method of correlating numbers with signs and expressions. He therefore borrows the technique of arithmetization, right down to the particular definitions, from Gödel.[59]

The Procedure of Arithmetization

The main interest of the method of arithmetization for the project of general syntax is that it reduces the descriptive functors necessary for applying the syntax to a given language. Every symbol of the object language will be correlated with a natural number, according to assignments that are purely conventional without, however, being completely arbitrary. For from the choice of assignments must follow the possibility of recognizing univocally the type of sign thus defined. The numerical description corresponding to each symbol of the object language is called a "term-number" (*Gliedzahl*). Carnap takes up exactly the assignments chosen by Gödel in his incompleteness theorems. To guarantee the univocity of the decomposition of term-numbers into constituent terms, one stipulates that the predicates will be represented by prime numbers or prime numbers raised to a power. The numbers of the object language will be represented by prime numbers $p > 2$, the defined numerical expressions by p^2, the undefined predicates by p^3, the defined predicates by p^4, the undefined functors by p^5, the defined functors by p^6. Finally, the logical constants receive purely arbitrary numerical assignations in terms of nonprime numbers: "0" is expressed by 4, "(by 6)," by 10, " $\exists$ " by 18, and so on. One can finally correlate a "series-number" (*Reihezahl*) with a series of expressions of the object language.

That arithmetic *carries with it its own combinatory means* explains the import of Gödel's theorems. The first theorem proved not only that the system of arithmetic is *incomplete* but also that it is *incompletable*. The adjunction of the undecidable proposition to the system of axioms again brings about the possibility of building a new undecidable proposition in this new system. Arithmetization thus confers on syntax a determination that a descriptive syntax could not have reached. By its means can be expressed the *operative possibilities* of a formal system, such as derivability, demonstrability, undecidability, and finally analyticity. Arithmetization is the method that providentially saves the damage done to tautology by Gödel's results. Carnap "turns around," so to speak, Gödel's technique in order to make it the tool of a new logicism. With respect to the question of analyticity, arithmetization indeed makes it possible to achieve two major results. Arithmetic being analytic, every arithmetically expressed syntax will itself be analytic. The status of the logic of science is thus settled. Moreover, being self-referential, arithmetization makes it possible to embed the syntax language in the object language. Hence the unification of language, the only restriction being that everything will not be provable within the sole object language. However, if the syntactic axiomatic is arithmetized—in other words, if the syntax is modeled in arithmetic—it is not necessary to leave room for specific axioms regulating the relations between fundamental signs: the definitions of the syntactic symbols already include the relations these symbols bear among one another, insofar as they use the properties of numbers. For example, "a number is not a predicate" does not have to be set out as an axiom, since this sentence is immediately deducible from definitions 25–27 of the syntax of Language I. The *syn-*

tactic definitions will therefore suffice for determining completely the relations between the symbols. The conditions pertaining to the exponents of the prime factors of the numbers represent the different types of expressions, series of formulas, and series of series that make up the language. We thus have the following result: descriptivity and analyticity can be combined in *one* case, that of arithmetized syntax.

Now arises the question of what makes such a descriptive syntax *applicable*. It is the use of a single descriptive functor, built up by abstraction from the various descriptive predicates an axiomatic would have required, such as "variable sign," "constant sign," "numerical sign," and "identity sign." One recognizes the category of expressions this unique functor determines, *Zei* for *Zeichen*, "is the sign of," by their arithmetized definition, the values of *Zei* being the term-numbers of the corresponding symbols.

Although it accepts a multiplicity of physicalist realizations, the arithmetized descriptive syntax is on the same level of generality as pure syntax. The only difference is that instead of referring, as does the latter, only to series of term-numbers, it also has an operator of application. Up until now we only have the schema of a possible language, whose representability is only foreshadowed by syntax. Thus, what the possibility of an arithmetized descriptive syntax teaches us is that the question of application, if it indeed remains in the final analysis the locus of the synthetic, *is itself articulated in a purely analytic manner*. This science of the languages of science then offers the paradigm of a field of knowledge entirely subordinated to the formal: one in which the question submitting the given to the forms is fully *already conceived* in arithmetic.

Gödel's incompleteness theorems gave to the *Logical Syntax* the instrument of its generality. But their impact on the destiny of analyticity does not stop here. They map out both the *aim* of the concept of analyticity that will be expressible in this arithmetized syntax and the *specific constraints* that will weigh on it. To make the point clear, we will say in a schematic way that the first theorem governs a *liberalization* of the criterion of analyticity, whereas the second one specifies *the limits* within which this construction can take place.

From the "First Theorem" to "C-Concepts"

What does the first theorem of incompleteness actually state? That if the system *P*, composed of the *Principia* completed by Peano's axioms, is ω-consistent, it must be complete, Gödel's formula *G* relative to *P* being an undecidable formula in this system.[60] Moreover, the incompleteness turns out to be *essential*: even if Gödel's formula is added to the previous system, the resulting system again has a true but undecidable formula, and so on to infinity. The first theorem thus proves that there can be no "definite" criterion of validity, understanding thereby an *effectively* calculable process.[61] The first theorem therefore confronts foundationalist philosophers with a dilemma. Either they must exclude from the "purely logical" what goes beyond the strictly constructive possibilities of the formalism, by leaving room for the mathematical synthetic a priori in the continuation of the analytic of logic. Or else they must *enlarge* the concept of formal validity, so that it includes the undecidable propositions in the field of the logical. The first theorem obliges us to recognize that if a complete criterion of validity is still possible, effective procedures will not give it. Carnap clearly chooses the second branch of the dilemma. The concept of "analytic" will be *the noneffective substitute of tautology*. It will not be constructible itself as a "definite" concept. But one should not see in this feature a limitation, a defect of the concept, which a new finitist approach could remedy. After Gödel, the choice is no longer between the tautological and the analytic, but between an analytic enlarged to the nonfinitist and the return of the synthetic a priori. If there is any reason to continue to speak about "analytic," it will be with the dimension of a "*C*-concept." Such a concept will have to be built up for each object language studied.

Language I, which specifies the rules of a finitist language, acceptable in consequence for Schlick and Wittgenstein, is a "*definite*" language in the technical sense of the word: all constants and closed expressions are either primitive terms or terms reducible step by step to primitive ones, the definitions having only limited quantifiers (*LS*, §15, 45). However, even if such a language may contain only "definite" symbols, it must necessarily possess rules of inference that are not definite. Let us take derivability: it is an "effective" procedure in the sense that the primitive statements are finite in number and the premises used in the inferences are also finite; but as the length of the derivations is not limited, this method is noneffective in the sense that "derivable in *S*" can require an infinite number of individual steps of the kind "the statement *P* is directly derivable from the statement *Q*." In a system in which there are only effective rules of transformation, "to be derivable from . . . " and "to be a consequence of . . . " coincide.

However, derivability does not make it possible to acquire a complete criterion of validity for arithmetic; to remedy the incompleteness of an arithmetic restricted to "*d*-rules," one must bring in nonfinitist (i.e., a noneffective) types of rules of inference, already used by Tarski in 1927 and by Hilbert in 1931,[62] which Carnap calls "*c*-rules." In this second method of deduction, termed the method of "consequence" (*Folge*), even the individual step is noneffective: a class of propositions K_2 is said to be a "direct consequence" of another class K_1 when every sentence of K_2 is a direct consequence of a subclass of K_1. This form of inference makes it possible to take an infinite class of propositions as premises. In a system that has *c*-rules alongside *d*-rules, derivability and consequence cease to coincide: the statements considered as nonprovable in terms of derivation can be proved valid by resorting to *c*-rules.

Thus, to draw a demarcation line between analytic and synthetic propositions in Language I, one must bring in "noneffective" syntactic concepts, whose employment depends on *c*-rules. The latter, let us repeat, apply not to statements but to possibly infinite classes of statements: a proposition will be called "analytic" if it is the consequence of the null class of propositions, and "contradictory" when every proposition is its consequence. From the relations between derivability and consequence, it follows that if every provable proposition is analytic, there are nonprovable analytic propositions.

Analytic in Language II

The *Syntax* also yields the syntactic rules of a much richer language, Language II, sufficient for expressing the whole of mathematics. As this language is no longer "definite" (it contains nonlimited quantifiers), the noneffective concepts are also accepted in it. From these differences, it follows that the definition of *analytic in Language II* differs on at least three essential points from the corresponding definition in Language I. First, instead of defining "analytic" by "consequence," one begins with a recursive definition of "analytic" so as to build up with its help that of "consequence." Second, for this criterion of "analytic" to be applicable, one must have sentences in "standard" (i.e., *reduced*) form. Finally, and what concerns us primarily now, a definition of "analytic in Language II" presupposes that one takes for the domain of variation of the syntactic functions not the definite predicates in Language II but, following Gödel's phrase, "all sets and relations in general."[63] For if quantification is restricted to a limited domain of definable predicates, it could very well happen that, although, for example, the proposition $M(F)$ may be true of all the predicates contained in Language II, it might not be so universally because it may be false of a function remaining undefined in Language II. It has been known since Cantor that there are always such undefinable functions in Language II. The noneffective concept that will be the instrument of the definition of "analytic in Language II" is that of *valuation (Wertung)*: S is an analytic sentence of Language II if every sentence obtained by valuation on F in S is analytic.[64] A valuation is a class of accentuated expressions (numerical expressions) that are the values taken on by the symbols of the object language in their classical interpretation. One has here the development suggested by Gödel: a valuation ranges over *all the possible values* of a numerical expression, whether or not they are represented in the object language.

Provided with the possibility of valuating the constituents of sentences of the language in the metalanguage, one must then put it to use to reach an evaluation of the validity of the sentence concerned: one passes from *valuation* to *evaluation* by correlating the tautology $0 = 0$ with any true subformula in a valuation, and the contradiction $0 \neq 0$ with a false sentence in a valuation. A sentence will then be called *analytic* if its evaluation brings out only tautologies.[65]

The criterion proposed makes it possible to distinguish two categories of sentences in a language: "*L*-determinate" sentences are those that are analytic or contradictory (§52); the tautological character of each one of their valuations proves that their truth depends not on the world but on the rules of the language. All the other sentences of the language will be said to be *synthetic* (determinate sentences, but *P*-valid, or indeterminate sentences are concerned here). The occurrence of an evaluation in the metalanguage clearly indicates that analyticity can no longer claim to hold absolutely, as a sort of patent of unconditional validity, to which only "eternally" true propositions could aspire. The procedure of valuation reveals that the *completeness* of the criterion of formal validity — analyticity — is obtained by enriching the syntax language with nonconstructive means.

The "Second Theorem" and the Constructive Limits

The first theorem of incompleteness would suggest the need to make room for syntactic *C*-concepts, designed to complete the gaps of the *D*-concepts. The second theorem of incompleteness points out rather the restrictive condition under which the construction of the analytic can be carried out. Such a concept can indeed be constructed, but never *in the object language*. If the first theorem makes it possible to infer that "analytic" and "nondemonstrable" are not incompatible, the second theorem warns that, by seeking to express "analytic in *L*" (or "contradictory in *L*") while *remaining in L*, one brings about contradictions. The analyticity of *L* cannot be proved in *L*.

The second theorem then yields an equivalent subtheorem in general syntax: certain syntactic terms concerning *L* are undefinable in *L*, and certain syntactic propositions of *L* are undecidable in *L*. Yet these terms can be defined and these propositions be made decidable in a formalized language having predicate and function variables *not occurring in the object language*. Thus is formally justified the measure that until now only had an ad hoc prophylactic value: that of preventing a *regressus in infinitum*. When we mentioned the necessity of quantifying over "*all* sets and relations in general" and not over the predicate *represented* into, we meant the predicates that, although not represented in *L*, could be represented in a richer language. Of course, the transition from one language to another implies that one carries out valuations on predicates and functions of a *higher order* and a *different types*, which "complicates things," as Carnap remarks in a letter to Gödel.[66]

4

Conventionality, Tolerance, and Universal Syntax

Carnap illustrates his criterion by proving the analyticity of certain primitive propositions of Language II and, in particular, those whose "analytic" character appeared doubtful to the pre-Königsberg logicians. To establish it, one must assume that the axiom of choice is valid in the syntax language — that there exists a class of selection for every valuation (*LS*, §34 h, 123). This recourse in the metalanguage to a translation of the very axiom whose analyticity is to be proved raises the problem of a possible *circularity*: has one not presupposed the truth of these axioms, held to be logical, in order to derive their logical truth? Has one not simply satisfied oneself on this account with "pulling rabbits out of the hat"? From Carnap's point of view, this objection originates in a conception of truth that is still substantialist: it misses precisely what is made clear through the distinction between the object language and its syntax language. There would be circularity if the axiom of choice (whose analyticity is in question insofar as a primitive proposition of the object language) were used in the object language itself. But this recourse to a translation of the axiom of choice in the metalanguage only brings out the general procedure of proof:

> It is clear [observes Carnap] that the possibility of proving a certain syntactical sentence depends on the richness of the syntax language used, and especially on what is regarded as valid in this language. (*LS*, §34 h, 123)

The axiom of choice in its metalinguistic translation has therefore not been used as if it were a "materially correct" (*inhaltlich richtig*) proposition. One has only given the proof that the definition proposed for the concept "analytic in *L*" made it possible effectively to characterize every proposition that "in a material interpretation," that is, in the syntax language, is taken to be logically valid. This reveals the mutation that the problem of foundation undergoes at the same time. It is no longer a matter of returning to a set of logical propositions whose

222

truth would be in a way "immediate." To found henceforth means: to exhibit the metalinguistic resources necessary for a proof of validity, with the purpose of casting light on the linguistic conditions of a given operative practice, rather than with a normative and exclusivist intention. The concept of analyticity itself is an *indefinite*, noneffective concept; if one proves with its help that Language II is noncontradictory, one will not have gained thereby an absolute certainty of its consistency. To obtain it, the same proof must be carried out again for the successive syntaxes built on Language II, namely, on the syntax of Language II, then on its metalanguage, on the metalanguage of this metalanguage, and so forth. But the essential benefit will be in elucidating the decisions necessary to be able in the actual state of research to obtain a complete criterion of validity for a definite formalization of classical mathematics. One may then question the advisability of using in syntax ineffective concepts, emphasizing as does Gödel (in a letter to Carnap) that these concepts do not throw any light on the problems they are supposed to solve, but one cannot challenge resorting to them; no theoretical or doctrinal *reason* is appropriate where a pragmatic decision prevails. We thus see to what extent the question of foundations is bound up with the *principle of tolerance*: "It is not our business to set up prohibitions, but to arrive at conventions" (*LS*, §17). That is why "in logic, there are no morals."[67]

This freedom, however, could upset scrupulous positivists. Where will one stop in matters of symbolic invention, if one is to apply literally this tolerance that the principle states in syntactic matters? Do not the "noneffective" concepts for which this principle is put forward themselves transgress the principle of verifiability? Does calling on them not amount to granting oneself the right to dissimulate what one does not know *how to do*, by concealing the whole unknown realm under an indistinct syntactic concept, whose universality is not at all operative, but actually quasi-theological? Is one not obliged to restrict the application of the principle of tolerance in the name of the principle of verifiability, which prescribes retaining only concepts of which one can ascertain whether or not they apply? To this objection, Carnap can oppose two replies. The first one consists in establishing a necessity of indefinite concepts on account of the very nature of the system of arithmetic. The second one takes up directly the question of verifiability, revised and corrected by the theorems of incompleteness. These two answers introduce, so to speak, "Realpolitik" into syntax: it is time to draw the consequence from the fact that syntax is *nothing other than* a part of arithmetic, and that no transcendent criterion may occur henceforth.

Indefinite concepts are needed, and, moreover, in the case of "analytic" a translation of the definition into the object language cannot be obtained. At first sight two properties seem to be arbitrarily introduced into the syntax. But, as is known, the terms and sentences of the syntax are "nothing other than" the terms and propositions of *arithmetic* that are endowed with a *syntactic interpretation*. Thus the limitations that weigh on the syntax—owing to its recourse to noneffective concepts, or to the impossibility of defining everything in the object language—are of an *arithmetical origin.* What one pretends to ignore by incriminating the arbitrariness of the syntax is that arithmetic itself is subjected to a double "deficit": in every system of arithmetic there are *undefinable* terms and *undecidable* sentences; consequently, one cannot expect that an adequate syntax of classical mathematics can escape these two types of deficiencies. A general syntax must instead *reflect* them and seek to restore the completeness *by taking* these internal limitations *into account*.

The existence of this general syntax then places restrictions on the invention of forms that the principle of tolerance seemed to allow to proliferate without any kind of limitation. The principle of tolerance owes its liberalness to the prior recognition of the degree of freedom opened, but also delimited, by general syntax. What authorizes, in the final analysis, "tolerance" in logical matters is the certainty that arithmetic yields the horizon within which the forms can be freely deployed. But we must also measure the impact of these observations on the other fundamental principle of the constitutional or syntactic idea. If *noneffective concepts* refer above all to an arithmetical "fact," one must now attempt to reformulate the principle of verifiability—no longer saying as previously, following Wittgenstein, that "the sense of a concept lies in the method by which to determine its applicability or nonapplicability." For we may not know how *to look* for an answer, while knowing *what form it must have*, that is, under what conditions we would acknowledge having found it: for example, it would be a demonstrative series in which the last sentence is the one we are trying to establish. Thus the question of whether the solution *is the right one* is in fact determinable, even if the manner in which this solution *can be established* is not yet determined.

The Principle of Tolerance and the Universality of Syntax

When Carnap defines the principle of tolerance by mentioning the *conventional* nature of logical investigation, does he not run the risk of misleading his readers? The fact that one may study the various possible structures of a language of science must not lead one to believe that the rules of formation and transformation are *totally arbitrary*. The very project of establishing general conditions of scientific discourse shows that it is a matter of circumscribing the limits within which the invention of forms can take place. The principle of tolerance can thus be understood only against the backdrop of the thesis of the universality of the logical syntax of science. Let us go a step further: not only does the statement of the principle of tolerance refer to the antecedent existence of a universally valid syntax, but any metalogical recourse to a set of *conventions* is, in a way, justified a priori by the necessity of the rules of general syntax. Failing to perceive how the arbitrariness of the choice of a certain language rests on the necessity of the formal conditions regulating any language, one cannot understand what founds Carnap's assurance against eventual pragmatic difficulties in applying these concepts. This double level of analysis seems to us to recommend itself in light of the examination of the controversial question of *synonymy*.

Conventionality, Synonymy, and Pure Syntax

As the languages considered in general syntax are not all like Language I and Language II, L-languages whose rules of transformation are only logical rules of deduction, one must be able to discriminate the *origin of the validity* of a certain proposition in any formal language that also comprises physical axioms among its rules of transformation. One remarks in particular that in such a language, every *valid* proposition is not *analytic*, no more than every *contravalid* proposition is synthetic. A proposition P_1 will be called analytic if it is L-valid, that is, if its validity depends on the "logical sublanguage" of the total language to which P_1 belongs.[68] The existence of a *twofold key*, *logical and physical*, of the rules of transformation, leads us to recognize the equivocity of the presystematic, unspecified notion of *synonymy*. In general syntax this notion is now represented by two distinct concepts, L-synonymy and P-synonymy.[69] In a general manner, one can understand the contrast between P-synonymy and L-synonymy as the syntactic explanation of Frege's distinction between sense and denotation. Two expressions are synonymous if they denote the same object; if they are, moreover, L-synonymous, then they have the same sense. The senses and the denotations thus understood both depend on the rules of the language under consideration. And the P-rules as much as the L-rules are a matter of choice:

> Whether in the construction of a language S we formulate only L-rules or include also P-rules, and, if so, to what extent, is not a logico-philosophical problem, but a matter of convention and hence, at most, a question of expedience. If P-rules are stated, we may frequently be placed in the position of having to alter the language; and if we go so far as to adopt all acknowledged sentences as valid, then we must be continuously expanding it. (*LS*, §51, 180)

It is therefore the preliminary *convention* of L-and P-rules that, in the construction of the language S, determines the synonymy under both of its kinds. In other words, general syntax traces the explanation of synonymy back to a *fiat* that coincides with the exposition of the rules of the language under consideration. For example, if this language comprises among its L-rules of transformation the reduction

"Bachelor" $\rightarrow$ "unmarried man,"

the corresponding sentence

"A bachelor is an unmarried man"

will be analytic (L-valid). But if such a rule of transformation does not occur in another language S with the same primitive vocabulary, the same statement may be P-valid, that is, synthetic. The principle of tolerance thus liberalizes the application of the distinction L-P-synonymous; some languages may extend L-synonymy at the expense of P-synonymy, and reciprocally. This freedom in the choice of language, which enables a statement of synonymy to be sometimes P-

valid and sometimes L-valid, is topically associated with the strictly determinate character of pure syntactic categories. One notices the connection between these two theses, which we could call, respectively, "the thesis of the variability of forms of language" (governed by the principle of tolerance) and "the thesis of the invariability of the categories of pure syntax," by examining Carnap's answer to Quine's objections concerning the syntactic construction of the notion of synonymy.

Directed against the subsequent developments of *Meaning and Necessity*, Quine's objections already make their mark in the *Syntax* with this explanation of synonymy. What Quine refuses to admit is that synonymy should be reducible to a definition or a rule, thus making it possible to define beyond the logically true, the broader category of the analytic (as providing the definitional abbreviation of a logically true proposition). For the definition does not add any clarity. Its occurrence is a contrivance, imported from the theory of constitution (tentatively accepted as holding), designed to eliminate immediately from syntax the problem of determining actual synonymies in a certain language.[70]

For Quine, the legitimate use of definitions in logic is of an essentially *critical* nature: they allow us to paraphrase a richer logical language that one wishes to evaluate in terms of a poorer logical language to which one could more easily apply a metalogical analysis. But they cannot receive an autonomous status in the language, nor can they authorize linguistic revisions. Rather than explaining synonymy in a conventional manner, by exhibiting an L-rule of transformation, Quine seeks to approach it as a *pragmatic* concept, "which refers to the criteria of behaviorist psychology and empirical linguistics."[71] Carnap, on the other hand, is not hostile to the idea of giving a pragmatic definition of synonymy, on the condition, however, that the latter is not made "the *base* of semantic theory." Although the term "semantic theory" now supersedes "syntax," the idea is the same: a pure theory of language can be grounded only on (purely analytic) rules of construction: If the concept "synonymous" is to be used at all in pure semantics, you have to state rules for it.[72]

One could therefore approach the question of the universality of pure syntax by examining its relation to pragmatics. From Quine's point of view, the concrete conditions of communication are what form the touchstone of the concepts of syntax: one cannot speak of the a priori universality of syntactic statements because the syntactic concepts themselves refer to certain conditions of verbal production. If, for example, the sentences of a certain language can be specified in pure syntax (or semantics), it nevertheless remains that, from Quine's point of view, the very notion of sentence must be borrowed from pragmatics. Like the notion of *sentence*, that of *analyticity* acquires sense only if one is able to explain positively what it means, for an individual, that such a series of words is analytic:

> Thus the requirement which I have in mind isn't met by saying that the analytic statements are those which follow from the semantical rules of language; any more than the general notion of sentence would be satisfactorily

provided by saying that a sentence is anything that is a sentence by virtue of the grammatical rules of language.[73]

For Carnap, on the other hand, the analytic and consequently a priori character of the statements of pure syntax entitles the latter to hold universally, and independently from experience. Already in the *Syntax*, the main point of divergence between Carnap and Quine concerns not the way to define a particular metalogical concept, but the question of the *application of forms*: the relation of the logic of science to the sciences. For Carnap, general syntax, later relayed by pure semantics, can take care of the application of the formal to empirical domains. The *P*-rules are constructed on the model of the *L*-rules. Considered metalogically, the *P*-rules make up just another syntactic category. A purely logical description of the empirical is for Carnap perfectly legitimate. Like the Wittgenstein of the *Tractatus*, he considers the logic of science to be either below or above but not on the same level as science. Quine, in contradistinction, admits the interest and even the legitimacy of the edification of a system only to the extent that a *translation* of this system into "the native language" or, if one prefers, into the terms of a *certain concrete speaker* is truly possible. But this possibility can no longer be measured on the basis of the system. It is the empirical sciences, psychology and linguistics, that arise to bound from the "outside," so to speak, the logician's work. This means that experience (scientifically registered) alone makes it possible to account for the application of forms. The philosopher loses at the same time his perspective on unified science.

The principle of tolerance must thus be restored to its true function: to ascertain the *combinatory* character of syntactic virtualities, without for that matter giving up the higher unification provided by arithmetized metalogic. The freedom to invent forms and to base the relation to experience on them culminates in the construction of the syntactic concepts themselves. As for the very delimitation of the logical or physical character of rules of transformation, it is not grounded on the recognition of logical reasons; but the logician has a right to emphasize the extreme variability that the distinction between *L*-and *P*-rules authorizes in the matter.

Implicitness from Kant to Carnap

Universal syntax thus plays a role topically similar to that of Kantian a priori forms and concepts: just as transcendental logic states the principles according to which is represented the general a priori condition under which things can become objects of our knowledge, so universal syntax specifies the a priori formal conditions of possibility of any scientific discourse—logical or descriptive, determinate or not[74]—and of the relation of language to experience. However, because the purely analytic universal syntax takes up the role Kant allotted to the synthetic functions belonging to distinct faculties, Carnap is able to follow Leibniz and Frege rather than him and to evade the Kantian distinction between the nominal and the real, between the synthetic derivation of constructed concepts and the analytic deduction of given concepts. Indeed, a sentence can be classed "*P*-valid" or "indeterminate" only in accordance with particular conventions that govern the language considered. It is thus impossible to guess a priori (i.e., from one sentence taken in isolation) its status in the language. This means that a sentence can pertain either to *L*-rules or to *P*-rules of deduction. As Kant remarked, there are indeed two ways of producing the "implicit" content of a proposition, according to the nature of the rules employed in its deduction. But one must not infer a dualism between the sensitive and the intellectual that would be formally unverifiable and would confine logic to subordinate roles, since these two kinds of rules can actually be combined in a single language. By suggesting making room for *P*-rules, Carnap at the same time makes accessible to deduction contents that are in fact synthetic. Let us take the two sentences:

(P_1) The body *a* is of iron.

(P_2) The body *a* cannot float on water.

Will we say that P_2 is "implicitly contained" in P_1? If we intend to restrict the idea of implicitness to what is *logically deducible* from P_1, the answer is negative. But we can choose to extend implicit to cover *P*-deducible, which makes P_2 a proposition "already contained," in *P*-sense, in P_1 completed by the rules of transformation (*LS*, §52, 185). There is therefore a *P*-implicitness a little like there was in the *Aufbau* a "quasi analysis." In both cases it is a matter of extending the purely formal procedures to areas that were traditionally outside logic.[75] If the division between analytic and synthetic propositions has a major foundational role and must appear as one of the universal features of the syntax of science, it is no longer because synthetic propositions belong to a different cognitive source, which would make them unfit for a purely formal treatment. The opposite is true: Carnap inscribes the division among the rules of formation (by contrasting logical terms with descriptive terms) and those of transformation (by juxtaposing *L*-and *P*-rules) only to more easily set on a par deduction, explanation, and prediction (*LS*, §82, 319). A *homogeneous* formal treatment (although not identical) of all the discursive operations of a scientific language is possible. It suffices for that purpose to translate this language in an adequate manner, into what is still a "rational reconstruction." In this sense, remark 6.113 of the *Tractatus* retains its value. It is not the synthetic proposition of the natural theory that reveals its own (*P*-) validity, but the metalogical translation offered by the logician's reconstruction.

Translation and Interpretation

To bring out the legitimacy of general syntax supposes the elucidation of a concept that governs its own applicability (as well as simultaneously determining the generality Carnap demands for it), and pertains to what could be called interlinguistic synonymy. For a syntax to be truly universal, its concepts *must* be translatable into any language chosen (eventually at the cost of certain adjunctions and constraints of correct formation). For a syntax to be applicable, the logical language S_1 and the physical language S_2 *must* both be able to be embedded in a language S_3 that encompasses them, and whose statements comprise a translation of the statements of S_1 and S_2.[76]

The formal notion of translation has an essential role to play, not only to account for the possibilities of a switch of language—so fundamental in theoretical analysis (in physics, for example)—but also to characterize the nature of philosophical analysis. In the two senses of the word "interpretation"—"interpreting" a formal system and "interpreting" a philosophical claim—*interpreting henceforth amounts to translating*. In the ordinary sense, translating consists in correlating the statements of a language S_1 (e.g., French) with the statements of a language S_2 (e.g., German) by means of a language S_3 that makes it possible to assert that synonymy of pairs of statements belonging to S_1 and S_2, respectively. Translating always presupposes that a language $S_1 + S_2$ has been formed (at least implicitly) in which the syntactic relations between S_1 and S_2 will be expressed.[77] What holds for natural languages holds in the same way for the interpretation of a symbolic calculus in a physical theory. If S_1 is vector analysis and S_2 a physical language lacking this analysis, to "interpret" the analysis is to construct a language comprising S_1 and S_2 as sublanguages, that is, to translate vector analysis into the language S_3 of physics. One can require either such a translation to be "equipollent" with respect to S_3 or to respect a stronger criterion, like that of the synonymy of the corresponding expressions of S_1 and S_2 in S_3 (in a conservative sublanguage, this criterion is always satisfied).

We note again here that, even if the interpretation is of the *descriptive* sort—that is, if descriptive expressions are added to the uninterpreted calculus, and on this account interpretations "yield something new that has not already been given in the construction of the calculus" (§62, 232)—the syntax in which the interpretation is carried out concerns only classes of symbols, of expressions, and of sentences. The essence of interpretation thus conceived is to never depart from the field of formal syntax. We recall the difficulty Carnap faced at the time of the *Aufbau* in making clear the nature of philosophical analysis in respect to the construction of a system of concepts. To the extent that a system of constitution included empirical and analytic axioms, the properly analytic contribution, which was that of the *theoretician* of constitution, was masked by the concern for the content of the derivations, a content that was, however, called on only as an illustration of the formal procedures. The notion of translation makes it possible now to define more clearly the nature of the task of the "logician of science" and to reveal the purely analytic character of his statements. This does not mean, one should hastily add, that every syntactic statement is analytic (one part of syntax is applied syntax, a part of physics). But the manner in which the philosopher addresses problems of science, from his metalogical standpoint, is analytic, since even "questions . . . that appear . . . to be the very opposite of formal," namely, the "concepts of meaning" (relations of consequence, concepts of content and of interpretation), "can be handled within the domain of formal syntax" (*LS*, §62, 233).

The *Logical Syntax* does not only have a "constitutive" function. It is not limited to specifying the properties and the formal relations between different possible types of languages. It also has a polemic use, in which translation will play a major role in dispelling appearance. There is a dialectic of pure syntax, which should make it possible to locate the error exploited by metaphysics (an error to which it also falls victim). The central concept of this dialectic is that of *quasi-syntactic* statement.

Dialectic of Pure Syntax and Analyticity

The Quasi-Syntactic

Carnap calls "quasi-syntactic" a property that looks like an object property, but which "according to meaning" in fact characterizes the *designation* of the object in the metalanguage. The relevance of introducing this category of properties (and corresponding statements) will become clear if we examine the following two examples:

(1) No one shaves himself on January 19, 1984.
(2) No one is his own brother.

The first statement expresses the irreflexivity of the property "to shave oneself at a given time"; similarly, the second statement expresses the irreflexivity of the property "is his own brother." Yet these two statements are, of course, distinguished by the fact that (1) can well be false, and in all likehood is (its truth-value is of a *synthetic* nature), whereas by virtue of the rules of the language "no one is his own brother" is an analytic statement.

One must conclude that irreflexivity has a different status in (1) and in (2). In (1), irreflexivity is an empirical property of a domain of objects. In other words, (1) truly states a property of the world. In (2), on the other hand, irreflexivity is founded on a logical necessity. Consequently, although (2) seems to describe the world, it is only the *transposition* in the object language of a property that initially characterizes the use of the expression "is a brother of." Therefore, (2) is a *quasi-syntactic* statement. For every quasi-syntactic statement, there always exists by definition a corresponding syntactic statement that presents in the metalanguage the property from which the quasi-syntactic sentence derives its validity. For example, " 'is a brother of' is an *L*-irreflexive expressions of relation" is a sentence of the syntax justifying (2).

It is now possible to analyze rigorously, that is, in terms of a general syntax, what led philosophers to believe that their statements *had an object*, or, in other words, what hid from them the true nature of their inquiries. Quasi-syntactic sentences can indeed receive two sorts of *interpretations*. In the first interpretation, the quasi-syntactic sentence is "of the same denotation" as the corresponding syntactic sentence; in other words, it also designates a syntactic property, but it does so in an *autonymous* way: substituting for the syntactic designation of its argument the corresponding designation of the object language. For example, if we consider the syntactic sentence

"5" is a number-word

the corresponding autonymous quasi-syntactic sentence will be

"5" is a number-word.

In fact, the autonymous mode is not very far removed from the syntactic mode, named "formal." In this case quasi syntax will not be able to create an extralinguistic illusion. However, sentences in the autonymous mode have an essential particularity, that of being *intensional*. Put differently, they do not allow the autonymous constituent to be replaced *salva veritate* by a synonymous expression. Autonymy is, of course, one of the characteristics of unilingual formal systems and, consequently, explains the restrictions on the principle of extensionality that these systems suggest. The important consequence of the correlation between these autonymous intensional sentences and the syntactic sentences that are equivalent (*gleichbedeutend*) to them is that henceforth we are guaranteed an *extensional* translation of every autonymous sentence.

There is the second type of interpretation: the quasi-syntactic sentence ascribes this time not a syntactic property to an object, designated in an autonymous manner, but an object property to an object. The latter is, however, only an appearance, attached to a choice of expression or, more precisely, of style, which is sometimes unconscious. For the mark of the quasi-syntactic is revealed by the possibility of translating the sentence considered into a syntactic statement. If we go back to the example given earlier, the quasi-syntactic sentence in the "material mode" would be expressed thus:

"5" is a number.

This sentence is constructed like an observation sentence of the type "Reagan is a president." It has the linguistic appearance of an object statement in that it too seems designed to convey a fact. To bring out the sort of transcendental illusion created by an employment of language such as this, we will say that a "pseudo-object statement" (*Pseudo-objektsatz*) is concerned here. In fact, the sentence does not teach us anything about the *object* 5, but does specify the syntactic category to which "5" belongs.

Translating into an explicit syntactic language of statements that seem to characterize synthetically an object, but that are really confined to stating the syntactic properties of a language and are therefore purely analytic (*L*-valid), appears to Carnap from the outset to be promising. The method of translating *can* be put to use in any situation, since every statement must be able to receive a determinate status in a syntax one will eventually have to exhibit. Moreover, this method *must* make it possible to solve the conflicts taken to be "ideological," but which for the most part are mere pragmatic alternatives between different manners of speech: philosophical contrasts (realism-idealism, logicism-formalism, etc.) are transformed into conflicts of usefulness that can no longer be the object of a controversy. One of the most important problems the method of translation, applied in this manner, allows us to raise again (and which it is supposed to be able to dissolve) is that of the principle of extensionality and in particular of the legitimacy of intensional languages.

Analyticity and Extensionality

In the *Aufbau* the thesis of extensionality forms one of the conditions of possibility of the system of constitution. The thesis defended there applies to the unified language of science, which it characterizes in an "absolute" manner, in accordance with proposition 5 of the *Tractatus*:

> 5. A proposition is a truth-function of elementary propositions.
> 5.01. Elementary propositions are truth-arguments of propositions.

As the *Logical Syntax* is precisely defined by the giving up of the absolute point of view that was still that of the *Aufbau*, the logician is faced with the new task of enlarging (or completing) the extensionality thesis so as to make it compatible with the existence of a multiplicity of languages eventually nonequivalent among each other and possessing very diverse formal properties. The question then arises whether one should admit intensional languages, or, in other words, if syntax, which is by definition extensional (cf. §67, 246–47), can also apply to languages containing expressions that do not follow the principle of substitutivity of equivalents.

The problem of intensional languages represents for general syntax a sort of challenge, quite comparable to that of Frege's system or that of the constitution system in their times. The universal capacity of the syntax to account for *every* language must now be ascertained:

> For this reason we will not formulate the *thesis of extensionality* in a way that is at the same time more complete and less ambitious, namely, a *universal language of science may be extensional*; or, more exactly, for every given intensional language S_1, an extensional language S may be constructed such that S_2 can be translated into S_1. (*LS*, §67, 245)

Just as in the previous cases the venture was in danger of being lost when it seemed to be won, through the discovery of a special case the system could not translate adequately (in the *Aufbau*, disposition terms) or through the exhibiting of an unperceived contradiction (in Frege's system). Thus one must now test the universality of the syntax by making the thesis of extensionality a *hypothesis*, of which one knows from the outset that it will never be fully "verified," but at most may be contradicted if a language resists extensional translation:

> Since we are ignorant of whether there exist intensional sentences of quite another kind than those known, we are also ignorant of whether the methods described, or others, are applicable to the translation of all possible

intensional sentences. For this reason the *thesis of extensionality* (although it seems to me to be a fairly plausible one) is presented here *only as a supposition.* (*LS*, §67, 247)

A language is "intensional" if it contains certain constituents that call for the limitation of the rule of substitutivity of *L*-equivalent expressions. To give an extensional translation of these sentences, one must find a syntactic explanation accounting for this limitation and, finally, find a way to avoid it. In regard to these expressions, Carnap discovers that they all have a common feature: that of expressing in the "material mode" and, more often still, in the "autonymous" mode, a purely syntactic property.

Let us take the case of "propositional attitudes." The sentence

(1) Charles believes *A* (*A* being taken here as a symbol for the object believed, and not as the designation of this object)

is *intensional.* Carnap does not question the "authentically intensional" nature of this statement, unlike Russell who in Appendix C of the *Principia*, translates away the supposedly intensional statements into conventional extensional ones. The principle of tolerance calls for accepting the "reality" of intensional languages that in certain cases may be preferred to the corresponding extensional languages. To make (1) extensional, one needs only interpret it in such a way that *A* is in (1) an autonymous designation. Sentence (1) can then be translated as:

(2) Charles believes *A*.

Sentence (2) is a statement of descriptive syntax, "to believe" being a descriptive predicate, defined or undefined *A* being the name of a sentence, that is, a concrete series of symbols in the language concerned. To characterize the transition from (1) to (2), we would say nowadays that we are proceeding from the *use* of *A* to its *mention.*[78] The same kind of argument allows us to translate into the extensional language the following intensional statement:

(3) Prim (3) contains "3."

If the number term "3" is replaced in (3) by the equivalent expression "2 + 1," (3) becomes false. Yet it is possible to translate (3) into the formal language, by interpreting the intensional constituent "3" in (3) as self-designating in the autonymous mode. Once translated, (3) becomes:

(4) "3" occurs in "prim (3)."

Now, (4) is a statement of pure syntax, since it puts forth an analytically true relation between the complex expression and its constituent symbols (§68, 248–49).[79]

Universal Words

The inquiry into the analyticity characteristic of philosophical discourse — or, more strictly, characteristic of the logic of science, since metaphysical statements prove most often to be nonsensical owing to a mistake concerning the types of expressions they use or for want of a uniform syntactic adjustment—presupposes that we make clear the precise function of a category of predicates that is destined to play an essential role therein (and moreover which already makes up the greater part of what are called "philosophical concepts"). What is concerned is "universal predicates," which correspond in the logic of science to the "universal words" (*Allwörter*) of traditional philosophical discourse.

In the dialectic of syntax, *Allwörter* acquire from this *intermediate* position (due to their belonging both to traditional philosophy and to the logic of science) a major strategic function. Their role as go-between, in fact, bestows on them two tasks. The first task is *descriptive*: universal words appear in traditional philosophical discourse; they even make up the greater part of the concepts of metaphysics. The second task is *constructive*: universal words receive a definite syntactic status in general syntax.

What explains once again the *appearance*—that is, the nonimmediate character of the transition from the universal word in its usual philosophical use to the universal predicate of the logic of science—is the "material" use most often made them in philosophy. The material mode always functions as an opaque medium, distorting, potentially generating illusion, somewhat like in psychoanalytic theory where the reregistering of unconscious representations in the conscious system dissimulates their real mental function.[80] Thus, universal words are the touchstone of the efficiency of syntax as a *critical instrument*. On this issue one could compare Kant's dialectic with Carnap's dialectic: Kant subjects the concepts of traditional metaphysics to a critical examination by relating them to a priori sources of knowledge, whereas Carnap relates philosophical statements to the general conditions of the formation of statements in any language. A universal word is a constituent that defines a "kind" within which every substitution will lead back to a true proposition. For example, the statement:

(1) "7" is an odd number.

The proposition is analytic (insofar as it is *L*-valid). Yet if the constituent "7" is varied, the truth-value of (1) can change for certain substitutions.

Let us now examine the statement

(2) '7" is a number.

In some languages such as Language I or Language II in which the set of numbers forms a closed kind, so that the accepted substitutions concern only number expressions,[81] sentence (2) remains true for every expression substitution for "7," as long as the variants of (2) retain a sense (*LS*, §76, 293). The analogy of this case with the one studied by Bolzano is striking ("the sum of the angles of this triangle is equal to two right angles"). It is due to the fact that as one goes from (1) to (2) the content of the predicate diminishes until one reaches the largest predicate, lacking any specific content, and applying without any restriction to the whole of a kind. But although the parallel is worth outlining, owing to the common application of the method of variation within the limits of a kind, it is more interesting to bring out the limits of the analogy.

One notices at first that Carnap takes to be "eminently analytic," so to speak, the predication that *determines* the boundaries of the kind—boundaries within which any variation on the argument will give an analytic statement. What allows him to assert this is that he has a clause of meaning (delimiting the possible substitutions) that is extremely restrictive and easily testable since it is the result of a notational convention. Statement (2) therefore owes its analyticity to its being derived from a rule of notation specifying the syntactic category to which the expression "7" belongs. It is obvious under such conditions that every statement of the form "*X is a number*" *will be either syntactically L*-valid or badly formed. Bolzano, on the other hand, does not have the same reasons for regarding as analytic the proposition that delimits the "dominant" kind within which any substitution *salva veritate* is allowed. We already know that his criterion of objectivity (*Gegenständlichkeit*) does not function in the manner of a clause excluding meaninglessness. For example, in Bolzano's logic one may vary the constituent "7" in statement (2) ("7 is a number") to yield the proposition

(3) "Caesar" is a number.

To this seemingly technical reason is added a motivation of an ontological nature. Generally speaking, for Bolzano, truth has a content (it is not purely nominal). He therefore can conceive *analytic* truth only against the backdrop of *synthetic* truth. In the *Syntax*, Carnap develops, on the contrary, a category of *L*-valid that is no longer dependent on the existence of "nonnominal" truths. In other words, Carnap allows himself to *nominalize* the *genus*: to say that generic predication is analytic is to say that the genus applies to every expression that, in a language, can be ascribed to it. The nominalization of generic predication leads then to its being emptied of all content. To say that "7 is a number" or that "Caro is something" only amounts to specifying the syntactic category of the expression that stands in subject position.

Carnap distinguishes two types of *use* of universal words; this duality corresponds, as we have noted, to the dual function, explanatory and critical, of the general concept of "quasi syntax." In its properly syntactic use, the universal concept is "dependent." It serves as an "auxiliary grammatical symbol"; it functions, in fact, somewhat like an "index," by bringing out the syntactic genus of an expression that is then used in a genuine object sentence (*LS*, §76, 294). For example, the expressions "integer" or "real number" make it possible in the following sentential functions to characterize the syntactic type of the symbol they qualify:

The integer "7 . . . "
The real number "7 . . . "

In this use, the universal predicate is the syntactic transposition of what Wittgenstein called, in the *Tractatus*, a "formal concept," the latter having therein precisely an essentially critical and preventive function. For Wittgenstein, the formal concept only has a *dependent* use, insofar as it delimits the range of a variable (cf. 4.1272). Carnap can now show that Wittgenstein's conclusion, according to which no other *type of use* of formal concepts is legitimate, arises from a too narrow conception of the "limits of language." There is no longer any reason to consider as does Wittgenstein that the expression of the type "1 is a number" is nonsensical. It would be better to say that an *independent* use is concerned, in the material mode, of a quasi-syntactic predicate. This use is independent to the extent that, instead of serving as index in an object sentence, the generic term stands alone in predicate position. What makes the statement "1 is a number" perfectly legitimate is that it expresses in the material mode the "parallel" or "transposed" syntactic quality (*PLS*, 63; *LS*, §80, 308) asserted by

"1" is a number expression.

From the "dialectic" standpoint, which is the real argumentative locus of the concept of quasi-syntactic, the material mode seems thus to have a fundamentally ambiguous role (which already appeared to us with respect to intensional languages). By virtue of the principle of tolerance, its statements cannot be excluded as being ill-formed. One may have reasons for preferring the material mode, for example, its flexibility of use or its convenience (§81, 312). But one must also know that it is only a *derived* mode of expression. It would be dangerous to stick to the objective appearance of its statements, and to ascribe to them a *representative* value. Into this trap fall common sense as well as traditional philosophy.

It is therefore a *fact*—a fact that could be called "natural," psychosociological—that explains that philosophers were misled for so long concerning the status of their own discipline, that they believed their "claims" to be comparable to scientific truths, and that some of them went as far as to imagine an independent source of philosophical knowledge in synthetic a priori powers. The dynamic illusion here is none other than a natural tendency, which lies in preferring the "transposed mode" because it strikes the imagination (*LS*, §80, 309). This tendency can only be strengthened by the absence of a syntactic approach. Carnap brings out here what could be called the "resistance" of scientists themselves to accepting the syntactic mode concerning metaphysical questions: it is not freely that one abandons object speech in favor of a strictly linguistic attention (*LS*, §80, 309). Finally the material mode hides the *relativity* of syntactic decisions for a given language. This remark applies not only to almost every philosophical proposition, but also to the constitutional theses of the *Aufbau*.

When the axioms of the *Aufbau* were divided into analytic (if they were a consequence of the definitions) and synthetic (if they expressed a relation between constituted objects nonderivable from their definitions), the former alone deserving to be called "theses of constitution," appeal was made to what the syntax now allows us to distinguish more clearly as the contrast between linguistic forms (which the analytic propositions explore by specifying their relations, the rules that govern them, etc.) and empirical observations. But propositions such as "colors form a continuum" still had in the *Aufbau* an uncertain status: inherited from the state of positive sciences, they had no less a quasigrammatical character making it possible to distinguish the essential overlapping from the accidental overlapping of color-similarity circles.

It is now possible to give a complete answer to the question of the *nature* of such a knowledge. Let us assume that the following conventions are given in the syntax of the *P*-language in question:

> A colour-expression consists of three co-ordinates; the values of each co-ordinate form a serial order according to syntactical rules; on the basis of these syntactical rules, therefore, the colour-expressions constitute a three-dimensional order. (*LS*, §79, 306, trans. Smeaton)

One will infer that the continuity of colors is in fact a property of the color expressions of this language and, consequently, a syntactic property stated in a purely analytic fashion. But a language in which the continuity of colors is an empirical property can be imagined:

> The colour-expressions are not compound; they are primitive symbols; further, a symmetrical, reflexive, but not transitive, ᴘrδ to which the colour-expressions are suitable as arguments, occurs as a primitive symbol; the theorem of the three-dimensionality of the order determined by this predicate is P-valid. (Ibid.)

This example proves that one can no longer hope to know the cognitive species of a statement — its analyticity or syntheticity — merely by examining its content; a sentence must be referred to the rules of formation and of transformation of the language in which it was formed. Some languages introduce color expressions by *definition* (such as "a color expression has three coordinates"), so that the continuity of each dimension is posited prior to the empirical evidence as a syntactic rule. Other languages postulate color expressions as undefinables with regard to which a relation of resemblance makes it possible to define an order. Depending on the case, this order may be established following empirical laws contained in this language (which makes three-dimensionality a *P*-valid statement), or else empirically constructed, by comparison with pairs of colors (three-dimensionality then becomes an "indeterminate" statement). But there are also languages that, because they fail to state their syntactic rules clearly, will leave us in the dark as to the status of their statements.

Philosophy Nominalized

Philosophy is to be replaced by the logic of science — that is to say, by the logical analysis of the concepts and sentences of the sciences, for *the logic of science is nothing other than the logical syntax of the language of science*. (*LS*, xiii)

The previous developments could lead us to see a dispersion of logico-philosophical inquiry: relativizing analyticity (and other fundamental syntactical concepts) to a given language leads to an indefinite construction of logics that seem no longer to claim to found the unity of science. From this point of view, the logic of science seems to come "after the sciences," merely elucidating the status of theoretical statements produced elsewhere; its function seems strictly descriptive and clarifying.

But this would be to forget that a "reunification" of these particular syntaxes is accomplished in general syntax, which in principle is "applicable to languages of any form whatsoever" (*LS*, xv). There is therefore more to be expected from the logic of science than simply bringing to light a posteriori the linguistic structures of "natural" theories. As I noted earlier, the logic of science reveals the conditions of possibility of scientificity, that is, of rationality in general. Yet it is not the linguistic element that plays the founding role here. Linguistic expressions are an object of study only insofar as they bring out a system of formal rules; these formal rules replace, in the transcendental function, the a priori forms and concepts of Kant, the hierarchized "propositions in themselves" of Bolzano and the "logical laws" of Frege.

What allows us to award such a topical role to the Carnapian formal is its double characteristic of making possible a logical discourse in general and of escaping any empirical test. Thus, although the logic of *science* in a sense comes "after" the sciences (insofar as it does not have to deal with experimental contents, while presupposing the existence of fully developed sciences), it still retains the traditional status of First Philosophy, in that it alone makes it possible to exhibit the foundation of the legitimacy of scientific discourse in its universality. The dispersal of logical tasks must not hide the major endeavor: to build a "unique" system of science—unique not in the former sense of a "monolingual" discourse, but in the sense that a single general syntax applies to regional theories and therein uncovers the strict separation between logical and descriptive constituents, between analytic and synthetic statements, which scientific activity always presupposes. The logic of science delimits the thinkable: what is neither a syntactic (that is, logical) statement nor an empirical (*P*-valid or indeterminate) statement is meaningless.

The war against metaphysical statements should be set in the context of this "pretension."[82] Logic can let nothing remain outside the system of unified science of which it must, so to speak, "take care." Traditional philosophy is indeed subjected to the most drastic of treatments. Either its statements are translatable into general syntax, and this translation reveals thereby their real vacuousness. Meaningful philosophical statements are only grammatical observations concerning the language of science or suggestions for the uses of a future language—

observations and suggestions, however, of little use, to the extent that they are not explicitly given in syntactic language, which makes them liable to encourage "obscurities and contradictions" (*LS*, §78, 298, 300, 301; §80, 308, 310, etc.). Or else the statements of traditional philosophy cannot be adequately translated even with ordinary adjustments and supplements, and are declared nonsensical (which means, practically, that no commentary or, a fortiori, any debate can dwell on these theses). When the metaphysician "milks the he-goat" by asserting, for example, that the world is the development of God, it would be to hold a sieve underneath if one were to object that the world is not the development of God:

> This metaphysical statement has no more sense than the children's rhyme "eeny meeny mink monk"; the only difference is that many elevated feelings are associated with the metaphysical statement.[83]

The inventive freedom granted to the logic of science arises, on the contrary, from the recognition of its empirical vacuousness and from the purely pragmatic character of the choice of a given language. The logic of science can, of course, state the syntactic rules of a language or a family of languages (which is purely the object of general syntax). But it can also, in turn, *propose* new syntactic forms: "for a language (not previously stated) that is proposed as a language of science (or of a subdomain of science)," or even, on a purely exploratory basis, "for a language (not previously stated) whose formulation and investigation is proposed (apart from the question whether it is to serve as a language of science or not)" (*LS*, §17, 52) — unlike what traditional philosophers, concerned with truth, somewhat naively believed.

However, the amoralism Carnap mentions, here concerns the investigation of various possible syntaxes and not the metasyntax that makes it possible to bring together all these divergent symbolic attempts. The logic of science does not have to "believe" in the language it proposes: it is just a linguistic schema. On the other hand, when logicians state in general syntax that all possible scientific propositions are either analytic or synthetic, and that this is again an *analytic* division with respect to a higher syntax, they are not resorting to "aesthetics," so to speak, but describing a universal feature of scientific language.

Philosophy or rather the logic of science, as Carnap understands it,[84] undeniably is entirely nominal, purely analytic, and therefore without "consequence." But considered in its relation to the system of unified science, it paradoxically indicates the limits of all rational knowledge. Moreover, this twofold value of logical activity (which Carnap never made explicit, but which appears clearly in the double aspect — assertive and normative — of the syntax), led Quine to show the insufficiency of the point of view that is implicit under the word "convention": arbitrary and nominal with respect to its application, the convention must nevertheless possess, in metalogical discourse, grounds that in the final analysis are legitimating.[85] As we already observed, however, it is from the general syntax that the "convention" receives its twofold value, nominal and foundational.

Conclusion

The Analytic-Synthetic Division:
A Dogma of Empiricism?

In spite of the tactical differences of employment, which I have had the opportunity to bring out, the distinction between analytic and synthetic propositions seems to present at least one persistent feature: it always served as a foundational strategy of rationalist inspiration. In the four systems analyzed, we indeed observed the recurrence of the type of question to which Kant subordinated the relevance of the demarcation between judgments. For Kant, the problem of the foundation of a universal and necessary science was that of the possibility of synthetic a priori judgments; Bolzano attempts to solve the same problem by "redogmatizing" the Kantian theses. It is the objective articulation of the truths of "science in itself" that founds our effort to bring out truth. When Frege reconstructs arithmetic, hoping to reveal its logical essence, it is again the objective existence of logical truths that determines the possibility of the formulary system. Undoubtedly, Bolzano and Frege broke off with Kantianism by making the conditions of the objectivity of science antecedent to the knowing subject. Yet the very way in which they describe this independent domain—the reign of propositions in themselves or of thoughts and their denotations—recalls Kantian deduction: since science exists, there must be a priori conditions making its knowledge possible; the philosopher's task is to exhibit—that is, to bring to light in their pureness—these a priori conditions.

It may be objected here that if the topical description of the change of key affecting the concept of analytic proposition and the discursive constellation in which it receives its meaning leads us to map out thematic mutations, any continuist interpretation seems henceforth precluded. Is it not somewhat artificial to suppose the permanence of the "transcendental question" when the whole critical problem has disappeared? Is the "same question" still involved, when it is granted elsewhere that the concepts of logic, form, analytic proposition, and so forth, have changed content? Why then continue to give preference to this unique question regarded as the only persistent one?

The answer to such an objection must be both general and specific, since it determines simultaneously the methodology of this work and its application. For the historian of systems it is foremost a matter of principle: if one only brings out thematic ruptures, changes of significance, one prevents oneself from explaining what, nevertheless, forms the condition of possibility of the comparative approach; moreover, one loses sight of what constitutes the philosophical and not strictly historical interest of the systems considered. To speak of discontinuity presupposes beginning with the existence of a link—however weak—between the systems, a link on which talk about dispersion rests, but which one often finds more convenient to leave in the dark. If it claims to be *comparative*, any discontinuist discourse must necessarily bring in, even if tacitly, minimal *continuist hypotheses*, which serve to sustain subsequent distinctions. On the other hand, the question of the *philosophical interest* cannot be raised in a purely discontinuist perspective: following the skeptical thesis that forms the usual backdrop of discontinuism, some kind of stylistic pleasure is assumed to motivate the formulation as well as the interpretation of a philosophical system; it is the singularity of a thought that captivates us, since in the final analysis this singularity does not seem to refer back to anything except the author's will or the system of statements making up his or her work. In demanding of a comparative analysis that it cast light on what remains common to two systems (one of which took leverage on the other in order to distinguish itself), the historian realizes that a system is not purely and simply a captive of its themes and its combinations, but that it can *communicate* (i.e., share) with another system some fundamental goals, patterns of inquiry, paradigmatic solutions and examples, and even the canon of the form of a systematic work. The existence of this fundamental level would therefore explain why an author can be said to be *interesting*: taken absolutely and without any counterbalance, the thesis of discontinuity implies that the major perlocutionary effect of a system is of the nature of a *peculiarity*. If one wishes, rather, to account not for the rhetorical or the psychological *interest* but for the properly philosophical *interest*, which rewards reading, commenting on, or even annexing other philosophical texts, room must be spared, in my opinion, for a global strategic community that delimits a realm of relative difference and discursive conflict.

Around the axis of the same foundational strategy, the four systems studied appeared to me to follow respectively analogous tactics. Should I have stressed their analogy by applying to them the adjective "transcendental"—a term acknowledged to be bound up with Kant's critical project, and which on this account, seems to have a clearly discontinuist vocation? The problem consists precisely in discovering what type of *connection* the concept of "transcendental" may have with the idea of a critique of the origin of knowledge. In one of his *Reflections*, Kant points out that "transcendental philosophy is the critique of pure reason." "The question is what reason can know without resorting to any experience and what the condition, the objects and limits of knowledge are."[1] In the texts commented on here, we often encountered the standard sentence or answer that indicates the presence of this kind of inquiry, without, however, the properly Kantian solution being associated with it. The standard question: Under what conditions is science (a particular science) possible? The standard answer: For the statement *P* to be true, it is *necessary* that . . . (followed by the statement of a universal a priori condition, constituting the object of *P* as the object of knowledge, independently of any recourse to experience). The underlying analogy of different foundational procedures consequently obliged us to distinguish the "transsystematic" transcendental theme from its realization in Kant's critical philosophy. To separate more distinctly the schema common to the various transcendental tactics from its use in the Kantian system in terms of cognitive functions (*Erkenntnisfunktionen*), it would undoubtedly have been desirable to have indexed the concept so as to differentiate, for example, what might be called the transconcept of "transcendental$_t$" from the concept of "transcendental$_k$" (transcendental in the Kantian system); the typographical difficulties of such a notation, however, do not seem to be compensated for by the clarity achieved, additional explanations being necessary in each case.

I was therefore able to bring out three types of tactics within the same foundational strategy: the *transcendental-subjective* tactic, which locates the legitimating instance in the act of judgment of a knowing subject, insofar as this act obeys certain formal constraints arising from its original faculty (form of intuition, function of understanding, etc.); the *ontotranscendental* tactic, which eliminates from the subject the foundational instance and places it in an objective and presubjective space; finally, the *syntactic* tactic, which "secularizes" recourse to preliminary conditions by emptying them of all content and by reducing them to pure linguistic forms. Each of these "tactics" handles the demarcation between propositions in view of its own ends. Thus it has in Kant, as we saw, the essential function of subordinating the logical to the transcendental, the analytic to the synthetic, while circumscribing the specificity of philosophy, since its concepts are reached by analysis, unlike mathematics and physics, whose concepts are constructed, that is, synthetic. In Bolzano, the function of analytic propositions is to make knowledge possible for us finite beings, who can understand but a portion of each universal truth. Analytic truths are thus stages in the quest for general laws, intermediaries that have sometimes a propaedeutic value, sometimes a protreptic value.

Let us return to the discontinuities. To describe the changes the concept of analyticity undergoes from the Frege of the *Basic Laws* to the Carnap of the *Logical Syntax* is to bring out the simultaneous shift of the logicist requirement. In Frege, the analyticity of mathematics is the essence of this science; the unraveling of the system of arithmetic revealed the operative potentialities of pure logic, which formed in turn the foundation of rationality in general. Carnap gives up piece by piece this conception of the unitary system—not, however, under the influence of skepticism, which is often ascribed to him, but in my opinion precisely because he understands that the unitary ideal can very well go along with the atomization of logical tasks. The multiplicity of formal languages, of rules of formation and transformation, only brings out better the deep unity of universal syntax. Being part of arithmetic, universal syntax is the framework within which every formal exercise delimits its "regional" rationality. One cannot depart from such a framework. The liberalism of the principle of tolerance is founded on the certainty that there is an a priori set of general conditions of formal thought, these conditions being in turn of an *analytic* nature. This shift of the logicist requirement therefore explains both how logicism survived Gödel's theorems and how the notion of *analytic proposition* played a crucial role in the strategy of its salvage. In unpublished course notes from 1936, Carnap summarizes very clearly the main features of this "shift," that is, the change of content of the logicist thesis. A superficial reading could lead one to believe that the logicist thesis is finally abandoned. Actually, it is *widened* and *generalized*, the concept of "analytic proposition" playing since the *Logical Syntax* the role of a unifying category of the formal. Carnap explains here why it is not essential for the logicist thesis that the axioms of choice and of infinity should be considered as purely logical in spite of their aspect of existential propositions:

> This controversy is, however, not considered today to be as fundamental as it seemed to be ten years ago. We think now that the question is rather a technical one concerning the choice of the form of the mathematical system. We may construct this system either by adding new primitive sentences of a specific mathematical nature to the logical ones if that turns out to be necessary or seems to be convenient without being necessary, or we may take merely logical primitive sentences if it is possible; and further we may add new primitive terms of a specific mathematical nature to the logical ones, as for instance Hilbert prefers to do, or we may take only logical primitive symbols; that is certainly possible and has been done by Russell. Here we have some theoretical questions as to which forms of a system of mathematics are possible, and some practical questions concerning our choice among those possibilities. In some of the forms mathematics would be a branch of logic; in others it would be associated with logic. The essential point is that in each of these cases the system can be constructed in such a way that all theorems of mathematics like those of logic are *analytic*; that is to say, their truth is not dependent upon any facts outside of language, but is determined solely by the rules of language.[2]

What explains why the debate concerning the "purely logical" character of the axiom of choice lost its relevance is that one now has a more liberal idea of the construction of mathematical systems. Any proposition that does not depend on facts — that is, any statement whose *function* is formal — is analytic. The function of a proposition depends, so to speak, on the *act* of the builder, who asserts the corresponding rule. In speaking of an "act," I do not mean that Carnap restores in its prerogatives "reflection," which, in Kant, subordinates the formal logical inquiry to a transcendental investigation. The *function* of a statement — in the language considered — is clearly either formal or empirical, and is bestowed on the statement by setting up rules that constitute this language. These rules indeed proceed from a decree, although the alternative they comprise goes beyond simple stipulations.[3] Even if this duality seems, at first sight, to follow from a convention, it also governs syntax, and consequently represents a quasi-transcendental condition of the formation of a theoretical language. These reflections bring out the status of the analytic-synthetic division in respect to the actual science of mathematics; the division is part of the conditions of possibility of the unity of science insofar as it applies to forms. It does not need, therefore, to be subjected to an empirical inquiry. For reciprocally, any empirical inquiry presupposes it.

In its main features, this general schema seems to us to belong again to a project parallel to that of Kant's transcendental philosophy. If "transcendental principle" means a principle "through which we represent the general a priori condition under which alone things can become the objects of our recognition,[4] we notice the analogy between Kant's procedure and Carnap's. Let us spell it out again: speaking of an analogy is not tantamount to making Carnap a philosopher of the transcendental subject. The transcendental is no longer associated, as in Kantianism, with a relation of our cognition with *our power of knowing*. The "general a priori condition" applies no longer to *cognition*, but to the *language of science*. This difference of application of the transcendental should not hide the topical relationship between the system of Kant and that of Carnap. Like Kant, Carnap starts from science as given, with the intention of understanding what made it possible. Like Kant, he brings to light the general conditions of a universal and necessary objective knowledge. Like Kant, finally, he locates these conditions in a priori forms, with, however, *this essential shift*: *a priori* legitimacy comes totally under the jurisdiction of syntax. All the synthetic functions of Kantian transcendental philosophy (unity of matter and form in the description of the phenomenon, as well as architectonic unity) are henceforth ensured by the universal forms of a possible language: this constitutes, in my opinion, the underlying continuity between the *Aufbau* and the *Logical Syntax*.

How are we to explain then that Carnap identifies his own attempt as empiricist? Why does he call on Hume rather than Kant? I have often had the opportunity of remarking in this book how in the imaginary dialogue between Hume and Kant that we can set up, Carnap does not fail on several essential issues to side with Kant: although it does not have a foundation independent from the subject of knowledge, causality is not purely imaginary; it must, therefore, have some foundation. Instead of defending Hume, by arguing that such a foundation is not necessary, and that even without rational certainty we continue to expect, with equal assurance, to be in the truth, Carnap pursues, throughout his career, a project whose Kantian origins I have emphasized, by seeking to discover the logical foundation of induction.

By adopting an external point of view with the help of comparative topics, we could characterize Carnap's philosophy by saying that it substitutes the jurisdiction of the formal for that of Kant's transcendental subject. This means that henceforth formal logic tacitly ensures the transcendental function, by providing the "general a priori condition" that makes a language of science possible in general. Universal syntax exhibits the conditions of possibility of any science. Rationality being assumed, logic is able to account for the constitutive features of language that found this rationality. Hume, on the contrary, submits empirical knowledge to the question of its natural genesis; beneath the forms, what about the effective means of knowing, that is, of generalizing, abstracting, predicting? Unlike Kant and the reading he suggests, Hume does not require that one should renounce knowing, but that one should have no illusions concerning the natural character of a knowledge that cannot be rationally founded *and that need not be either*. Whether they are the result of habit or another principle of the imagination, the adjunctions to the pure empirical given represent an obstacle of principle to any reductionist amibition.

Carnap's logicism shares with the "ontotranscendental" philosophies of his predecessors the quest for the conditions of possibility of a scientific discourse in the constitutive objective structure described by the universal syntax. An exhaustive presentation of such a syntax can be given in an appropriate language (the syntax remains therefore internal to the language; it is not its limit, as Wittgenstein thought). As long as the concepts of this pure syntax are not established in a rigorous manner, one cannot be certain about the foundations of rationality, nor about the limits of the knowable. I suggest understanding Carnap's logicism as one of the attempts to dissociate criticism from the examination of the subjective power of knowing, in order to associate it with bringing out the objective *medium* that knowing already presupposes. What constitutes the novelty of this endeavor, compared with the antecedent ones of Bolzano and Frege, is that the universality of truth (the set of truths in themselves, or logical laws) is now shifted to the universality of the rule (the rules of universal syntax).

By drawing the conclusion that the analytic-synthetic demarcation is the instruction of an essentially rationalist tradition, we are, of course, faced with a problem that must be accounted for if we wish to ascertain the adequacy of the method followed: very early, around 1923, Carnap adopts empiricism, and he will never cease to conceive his own philosophy as belonging to the antimetaphysical current originating in Hume. But exactly which philosophical attitude does Carnap adopt when he speaks of "empiricism"? As a matter of principle, the historian has a right to confront with the evidence—that is, with the examination of the precise network of theses, demonstrative means, and implications—the filiation the author proposes for his own system. The fact that Carnap judged the orientation of his research and that of his friends of the Vienna Circle to be "empiricist" is not enough to prove the relevance of this judgment, nor to determine the real function—theoretical, expressive, promotional, polemic—of the adherence.

If we take into account the texts published in the 1920s by the members of the Vienna Circle, we notice that the term "empiricism" qualifies a rather vague doctrinal position, which resembles a rallying cry rather than a precise set of claims: the label "empiricist" may be applied to any "antimetaphysical" and "pro-scientific" attitude, any manner of thought founded on experience and rejecting speculation.[5] Even while defining the philosophical position of the Circle as "empiricist and positivist," the group's 1929 manifesto, eloquently titled *Wissenschaftliche Weltauffassung: Der Wiener Kreis*, provides a glimpse of what distinguishes the new from the traditional empiricism:

> It is *the method of logical analysis* that essentially distinguishes recent empiricism and positivism from the earlier version that was more biological-psychological in its orientation.[6]

Nothing in the method of logical analysis appears at first to go against the empiricist orientation of the Circle: the application of logic in *reducing* the empirical given to its basic elements does not contradict the fundamental empiricist claim according to which all knowledge derives from experience, the latter consisting of what is immediately given; it seems rather to form with this thesis an organic whole. Reduction seems to constitute the empiricist method par excellence, recourse to logic being perfectly legitimate since the latter is made up of analytic propositions, lacking empirical content.

Yet, the very radicalness of the reductionist attempt brings out the strangeness of the "empiricism" on which it calls. To account for the uneasiness the "classical" empiricist feels in regard to the unitary and foundational ambition of the logical empiricists, one must exhibit the recourse they make to *two languages*, the first being relative to scientific procedure, the second to philosophical activity; the "scientific" empiricism of logical empiricists consists in demanding that every positive theory be confirmed by experience, and that it should not claim a validity beyond that allowed by experience. But what holds for the sciences does not hold for the theory of science. The latter indeed mobilizes concepts that no longer need to be compared with the given, precisely because they say nothing about the facts. Having from the outset emptied the syntactic concepts of any content, the philosopher no longer has to take experience into account.

The previous discussion brings out the *constitutive* status of the analytic-synthetic division: to be a "logical empiricist" is to accept that the universality of the demarcation between analytic and synthetic propositions is at the base of the "empiricist" character of the logic of science. It is through this distinction that logic acquires its status as a science and can thus take on a wide radius of action, coextensive with philosophy. Successively called "constitution theory," "universal axiomatic," "syntax of science," and "semantics," logic is henceforth entrusted with all the "formal" aspects of the scientific construction of experience.

The "empiricist" claim of the Vienna Circle is therefore tenable only if one antecedently accepts the thesis of strict division between analytic and synthetic propositions; for, indeed, we can be assured that the logical analysis of the given does not bring in any content "outside the frame of possible experience"[7] *only if* all the propositions of logic are analytic. At this juncture, the popular interpretation of the Humean distinction between relations of ideas and matters of fact leads us providentially to believe that the analytic-synthetic division is not the exclusive property of the rationalists, assimilated with the advocates of synthetic a priori judgments. Once it is granted that "logical analysis" does not play any role other than that of a simple means of translation or abbreviation of empirical contents, one can indeed consider that synthetic a priori judgments and, along with them, metaphysical speculation are definitively discredited, this appearing as a "victory of empiricism."

A fussy empiricist may hesitate, however, to agree with the official proclamation of the vacuousness or the neutrality of logic. The construction of universal syntax, then of semantics, shows, on the contrary, that recourse to forms of language dissimulates real "ontological" commitments, which the principles of tolerance and of the analyticity of logic manage only with difficulty to render commonplace. In this respect, Carnap's 1950 "Empiricism, Semantics, and Ontology" appears to be very enlightening; in this article he tries to prove against Quine that to use a language referring to "abstract entities," such as properties or propositions, is perfectly compatible with an empiricist attitude. As Quine correctly points out, the way Carnap brings out the purely linguistic and therefore realist-free character of the construction of any system of reference whatsoever assumes the validity of the strict demarcation between analytic and synthetic propositions: "external questions" do not need any theoretical justification because they assert nothing concerning the *reality* of the denoted entities. In other words, because semantics is purely analytic it can be held to be free from any extralogical constraints. The metaphysician, for Carnap, is the one who defends the claim that the abstract entities to which a semantic system refers "can be experienced as immediately given either by sensation or by a kind of rational intuition."[8] It is therefore not astonishing that Carnap refuses to admit that a language accepting variables of a higher order can be qualified as "Platonist"; for according to him, to be a Platonist actually presupposes that one goes beyond the analytic-synthetic distinction, transgressing at the same time the distinction between internal and external questions by adhering, for example, to the doctrine of universals.

Thus, when Carnap, in his own words, "translates" Hume after quoting the passage of the *Enquiry* in which metaphysicans are criticized,[9] we have the impression that he is mistaken concerning those whom Hume called "metaphysicians": the most dangerous among them, according to Hume, are those who ignore themselves, like the essentialist mathematicians, by raising to the level of standards a rigor and a precision beyond our capacities of perceptual discrimination. By deploying a distinction beyond that which experience allows us to ascertain, does the logicist not meet the essentialist mathematician? If he had really taken Hume seriously, Carnap would not have allowed himself to "constitute" concepts in favor of an "objective" unity of sciences—an objective unity presupposed then proved.

For what unity is achieved at the level of language, as in the *Logical Syntax*, or when the action of going beyond the given is rendered commonplace by the hypothesis of an analogical transfer of constructive procedures, as in the *Aufbau*? Had he been Humean, or even simply empiricist, Carnap would not have thought of suspending the possibility of philosophy on a distinction that, although "constitutive," is not empirical. He would have discredited from the outset the whole array of "foundational" questions insofar as they idealize the cognitive process, instead of continuously raising the question of justification as a preliminary to any question of fact.

That Carnap and his friends of the Vienna Circle nevertheless stuck to the label "empiricist" is inseparable from the rationalist conviction that the forms of language are in themselves empty and independent of experience. The thesis was, moreover, irrefutable since no fact of experience, by definition, could be turned against it. Thus, when Quine attacks the dogma of analyticity, he questions the constitutive role of the status of philosophy rather than the difficulty implied by the definition of the concept of analytic proposition. It is striking to observe that the numerous "replies to Quine" seem to have missed the real point, which is not to solve the technical problem represented by a noncircular definition of "analyticity," nor even to challenge the strictly descriptive interest of the demarcation for certain classes of statements, but to show how the foundational use of this contrast is necessarily an obstacle to establishing an empiricist epistemology. Quine therefore suggests separating philosophical research from the topical influence of the Kantian division between propositions. Semantics must be built up in compliance with an empiricist reappraisal of epistemology, which subjects the metalogical concepts to the existence of *pragmatic* criteria. Does this mean that nonconstructive concepts or procedures should be banished from logic? Should one out of empiricist purism give up, for example, the latent Platonism of nonfinitist logics? Not at all: Quine refuses to subject logical invention to purely philosophical criteria of adequacy. It is supposed that mathematicians must, in their own practice, posit objects. But the case of concepts like analyticity is quite different: unexplained concepts are brought in, without a real pragmatic or epistemological foundation, and are assigned the task of founding the whole of discourse. If the philosopher takes such liberties with the language of science, if he puts himself in the position of universal legislator, empiricism is over with. Unlike the particular sciences, philosophy cannot take the risk of going beyond the given. At the same time logic ceases to be entitled to the primary status of a "first philosophy": it is neither the instrument of the philosopher alone, nor his sole instrument.

Quine's empiricism thus allows us to reach a topical point of comparison from which to understand the profound unity of the systems of Kant, Frege, Bolzano, and Carnap. *Focusing like them on the questions of the unity of science, he sets himself apart by not recognizing the legitimacy of a transcendental point of view.* To adopt a point of view strictly immanent to scientific practice leads one to give up the analytic-synthetic dualism, which is functionally bound up with a foundational procedure, whether of an "ontotranscendental" or a "syntactic" type.

Such a line of demarcation between empiricists and rationalists will surely prompt the reader to look for counterexamples. Let us therefore try to refute comparative topics by confronting it with the facts, by applying it to the philosophical system that appears the least likely to submit to it. Karl Popper's philosophy seems to single itself out here; equally removed from the logical empiricists and from the advocates of "psychologism" (among whom he would probably count Quine), Popper could be difficult to class. Does he not call himself an empiricist while labeling his own philosophical orientation "critical rationalism"?[10] If we must take Popper literally when he proclaims that he synthesizes rationalism and empiricism, then our whole enterprise will prove to be inadequate: if rationalist foundationalism can merge into empiricist naturalism — in Popper, the objectivity of laws is anticipated by the "instinctive expectations" of finding regularities, an expectation that is generalized to every living being — if the transcendental thesis, in the final analysis, integrates the temporary character of acknowledged truths, why continue to draw careful distinctions among discursive constellations? Does the metasystem not prove ultimately to be the realm of confusions and compromises, in which it would be useless to look for stable configurations?

It is true that Popper's system does present the originality of bringing together theses that at first appear to challenge the traditional contrasts (rationalism and empiricism, realism and idealism, etc.). I may also add that the subtlety of some of his analyses has given rise to major misinterpretations that he himself carefully recorded. Lacking space to give more than an outline, I should nevertheless like to show how Popper's system can be located in comparative topics as developed here.

What should we think of Popper's "empiricism," to begin with? We saw earlier why one could not believe the "empiricist" proclamation of philosophers; the thematic use of the term "empiricist" is indeed conditioned in turn by a network of interpretative hypotheses. To judge its real function, it is not enough just to observe the *fact* of the use of the term; it is necessary to refer this use back to the general strategy in which it occurs. I will assign only a minor value to the fact that Popper defends "the fundamental thesis of empiricism according to which experience alone makes it possible to determine the truth or falsity of a statement concerning reality."[11] For this is the "weak" sense of the word "empiricism" and not the technical sense that concerns us here.

I have a clue for guiding me in briefly portraying Popper's strategy: his reading of Hume. I described earlier the bias implicit in Kant's interpretation. Let me note from the outset that Popper takes up all the assumptions of this interpretation. We recall the succession, brought out in the introduction of this book, between the assimilating and the critical phase: one encounters it again in Popper in a striking manner. There is no doubt that "Hume *was right* in stressing that our theories cannot be validly inferred from what we can know to be true." But he was wrong when "he concluded from this that our belief in them was irrational": *he was wrong* to despair of reason (one has the impression that one is rereading the *Progelomena* here).[12]

To have recognized that we cannot know nature (that is, acquire a valid knowledge, following the logico-mathematical model of deductive validity) and that there is no "inductive knowledge" represents for Popper the definitive contribution of Hume. But he immediately departs from Hume in asserting two completely rationalist theses.

On the one hand, although one cannot know "by proof" in the experimental sciences, one can nevertheless have a "tentative critical acceptance" of scientific theories. Such an agreement displays a perfectly rational course of action: "There is not even anything irrational in relying for practical purposes upon well-tested theories, for no more rational course of action is open to us."[13] We know indeed what founds for Popper the rationality of this attitude of relative confidence: the logical notion of *verisimilitude*, which itself is relative. Of course, the truth of a theory cannot be *proved* like a theorem of mathematics; one can nevertheless say that a theory T_1 is closer to the truth than a theory T_2, if T_1 contains at least as many true statements but fewer false ones than T_2 (or if T_1 has more true statements but no more false ones). Once we have determined the *truth content* of a theory—all the nontautological true statements that are deducible from it—and its *falsity content*—the class of false statements it contains[14]—we could in principle know deductively which of the theories is the best, both logically, according to its predictive ability, and even empirically, according to the effective resistance it opposes to the attempts to refute it. For example, although Copernicus's heliocentric theory cannot be said to be "true," one can nevertheless assert that it is closer to the truth than the geocentric theory of Ptolemy: the latter leaves unexplained a large number of phenomena that the former, on the contrary, anticipated (the rotation of Foucault's pendulum, the movement of the winds, the flattening of the Earth at the poles, etc.).[15]

It is thus perfectly rational to consider that the Copernican theory, although false, is nevertheless closer to the truth, "more truthlike," than the Ptolemaic theory. Although Popper discredits the "determinative" claim of the idea of truth in the experimental sciences, he maintains its *regulative* function:[16] in a manner quite similar to Kant's gesture restoring the regulative role of the idea of liberty after having excluded it from the phenomenal realm, and thus saving the possibility of rational morals, Popper undermines skeptical speculations; we think and act within a horizon of rationality. Even if we never cease to behave like metaphysicians, by postulating regularities under the impulse of biological tendencies, the rigorous control of these more or less haphazardous conjectures through systematic tests restores immediately the prerogatives of reason over the natural impulse.

We come now to Popper's second correction of Hume in the "critical" direction. Popper's objection to Hume could be reformulated by saying that, since repetition is not "in itself" but "for us," it would be useless to seek its trace in some "given."[17] Hume saw quite well that each case is independent from the other, but he did not go far enough: each case is in itself entirely singular, and if we perceive a resemblance between several events, it is because we projected our anticipation on experience: repetition is a "determinative" function and not, as Hume took it, a "passive synthesis," to use Gilles Deleuze's phrase.[18] By requiring that receptiveness be thus submitted to criticism, Popper again closely follows Kant; as one knows, in Kant, the synthesis of reproduction (that is, the grasp of an observation as being "similar" to another) is governed by a transcendental principle: if phenomena were not subjected a priori to a rule — if cinnabar were sometimes red and sometimes black — empirical imagination could not form a coherent representation of empirical objects.[19] Likewise for the notion of cause: the universal affinity of phenomena cannot result simply from an empirical rule of association; *empirical* affinity depends on *transcendental affinity*, which is founded on the principle of the unity of apperception.[20] No repetition, no regularity are *given* in experience.

Popper is therefore very close to Kant when he objects to Hume that every observation already assumes the selective and anticipating occurrence of understanding. This means that there can be no pure "sense-datum," that no impression can be imposed by imagination. Hence the necessity of modifying the empiricist map of the human mind: the imaginative custom — an effect of the passive repetitive syntheses — is set aside along with outdated associationist ideas. Popper replaces it by a prediction-anticipation function that is pure spontaneity: there is no longer any passive synthesis; every synthesis involves a categorical and theoretical projection process; every activity, even perception, presupposes a choice and brings in an incipient theory. "It never occurred to David Hume that the understanding might itself, perhaps, through these concepts, be the author of the experience in which its objects are found; he was constrained to derive them from experience." The quote is from Kant,[21] but it could be attributed word for word to Popper, even if the Popperian system of theoretical hypotheses, unlike the Kantian system of pure a priori concepts, is as a matter of principle rectifiable as a function of the refutations of experience.[22]

The preceding discussion allows us to judge the import of the denomination "critical rationalism." Critical? But what plays the role of agent of lawfulness and objectivity, once the transcendental subject is discredited from any foundational role? What foundational, or at least normative, pretense can this critique still claim? As we expected, Popper follows here the road taken by the logical philosophers who sought to change Kantian philosophy of science in an objective direction. From the genealogical point of view, the transcendental solution he adopts constitutes, in the transcendental lineage represented by Bolzano and Frege, a new tactic within an essentially identical strategy. The latter is characterized by four theses whose combination and articulation we already observed.

(1) *There is only objective epistemology.* Following Bolzano and Frege, Popper contrasts two senses of knowledge and of thought: on the one hand, knowledge in the subjective sense, as a set of states of consciousness, of beliefs or dispositions of a subject; on the other, knowledge in the objective sense of content "in itself." Epistemology for Popper, as for the authors studied in this book, consists not in analyzing the subjective conditions producing grounded beliefs, but in studying the content and the relations of mutual dependence between scientific statements, without concern for the question of when and how these statements were acknowledged to be true.

In other words, the theory of knowledge is the "science of science":[23] the facts displayed by the development of empirical sciences form the ground for testing the assertions of this theory. The existence of an objective science, being a condition for the development of this "epistemology without a knowing subject," plays the role here of a principle, that is, of a fundamental assumption, as in the authors of the rationalist tradition brought together in this book. "The existence of theoretical sciences of nature is a fact. The purpose of the theory of knowledge is not to cast doubt on this fact, but to explain it," writes Popper in 1933, and he recalls the similar passage from the introduction of the *Critique of Pure Reason*.[24] However, as he himself remarks, objectivity cannot be explained by the *fact* of science: only a *transcendental legitimacy* can give substance to an objective epistemology. In subsequent texts, Popper acknowledges that the rules of method that the theory emphasizes are themselves fallible. This does not mean that they are subjective. If they are not properly speaking sufficient to found objective knowledge, they retain nevertheless the value of regulative ideals in the theory of the growth of knowledge.

(2) *The transcendental character of the objective foundation of epistemology.* Unlike the authors who were subjected to the trial of comparative topics, Popper in his 1933 book explicitly claims the transcendental character of the approach chosen. He uses the concept of "transcendental," as I did earlier, by cutting it off from any reference to a subject: "The analysis of scientific knowledge as an objective state of affairs" is transcendental.[25] Popper clearly draws his inspiration here from paragraph 3 of *The Foundations of Arithmetic* in which Frege, as we saw, corrects the Kantian account of validity: when one analyzes the nature of a scientific statement, one is not interested in "the conditions, psychological, physiological and physical, which have made it possible to form the content of the proposition in our consciousness," nor in "the way in which some one man has come, perhaps erroneously, to believe it true," but rather in "the ultimate ground on which rests the justification for holding it to be true."[26] This analysis of the legitimating ground is not psychological in nature, nor is it strictly logical

either, even if logic is considered "in its relationship with the methodology of the natural sciences"; it is "transcendental."[27] Its constitutive value is to be taken, as in Bolzano and Frege, in the literal sense of the term: the objective set of truths and of their relations have more than an explicative value; they have a causal role.

(3) *The ontotranscendental thesis: the autonomy of "world 3."* While acknowledging, like Frege, his debt to Kant—a debt he precisely accuses the different representatives of modern positivism of not having admitted, and rightly so, as my investigations prove—Popper discerns in Kant, as in contemporary positivists, impure adjunctions that in his opinion contaminate the transcendental enterprise. It is not of minor interest for us to observe that among these elements, improperly mingled with transcendental reflection, Popper points out precisely the alternatives to the version of transcendentalism we named "ontotranscendentalism": the "psychological" version of the transcendental, represented by Kant, and the "linguistic" version, which appears in Wittgenstein and, I believe, in Carnap.[28]

Even if the term "transcendental" no longer occurs in the subsequent texts, the later Popper seems, on this issue, to remain faithful to his analysis of 1933: the development of an "objective epistemology" must be founded on the "thesis of the three worlds." What we have here is more than a mere analogy with the philosophies of Bolzano and Frege; Popper calls on both of them, and designates the entities making up world 3 by the Bolzanian term "in themselves." There is a shade of a difference, however: the choice between the realist and the idealist interpretation is left open, both options being equally acceptable (insofar as irrefutable by nature), even if the first is judged preferable:

> The first is the physical world or the world of physical states; the second is the mental world or the world of mental states; and the third is the world of intelligibles, or of *ideas in the objective sense*; it is the world of possible objects of thought: the world of theories in themselves, and their logical relations; of arguments in themselves; and of problem situations in themselves."[29]

Combined with the theme of the tentative character of discovery, by "trial and error," that of objectivity gives rise spontaneously to an epistemology of the Bolzano-Fregean type; the world of subjective consciousness (world 2) can be elucidated by world 3, but not reciprocally. The system of truths in themselves can only be indefinitely approached; objective truth constitutes an aspect of reality distinct from the physical and the mental levels and interacting with them: like Bolzano and Frege, Popper acknowledges that objective truth plays to a certain extent a causal role in theoretical construction. Only a certain verisimilitude can be claimed for well-tested theories: we encounter again here exactly the Bolzanian contrast between science in itself and the treatise, a contrast occurring equally, although in different terms, in the Fregean conception of the system.

(4) Although obviously less clear-cut than in the authors of the same tradition examined earlier in this book (owing to the intermediate status of the propositions

of the logic of discovery, which are neither empirical nor formal), *the contrast between analytic and synthetic propositions* retains a role in the theory of method, by making it possible *to distinguish clearly the deductive constituents from the factual ones*, at least in the case of formalized theories. Logic is above all for Popper a theory of deduction, that is, of the transmission of truth and of the retransmission of falsehood. The statements of the natural sciences are refutable only because of the possibility of carrying falsehood back from the conclusions to the premises, according to *modus tollens*. Deductive rationality can thus, in a way, spread over the empirical domain owing to the perspective logic allows us to take on the attempts made in view of predicting events. It is this type of occurrence that raises logic (including Tarski's theory of truth and calculus of systems)[30] to the level of "organon of rational criticism."[31]

The imbroglio of Popper's theses is thus only apparent. The method that consists in identifying the underlying continuity of systems brings to light, as a three-dimensional map, the different layers of his thought: a continuous theme of an "ontotranscendental," in the lineage of Bolzano and Frege, accompanied by a series of objections against linguistic or phenomenalist extensions of the transcendental; the adjunctions to this theme can now be precisely evaluated, by determining if it is a "central thesis, governed by an arrangement of principles, or if it is a connected thesis, a stylistic variant, or a novel thesis. For example, I could suggest considering as one of Popper's "central" theses the idea that the critical approach is characteristic of rationalism, and as a connected thesis, the proposition that only a formulated theory can be objective. On the other hand, the rejection of the principle of induction as well as the assertion of the theoretical character of any observation would form novel adjunctions within the ontotranscendental *episteme*.

As we saw in the case of Popper, the history of "post-Kantian" philosophical logic does not end with Carnap. Only the necessary limitation imposed on my field of investigation in this book could lead one to believe that it does. If the controversy between Carnap and Quine largely dominated the philosophical scene during the 1950s, one cannot infer that the fate of apriorist foundationalism was decided once and for all. By recalling the structure of the arguments opposed, my intent was not to record the surpassing of rationalism by a finally triumphant empiricism, but to emphasize the historical nature involved in the distinction between analytic and synthetic propositions, which is often ill-perceived.

The time has come now to try to evaluate the method I have labeled "comparative topics." The descriptive and analytic interest must be judged by the evidence, but I would like to indicate finally some of the difficulties I have had to overcome — not those that concern the contents to be analyzed, but those that pertain to language, to the presentation of theses. On account of the continual, to-and-fro between the object system and the comparative language that an inquiry of this kind imposes and the danger of a lapse that this implies, confusions of level continually imperil the clarity of the analysis.

On the other hand, the requirement the method suggests of making functional distinctions (according to the role played by a given concept, distinction, or thesis in different systems) and discerning behind homonymies the different valencies of homophonic concepts tends to lead to a terminological proliferation that must be kept to a minimum. I strove for parsimony in this study whenever this did not compromise comprehension. While showing what sets them apart, I continued to speak of the "analyticity" of Bolzano and that of Quine. In the continuity of use of the same term there is a deep reason: although the concept of "analytic proposition" is in each case used in a different strategy, it is nevertheless the "same concept," *at least to the extent that such an expression remains meaningful when one passes from one system to another*. In this case the difficulty of presentation consists in allowing the diversity of meaning to appear clearly behind the terminological identity. It arises from the necessity of distinguishing the naming of concepts in the system from the designation of elements of the system in the metalanguage. Comparative topics is not an exception when it encounters the contradictory effect of these two requirements: the requirement of continuity that the preservation of the condition of philosophical communication determines (one need only recall the assimilating interpretation, the references shared among philosophers, often for quite different reasons, and the very notion of "philosophical problem," presented as the invariant of various sytems); and the requirement of innovation or critical appraisal, which tends to favor the coining of neologisms. They are present in every philosophical text and contribute, in respect to their proportion, to individualize a philosophical "style."

The second type of methodological constraint impelled me, on a few occasions, to resort in the comparative language to neologisms, or seemingly deviant and even paradoxical terminological uses, in order to describe what was not perceptible when one focused on a single system: the existence of persisting argumentative structures, for example, appeared to me to justify a description of the "transcendental" in terms of a generic strategy, which branches off into different but related tactics. The main pitfall historians must avoid here is that of not distinguishing sufficiently, in the topical presentation, the strategic level and its tactical instance and letting themselves believe, for example, that the transcendental is identified with its Kantian use, which would unfailingly obscure the very possibility of subsequent metamorphoses. It is to be hoped that the neologism of "ontotranscendental" contrasted with "subjective transcendental" and "syntactic transcendental" brings out both the continuity of an argumentative structure and the discontinuity of the particular tactics in which it is instantiated. One may object here that no tradition supports the expression "ontotranscendental," which also violates the well-established rules of the language of historians of philosophy. How can one dogmatically put forth an ontology and pursue a transcendental inquiry? The answer, as we know, is to recall that the "transcendental" concerned is no longer that of the Kantian system; while answering a similar question, the transcendental is now set in another discursive formation. It obeys other constraints, the Kantian subject having been discredited for a while.[32]

Other difficulties threaten the comparative enterprise: let us finally cite the reductionist danger, and also the closely related one of the normative approach. It was not the purpose of this book to diminish the originality of logical empiricism: Carnap would have (without knowing it) only reproduced Kant—just as Popper did Bolzano and Quine, Hume. What is shown by expressing the general strategic substructure is, on the contrary, the novelty of each author, not only the nature and the extent of the tradition in which they take part, but also the common base, the conceptual or doctrinal reformulations they bring about.

Another obstacle to the free use of the method would lie in making a value judgment on the evolution of the discursive formations; one could deplore, for example, that the ontotranscendental approach loses sight of what for a Kantian forms the essential feature of the criticist project, or even, as already considered, one could be taken aback by the anti-Kantian violence of the neologism "ontotranscendental." Comparative topics claims to be *descriptive*: it therefore analyzes Frege's system and Bolzano's as obeying an argumentative form derived from Kantianism, generated by varying the nature of the general a priori condition required to account for what makes an object of knowledge or scientific discourse possible. In doing so, we do not distort the texts; on the contrary, we let them express their conflict with Kant and recover what from their point of view can be preserved in the *Critique*.

We discover once again here the twofold orientation, assimilating and accommodating, of every philosophical reading. This is not surprising: every "interested" reading exerts some ascendancy on the text studied. In this book I have tried to free us from this ascendancy by revealing the motivations from which it arose.

Notes

Notes

Introduction

1. *Philosophisches Magazin* (Halle), I—III; see Kant's letters to Reinholdt, May 12 and 19, 1789, and *The Kant-Eberhard Controversy.*

2. My use of the concept of "topics" concurs with Gilles Granger's use of the corresponding adjective with which he describes the "strategical" dimension of rationality: "[At the strategical level] rationality is *topical* rather than logical, reflexive and metacritical in respect to the logically rational. . . . This determination . . . does not have its source and motor in logical derivations, and prerational *choices* determine its rules" ("Les deux niveaux de la rationalité," *Entretiens d'Oxford*, September 3–9, 1984, Institut International de Philosophie; see also *Pensée formelle et sciences de l'homme*, postface). Yvon Belaval also uses the word "topical" in a sense similar to mine and applies the correlative methodology, for instance, in his article "La doctrine de l'Essence chez Hegel et chez Leibniz," in *Etudes leibniziennes*, 264–378.

3. Wolff, *Philosophia prima sive ontologia*, 1729, §495; on this issue, see G. Lebrun, *La patience du concept: Essai sur le discours hégélien*, 390.

4. We can only refer here to the essential analyses presented by Lebrun, *Patience*, 393.

5. By "rationalist" I understand here any doctrine that postulates the intrinsic rationality of scientific knowledge — that is, one that presents it as universal and necessary, these two conditions guaranteeing the objective legitimacy of knowledge (whether the foundation of this legitimacy is ascribed to an a priori structure of reason or to a universal structure of syntax). "Rationalist" is contrasted here with "empiricist," by which I refer to any doctrine that subordinates the critical analysis of knowledge to the type of genesis that actually made it possible, and thus does not posit an absolute criterion of objectivity. For objectivity it substitutes objectification, which is relative to the natural conditions (historical, linguistic, psychological, etc.) in which cognition occurs, and thus typically brings in something going beyond the given that escapes any rational legitimation.

6. To avoid confusion between the Kantian concept of transcendental, as such bound up with the objective nature of the forms of intuition and with intellectual functions, and the metasystematic concept used here to designate *any* inquiry into a general a priori condition insofar as it makes possible an object of knowledge, it might be desirable to use two forms of writing, flanking topical concepts with indices, following Carnap: "*t* transcendental *t*." For technical reasons I will not carry out this suggestion, but I urge the reader to be sensitive to this essential difference in the level of analysis.

7. Michel Foucault, *L'archéologie du savoir* (Paris: Gallimard, 1969), 44ff.

8. On the doxographical genre in the history of philosophy, Richard Rorty, "The Historiography of Philosophy: Four Genres," in Rorty et al. (eds.), *Philosophy in History* (Cambridge: Cambridge University Press, 1984), 61–67.

9. Foucault, *Archéologie*, 23.

10. See Richard Rorty, *Philosophy and the Mirror of Nature* (Princeton: Princeton University Press, 1979), 315ff.

11. I wish my first tutors in philosophy, Gilles Granger and Gérard Lebrun, to know that I am not merely bowing to custom when I express my indebtedness to them; all that I owe them cannot be easily assessed. Gilles Granger inspired and supervised the thesis from which this book originated. He did not cease over the years to give me his encouragement, his observations, and sometimes his criticisms, in a spirit of tolerance and freedom for research that was very precious to me. Gérard Lebrun, too, marked strongly this inquiry; I am indebted to him for my reading of Hume and, more generally, for a style of approaching texts that later led me to bring out the "topical" dimension of philosophical concepts.

I am also grateful to those who helped me at different stages of this inquiry by their suggestions and comments, in particular Daniel Andler, Jacques Bouveresse, Alain Boyer, Alberto Coffa, Pascal Engel, Louis Guillermit, Françoise Hock, Pierre Jacob, Francis Jacq, Philip Kitcher, Françoise Longy, Philippe Minh Nguyen, Jean-Claude Pariente, Elisabeth Schwartz, Eric Vigne, and Jules Vuillemin. I thank Richard Nollan, curator of the Rudolf Carnap Archives at the University of Pittsburgh, for having facilitated access to the unpublished manuscripts of Carnap and for permission to quote from them, and likewise Willard Van Orman Quine for permitting me to publish extracts of his correspondence with Carnap. I am indebted to the Alexander Von Humboldt Foundation, whose research scholarship for the university year 1972–73 made it possible for me to start this study, and to the Centre National de la Recherche Scientifique, with whose help I was able to finish it. Finally, I wish to thank especially Réda Bensmaïa, who has given me since the beginning of this work all the moral support, intellectual stimulation, and material aid necessary for carrying out this long-term enterprise.

Chapter 2 of Section 1 draws on an article published in *Kantstudien*, 66 (1975), 1–34. Part of Chapter 3 of Section 2 appeared in *The Monist*, 64 (1981), 214–30. Chapter 2 of Section 4 takes up, with some changes, a speech delivered at the Journées Internationales sur le Cercle de Vienne (Paris, 1983) and was published in *Fundamenta Scientiae*, 5 (1984), 285–303. And I thank all the editors and publishers who have allowed me to reproduce other texts here.

Section 1. Kant and His "Precursors"

1. "As for *our own existence*, we perceive it so plainly and so certainly that it neither needs nor is capable of any proof. For nothing can be more evident to us than our own existence" (IV, IX, §3).

2. For instance, here is what Locke writes in his *Draft A*: "Thus in propositions where the predicate is part of the definition of the subject, I have a certain knowledge of the truth of the proposition, which is no more but that the Idea I have framed which I call *man* contains in it the Idea which I call *rational*, and so is but a predication of names suited to my Idea but not knowledge of things existing *in rerum natura*: it being evident that children for some time and some men all their life times are not so rational as a horse or dog; . . . so that of these we have no further knowledge of things than we have by our senses" (§13; cf. §15).

3. The notion of "identical proposition" is generally taken by Locke in the sense of the explicit tautology "a circle is a circle." However, because he takes as an example of the negation of identical "blue is not red," it seems legitimate to extend identical propositions to numerical equalities, which he sets elsewhere among "relations" (which we know from another source to designate in fact any kind of proposition). See IV, VII, §§4 and 6.

4. *Draft A* specifies that *demonstrations* pertaining to numbers are more evident than those pertaining to extension, precisely because each step of the proof rests on an immediate grasp of the equality or inequality in the sole case of arithmetic, whose objects are always distinct, which is not the case with every idea of extension. The *Essay* returns to this assertion: "Demonstrations in num-

bers, if they are not more evident and exact than in extension, yet they are more general in their use, and more determinate in their application'' (II, XVI, §4).

5. For one could, on the other hand, consider that each stage of the proof is ''analytic'' (in Kant's sense) to the extent that one must grasp, through an examination of the idea, what it ''contains.'' Such an interpretation could, moreover, be supported by the fact, already noted here, that Locke apparently conceives no relationship between a subject and a predicate other than the ''inherence'' of a contained in a containing. But one could argue, on the other hand, that in order to find the right intermediate step one must first form an idea of mode capable of serving as a rule — a *regula*, as in Cavalieri's method. Is this, then, a synthesis? We have seen here that the composition of simple modes occurs without any limitation, owing to the nominal character of this mode. Now, there is more to the idea of synthesis than simply that of arbitrary composition; synthesis must proceed according to a ''principle of unification,'' which is precisely what seems to be lacking in the case of complex modes.

6. This is not to go back on what was established earlier here and to restore somehow the mathematical object in existence. For we cannot infer from the fact that the modes lack an existence separate from a substance that they lack ''being''; they do not have the type of existence characteristic of substance, but can nevertheless be observed in the mode of abstraction. The ''relations of proposition between numbers and extensions'' are regulated *ex necessitate rei* (ibid., §12). In other words, they are properties ''inseparable'' from the idea we have of *the thing*.

7. We should ward off here an objection concerning the type of certainty of sentences of the kind ''blue is not red.'' One could indeed doubt that this proposition can be proved, for Locke specifies in IV, VII, 4, that it is a self-evident proposition. Yet elsewhere he takes this same example to be ''as capable of demonstration as [are] ideas of number and extension'' (IV, II, §13). It seems that the difference of doctrines merely concerns the fact that in matters of color all is a question of degree; according to the context, one may have to prove that this green is qualitatively different from this blue, and succeed by producing an intermediate color that will be recognized as distinct from both of them. It may also happen that one does not need a proof, knowing in a prereflexive manner that two colors are distinct.

8. On Kant's hesitations concerning the mediation of Humean philosophy, see Michel Malherbe, *Kant ou Hume*, 21.

9. See, for example, A. J. Ayer, *Language, Truth, and Logic*, 31; W. Stegmüller, *Das Wahrheitsproblem und die Idee der Semantik*, 291; H. Reichenbach, *The Rise of Scientific Philosophy*, 86; D. G. C. MacNabb, *David Hume, His Theory of Knowledge and Morality* (New York: Hutchinson Press, 1951), 46; A. Flew, *Hume's Philosophy of Belief* (London: Routledge & Kegan Paul, 1961), 54–55; J. Bennett, *Locke, Berkeley, Hume: Central Themes* (Oxford: Clarendon Press, 1971), 252.

10. On this issue, see G. Deleuze, *Empirisme et subjectivité* (Paris: PUF, 1953), 110ff., whom I follow here.

11. It might be objected here that, if it is true that the ''natural'' relationship is external to its terms and, moreover, unthinkable, insofar as a condition of the activity of comparison that *precedes* the formation of the complex idea, this reason no longer holds for the ''philosophical'' relationship, for instead of producing a comparison, it results from one. Why not admit that at the same time that it produces understanding as a system of philosophical relationships, imagination makes possible the development of ideas on the model of an inclusion of classes? If the capacity of establishing a logical hierarchy of ideas may therefore be legitimately denied of ''natural'' relationships, may one not expect, with respect to ''philosophical'' relationships and the abstracting process of understanding, the ''common parts'' of compared ideas to be brought to the fore? This argument, which appears to be followed at least implicitly by certain commentators, arises in all likelihood from an illegitimate extension of the principle of difference. According to this principle, ''whatever objects are different are distinguishable, and . . . whatever objects are distinguishable are separable by thought and imagination'' (*T*, I, I, 7, 18). If, for example, we compare this green and this blue with this scarlet, will we

not discover the common property of these two terms, by noting that this green and this blue are more similar to each than this green and this scarlet? However, the principle of difference does not state that distinguishability also applies in intension: as Hume remarks with respect to abstract ideas (*T*, I, I, 7, 21), even abstract ideas are ideas "in themselves" individual, which become general only in their "application." Abstraction therefore does not at all imply the decomposition of the individual concrete idea, or the separability of a property common to a class. The transition from intension to extension, from one singular idea to other singular ideas "according to a certain custom," precisely dispenses Hume from having to constitute an "ontology" of classes or properties: "That custom produces any other individual idea, for which we may have occasion."

12. See Deleuze, *Empirisme*, 110.

13. Hume indeed writes: "And tho' it be impossible to judge exactly of the degrees of any quality, such as colour, taste, heat, cold, when the difference betwixt them is very small; yet 'tis easy to decide, that any of them is superior or inferior to another, when their difference is considerable. . . . We might proceed, after the same manner, in fixing the *proportions* of *quantity* or *number*, and might at one view observe a superiority or inferiority betwixt any numbers, or figures; especially where the difference is very great and remarkable" (*T*, I, I, 7, 70).

14. I treated the problem of Humean geometry in "Comment appliquer les mathématiques en restant empiriste? Quelques problèmes relatifs à l'unité de la science," *Appliquer les mathématiques*? 10 and 14ff. On this issue, see also Malherbe, *Kant on Hume*, 52ff.

15. Jean Laporte, "Le scepticisme de Hume," 1933, 115; 1934, 117.

16. As Hume observes at the beginning of his reflections on the divisibility of space and time: "Wherever ideas are adequate representations of objects, the relations, contradictions, and agreements of the ideas are all applicable to the objects; the plain consequence is, that whatever *appears* impossible and contradictory upon the comparison of these ideas, must be *really* impossible and contradictory, without only farther excuse or evasion" (*T*, I, II, 29). This text reveals that it is a natural relationship of "contrariety" between ideas that accounts for objective contradiction and not the opposite, which amounts to saying that contradiction is perceived in an act of comparison—that is, in a judgment.

17. Pappus defines it in this way: "Now analysis is the way from what is sought—as if it were admitted—through its concomitants in order to something admitted in synthesis. . . . And we call such a method analysis, as being a solution backwards" (in J. Hintikka and U. Remes, *The Method of Analysis, Its Geometrical Origin, and Its General Significance*, 8). Also F. Hultsch (ed.), *Pappi Alexandrini Collectionis Quae Supersunt*, II, 634ff.

18. Georg Friedrich Meier, ed. (Halle, 1752). The announcement of the program of Kant's courses for the winter semester 1765–66 mentions it; partially reproduced at the beginning of L. Guillermit's French translation of the *Logic* (7–8).

19. "In identicis quidem connexio illa atque comprehensio praedicati in subjecto est expressa, in reliquis omnibus implicita ac per analysin notionum ostendenda, in qua demonstratio a priori sita est" (Leibniz, *Opuscules*, ed. Couturat, 519).

20. G. W. Leibniz, *Philosophische Schriften*, ed. Gerhardt, VII, 168–69.

21. Ibid., IV, 296.

22. Ibid., VII, 295: *De Synthesi et Analysi Universali*.

23. Ibid., VII, 219.

24. Leibniz, *Opuscules*, 16–17.

25. This first Kantian criticism of the characteristic comes from 1764 to 1770. The *Inaugural Dissertation* no longer addresses the status of *what is to be represented*, but more profoundly *what it is possible to say with concepts*. "Intellectual characters" are no longer reserved for the mathematical realm. On the contrary: they are dismissed on account of their inability to characterize what appears only in pure intuition. What now guides Kant's criticism is no longer the "arbitrary-real" contrast, but the "discursive-intuitive" contrast: he speaks in terms of *faculties*, and no longer of objects

to know. Intuition is the ability to see immediately something singular—immediately, that is, concretely. The object is then grasped in the singularity of a sense-datum: *the* left hand, *the* right hand. The relationship of nonsuperposability between the two hands I can *see*, but not *deduce*. Discourse can, on the contrary, only infer that they can be substituted for one another. It is therefore because the discursive cannot found *everything* that one must *limit* it. It is because intuition teaches us *something else* that one must grant it a specific mode of demonstration: not by universal concepts, but by direct presentation of singular objects (§15).

26. On the dogmatism of Descartes and Leibniz, see Y. Belaval, *Leibniz critique de Descartes*, 62ff.

27. Seneca, *Letter to Lucilius*, reference given by F. Courtès in his notes to the French translation of the *False Subtlety*, 108.

28. Leibniz, *Philosophische Schriften*, V, 6.

29. Leibniz, *Opuscules, Elementa Characteristica Universalis*, 42.

30. J. Cavaillès, *Sur la logique et la théorie de la science* (Paris: PUF, 1960), 3ff.

31. Akad, XXIV: *Logik Politz*, 533; *Logik Dohna Wundlaken*, 726; *Wiener Logik*, 836.

32. "Insofar as a foundation of knowledge, the partial concept can be represented a priori before any comparison [*Vergleichung*] owing to the powers of the faculty of productive imagination" (*R*, Akad, XVI, 2884).

33. *Auszug* §15: "Unterscheidungsstücke der Erkenntnis."

34. Leibniz, *Opuscules, Consilium de Encyclopaedia Nova*, 37.

35. "It is to compare with a thing something taken as a character" (§1).

36. One *Reflexion* states similarly: "In every *conceptus communis* comparisons must be set up, failing which there would be no *conceptus communis*; but it must not be formed from comparative representations" (*R*, 2875).

37. It may be objected here that the first edition of the *Critique of Pure Reason* defines knowledge as a "whole in which representations stand compared and connected" (97, IV, 76). But one must not understand here any preeminence of the logical in the formation of the knowledge: by means of this definition there is introduced the threefold synthesis necessary for any knowledge. Comparison is second with respect to connection. During the critical period, Kant no longer refers judgment to comparison, but to *connection* (*Verbindung*), which comprises at the same time the internal aspect of the characterization of an object and the external aspect of the confrontation of concepts.

38. "All my rational concepts can be completely distinct, but the empirical concepts are excluded from this property and remain always incompletely distinct" (*LB*, Akad, XXIV, 134).

39. This is indeed how Hegel understands it: "Although analytic cognition proceeds upon relations which are not a material given externally, but thought-determinations, it still remains analytic, since for it these relations too are *given* relations" (*Science of Logic*, III, III, 2, ed. Lasson, p. 450). Although analytic, the purely given is not to be confused with a principle of purely formal thought. Already in the *Unique Foundation*, Kant emphasizes the specificity of these "givens and materials of the thinkable," which make up the "first *real* foundation of possibility." From this analytic a *real* knowledge can be derived. In the next chapter I will return to the problem that arises in attributing this property to the analytic.

40. "The given things of nature, when they are expressed under a collective character, fall by way of this character under a certain concept, which is their nominal definition. Therefore names must be markings [*Anzeichnungen*], serve as classes, exhibit a unity in fragmentation [*Stücken*] but not the properties and the intrinsic, consequently not the foundations of the explanation, but the foundations of the division" (*R*, 3004). Likewise in his *Inquiry Concerning Evidence* Kant contrasts with the simple word the algebraic sign and the geometric figure, which have both a designative and an explicative value (First Remark, §2).

41. See also *Reflexionen*, 2921 and 2927.

42. See *Reflexionen*, 2992–93. This contrast between simple recognition and the integral production of a concept recalls the Spinozist distinction between knowledge by signs and adequate knowledge. The sign, a purely *indicative* image, is incapable of expressing the nature of things: as the trace of a thing or an idea, it merely makes possible simple representative recognitions (*Ethic*, II, 18, Sc.; II, 16, Cor. II; IV, 1, Sc.). Hegel will make an anti-Kantian use of this same contrast. The typical case of indicative knowledge for him is mathematics, which singles out its objects, but fails to produce them (*"Begriffloses Kalkulieren,"* *Science of Logic*, introduction, ed. Lasson, 34). Philosophy, on the contrary, groups thing in its complete development. Mathematics should therefore not be set as Kant does on the side of concrete and genetic knowledge, whereas philosophy should be raised to the level of an abstract discipline. If mathematics can lay claim to the status of a science, it is because the intuition from which it starts is "raised to its abstraction," because its object is a "nonsensible sensible" (*ein unsinnlich sinnliches*) (ibid., III, III, 2, 472). Moreover, in contradistinction to philosophy, mathematics is incapable of overcoming the contrast of being and knowledge. It succeeds in proving something only by calling on procedures contingent in content, pure means of knowledge foreign to the internal nature of the thing (*Phenomenology of Mind*, preface, iii). Philosophy is therefore alone capable of producing completely the concept, and of putting an end to the dualism of being and knowing.

43. It therefore seems contradictory to speak, as does Lewis White Beck, of a "nominal synthetic" definition ("Kant's Theory of Definition," *Philosophical Review*, 65 [1956], 179ff.; reprinted in *Studies in the Philosophy of Kant* Bobbs Merrill Co, Indianapolis, 1965). Beck asserts that this expression refers to the "declarations" by which a concept is created intentionally by means of definition. Actually, what Beck is describing here is nothing more than what Kant calls a "real declaration," which is precisely distinguished by Kant from nominal definition: "Either I ascribe to a word its concept (name determination) following usage or I ascribe to an arbitrary concept a word and I thus create a usage; in the first case, we have nominal declaration, in the second real declaration" (*R*, 2931). See also *Reflexion*, 2924.

44. L. W. Beck, "Kant's Theory of Definition," 184.

45. Leibniz, *Philosophische Schriften*, ed. Gerhardt, IV, 422–26.

46. Leibniz, *New Essays Concerning Human Understanding*, II, 31, §1.

47. Leibniz, *Philosophische Schriften*, ed. Gerhardt, VII, 293.

48. Ibid., 294; *New Essays*, II, 31, §1.

49. Leibniz, *Discours de métaphysique* , in *Oeuvres* (Paris: Montaigne, 1972), §24; *New Essays*, II, 31, §3.

50. On nominal definition of given empirical concepts, see *Reflexionen*, 2918, 2934–36, 2945; on given a priori concepts, see 2914, 2918, 2926, 2968, 2995.

51. See also *R*, 3006.

52. Texts in which Kant considers the definitions of rational concepts *real* and *capable of completeness*: *Reflexionen*, 2913–94, 3002. Texts in which he holds them to be incomplete: *Logik*, 142; *KRV*, A 241–42, note; A 242, IV, 159.

53. "The definitions of concepts are relative to concepts that are either a priori or a posteriori. Concerning the first, a complete explication can be given. Concerning the second, the logical definition is only nominal" (*R*, 2994). What allows Kant here to place on a par the intellectual or rational a priori principle and the a priori intuition? It is because synthesis, on the one hand, and analysis, on the other, make it possible to delimit an a priori object whose essence is not only logical, but also real: "Real definitions are not always genetic; they do not follow from the way the object appears in its consequences, but from the way it is in its origins" (*R*, 3002).

54. *KRV*, B 757, 478; *Logik*, §§102, 141, 151.

55. Paragraph 103 of the *Logik*, which relies on paragraphs 101–2, offers an example of this rupture in classification.

56. This *Reflexion* is in all likelihood subsequent to Lambert's letter to Kant of November 1765, in which one can read: "It is not the definitions that come first, but what one must necessarily know beforehand in order to formulate the definition" (*Lamberts Philosophische Schriften*, IX, 338). The fact that the empiricists miss the "purely given" does not exclude Kant's being influenced by the demarcation they draw between realms of knowledge according to whether or not an exhaustive definition is possible in them.

57. *Reflexionen*, 3127–62; for "occult qualities," see *Metaphysical Foundations of Natural Science*, chapter 2, "General Corollary of Dynamics," 4.

58. *Rezension von Eberhards Magazin*, XX, 408.

59. Lambert levels the same objection at Wolff: "Wolff could link conclusions and infer consequences without end; thereby he merely transferred any difficulties to the definitions. He showed how one must advance, but what he ignored is how one must start. . . . Wolff seems also not to have noticed sufficiently with what care Euclid sets up the order of his exposition in order to prove the *possibility* of figures and to determine their *limits*" (*Lamberts Schriften*, IX, 337–38).

Section 2. Bolzano's Renovation of Analyticity

1. The explanation of the proposition in itself as "content which is abstracted from a mental act," given by Ursula Neemann in her article "Analytic and Synthetic Propositions in Kant and Bolzano," is therefore inadequate. As Bolzano states against Gerlach: "We would not have propositions *in thought* if there were no propositions *in themselves*" (*W*, §21, I, 86).

2. G. Frege, "Logik," in *Nachgelassene Schriften*, I, 36.

3. H. Scholz, *Mathesis universalis*, 262.

4. Likewise there are no two identical representations in themselves (*W*, §91, I, 428).

5. Günter Buhl ("Ableitbarkeit," 1961) analyzes in a similar way "the composition of propositions in themselves into clearly defined parts" (see 15).

6. As Bar-Hillel shows (in "Bolzano's Definition of Analytic Propositions," *Aspects of Languages*, 11) the criterion of equivalence between propositions is for Bolzano an extensional homomorphy, without reaching isomorphy, for constraint is attached to the smallest subdesignators. But the criterion of propositional identity (or unicity) is an intensional isomorphism, that is, an identical composition of *L*-equivalent parts.

7. On this issue, see P. Boehner, *Medieval Logic*, 24; J. M. Bochenski, *Formale Logik*, 179ff.

8. See, e.g., Buhl, "Ableitbarkeit," 14ff.

9. Husserl quotes this text in his *Logical Investigations*, II, 2, §4. After commenting on Bolzano's conception, Husserl finally retains a rigorously dualist conception of constituents, according to the "dependent" or "independent" character of the meanings they express.

10. Bochenski, *Formale Logik*, 157.

11. Albert of Saxony, *Perutilis Logica*, tract. 4, c. 1, fol. 24 ra-b, Aurelianus Sanutus, ed., Venice 1522; quoted in Boehner, *Medieval Logic*, 25.

12. Cf. the phenomenological approach to this question in *Logical Investigations*, II, 2, 107ff.

13. The "in itself" is both representation in itself and represented, indissociably "asserting sense" and "asserted sense." On this ambiguity, see Husserl's note, *Logical Investigations*, 97.

14. See also §147, II, 82, where Bolzano takes the (German) terms *Form* and *Art* to be interchangeable.

15. Bolzano continues in these terms: "This whole definition probably stems only from the fact that in the examples which are used in logic, e.g. in the syllogism: all *A*s are *B*, all *B*s are *C*; therefore all *A*s are *C*—the signs *A*, *B*, and *C* may mean, as we say, 'anything' [*was immer bedeuten*]. But this statement is not altogether precise. The signs *A*, *B*, and *C* can here mean very different things, but not quite anything we may choose. They must signify representations such that *B* is a representation which can be predicated of all *A* and *C* one which can be predicated of all *B*s. Thus it can be seen that

the objects *A, B,* and *C* are not left indeterminate as to all their characteristics, but only as to some of them'' (*W*, §7, I, 28; George trans., 9).

16. On this issue, see E. Gilson, *L'être et l'essence*, 174–76.

17. *Posterior Analytics*, I, 4, 73a. On the Aristotelian conception of analyticity, see Granger, *La théorie aristotélicienne de la science*, 224–29.

18. Aristotle, *Posterior Analytics*, I, 4, 736 (Granger's *Théorie*, 227).

19. Aside from the advocates of relativism whom Bolzano names, one should mention the original conception of Schleiermacher. According to him each concept is provided with a capacity of *development* such that the content it has at a given time cannot be considered to be closed. If the concept originally only gives rise to synthetic judgments, analytic judgments progressively appear as a sign of its internal enhencement. See ''Dialektik,'' *Sämmtliche Werke*, IV, 2, 88–89.

20. If the same term expresses concepts whose definitions are distinct (although eventually equivalent), there is but homonymy between the representations expressed, which are no more identical with one another than Euclid of Megara and Euclid Ptolemy Soter.

21. The term *gegenständlich* has no equivalent in French or English. In order to remain as close as possible to the root *Gegenstand* (''object''), I will translate it by ''objective.'' Yet this translation threatens to confuse the two concepts *gegenständlich* and *objektiv*, the latter being the antonym of *subjektiv*, ''subjective.'' But, because both terms belong to different spheres, the danger is not great. Actually, unless one coins a neologism such as ''objectity'' — which serves to translate the Husserlian concept of *Gegenständlichkeit* — or one resorts to other concepts (e.g., ''realizability'' or ''denotation''), the suggested translation remains the most ''natural'' in English.

22. *Logique de Port-Royal*, 47–48.

23. *Philosphische Schriften*, ed. Gerhardt, IV, 147. On this issue, see R. Kauppi, ''Ueber die leibnizische Logik,'' 36.

24. Which does not mean that the fulfillment of the clause of objectivity *depends* on such an inquiry: this is an objective fact that anticipates any knowledge acquired by a subject.

25. See, e.g., Buhl, ''Ableitbarkeit,'' 18ff.

26. J. Lukasiewicz, *Die logischen Grundlagen der Wahrscheinlichkeitsrechnung*, 64.

27. Granger, *Théorie*, 116.

28. H. R. Smart, ''Bolzano's Logic''; Y. Bar-Hillel, ''Bolzano's Definition,'' 7, note 4.

29. W. V. O. Quine, ''Carnap and Logical Truth,'' in *Ways of Paradox*, 110.

30. Bar-Hillel, ''Bolzano's Definition,'' 6.

31. Ibid., 12.

32. Ibid., 13.

33. First of all there is an occurrence of the term ''logically analytic'' in remark 1 of §148; moreover, the distinction drawn in subsection 3 between a ''logical'' or ''narrow'' sense and a ''material'' or ''large'' sense of analyticity is repeated for derivability: §223, II, 392; see J. Berg, *Bolzano's Logic*, 99ff.

34. Neemann, ''Analytic and Synthetic Propositions,'' 8.

35. *Posterior Analytics*, I, 5, 18.

36. *Metaphysics*, Z 4 1029b15. On this issue, see Granger, *Théorie*, esp. 8.8.

37. Leibniz, *New Essays Concerning Human Understanding*, IV, VIII, §4.

38. Unlike Bolzano, Bar-Hillel considers the proposition quoted, ''Even a wise man is fallible,'' to be analytic, and suspects Bolzano of having omitted the word ''man'' from his translation in order to have a more favorable example for his thesis. As this false variant formulation shows — ''Even a god is fallible'' — the proposition remains synthetic in both cases.

39. Bolzano resorts to this type of argument in order to discredit the supposed ''proofs'' of his predecessors in the famous study of 1817 where he proves the theorem: ''There must always be, between any two values of an unknown magnitude that give two results of opposite sign, at least one

real root of equation'' (*Reinanalytischer Beweis des Lehrsatzes, dass zwischen je zwei Werten . . .* , 1817).

40. This twofold regulation is what explains Bolzano's apparent ambivalence on this issue: sometimes the barrenness of analytic propositions is emphasized (§12, I, 52), sometimes analytic truths are presented in their pedagogic potentialities and a number of interesting cases are investigated (§447, IV, 116).

41. This second factor should be associated here with the first, on account of a specific obstacle, which pertains both to the discipline and to the subject. Bolzano indeed observes that certain particular truths tend to encounter a ''resistance'' on the part of readers if they suspect that what is being taught brings their conduct into question or challenges their received ideas. Certain disciplines will of course be more liable to prompt such ''resistance''; ethics, for example (which for Bolzano is an objective science), will resort more than another to analytic propositions for their exemplary value.

42. As in the previous cases, this factor is associated with the two others. The most favorable cases for analytic propositions are those in which all three factors reinforce their effects. The discipline that, alongside mathematical analysis, would deserve the title of analytic science is *casuistry* (the science of the interpretation of individual cases in ethics; see §444, IV, 113). It indeed brings together the three favorable conditions. First of all it is a science of concrete facts. As such, it must combine in its problems and deductions a very large number of constituents that, on account of their diversity and their eventual incompatibility, make up the substance of the ''case of conscience.'' Furthermore, it is of course directed at the largest class of readers. Finally, it has an essentially practical aim and therefore brings in an ectypical reasoning.

43. In their first two uses, propositions are most often intuitive, as is indicated by the presence in the statement of a deictic word or a proper name, as in these two examples: ''This triangle is a figure,'' and ''Caius, who is morally bad, does not deserve any respect.'' Explicative propositions can be purely conceptual, as is the case of the definition of the triangle, or intuitive if in the explanation appear representations of experience, such as ''Amaranth is reddish purple.'' The departure from the Kantian criterion, which associated the two distinctions, analytic-synthetic and conceptual-intuitive, is thus confirmed.

Section 3. Frege and the Hypothesis of Analyticity

1. Kant, *Kritik der reinen Vernunft*, Akad, III, 22 and 538–39. On the notion of system in Frege, see *Logik in der Mathematik, in Nachgelassene Schriften*, I, 221; *Formale Theorien der Arithmetik*, in *Kleine Schriften*, ed. I. Angelleli, 104; *Begriffsschrift*, preface and §13; *Grundlagen der Arithmetik* §1, 1; *Grundgesetze der Arithmetik*, I, ivff.

2. *Logik in der Mathematik, N*, I, 221; *G*, vi.

3. *KS*, 104. Claude Imbert sees in this metaphor the sign of the inability of the *Grundlagen*, ''a nontechnical work, written before ideography reached completion in its new version,'' to describe otherwise the fruitfulness of formula (cf. introduction to the French translation of the *Foundations, Les fondements de l'arithmétique* [Paris: Seuil, 1969], 85). The occurrence of the same metaphor in a text of 1914, *Logik in der Mathematik* (*N*, I, 221), indicates that the metaphor has the function of a presystematic elucidation, in accordance with the Fregean doctrine of *Winken*.

4. On this issue see J. C. Pariente, ''Le système des propositions catégoriques à Port-Royal,'' in *Mérites et limites des méthodes logiques en philosophie* (Paris: Vrin, 1986), 227–49.

5. Concerning this problem Frege writes: ''The *particular* affirmative proposition on the one hand indeed says less than does the *universal* affirmative, but on the other hand (what is easily overlooked) also says more, since it asserts the realization of concepts, whereas subordination occurs also in the case of empty concepts—with the latter, even occurs invariably. Many logicians seem to assume without ado that concepts are realized, and to overlook entirely the very important case of empty concepts, perhaps because they quite wrongly do not recognize empty concepts as justified.

This is why I use the expressions 'subordination,' 'universal affirmative,' 'particular affirmative,' in a sense somewhat different from theirs, and arrive at statements that they will be impelled to hold (wrongly) to be false'' (*G*, I, 24–25, note 2). Let us note that Bernard Bolzano also made similar remarks; but the use of these properties in a formula language obviously gives these remarks a different import in each case.

6. The question of Frege's *realism* gave rise to an important controversy in the 1970s, following the publication of Michael Dummett's *Frege, Philosophy of Language*, in which the author presents what makes Frege a realist (see also Dummett's ''Frege as a Realist''). This interpretation was questioned by Hans D. Sluga both in articles: ''Frege as a Rationalist,'' in *Studien zu Frege*, ''Frege and the Rise of Analytic Philosophy,'' and in his book *Gottlob Frege*. See also G. Currie, ''Frege's Realism''; M. Dummett, *The Interpretation of Frege's Philosophy*, Chapter 20 (''Realism''), and his review of H. Sluga's book, in the *London Review of Books*, September 18–October 1, 1980.

7. See, e.g., Max Black, ''Frege on Functions''; W. Marshall, ''Frege's Theory of Functions and Objects'' (criticized in Michael Dummett, ''Frege on Functions: A Reply''), and ''Sense and Reference: A Reply.''

8. W. Wundt, *Logik*, I, 154–55.

9. The same idea is expressed in *Einleitung in die Logik, N*, I, 76ff.

10. Letter to Husserl of May 24, 1891.

11. Marshall, ''Frege's Theory of Functions and Objects,'' in Klemke, *Essays on Frege*, 250, n. 2.

12. Reinhart Grossmann, *Reflections on Frege's Philosophy*, 116.

13. The necessity of a twofold approach to definition receives a detailed account in *Logik in der Mathematik, N*, I, 225ff. and *Ueber die Grundlagen der Geometrie, KS*, 288–90.

14. On this issue see Christian Thiel's remarkable article ''Zur Inkonsistenz der Fregeschen Mengenlehre,'' in *Frege und die moderne Grundlagenforschung*, ed. Thiel, 134–59.

15. G. Peano, *Revue de mathématique*, VI, quoted by Frege, *G*, II, §58, n. 1.

16. Peano's definition of addition goes against these two rules: the closure of the numerical field is not demonstrated a priori, nor is it ''obvious by the form of the conditions'' stated by the successive definitions of the plus sign (+). Nothing therefore guarantees the closure of the definition on the numerical domain taken in its entirety. Furthermore, a given number can belong to two different senses of the additive operation, for example, whether they are expressed by the integer or the equivalent rational number.

17. One understands then what makes these definitions ineffectual: they render the theorems uncertain and fluctuating, in the image of meanings also taken ''*im Flusse*.'' How are we to answer, for example, the following question: ''How many square roots of 9 are there?'' If the definition of the concept of square root has the positive integers for domain, we will prove that there is only one. But this theorem will become void when the definition is reformulated so as to include negative integers. Who can tell when we have reached the final theorem? ''Who can tell but that we may see ourselves driven to recognize four square roots of 9?'' (*G*, II, §61; see also §66, 79).

18. See also *G*, II, §66, 79.

19. J. D. Gergonne, ''Essai sur la théorie des définitions'' in *Annales de mathématiques pures et appliquées*, 9 (1818), 1–35.

20. This for Hilbert is not a formal imperfection but an advantage (heuristic fruitfulness, independence proofs, etc.): letter to Frege of December 29, 1899, *N*, II, 67.

21. ''To the objection that the equals sign to be defined occurs already as known I reply with Peano that ' = . . . Df' counts for me as a symbol that does not express the same thing as ' = '. Definitions are not really part of the theory, but typographical stipulations. ' = . . . Df' is not one of the primitive ideas of mathematics, but merely an expression of my will'' (*N*, II, 251; see also *N*, II, 248, and *Principia Mathematica* 13.01, I, 168). The same problem appears in the Frege-Peano correspondence, *N*, II, 184 and 191.

22. M. Schirn, *Studien zu Frege*: "Identität und Identitätaussage bei Frege," 181–215; ibid., B. Kienzle, "Notiz zu Freges Theorien der Identität," 217–19; R. E. Nusenoff, "Frege on Identity Sentences."

23. A. N. Whitehead and B. Russell, *Principia Mathematica*, I, 57–58.

24. *G*, I, preface, xvii; *GA*, §74, 87; *KS*, 247.

25. In L. Couturat, *La logique de Leibniz*, 228.

26. *KRV*, Akad, III, 111.

27. On this issue see my article "Sens frégéen et compréhension de la langue," in *Meaning and Understanding*, 304–23.

28. *Philosophische Schriften*, VII, 31.

29. E. Husserl, *Philosophie der Arithmetik, psychologische und logische Untersuchungen* 97–98.

30. In "Frege on Sense Identity," Jean Van Heijenoort tries to reconcile the two criteria by suggesting interpreting the term "immediate consequence" (in the expression "the recognition of the content of *A* has as an *immediate consequence* the recognition of the content of *B*") as the relation from premises to conclusion in a system of natural deduction, Frege's "purely logical laws" making up the rules in question. As the author points out, synonymy under this hypothesis ceases to be a transitive relation.

31. *KS*, 226. See also on this issue C. Thiel, "Zur Inkonsistenz der Fregeschen Mengenlehre," 131–39.

32. For example, *KRV*, 143.

33. By "epistemology," we do not mean here the critical study of science, but that part of the theory of knowledge that characterizes cognitive contents by relating them to types of psychological processes.

34. The main representatives of this interpretative trend are Philip Kitcher, "Frege's Epistemology"; M. D. Resnik, "The Frege-Hilbert Controversy," and *Frege and the Philosophy of Mathematics*, Hans Sluga adopts a similar but more circumstantial position in his *Gottlob Frege*.

35. "Sinn und Bedeutung," *KS*, 149.

36. " . . . Unbeholfenheit des Schriftsteller und der Sprache mögen daran Schuld sein" (*Logik, N*, I, 139).

37. Preface to *Gelassene Schriften*, xxii.

38. *KRV*, Einleitung, III, 29.

39. Ibid., 34–35.

40. Cf. *LM*: "Wenn man nun die Logik zur Philosophie rechnet . . . " (*N*, I, 219).

41. Ibid., in particular, 323.

42. The definability of mathematical notions in purely logical terms and the deducibility of mathematical truths from logical truths are in Frege's philosophy two equivalent formulations in accordance with the second principle of the *Grundlagen*. Alan Musgrave distinguishes them in his study on Russell's logicism ("Logicism Revisited," 101).

43. On Russell's antinomy, see R. Carnap, *Logical Syntax of Language*, 138; W. O. Quine, "On Frege's Way Out," *Mind*, 64 (1955), 145–59, and Klemke, *Essays on Frege*, 485–501; Boleslaw Sobocinski, "L'analyse de l'antinomie russellienne par Lesniewski," *Methodos*, (1949), and Thiel, "Zur Inkonsistenz der Fregeschen Megenlehre."

44. In "What Is Cantor's Continuum Problem?", Gödel writes: "But, despite their remoteness from sense experience, we do have something like a perception also of the objects of set theory, as is seen from the fact that the axioms force themselves upon us as being true" (*American Mathematical Monthly*, 54 [1947], 515–25; reprinted in P. Benacerraf and H. Putnam (eds.), *Philosophy of Mathematics: Selected Readings*).

45. Hao Wang judges in this way what he takes to be the real contribution of Frege's enterprise: "Dedekind and Frege speak of reducing mathematics to logic, and a great philosophical significance

has been attributed to this achievement. While their definition of number in terms of set is mathematically interesting in that it relates two different mathematical disciplines, it is not so powerful as to provide a foundation for mathematics'' (*A Survey of Mathematical Logic* [Amsterdam: North-Holland, 1963], 37). On this issue, cf. J. Bouveresse, *La parole malheureuse* (Paris: Minuit) 46ff.

46. A. Tarski, *Undecidable Theories* (Amsterdam: North-Holland, 1953).

47. Concerning Gödel's theorems of incompleteness, see Section 4. Church's theorem states that for a formal system, such as is obtained by adding to the axiom of Peano the logic of the *Principia*, there is no effective method of decision that allows us to know which propositions of this system are provable. See ''A Note on the Entscheidungsproblem,'' *Journal of Symbolic Logic*, 1 (1936), 40–41.

Section 4. The Foundational Strategies of Rudolf Carnap

1. Cf. R. Carnap, ''Die logizistische Grundlegung der Mathematik.''

2. B. Russell, ''The Relation of Sense-Data to Physics,'' in *Mysticism and Logic* (London: Allen & Unwin, 1917), 146.

3. If the concept *a* is reducible to the concepts *b* and *c*, and if the concept *b* in turn is reducible to the concepts *x* and *y*, then *a* is reducible to the concepts *x, y* and *c*, but it is obviously false that the concepts *x, y,* and *c* are reciprocally reducible to *a*.

4. Leibniz, *Philosophische Schiften*, ed. Gerhardt, VII, 23.

5. This duality amounts to asserting that the determination of sense is of the same power as the possible determination of facts. The space of states of affairs, according to Wittgenstein, is what allows us to determine the things. Reciprocally, the space of things, through the relations between elements that occur there, indicates what the possible configurations of objects are. See Wittgenstein, *Tractatus Logico-Philosophicus* (London: Routledge & Kegan Paul, 1922), 2.011 and 2.0141. On this whole issue, cf. Gilles Granger, ''Sur le problème de l'espace logique dans le *Tractatus*.''

6. The form of this definition makes it impervious to the procedure of reduction as it is presented in the *Aufbau*. Carnap will later attempt to remedy this, in ''Testability and Meaning,'' I–IV, *Philosophy of Science*, 1936–37.

7. *A*, 13, 16.

8. Simultaneously, the extensions that are constructed have no *objectivity* independently of the statements in which they occur. Carnap thus departs from the essentialism of early logicism. The number 5, for example, cannot be recognized as an independent entity, even in the definition given by Frege and Russell: ''One cannot say what the class of my five fingers is. It is only a quasi object (i.e., an autonomous complex). A sign introduced for the purpose of designating it would have no meaning in itself, but would merely serve to make statements about the fingers of my right hand, without having to enumerate these objects one by one. . . . Likewise, one cannot say what the class of all classes of five objects itself is'' (*A*, §40, 54).

9. N. Goodman, *The Structure of Appearance* (Cambridge, Mass.: Harvard University Press, 1951), 3.

10. Ibid., 7.

11. See W. V. Quine, *Word and Object*, e.g., §5, 17.

12. J. Vuillemin, *La logique et le monde sensible*, Goodman, *Structure of Appearance*, 102, and Carnap's letter to Goodman of July 2, 1939, Carnap Archives, University of Pittsburgh Libraries, 102–44–01; there Carnap writes: ''Today I should prefer a construction of the language of science on a physical basis, beginning with physical predicates designating observable properties of things and therefore being intersubjective, to the '*eigenpsychische*' basis taken in the *Aufbau*. At that time I recognized already the possibility of a physical basis (see section about physical basis), and today I admit of course the possibility of an '*eigenpsychische*' basis (see ''Testability and Meaning,'' section on perception terms as basis), since my general attitude is now more tolerant, liberal, or relativistic, as you would probably say (the germ to this attitude of tolerance may be found, I think, in the attitude

of neutrality toward different points of view or ways of expression, e.g., the realistic and the idealistic one, in the '*Aufbau*'). Thus, in the first place, it is a difference in emphasis or practical preference rather than in theoretical belief; but, to a smaller degree, there is also a theoretical difference. I have now serious doubts concerning the view that the construction on the '*eigenpsychische*' basis pictures the actual development of knowledge. I do not know whether I should dare to assert the negation of that assertion. I should rather think that the question is not formulated precisely enough to try to give an answer to it. (In some sense, I believe we may speak of something like 'an immediate knowledge of things'; Reichenbach, in his new book, contributes something to this discussion; but, as mentioned above, the whole problem is very much in need of further clarification.)''

13. W. Köhler, ''Gestaltprobleme und Anfänge einer Gestalttheorie.''

14. W. Wertheimer, *Ueber Gestalttheorie* (Berlin, 1925); translated in *Social Research*, 11 (1944), 81–99.

15. Or else we will say, what amounts to the same thing, that the notion of *composition* has two different senses. This option is taken by Ziehen in this text of 1920: ''The term 'composed' has a double sense. It can mean 'formed by synthesis' or else—as opposed to simple—'divisible into partial representations.' A complicative representation [*Komplexionvorstellung*] is always 'composed' in both senses. A contractive representation [*Kontraktionsvorstellung*] just as a general representation is, on the contrary, always composed in the first sense, and can on this account very well be simple. For example, the representation 'color' is not divisible into 'partial representations,' but can nevertheless be formed by synthesis from 'members' red, green, etc.'' From the distinction made here between ''part'' (*Teil*) and ''member'' (*Glied*), Ziehen draws the following consequence, which he correctly judges to be remarkable: ''In certain cases an analysis (isolation, abstraction) is possible without the occurrence of a synthesis of which as such we are conscious'' (*Lehrbuch der Logik* [Bonn: Marcus & Webers Verlag, 1920], 346).

16. ''What is concerned here is a degenerate case: all the elements (with the exception of the isolated elements, that is, those that are only related to themselves) are related to one another; the set is therefore homogeneous, there are no longer any distinctive properties, and on this account there is no longer any possibility of setting up an order'' (*Die Quasizerlegung*, 3).

17. This qualitative difference between the two types of obstacles is well brought out in Gilles Granger's article, ''Le problème de la *Construction logique du monde*,'' 36. The author emphasizes that the difficulty of companionship arises only if quasi analysis is confronted with the ''foreign postulate'' of analysis in the strict sense. The texts used in my study confirm that such was indeed the strategy adopted by Carnap so as to protect quasi analysis from the objection of incompleteness. Gilles Granger believes, on the other hand, that Carnap did not succeed in overcoming the second obstacle concerned here.

18. Paragraph 108 of the *Aufbau* seems to us to belong to the type of reflection of which the architectonic of pure reason constitutes the prototype. Our recourse to the concept of ''schema'' is inspired by the well-known passage of this text where Kant contrasts ''technical'' and ''architectonic'' unity: ''To be realized, the idea calls for a *schema*, that is, a diversity and an ordering of parts that are essential and determined a priori after the principle of the end. The schema that is not outlined following an idea, that is, following a capital end of reason, but empirically, following ends that occur accidentally (whose number cannot be known in advance) gives us a *technical* unity, but one that results from an idea (where reason gives a priori the ends, and does not wait for them empirically) founds an *architectonic* unity'' (*KRV*, B 861, III 539).

19. ''The construction of an object corresponds to the indication of the geographical coordinates for a place on the surface of the earth. The place is uniquely determined through these coordinates; any question about the nature of this place (perhaps about the climate, nature of the soil, etc.) has now a definite meaning. To answer all these questions is then a further aim which can never be completed and which is to be approached through experience'' (*A*, §179, 253; trans. George, 289).

20. "The first aim, then, is the construction of objects; it is followed by a second aim, namely, the investigation of the nonconstructional properties and relations of the objects. The first aim is reached through convention; the second, however, through experience" (ibid.).

21. *KRV*, III, 330 and 497.

22. *A*, §180, 253ff.; trans. George, 290. The solubility in principle of meaningful questions assumes in particular that the propositions stating the relations between experiences are always decidable. As Arne Naess observed (*Four Modern Philosophers: Carnap, Wittgenstein, Heidegger, Sartre*, 52), the status of this last presupposition in the *Aufbau* is not clear. Carnap makes it a "thesis of constitution" and calls on it to justify, against the teachings of the psychology of knowledge, the fiction of the persistence of the given (§101, 139–40). The only way to understand this assumption is to consider it as a condition of the possibility of constructing concepts that in a sense is already established, the sole function of constitution being to imitate logically the formal genesis. In other words, if the lapses of memory have a devastating effect, no knowledge would be possible.

23. Jürgen Habermas, *Erkenntnis und Interesse* (Frankfurt: Suhrkamp, 1968), Chapter 4.

24. H. Bergson, *La pensée et le mouvant* (Paris: PUF, 1963), 1286; cf. *A*, §182, 258; trans. George, 295.

25. "Ueber die Aufgabe der Physik und die Anwendung des Grundsatzes der Einfachsheit," *Kantstudien*, in particular pp. 90 and 97.

26. Hans Hahn, *Logik, Mathematik und Naturerkennen, Einheitswissenschaft*, II, 1933; translated in Ayer, *Logical Positivism*, 158ff.; and R. Carnap, *Die alte und die neue Logik*, translated in Ayer, ibid., 141ff. On the notion of tautology see *Wissenschaftliche Weltauffassung: Der Wiener Kreis*, in Otto Neurath, *Empiricism and Sociology*, 311; see also Neurath, "Sociology and Physicalism," in Ayer, *Logical Positivism*, 284; Hans Reichenbach, "L'empirisme logique et la desagregation de l'*a priori*," *Actes du Congrès International de Philosophie Scientifique*, I, 30. Concerning Russell's use of the concept "tautology," we will refer to the following texts: *Introduction to Mathematical Philosophy* (204–5 and note), where the author mentions the purely heuristic aspect of this concept ("For the moment, I do not know how to define 'tautology' "); *Logic and Knowledge*, 240; *My Philosophical Development*, 119; see also J. Vuillemin, *Leçons sur la première philosophie de Bertrand Russell*, 244.

27. "Of course the proof of the tautological character of mathematics is still not complete in all its details. It is a difficult and arduous task; yet we do not doubt that faith in the tautological character of mathematics is essentially correct" (Hahn, ibid., 158).

28. Russell and Whitehead, *Principia Mathematica*, II, 183; I. Grattan-Guiness, *Dear Russell-Dear Jourdain* (New York: Columbia Press University 1977), 173; see also B. Russell, *Introduction to Mathematical Philosophy*, 131ff.

29. *Dear Russell-Dear Jourdain*, 173. Russell at first believed that the axiom of infinity *could be proved*. If *n* is a finite number, there is at least one class that has *n* members. Nothing then seems to preclude the construction of an infinite series n, (n), $[(n)]$, $\{[(n)]\}$, etc. *But the theory of types destroys any hope of proving the existence of such a series, since, each term being of a different type from its predecessor, the terms of the series cannot be brought together in a set. On this issue see Vuillemin, Leçons, 144.*

30. See B. Russell, *Principles of Mathematics*, Chapter 1, §1: "Pure Mathematics is the class of all propositions of the form '*p* implies *q*,' where *p* and *q* are propositions containing one or more variables, the same in the two propositions, and neither *p* nor *q* contains any constants except logical constants" (p. 3).

31. R. Carnap, "Die logizistiche Grundlegung der Arithmetik," translated in Benacerraf and Putnam, *Philosophy of Mathematics: Selected Readings*, 35.

32. This is why Russell presents his "solution" not as a real way out, but, on the contrary, as the very mark of the limits against which the logicist endeavor comes. Russell continues nevertheless to commit himself to the heuristic principle of logicism, and sees in the tautological interpretation of

mathematical propositions the only satisfactory approach, while admitting that he still does not know how to define "tautology" (see *Introduction to Mathematical Philosophy*, 205, and *Dear Russell-Dear Jourdain*, 162–63). Carnap's "Autobiography" gives us a hint concerning the way he judges afterward the value of this first attempt at a solution: "I was inclined towards analytic interpretations of the axiom of infinity and the axiom of choice; but during my time in Vienna we did not achieve complete clarity on these questions" (Schilpp [ed.], *Philosophy of Rudolf Carnap*, 47).

33. Russell, *Introduction to Mathematical Philosophy*, 122; cf. *Principia*, I, 88, and III, 257–58.

34. *Mathematische Annalen*, 59 (1904), 514–16.

35. Russell, *Introduction to Mathematical Philosophy*, 123. Russell illustrates the difficulty by comparing the construction of a class of selection respectively for an infinite set of pairs of boots and for an infinite set of pairs of socks. In the first case—each pair of boots comprising two distinct elements, a "right foot" and a "left foot"—we have a criterion of choice that is lacking in the second case, socks being identical two by two. The possibility of reaching a good order for an infinite class of nonordered pairs is therefore not at all guaranteed. Zermelo believed that it was always possible to organize a class of subclasses into sequences in which every subclass has a first term. But he did not see that in certain cases there would be no criterion of selection for the representative of the subclass.

36. *Dear Russell-Dear Jourdain*, 172.

37. Carnap, in Benacerraf and Putnam, *Philosophy of Mathematics*, 34.

38. "Die Mathematik als Zweig der Logik," 308.

39. In Benacerraf and Putnam, *Philosophy of Mathematics*, 36.

40. Wittgenstein, *Tractatus*, 6.1232.

41. F. P. Ramsey, *Foundations of Mathematics*, 1–61.

42. Ibid., 29.

43. "Whether there are indefinable classes or not is an empirical question; both possibilities are perfectly conceivable. But even if, in fact, all classes are definable, we cannot in our logic identify classes with definable classes without destroying the apriority and necessity which is the essence of logic" (ibid., 22–23).

44. Carnap, in Bonacerraf and Putnam, *Philosophy of Mathematics*, 39.

45. Carnap borrows this distinction from F. Kauffmann, *Das Unendliche in der Mathematik und seine Ausschaltung: Eine Untersuchung über die Grundlagen der Mathematik.*

46. See *Foundations of Set Theory*, 178, and Carnap, in Benacerraf and Putnam, *Philosophy of Mathematics*, 41.

47. See Carnap, "Die logizistische Grundlegung der Arithmetik," for instance this passage: "The logicist does not establish the existence of structures which have the properties of the real numbers by laying down axioms or postulates; rather, through explicit definitions, he produces logical constructions that have, by virtue of these definitions, the usual properties of the real numbers. . . . This 'constructivistic' method forms part of the very texture of logicism" (in Benacerraf and Putnam, 44; cf. Russell, *Logic and Knowledge*, 239–40).

48. "Eigentliche und uneigentliche Begriff," 358.

49. *Erkenntnis*, 2 (1931), 143–44.

50. *Wittgenstein und der Wiener Kreis, Aus dem Nachlass*, 218.

51. "Ueber formal unentscheidbare Sätze der Principia Mathematica und verwandter Systeme," *Monatshefte für Mathematik und Physic*, 38 (1931), 173–98, translated in Jean Van Heijenoort, *From Frege to Gödel: A Source Book in Mathematical Logik, 1879–1931, 596–617; see Gödel's summary in Erkenntnis*, 2 (1931), 149–51.

52. Letter consulted at the Archives of the Rudolf Carnap Collection, University of Pittsburgh Libraries, ref. 029–08–03.

53. See P. Bernays, "Die Philosophie der Mathematik und die Hilbertsche Beweistheorie," *Blätter für deutsche Philosophie*, 4 (1930).

54. Letter to Neurath of December 23, 1933, quoted with the permission of the curator of the Archives of the Rudolf Carnap Collection.

55. See Alfred Tarski, "Fundamentale Begriffe der Methodologie der deduktiven Wissenschaften," I: "Metamathematics should not be considered in its principle as a unique theory; one must on the contrary construct a special 'metadiscipline' adapted to the needs of the examination of each deductive discipline. However, the current reflections are of a more general character: they have for their aim to *make precise the meaning of a series of important metamathematical concepts and to determine the fundamental properties of these concepts* which the special disciplines share in common" (*Collected Works of A. Tarski*, 353).

56. D. Hilbert, "Neubegründung der Mathematik, erste Mitteilung," in *Gesammelte Abhandlungen*, III (Berlin: Julius Springer, 1935), 163.

57. *LS*, §2, 7; Carnap uses the same metaphor in a speech given on June 18, 1931, at a meeting of the Vienna Circle: "The difference between arithmetized metalogic and the metalogic presented until now is the following: arithmetized metalogic deals not with empirically present configurations [*Gebilde*], but possible configurations. The old metalogic is therefore comparable with the geography of language forms; arithmetized metalogic on the other hand is the geometry of language forms" (*Vortrag über Metalogik*, Carnap Archives, University of Pittsburgh Libraries, 081–07–18, 9).

58. Cf. on this issue W. Kneale and M. Kneale, *The Development of Logic*, 714.

59. In a letter of December 23, 1963, Ina Carnap clears up what remained for many commentators and in particular her correspondent, Herbert G. Bohnert, a marvel: how did Carnap so quickly after the publication of Gödel's results not only take them into account, but also construct a "substitute" concept of formal validity? The answer is simple: "Carnap said that during his conversations with Gödel he had assimilated his ideas before Gödel's article on undecidability was published, which explains the briefness of the interval."

60. A system of formalized arithmetic is said to be "ω-consistent" if for any variable x and a formula $A(x)$ we cannot have in this system at the same time $\vdash A(0)$, $\vdash A(1)$, $\vdash A(2) \ldots$ and $\vdash \sim \forall x\, A(x)$. A system is "simply consistent" if it is not possible to derive both a proposition and its negation. The criterion of ω-consistence is thus stronger than that of simple consistence; there are systems of arithmetic that are consistent but not ω-consistent. In an article of 1932, "Einige Betrachtungen über die Begriffe der ω: Widerspruchsfreiheit und der Vollständigkeit," Tarski points out that he had already outlined the distinction between the two types of contradiction as early as 1927 (see *Logic, Semantics, Metamathematics*, vol. 2).

61. To avoid ambiguity in translating the two pairs of German expressions formed on the same root: *definiert-undefiniert* and *definit-undefinit*, I will translate *definit* by "effective" (and *indefinit* by "ineffective" or "noneffective").

62. D. Hilbert, "Grundlegung der elementaren Zahlenlehre," *Mathematische Annalen*, 1931, 104. In the article quoted in note 60, this section, Tarski establishes against Hilbert the nonfinitist character of the rule in question. See Carnap's commentary, *LS*, §48, 173.

63. K. Gödel, letter to Carnap of November 28, 1932.

64. *LS*, §34c. In his 1963 article (Schilpp, *The Philosophy of Rudolf Carnap*, 478), E. W. Beth shows that the proofs of the *Logical Syntax* can escape the consequences of the Löwenheim-Skolem paradox only if it is assumed that they refer to an intuitive model. This kind of assumption, already present in the *Aufbau*, appears to me to be characteristic of the logicism of the second Carnap, insofar as it reflects the universalist requirements of the syntax (see Chapter 4).

65. But from the mere fact that an evaluation contains a contradiction for a given valuation, one cannot infer that the sentence considered is contradictory. This is the case only if the sentence is logical. If it contains a descriptive predicate on which the valuation occurs, the sentence is contradictory (logically false) only if there is no property that makes it true (*LS*, §34c, 108).

66. Carnap's letter to Gödel of September 27, 1932.

67. *LS*, §17, 52; see also §44, 164.

68. The definitional characteristic of the *L*-rules of a language *S* lies in the general substitutivity they permit for descriptive expressions. The *L*-sublanguage of *S* is therefore that part of *S* that contains the same sentences as *S* but only has *L*-rules of transformation (*LS*, §51, 181). Concerning the problem of the "conservatism" of mathematics, see Hartry Field, *Science Without Numbers*, 16ff.

69. Two statements are *L*-synonymous if they are consequences of one another, their mutual deduction only calling for logical rules of transformation. For example, two tautologies are *L*-synonymous. Two *expressions* are *L*-synonymous if they are substitutable *salva veritate* in every sentence of the language in accordance with the rules of designation present in its syntax. For example, the expression "bachelor" is *L*-synonymous with the expression "unmarried man." On the other hand, "evening star" and "morning star" are two *P*-synonymous expressions. All that is said of the one holds for the other, insofar as they designate the same "rock sphere," following the expression Quine uses in one letter, which the *P*-rules of transformation of the language should allow us to establish. Finally, the *P*-equipollence between statements, which corresponds to the *P*-equivalence between expressions, can be illustrated by two physical statements that are *P*-consequences of one another: (1) In this 5,000-cm^3 volume tube there are two grams of hydrogen at such and such a pressure. (2) In this 5,000-cm^3 tube there are two grams of hydrogen at such and such a temperature.

70. W. V. Quine, letter to Carnap of January 5, 1943; see also *Word and Object*, Chapter 2; "Epistemology Naturalized," in *Ontological Relativity and Other Essays* (New York: Columbia University Press, 1969), 69–90.

71. W. V. Quine, letter quoted.

72. Carnap's letter to Quine of January 21, 1943.

73. Quine's letter to Carnap of May 7, 1943.

74. Carnap calls "determinate" every statement whose truth or falsity depends on the rules of transformation of the language under consideration, whether *L*-or *P*-rules are concerned (*LS*, §48, 173–74). Validity (as the contravalidity) therefore generally subdivides into *L*- and *P*-valid. For instance, a proposition deduced from a physical law is *P*-valid. A proposition (even a descriptive one) whose truth is obtained by the rules of *L*-consequence (such as "Caesar is or is not bald") is *L*-valid. All the other statements are indeterminate. As all analytic propositions are by definition determinate, all indeterminate statements are *synthetic*. There are therefore two categories of synthetic sentences: *P*-valid and *P*-contravalid ones on the one hand, and indeterminate ones on the other (*LS*, §52, 185).

75. On this issue, Carnap is quite significantly opposed not only to Kant, but also to Wittgenstein. For the *Tractatus* observes (correctly, from Carnap's point of view) that the truth of tautologies can be recognized "from the symbol alone," which is true only if the *L*-rules are given at the same time as the statements. But he mistakenly takes this to be a distinctive feature of tautologies: "And so too it is a very important fact that the truth or falsity of non-logical propositions *cannot* be recognized from the propositions alone" (6.113). For if, in the case of tautologies, *L*-rules of transformation must be taken into account for their *L*-validity to be recognized, one does not see why the *P*-rules could not *also* be taken into account in order to recognize "from their symbol alone" the *P*-validity of determinate synthetic statements (*LS*, §52, 186).

76. The syntactical construction of the concept of *translation* uses the concepts of *reversible transformance* and *conservative sublanguage*. Carnap calls the *transformance* of *S* into S_2 the syntactical correlation between all sentential classes (sentences, expression, symbols) of S_1 and those of S_2 that replace the consequence relation in S_1 by the parallel relation in S_2. If the transformation on the symbols is reversible (i.e., if its converse is the transformation of S_2 into S_1), the two languages S_1 and S_2 are *isomorphic*. A translation of S_1 into S_2 is so obtained when the transformance of S_2 into S_1 is a sublanguage of S_3 (*LS*, §61, 224).

77. It is precisely, among other things, the theoretical existence of this syntactic language of reference that Quine questions in *Word and Object*. Radical translation (i.e., of translating a hitherto unknown language) calls for *pragmatic* concepts and not purely syntactic ones (nor purely semantic ones).

78. On this issue see F. Récanati, *La transparence et l'énonciation* (Paris: Seuil, 1979).

79. One could also consider (4) as a statement of the descriptive syntax, by taking the symbol "3" in its value as a material sign related by *Zei* to the corresponding syntactic form. Understood in this manner the statement is still analytic, as we saw above.

80. Following up this analogy, one could compare the *translation* of statements in the formal mode to psychoanalytic interpretation, *the syntactic elucidation* dissipating pseudoproblems to Freud's "Wo es war, soll Ich Werden", the *resistance* to the interpretation being likely to arise in both cases.

81. Unlike Frege's and Russell's constructions, which admitted, for example, that every expression of the property of a concept should be substituted for a numerical expression.

82. We are only briefly alluding here to the question of metaphysics, which has often been commented on; Carnap's major articles on this subject are "Ueberwindung der Metaphysik durch logische Analyse der Sprache"; "Theoretische Fragen und praktische Entscheidungen"; "On the Character of Philosophic Problems."

83. "Theoretische Fragen und praktische Entscheidungen," 257.

84. In a letter of July 27, 1932, which Neurath addresses to Carnap while the latter is finishing the writing of the *Logical Syntax*, Neurath exclaims in his usual vehement way: "I hope that the nauseating word 'Philosophy' no longer occurs there." The term "syntax" was finally retained although for some time the word "semantic" was held in favor (under Gödel's and Behmann's influence).

85. W. V. Quine, "Truth by Convention," in Lee (ed.), *Philosophical Essays for Alfred North Whitehead*; reprinted in Benacerraf and Putnam, *Philosophy of Mathematics: Selected Readings*, 329–54.

Conclusion

1. Kant, *Handschriftliche Nachlass, Reflexion* 4455.

2. Extract from the course "Philosophy and Logical Analysis," 1936, Archives 081–03–01, p. 10. Quoted with the permission of the curator of the R. Carnap Collection, University of Pittsburgh Libraries.

3. Cf. this volume, Section 4, Chapter 4.

4. Kant, introduction to *Critique of Judgment*, v.

5. See Hans Hahn, Otto Neurath, Rudolph Carnap, *Wissenschaftliche Weltauffassung: Der Wiener Kreis*, "Historical Background," in O. Neurath, *Empiricism and Sociology* (Dordrecht: Reidel, 1973), 301.

6. Ibid., 306.

7. Kant defines the "speculative interest" of empiricism thus: "In following it understanding always keeps to its own territory, that is, within the field of simply possible experiences; it can always inquire into its laws and, by means of these laws, extend without end its comprehensible and sure knowledge" (*KRV*, Akad, III, 325).

8. "Empiricism, Semantics, and Ontology," reprinted in *Meaning and Necessity*, 220; see also Gustav Bergmann's reply to Quine, in "Two Cornerstones of Empiricism," *Synthese*, 8 (June 1953), 435–52; reprinted in G. Bergmann, *The Metaphysics of Logical Positivism* (Madison: University of Wisconsin Press, 1954), 78–105.

9. *EHU*, 165; R. Carnap, *PLS*, 36: after having quoted the passage of the *Enquiry* concerned, Carnap writes: "We agree with this view of Hume, which says—translated into our terminology— that only the propositions of mathematics and empirical science have sense, and that all other propositions are without sense."

10. *The Philosophy of Karl Popper*, ed. P. A. Schilpp, 1121. See also Karl Popper, *Die Beide Grundprobleme der Erkenntnistheorie*, abbreviated as *BGE* in the following notes.

11. *BGE*, 8.

12. Karl Popper, *Conjectures and Refutations: The Growth of Scientific Knowledge*, 51 (*CR*). Compare with Kant, introduction to *Prolegomena to Any Future Metaphysics*, and *Kritik der reinen Vernunft*, A 760-B 788, Akad, III, 496.

13. Popper, *CR*, 51; see also 216, 312–13 and 383.

14. *Objective Knowledge: An Evolutionary Approach*, 49 (*OK*). These notions must, in fact, be relativized in order to fulfill the conditions of adequacy (since from a false proposition it is logically possible to deduce true statements): one will speak of the content of a statement *a* given *B*, and one will define the falsity content as the content of *a*, given the truth content of *a*). In fact, the definition of verisimilitude given by Popper in these passages was refuted in 1974 by David Miller ("Popper's Qualitative Theory of Verisimilitude," *British Journal for the Philosophy of Science*, 25 [1974], 166–77) and by P. Tichy ("On Popper's Definitions of Verisimilitude," ibid., pp. 155– 60). For Popper's subsequent autocritical reflection see among other texts "A Note on Verisimilitude," ibid., 147–59 and *OK*, Appendix 2, "Supplementary Remarks."

15. See "La signification actuelle de deux arguments d'Henri Poincaré," in R. Bouveresse (ed.), *Karl Popper ou le rationalisme critique* (Paris: Vrin, 1981), 194.

16. *OK*, 30.

17. "The central idea of Hume's theory is that of *repetition based upon similarity* (or 'resemblance'). This idea is used in a very uncritical way. We are led to think of the water-drop that hollows the stone: of sequences of unquestionably like events slowly forcing themselves upon us, as does the tick of the clock. But we ought to realize that in a psychological theory such as Hume's, only repetition-for-us, based upon similarity-for-us, can be allowed to have any effect upon us. We must respond to situations as if they were equivalent; *take* them as similar; interpret them as repetitions" (*CR*, 44).

18. Gilles Deleuze, *Différence et répetition*.

19. Kant, *KRV*, A 100–101.

20. Ibid., A 114, Akad, IV, 85.

21. Ibid., B 127, Akad, III, 105.

22. "When Kant said 'our intellect does not draw its laws from nature but imposes its laws upon nature,' he was right. But in thinking that these laws are necessarily true, or that we necessarily succeed in imposing them upon nature, he was wrong" (*CR*, 48).

23. *BGE*, 7; this expression will be subsequently rectified by Popper, who will prefer to speak of the "theory of empirical method" (see, e.g., *The Logic of Scientific Discovery*, §5).

24. *BGE*, 59. One no longer finds the explicit usage of the word "transcendental" in the indicated sense in the later works of Popper, with the exception of a page of *CR* (291) where he uses it for qualifying an argument of Carnap's in *Logical Foundations of Probability*.

25. Ibid., 58.

26. Frege, *Die Grundlagen der Arithmetik*, §3, 4.

27. Karl Popper, *OK*, 308; *BGE*, 58. Let us observe that Popper refers in the latter text to a number of authors who undertook to apply the transcendental method in the sense of the search for the objective conditions of possibility of science: he quotes Natorp, Cohen, Riehl, Schuppe, Wundt, Rehmke, and especially Külpe (*Vorlesungen über Logik*, O. Selz, 1923).

28. I have treated elsewhere the relationships between the use of the transcendental method in Wittgenstein and in Carnap in *Noûs*, "Formal Logic as Transcendental." Popper follows this analysis by seeking to prove the contradiction between the positivist and transcendental tendencies in logical positivism. What he believes to be a contradiction is one only if one keeps to a narrow meaning of the principle of tolerance; see this volume, Section 4, Chapter 4).

29. *OK*, 154.

30. Ibid., 335.

31. *CR*, 64; *OK*, 318. On the analytic character of statements rationally justifying the preference given to one theory over another, see *OK*, 83–84.

32. In this respect it would have been interesting to study the modification brought about in the Kantian conception of the transcendental by Husserlian phenomenology, and to locate his enterprise with respect to ontotranscendentalism. As my topical project in this book focuses on the concept of *analyticity*, the detour by Husserl did not seem relevant to us; it is self-evident that a topical study of the transcendental could not dispense with it.

Bibliography

Bibliography

LOCKE

Works

An Early Draft of Locke's Essay (Draft A). Ed. R. I. Aaron and J. Gibb. Oxford, 1936.
An Essay Concerning Human Understanding (E). 2 vols. Ed. A. C Fraser. London: Dover, 1959.
Of the Conduct of the Understanding. In *Works*, vol. 4. London, 1823; reprinted Aalen: Scientia Verlag.

Commentaries

Bennett, J. *Locke, Berkeley, Hume: Central Themes*. Oxford: Clarendon Press, 1971.
Mackie, J. L. *Problems from Locke*. Oxford: Clarendon Press, 1976.

HUME

Works

An Abstract of a Treatise of Human Nature (A). Ed. L. A. Selby-Bigge. Oxford: Clarendon Press, 1978 (following the *Treatise*).
Enquiries Concerning Human Understanding and Concerning the Principles of Morals (EHU). Ed. L. A. Selby-Bigge. Oxford: Clarendon Press, 1975.
Dialogues on Natural Religion. Ed. N. Kemp Smith. Oxford, 1935.
Treatise of Human Nature (T). Rev. ed., L. A. Selby-Bigge. Oxford: Clarendon Press, 1978.

Commentaries

Ayer, A. J. *Hume*. Oxford: Oxford University Press, 1980.
Bennett, J. *Locke, Berkeley, Hume: Central Themes*. Oxford: Clarendon Press, 1971.
Deleuze, G. *Empirisme et subjectivité*. Paris: PUF, 1953.
Flew, A. *Hume's Philosophy of Belief: A Study of His First Inquiry*. London: Routledge & Kegan Paul, 1961.
Kemp Smith, N. *The Philosophy of David Hume*. London: Macmillan, 1949.
Laporte, J. "Le scepticisme de Hume." *Revue philosophique*, 1933, 115; 1934, 117.
Lebrun, G. "La boutade de charing-cross." *Manuscrito*, 1 (1978), 65–84.
Malherbe, M. *Kant ou Hume*. Paris: Vrin, 1980.
Malherbe, M. *La philosophie empiriste de David Hume*. Paris: Vrin, 1976.
Michaud, Y. *Hume ou la fin de la philosophie*. Paris: PUF, 1983.

Pears, D. *David Hume: A Symposium*. London, 1963.
Stroud, B. *Hume*. London: Routledge and & Kegan Paul, 1977.
Zabeeh, F. *Hume: Precursor of Modern Empiricism*. The Hague, 1960.

KANT

Works

Anthropologie in pragmatischer Hinsicht (Anth), 1798. *Akad*, VII.
Kants gesammelte Schriften. Vols. I–IX: *Werke*; vols. X–XIII: *Briefwechsel*; vols. XIV–XXIII: *Handschriftlicher Nachlass*; vols. XXIV–XXIX: *Vorlesungen*. All references are to the edition of the Deutsche Akademie der Wissenschaften zu Berlin (abbreviated Akad). Berlin: Walter de Gruyter, 1966.
Kant's Inaugural Dissertation and Early Writings on Space (D). Akad, II. Trans. J. Handyside. Chicago: Open Court, 1929.
Kants Logik (L). Ed. J. B. Jäsche, 1980. Akad, IX. Trans. R. S. Hartman and W. Schwarz. New York, 1974.
Kritik der reinen vernunft (KRV), 1781, 1786. Akad, III (*Critique of Pure Reason*). Trans. N. K. Smith. London, 1929.
Logik Blomberg. Akad, XXIV, 1.
Logik Politz. Akad, XXIV, 2.
Prolegomena zu einer jeden künftigen Metaphysik, die als Wissenschaft wird auftreten können (P), 1783. Akad, IV (*Prolegomena to Any Future Metaphysics*). Trans. L. W. Beck. New York, 1951.
Reflexionen (R). Akad, XIV.
Vernunft durch eine ältere entbehrlich gemacht werden soll, 1790 (*The Kant-Eberhard Controversy [KEC]*). Trans. Henry E. Allison. Baltimore: Johns Hopkins University Press, 1975.
Welches sind die wirklichen Fortschritte, die die Metaphysik seit Leibnizens und Wolfs Zeiten in Deutschland gemacht hat? [WF], 1791. Akad, II (*What Real Progress Has Metaphysics Made . . . , [PM]*). Trans. T. Humphrey. New York: Abaris, 1983.
Wiener Logik. Akad, XXIV, 2.

Commentaries

Beck, L. W. *Essays on Kant and Hume*. New Haven, Conn.: Yale University Press, 1978.
Beck, L. W. *Studies in the Philosophy of Kant*. Indianapolis: Bobbs-Merrill, 1965.
Cohen, H. *Kants Theorie der Erfahrung*. Berlin, 1918.
Guillermit, L. "La conception kantienne de l'analyse et de la synthèse." To appear in *Ecrits*, ed. E. Schwartz and J. Vuillemin.
Kroner, R. *Von Kant bis Hegel*. Tübingen, 1921.
Lebrun, G. *Kant et la fin de la métaphysique*. Paris: Armand Colin, 1970.
Vleeschauwer, H. J. de. *La déduction transcendentale dans l'oeuvre de Kant*. Paris-The Hague, 1937.
Vuillemin, J. *L'héritage kantien et la révolution copernicienne*. Paris: PUF, 1954.
Vuillemin, J. *Physique et métaphysique kantienne*. Paris: PUF, 1955.

BOLZANO

Works

Beyträge su einer begründeteren Darstellung der Mathematik. Prague, 1810.
Der Briefwechsel mit F. Exner. Ed. E. Winter. 1935.
Einleitung in der Grössenlehre (EG). Ed. J. Berg, *Gesamtausgabe*, vol. III.
Functionenlehre. Ed. Rychlik. 1931.

Gesamtausgabe. Ed. E. Winter, J. Berg, F. Kambartel, J. Louzil, B. Van Rootselaar. Stuttgart: Frommann Verlag, 1977.

Paradoxien des Unendlichen (PU). Leipzig, 1831. Translated by D. A. Steele as *The Paradoxes of the Infinite*. London, 1950.

Reinanalytischer Beweis des Lehrsatzes, dass zwischen je zwei Werten . . . 1871.

Was ist Philosophie? Vienna, 1849.

Wissenschaftslehre (W). Vols. I–IV. Sulzbach, 1837; Leipzig, 1914. Partially translated by R. George as *Theory of Science*. Oxford: Basil Blackwell, 1972; and by Burnham Terrell, Dordrecht: Reidel, 1973.

Commentaries

Bar-Hillel, Y. "Bolzano's Definition of Analytic Propositions." *Theoria*, 16 (1950), 91–117, and *Methodos*, 2 (1950), pp. 32–55. Reprinted in *Aspects of Languages*. Magnes Press, 1970, 3–32.

Bar-Hillel, Y. "Bolzano's Propositional Logic." In *Aspects of Languages*, 32ff.

Berg, J. *Bolzano's Logic*. Stockholm Studies in Philosophy. Stockholm: Almquist & Wiksell, 1962.

Bergmann, H. *Das philosophische Werk Bernard Bolzanos*. Halle, 1909.

Beth, W. E. "Une contribution à l'histoire de la logique mathématique." *Actes du congrès international d'histoire des sciences*, September 3–9, 1956, 1104–6.

Buhl, G. "Ableitbarkeit und Abfolge in der Wissenschaftstheorie Bernard Bolzanos." *Kantstudien, Ergänzungshefte*, 83 (1961).

Cavaillès, J. *Sur la logique et la théorie de la science*. Paris: Vrin, 1976.

Church, A. "Propositions and Sentences." In *The Problem of Universals: A Symposium*. Notre Dame, Ind.: University of Notre Dame Press, 1956.

Danek, J. *Les projets de Leibniz et Bolzano*. Laval: Presses de l'Université de Laval, 1975.

Dapunt, I. "Zur Klarstellung einiger Lehren B. Bolzanos." *Journal of the History of Philosophy*, 7 (1969), 63–73.

Dubislav,, W. "Bolzano als Vorlaufer der mathematischen Logik." *Philosophisches Jahrbuch der Görresgesellschaft*, 1931.

Dubislav, W. *Ueber die Sogenannten analytischen und synthetischen Urteilen*. Berlin: H. Weiss, 1926.

Granger, G. "Le concept de continu chez Aristote et Bolzano." *Etudes philosophiques*, 1969, 513–23.

Grossmann, R. "Frege's Ontology." *Philosophical Review*, 70 (1961), 23–40.

Lukasiewicz, J. *Die logischen Grundlagen der Wahrscheinlichkeitsrechnung*. Cracow, 1913.

Neemann, U. "Analytic and Synthetic Propositions in Kant and Bolzano." In *Deskription, Analytizität und Existenz*. Weingartner, 1966. Reprinted in *Ratio*, 12 (1970), 1–20.

Raymond, P. *Matérialisme dialectique et logique*. Paris: Maspero, 1977.

Scholz, H. Review of Bar-Hillel's articles, "Bolzano's Definition of Analytic Propositions." *Journal of Symbolic Logic*, 17 (1952), 119–22.

Sebestik, J. *Mathématiques et théorie de la science chez Bernard Bolzano*. Paris: thèse d'Etat, 1974.

Sinaceur, H. "Bolzano est-il un précurseur de Frege?" *Archiv für Geschichte der Philosophie*, 1975.

Smart, H. R. "Bolzano's Logic." *Philosophical Review*, 53 (1954), 513–33.

Winter, E. J. *Leben und geistige Entwicklung des Sozialethikers und Mathematikers Bernard Bolzano, 1781–1848*. Halle: Max Niemeyer Verlag, 1949.

FREGE

Works

Begriffsschrift, eine der arithmetischen nachgebildete Formelsprache des reinen Denkens (B). Halle, 1879. Translated by T. W. Bynuum as *Conceptual Notation and Related Articles*, Oxford, 1972.

Die Grundlagen der Arithmetik: Eine logisch-mathematische, Untersuchung über den Begriff der Zahl (GA). Breslau: W. Köbner, 1884. Translated by J. L. Austin as *The Foundations of Arithmetic*. Oxford, 1950.

Grundgesetze der Arithmetik, Begriffsschriftlich abgeleitet (G). 2 vols. Jena: Hermann Pohle, 1893 and 1903; Hildesheim: Olms, 1962. Translated by M. Furth as *The Basic Laws of Arithmetic*, vol. 1, part 1. Berkeley: University of California Press, 1963.

Kleine Schriften (KS). Ed. I. Angelelli. Hildesheim: Olms, 1967. Articles translated in *Translations from the Philosophical Writings of Gottlob Frege*, ed. P. Geach and M. Black. Oxford, 1960; in *Logical Investigations*, ed. P. Geach and R. Stoothoff. Oxford, 1977; and in *On the Foundations of Geometry and Formal Theories of Arithmetic*, ed. E. H. Kluge. New Haven: Yale University Press, 1971.

Commentaries

Angelelli, I. *Studies on Gottlob Frege and Traditional Philosophy*. Dordrecht: Reidel, 1967.

Benacerraf, P. "Frege: The Last Logicist." *Midwest Studies in Philosophy*, VI, 1981.

Black, M. "Frege on Functions." In *Problems of Analysis: Philosophical Essays*, 229–54; reprinted in Klemke (ed.), *Essays on Frege*. Urbana, 1968.

Bouveresse, J. "Frege critique de Kant." *Revue Internationale de Philosophie*, 130 (1979), 739–60.

Burge, T. "Frege on Extensions of Concepts from 1884 to 1903." *Philosophical Review*, 93 (1984), 3–34.

Church, A. "On Sense and Denotation." *Journal of Symbolic Logic*, 7 (1942), 47.

Currie, G. "Frege's Realism." *Inquiry*, 21 (1978), 218– 21.

Dudman, V. H. "A Note on Frege on Sense." *Australian Journal of Philosophy*, 47 (1969), 119–22.

Dummett, M. *Frege, Philosophy of Language*. London: Duckworth, 1973.

Dummett, M. *The Interpretation of Frege's Philosophy*. Cambridge, Mass.: Harvard University Press, 1981.

Dummett, M. "Truth." *Proceedings of the Aristotelian Society*, 59 (1958–59), 141–62.

Dummett, M. "Frege on Functions: A Reply." *Philosophical Review*, 64 (1955), 96–107; reprinted in Klemke (ed.), *Essays on Frege*, 268–83.

Dummett, M. "Note: Frege on Functions." *Philosophical Review*, 65 (1956), 229–30.

Dummet, M. "Frege as a Realist." *Inquiry*, 19 (1976), 455–68.

Geach, P. T. "Frege's Grundlagen." *Philosophical Review*, 60 (1951), 535–44; reprinted in Klemke, *Essays on Frege*, 467–78.

Geach, P. T. "Quine on Classes and Properties." *Philosophical Review*, 62 (1953), 409–12; reprinted in Klemke, *Essays on Frege*, 502–4.

Geach, P. T. *Reference and Generality*. Ithaca, N.Y.: Cornell University Press, 1962.

Grossmann, R. *Reflections on Frege's Philosophy*. Evanston, Ill.: Northwestern University Press, 1969.

Heijenoort, J. Van. "Frege on Sense Identity." *Journal of Philosophical Logic*, 6 (1977), 103–8.

Heijenoort, J. Van. *From Frege to Gödel: A Source Book in Mathematical Logic, 1879–1931*. Cambridge, Mass.: Harvard University Press, 1967.

Heijenoort, J. Van. "Sense in Frege." *Journal of Philosophical Logic*, 6 (1977), 93–102.

Imbert, Cl. Introduction to *Les fondements de l'arithmétique*. Paris: Seuil, 1969.

Imbert, Cl. "Le projet idéographique." *Revue Internationale de Philosophie*, 130 (1979), 621–65.

Kambartel, F. *Introduction to Gottlob Frege, Nachgelassene Schriften*. Hamburg: F. Meiner, 1969.

Kienzle, B. "Notiz zu Freges Theorien der Identität." In *Studien zu Frege*. Ed. M. Schirn. Hamburg: F. Meiner, 1969.

Kitcher, P. "Frege's Epistemology." *Philosophical Review*, 88 (1979), 236.

Klemke, E. D. (ed.). *Essays on Frege*. Urbana: University of Illinois Press, 1968.

Largeault, J. *Logique et philosophie chez Frege*. Louvain: Beatrice-Nauwelaerts, 1970.

Marshall, W. "Frege's Theory of Functions and Objects." *Philosophical Review*, 62 (1953), 374–90; reprinted in Klemke, *Essays on Frege*, 249–67.

Marshall, W. "Sense and Reference: A Reply." *Philosophical Review*, 65 (1959), 342–61; reprinted in Klemke, *Essays on Frege*, 398–320.

Nusenoff, R. E. "Frege on Identity Sentences." *Philosophy and Phenomenological Research*, 34, 438–42.

Proust, J. "Sens frégéen et compréhension de la langue." In *Meaning and Understanding*. Ed. H. Parret and J. Bouveresse. Berlin: Walter de Gruyter, 1981.

Resnik, M. D. *Frege and the Philosophy of Mathematics*. Ithaca, N.Y.: Cornell University Press, 1980.

Resnik, M. D. "The Frege-Hilbert Controversy." *Philosophy and Phenomenological Research*, 34 (1974), 3.

Rouilhan, Ph. de. "Sur la sémantique frégéenne des énoncés." *Histoire, Epistémologie, Langage*, 5 (1983), 19–36.

Schirn, M. (ed.). *Studien zu Frege*. 3 vols. Stuttgart: Frommann Verlag, 1976.

Sluga, H. *Gottlob Frege*. London: Routledge & Kegan Paul, 1980.

Sluga, H. "Frege and the Rise of Analytic Philosophy." *Inquiry*, 18 (1975), 471–87.

Sluga, H. "Frege as a Rationalist." In Schirn, *Studien zu Frege*, 27–47.

Sluga, H. "Frege's Alleged Realism." *Inquiry*, 20 (1977), 227–42.

Schwartz, E. "Remarques sur 'l'espace des choses' de Wittgenstein et ses origines frégéennes." *Dialectica*, 26 (1972).

Thiel, Chr. *Sense and Reference in Frege's Logic*. Dordrecht: Reidel, 1968.

Thiel, Chr. "Zur Inkonsistenz der Fregeschen Mengenlehre." In *Frege und die moderne Grundlagenforschung*. Edited Chr. Thiel. Meisenheim and Glan: Anton Hain Verlag, 1975.

Tugendhat, E. "Die Bedeutung des Ausdrucks 'Bedeutung' bei Frege." In Schirn, *Studien zu Frege*.

Vuillemin, J. "L'élimination des définitions par abstraction chez Frege." *Revue Philosophique*, 1964.

Vuillemin, J. "Sur le jugement de recognition chez Frege." *Archiv für Geschichte der Philosophie*, 46 (1964).

CARNAP

Works

Abriss der Logistik. Vienna: Schriften zur wissenschaftliche Auffassung, 1929.

"Die alte und die neue Logik." *Erkenntnis*, 1, (1930). Translated by I. Levi as "The Old and the New Logic," in *Logical Positivism*, ed. A. Ayer. Glencoe, Ill.: Free Press, 1959.

"Die Antinomien und die Unvollständigkeit der Mathematik." *Monatshefte für Mathematik und Physik*, 41 (1934).

Die Aufgabe der Wissenschaftslogik. Vienna: Einheitswissenschaft, 1934.

"Autobiography" and "Replies." In P. A. Schilpp (ed.), *The Philosophy of Rudolf Carnap*. La Salle, Ill.: Open Court, 1963.

"Bericht über Untersuchungen zur allgemeinen Axiomatik." *Erkenntnis*, I (1930).

"Diskussion zur Grundlegung der Mathematik." *Erkenntnis*, 2 (1931).

"Dreidimensionalität des Raumes and Kausalität." *Annalen der Philosophie und philosophischen Kritik*, 4 (1924).

"Eigentliche und uneigentliche Begriffe." *Symposion: Philosophische Zeitschrift für Forschung und Aussprache*, Erlange, I, Book 4, 1927.

"Empiricism, Semantics and Ontology." *Revue Internationale de Philosophie*, 4 (1950).

"Erwiderung auf die vorstehenden Sätze von E. Zilsel und K. Duncker." *Erkenntnis*, 3 (1932).

Formalization of Logic. Cambridge, Mass.: Harvard University Press, 1943.

"Formalwissenschaft und Realwissenschaft." *Erkenntnis*, 5 (1935). Translated in Feigl and Brodbeck, *Readings in the Philosophy of Science*.

"Foundations of Logic and Mathematics." *International Encyclopedia of Unified Science*, vol. 1. Chicago: University of Chicago Press, 1939.

"Ein Gültigkeitskriterium für die Sätze der klassischen Mathematik." *Monatshefte für Mathematik und Physik*, 42 (1935).

An Introduction to the Philosophy of Science. Ed. M. Gardner. New York: Basic Books, 1966.

Introduction to Semantics. Cambridge, Mass.: Harvard University Press, 1942.

Der logische Aufbau der Welt (A). Berlin: Weltkreis, 1928. Translated by R. George as *The Logical Structure of the World*. Berkeley and Los Angeles: University of California Press, 1969.

Logische Syntax der Sprache (LS). Vienna: Julius Springer Verlag, 1934. English translation by A. Smeaton (Comtesse Von Zeppelin). London: Paul, Trench, Trubner, 1937.

"Die logizistische Grundlegung der Mathematik." *Erkenntnis*, 2 (1931). English translation by E. Putnam and G. Massey, in Benacerraf and Putnam, *Philosophy of Mathematics: Selected Readings*.

"Die Mathematik als Zweig der Logic." *Blätter fur deutsche Philosophie*, 4 (1930).

Meaning and Necessity. Chicago: University of Chicago Press, 1947.

"Meaning Postulates." *Philosophical Studies*, (1952).

"On the Character of Philosophic Problems." *Philosophy of Science*, 1 (1934).

Philosophy and Logical Syntax (PLS). London: Paul, Trench, Trubner, 1935.

"Physikalische Begriffsbildung." *Wissen und Wirken*, 39 (1926).

"Die physikalische Sprache als Universalssprache der Wissenschaft." *Erkenntnis*, 2 (1932). Translated as *The Unity of Science*. London: Psyche Min., 1934.

"Der Raum: Ein Beitrag zur Wissenschaftslehre." *Kantstudien, Ergänzungshefte*, 56 (1922).

Scheinprobleme in der Philosophie: Das Fremdpsychische und der Realismusstreit. Berlin: Weltkreis, 1928.

"Testability and Meaning." *Philosophy of Science*, 3 (1936).

"Theoretische Fragen und praktische Entscheidungen." *Natur und Geist* (Jena), 9 (1934).

"Ueber die Abhängigkeit der Eigenschaften des Raumes von denen der Zeit." *Kantstudien*, 30 (1925).

"Ueber die Aufgabe der Physik." *Kantstudien*, 28 (1923), 90–107.

"Ueberwindung der Metaphysik durch logische Analyse der Sprache." *Erkenntnis*, 2 (1932). Translated by A. Pap as "The Elimination of Metaphysics through Logical Analysis of Language," in A. Ayer, *Logical Positivism*.

In collaboration with H. Hahn and O. Neurath, *Wissenschaftliche Weltauffassung: Der Wiener Kreis*. Vienna: A Wolf, 1929. Translated by O. Neurath, *Empiricism and Sociology*. Ed. M. Neurath, R. S. Cohen, Dordrecht: Reidel, 1973.

Commentaries

Bohnert, G. H. "Carnap's Logicism." In J. Hintikka, *Rudolf Carnap, Logical Empiricist: Materials and Perspectives*.

Bouveresse, J. *La parole malheureuse: De l'alchimie linguistique à la grammaire philosophique*. Paris: Minuit, 1971.

Clavelin, M. "La première doctrine de la signification du Cercle de Vienne." *Etudes Philosophiques*, 4 (1973).

Clavelin, M. "Quine contre Carnap, la polémique sur l'analyticité et sa portée." *Revue Internationale de Philosophie*, 144–45 (1983).

Coffa, A. "Carnap's Sprachanschauung Circa 1932." *PSA*, 2 (1976).

Coffa, A. "Idealism and the *Aufbau*." In *The Legacy of Logical Positivism*. Ed. N. Rescher, forthcoming.

Coffa, A. "Logical Positivism and the Semantic Tradition." *Actes des Journées Internationales sur le Cercle de Vienne, Fundamenta Scientiae*, 5 (1984). Reprinted in A. Soulez, *Le Cercle de Vienne: Doctrines et controverses*. Paris: Klincksieck, 1986.

Coffa, A. *To the Vienna Station: Semantics, Epistemology and the A Priori from Kant to Carnap*. Cambridge: Cambridge University Press, forthcoming.

Goodman, N. "The Significance of *Der logische Aufbau der Welt*." In Schilpp (ed.), *The Philosophy of Rudolf Carnap*.

Goodman, N. *The Structure of Appearance*. Cambridge, Mass.: Harvard University Press, 1951.

Granger, G. "Logisch-Philosophische Abhandlung et *Logischer Aufbau der Welt*." *Proceedings of the 19th International Wittgenstein Symposium: Philosophy of Mind, Philosophy of Psychology*. Ed. Hölder, Pichler, Tempshy. Vienna, 1985.

Granger, G. "Le problème de la *Construction logique de monde*." *Revue Internationale de Philosophie*, 144– 45, fasc. 1–2 (1983).

Haach, S. "Carnap's Aufbau: Some Kantian Reflections." *Ratio*, 19 (1977).

Haller, R. "New Light on the Vienna Circle." *Monist*, 1982.

Hintikka, J. *Rudolf Carnap, Logical Empiricist: Materials and Perspectives*. Dordrecht: Reidel, 1975.

Jorgensen, J. "Carnap Logische Syntax der Sprache." *Erkenntnis*, 4 (1934), 419–22.

Kleene, S. C. Review of *The Logical Syntax of Language*. *Journal of Symbolic Logic*, 4 (1939), 82–87.

Krauth, L. *Die Philosophie Carnaps*. Vienna: Springer, 1970.

Naess, A. *Four Modern Philosophers: Carnap, Wittgenstein, Heidegger, Sartre*. Trans. A. Hannay. Chicago: University of Chicago Press, 1968.

Proust, J. "Empirisme et objectivité." In A. Soulez (ed.), *Le Cercle de Vienne, doctrines et controverses*. Paris: Klincksieck, 1986.

Proust J. "Formal Logic as Transcendental: Wittgenstein's *Tractatus* and Carnap's *Logical Syntax of Language*." *Noûs*, 1988.

Quine, W. V. "Carnap and Logical Truth." *Ways of Paradox*. Cambridge, Mass.: Harvard University Press, 1979.

Stebbing, L. S. "Logical Positivism and Analysis." *Proceedings of the British Academy*. London, 1933.

Vuillemin, J. *La logique et le monde sensible*. Paris: Flammarion, 1969.

OTHER WORKS AND ARTICLES CONSULTED

Ajdukiewicz, K. "Sprache und Sinn." *Erkenntnis*, (1934), 100–138.

Ajdukiewicz, K. "Das Weltbild und die Begriffsapparatur." *Erkenntnis*, 4 (1934), 259–87.

Aristotle, *The Works*. Ed. W. D. Ross. 12 vols. Oxford, 1908–52.

Arnauld, A., and P. Nicole. *The Art of Thinking: Port Royal Logic*. Trans. J. Dickoff and P. James. Indianapolis and New York, 1964.

Aubenque, P. *Le problème de l'être chez Aristote*. Paris: PUF, 1962.

Ayer, A. *Language, Truth and Logic*. London: Gollanez, 1936.

Ayer, A. (ed.). *Logical Positivism*. New York: Free Press, 1959.

Bar-Hillel, Y. "On Syntactical Categories." *Journal of Symbolic Logic*, 15 (1950).

Behmann, H. "Sind die mathematischen Urteile analytisch oder synthetisch?" *Erkenntnis*, 4 (1934), 1–27.

Belaval, Y. *Leibniz critique de Descartes*. Paris: Gallimard, 1960.

Belaval, Y. *Etudes leibniziennes*. Paris: Gallimard, 1976.

Benacerraf, P., and H. Putnam. *Philosophy of Mathematics: Selected Readings*. Cambridge: Cambridge University Press, 1983.

Black, M. *A Companion to Wittgenstein's Tractatus*. Cambridge: Cambridge University Press, 1964.

Bochenski, J. M. *Formale Logik*. Basel, 1956.

Boehner, P. *Medieval Logic*. Manchester: Manchester University Press, 1952.

Carnap, R., and Y. Bar-Hillel. *An Outline of a Theory of Semantic Information*. Report 247. Cambridge, Mass.: MIT Research Laboratory of Electronics, 1952.

Church, A. *Introduction to Mathematical Logic*. Princeton, N.J.: Princeton University Press, 1956.

Clavelin, M. "Elucidation philosophique et 'écriture conceptuelle' logique dans le *Tractatus*." *Wittgenstein et le problème d'une philosophie de la science*. Paris: CNRS, 1971.

Couturat, L. *La logique de Leibniz*. Hildesheim: Olms, 1969.

Driesch, H. *Ordnungslehre*. Jena: Dorderichs, 1912.

Feigl, H., and M. Brodbeck (eds.). *Readings in the Philosophy of Science*. New York: Appleton-Century-Crofts, 1953.

Foucault, M. *L'Archéologie du savoir*. Paris: Gallimard, 1969.

Fraenkel, A. A. *Einleitung in die Mengenlehre*. Berlin: Springer, 1919.

Fraenkel, A. A., and Y. Bar-Hillel. *Foundations of Set Theory*. Amsterdam: North-Holland, 1958.

Geach, P. T. *Logic Matters*. Oxford: Blackwell, 1972.

Gilson, E. *L'être et l'essence*. Paris: Vrin, 1962.

Gödel, K. "Ueber formal unentscheidbare Sätze der Principia Mathematica und verwander Systeme I." *Monatshefte für Mathematik und Physik*, 38 (1931). Translated in Van Heijenoort, *From Frege to Gödel: A Source Book in Mathematical Logic, 1879–1931*.

Granger, G. "The Notion of Formal Content." *Social Research* 49 (1982).

Granger, G. "Philosophie et mathématique leibniziennes." *Revue de Métaphysique et de Morale*, 1 (1981).

Granger, G. "Sur le problème de l'espace logique dans le *Tractatus* de Wittgenstein." *L'âge de la Science*, 3 (1968), 180–95.

Granger, G. *La théorie aristotélicienne de la science*. Paris: Aubier, 1976.

Granger, G. "Was in Königsberg zu sagen wäre." *Manuscrito*, 5 (1981).

Grattan-Guiness, I. *Dear Russell-Dear Jourdain*. New York: Columbia Press University, 1977.

Gueroult, M. *La philosophie transcendentale de Salomon Maïmon*. Paris: Alcan, 1929.

Hahn, H. "Logik, Mathematik und Naturerkennen." *Einheitswissenschaft*, 2 (1933). Translated in Ayer, *Logical Positivism*.

Hausdorff, F. *Grundzüge der Mengelehre*. Leipzig: Veit, 1914.

Hilbert, D. "Axiomatisches Denken." *Mathematische Annalen*, 78 (1918).

Hilbert, D. *The Foundations of Geometry*. Trans. L. Unger. La Salle, Ill.: Open Court, 1971.

Hilbert, D. *Gesemmelte Abhandlungen*. 3 vols. Berlin: Springer, 1932–35.

Hilbert, D. *Die Grundlagen der Mathematik*. Vol. 1. Berlin: Springer, 1968.

Hilbert, D. "Ueber die Grundlagen der Logik and Arithmetik." In O. Becker (ed.), *Grundlagen der Mathematik*. Freiburg: Verlag Karl Alber, 1964.

Hintikka, J. *Logic, Language-Games, and Information*. Oxford: Clarendon Press, 1973.

Hintikka, J., and U. Remes. *The Method of Analysis*. Boston Studies in the Philosophy of Science, vol. 75. Dordrecht: Reidel, 1974.

Husserl, E. *Logical Investigations*. 2 vols. Trans. J. N. Findlay. Atlantic Highlands, N.J.: Humanities Press, 1970.

Husserl, E. *Philosophie der Arithmetik, psychologische Untersuchungen*. Halle-Saale: Stricker, 1891.

Jacob, P. *L'empirisme logique: Ses antécédents, ses critiques*. Paris: Minuit, 1980.

Kauppi, R. "Ueber die leibnizische Logik." *Acta philosophica Fennica*, fasc. 12 (1968).

Kitcher, Ph. *The Nature of Mathematical Knowledge*. New York: Oxford University Press, 1984.

Köhler, W. "Gestaltprobleme und Anfänge einer Gestalttheorie." *Jahresbericht über Physiologie und experientielle Psychologie*, 3 (1922), 512–39.

Kneale, W., and M. Kneale. *The Development of Logic*. Oxford: Clarendon Press, 1962.

Lebrun, G. *La patience du concept: Essai sur le discours hégélien*. Paris: Gallimard, 1972.

Leibniz, G. W. *Mathematische Schriften*. 7 vols. Ed. Gerhardt. Berlin-Halle, 1849–63.

Leibniz, G. W. *New Essays Concerning Human Understanding*. Trans. A. G. Langley. Chicago, 1916 and 1949.

Leibniz, G. W. *Philosophische Schriften*. 7 vols. Ed. Gerhardt. Berlin, 1875–90. Partially translated by L. E. Locmaker in *Philosophical Papers and Letters*. 2 vols. Chicago, 1956.

Leibniz, G. W. *Opuscules et fragments inédits*. Ed. L. Couturat. Paris, 1903.

Mach, E. *Contribution to the Analysis of the Sensations*. Trans. C. M. Williams. La Salle, Ill.: Open Court, 1984.

Maïmon, S. *Versuch über die Transzendentalphilosophie*. Berlin: Voss, 1790; Brussels: Culture et Civilisation, 1969.

Minkowski, H. "Raum und Zeit." *Jahresbericht der deutschen Mathematiker Vereinigung*, 18, (1909).

Musgrave, A. "Logicism Revisited." *British Journal for the Philosophy of Science*, 28 (1977), 101.

Pariente, J. C. *Le langage et l'individuel*. Paris: Armand Colin, 1973.

Pariente, J. Cl. "Bergson et Wittgenstein." *Wittgenstein et le problème d'une philosophie de la science*. Paris: CNRS, 1971.

Popper, K. *Die Beide Grundprobleme der Erkenntnistheorie (BGE)*. Tübingen: Mohr, 1979.

Popper, K. *Conjectures and Refutations: The Growth of Objective Knowledge (CR)*. Rev. ed. London: Routledge & Kegan Paul, 1972.

Popper K. *Objective Knowledge: An Evolutionary Approach (OK)*. Oxford: Clarendon Press, 1972.

Porphyry. *Isagoge*. Trans. J. Tricot. Paris: Vrin, 1947.

Quine, W. V. "Truth by Convention." In *Philosophical Essays for Alfred North Whitehead*. Ed. O. H. Lee. New York: Longmans, Green, 1936. Reprinted in *Ways of Paradox and Other Essays*. New York: Random House, 1966.

Quine, W. V. "Two Dogmas of Empiricism." In *From a Logical Point of View*. Cambridge, Mass.: Harvard University Press, 1953.

Quine, W. V. *Word and Object*. Cambridge, Mass.: MIT Press, 1960.

Ramsey, F. P. *The Foundations of Mathematics*. London: Routledge & Kegan Paul, 1931.

Récanati, F. *La transparence et l'énonciation*. Paris: Seuil, 1979.

Reichenbach, H. "L'empirisme logique et la désagrégation de l'*a priori*." *Actes du Congrès International de Philosophie Scientifique*. Paris: Hermann, 1936.

Rorty, R. *Philosophy and the Mirror of Nature*. Princeton, N.J.: Princeton University Press, 1979.

Rorty, R., J. B. Schneewind, and Q. Skinner (eds.), *Philosophy in History*. Cambridge: Cambridge University Press, 1984.

Russell, B. *Introduction to Mathematical Philosophy*. London: Allen & Unwin, 1920.

Russell, B. *Logic and Knowledge*. London: Allen & Unwin, 1956.

Russell, B. *My Philosophical Development*. New York: Simon & Schuster, 1959.

Russell, B. *Mysticism and Logic and Other Essays*. London: Allen & Unwin, 1917.

Russell, B. *The Philosophy of Leibniz*. Cambridge: Cambridge University Press, 1900.

Russell, B. *Principles of Mathematics*. 2nd ed. London: Allen & Unwin, 1938.

Russell, B., and A. N. Whitehead. *Principia Mathematica*. 3 vols. Cambridge: Cambridge University Press, 1910–27.

Schilpp, P. A. *The Philosophy of Karl Popper*. La Salle, Ill.: Open Court, 1974.

Schlick, M. *General Theory of Knowledge*. Trans. A. E. Blumberg. New York: Springer-Verlag, 1974.

Schlick, M. *Gesammelte Aufsätze*. Vienna: Gerhold, 1938.

Tarski, A. *Logic, Semantics, Metamathematics*. Trans. J. H. Woodger. Oxford, 1956.

Van Heijenoort, J. *From Frege to Gödel: A Source Book in Mathematical Logic, 1879–1931*. Cambridge, Mass.: Harvard University Press, 1967.

Vuillemin, J. *Leçons sur la première philosophie de Bertrand Russell*. Paris: Armand Colin, 1968.

Waismann, F. *Einführung in das mathematische Denken*. Vienna: Gerhold, 1936.

Waismann, F. *Ludwig Wittgenstein und der Wiener Kreis*, notes published by B. F. MacGuiness. Oxford: Blackwell, 1967.

Wertheimer, M. "Gestalt Theory." *Social Research*, 11 (1944), 81–99.

Weyl, H. "Zeitverhältnisse im Kosmos, Eigenzeit, gelebte Zeit und Metaphysische Zeit." *Proceedings of the VIth International Congress of Philosophy*. London: Longmans, 1926.

Wittgenstein, L. "Some Remarks on Logical Form." *Knowledge, Experience and Realism*. Aristotelian Society, Supp. vol. 9, 1929.

Wittgenstein, L. *Tractatus Logico-Philosophicus*. London: Routledge & Kegan Paul, 1922.

Wundt, W. *Logik: Eine Untersuchung der Prinzipien der Erkenntnis und der Methoden wissenschaftlicher Forschung*. 2 vols. Stuttgart: Enke, 1880–83.

Index

Index
Prepared by Robin Jackson

297

Joëlle Proust is *chargée* of research at the Centre National de la Recherche Scientifique. She also teaches at the University of Paris VII. Proust received the Bronze medal of the CNRS in 1987 for *Questions de forme*. She contributes to *Fundamenta Scientiae* and *Les Archives de Philosophie*.

Anastasios Brenner is an assistant professor of philosophy at Compiègne University of Technology in France. He graduated from St. Paul's School in New Hampshire and holds a doctorate in philosophy from the University of Paris-Sorbonne.